T0295625

# Total Innovative Management Excellence (TIME)

# Total Innovative Management Excellence (TIME)

## The Future of Innovation

Edited by
H. James Harrington
Frank Voehl

CRC Press
Taylor & Francis Group
Boca Raton London New York

CRC Press is an imprint of the
Taylor & Francis Group, an **informa** business

A PRODUCTIVITY PRESS BOOK

First published 2020
by Routledge
52 Vanderbilt Avenue, New York, NY 10017

and by Routledge
2 Park Square, Milton Park, Abingdon, Oxon, OX14 4RN

*Routledge is an imprint of the Taylor & Francis Group, an informa business*

International Standard Book Number-13: 978-0-367-43242-3 (Hardback)
International Standard Book Number-13: 978-1-003-00455-4 (eBook)

---

**Library of Congress Cataloging-in-Publication Data**

Names: Harrington, H. James, editor. | Voehl, Frank, 1946- editor.
Title: Total innovative management excellence (TIME) : the future of innovation / [edited by] H. James Harrington and Frank Voehl.
Description: New York, NY : Routledge, 2020. |
Includes bibliographical references and index.
Identifiers: LCCN 2019058593 (print) | LCCN 2019058594 (ebook) |
ISBN 9780367432423 (hardback) | ISBN 9781003004554 (ebook)
Subjects: LCSH: Technological innovations–Management. |
Total quality management.
Classification: LCC HD45 .T665 2020 (print) | LCC HD45 (ebook) |
DDC 658.4/063–dc23 LC record available at https://lccn.loc.gov/2019058593LC
ebook record available at https://lccn.loc.gov/2019058594

---

*I dedicate this book to God who has given me so many riches– not in money but for my son, Jim, who makes me feel wanted every day, for the wife Marguerite's love, which has lasted long after "to death do you part," for my granddaughter, Grace, whose smile turns a rainy day into one filled with bright sunshine. And also for my friends like Candy Rogers, Chuck Mignosa, Frank Voehl, Neil Kuhn, and Doug Nelson who have given me much more than I can give them.*

*H. James Harrington*

# Contents

# Acknowledgments

My sincere thanks and respect for Candy Rogers, who translated all of my dictation into meaningful chapters, and to all of the following individuals who contributed chapters to the book.

Billy Arcement
Sid Ahmed Benraouane, PhD
Dr. Sorin Cohn
Bill Copeland
Ricardo R. Fernandez
Laszlo Gyorffy
Jane Keathley
Dana Landry
Mitchell W. Manning, Jr.
Mitchell W. Manning, Sr.
Chuck Mignosa
Langdon Morris
Doug Nelson
William S. Ruggles
Frank Voehl

# Editors

**Dr. H. James Harrington**
*Chief Executive Officer*

## HARRINGTON MANAGEMENT SYSTEMS

In the book, *Tech Trending*, Dr. Harrington was referred to as "the quintessential tech trender." The *New York Times* referred to him as having a "... knack for synthesis and an open mind about packaging his knowledge and experience in new ways – characteristics that may matter more as prerequisites for new-economy success than technical wizardry ... .". The author, Tom Peters, stated, "I fervently hope that Harrington's readers will not only benefit from the thoroughness of his effort but will also 'smell' the fundamental nature of the challenge for change that he mounts." William Clinton, former president of the United States, appointed Dr. Harrington to serve as an Ambassador of Goodwill. It has been said about him, "He writes the books that other consultants use."

Harrington Management Systems (formerly Harrington Institute) was featured on a half-hour TV program, *Heartbeat of America*, which focuses on outstanding small businesses that make America strong. The host, William Shatner, stated: "You (Dr. Harrington) manage an entrepreneurial company that moves America forward. You are obviously successful."

## PRESENT RESPONSIBILITIES

Dr. H. James Harrington now serves as the Chief Executive Officer for the Harrington Management Systems. He also serves as the Chairman of the Board for a number of businesses. Dr. Harrington also serves as the Chairman of the Walter L. Hurd Foundation. Dr. Harrington is recognized as one of the world leaders in applying performance improvement methodologies to business processes. He has an excellent record of coming into an organization, working as its CEO or COO, resulting in a major improvement in its financial and quality performance.

## PREVIOUS EXPERIENCE

In February 2002, Dr. Harrington retired as the COO of Systemcorp A.L.G., the leading supplier of knowledge management and project management software solutions when Systemcorp was purchased by IBM. Prior to this, he served as the Principal and one of the leaders in the Process Innovation Group at Ernst & Young; he retired from Ernst & Young when it was purchased by Cap Gemini. Dr. Harrington joined Ernst & Young when Ernst & Young purchased Harrington, Hurd & Rieker, a consulting firm that Dr. Harrington started. Before that, Dr. Harrington was with IBM for over 40 years as a Senior Engineer and Project Manager.

Dr. Harrington is past Chairman and past President of the prestigious International Academy for Quality and of the American Society for Quality Control. He is also an active member of the Global Knowledge Economics Council.

## CREDENTIALS

Dr. H. James Harrington was given a lifetime achievement award for his work in process improvement and in innovation by the International Association of Innovation Professionals.

H. James Harrington was elected to the honorary level of the International Academy for Quality, which is the highest level of recognition in the quality profession.

H. James Harrington is a government-registered Quality Engineer, a Certified Quality and Reliability Engineer by the American Society for Quality Control, and a Permanent Certified Professional Manager by the Institute of Certified Professional Managers. He is a certified Master Six Sigma Black Belt and received the title of Six Sigma Grand Master. H. James Harrington has an MBA and PhD in Engineering Management and a BS in Electrical Engineering. Additionally, in 2013 Harrington received an Honorary Degree of Doctor of Philosophy (PhD) from the Sudan Academy of Sciences.

H. James Harrington's contributions to performance improvement around the world have brought him many honors. He was appointed the honorary advisor to the China Quality Control Association, and was elected to the Singapore Productivity Hall of Fame in 1990. He has been named lifetime honorary President of the Asia-Pacific Quality Control Organization and honorary Director of the Association Chilean de Control de Calidad. In 2006, Dr. Harrington accepted the Honorary Chairman position of Quality Technology Park of Iran.

H. James Harrington has been elected a Fellow of the British Quality Control Organization and the American Society for Quality Control. In 2008, he was elected to be an Honorary Fellow of the Iran Quality Association and Azerbaijan Quality Association. He was also elected an honorary member of the quality societies in Taiwan, Argentina, Brazil, Colombia, and Singapore. He is also listed in the "Who's-Who Worldwide" and "Men of Distinction Worldwide." He has presented hundreds of papers on performance improvement and organizational management structure at the local, state, national, and international levels.

## RECOGNITION

- The Harrington/Ishikawa Medal, presented yearly by the Asian Pacific Quality Organization, was named after H. James Harrington to recognize his many contributions to the region.
- The Harrington/Neron Medal was named after H. James Harrington in 1997 for his many contributions to the quality movement in Canada.
- Harrington Best TQM Thesis Award was established in 2004 and named after H. James Harrington by the European Universities Network and e-TQM College.
- Harrington Chair in Performance Excellence was established in 2005 at the Sudan University.
- Harrington Excellence Medal was established in 2007 to recognize an individual who uses the quality tools in a superior manner.
- H. James Harrington Scholarship was established in 2011 by the ASQ Inspection Division.

Dr. H. James Harrington has received many awards; some of them are the Benjamin L. Lubelsky Award, the John Delbert Award, the Administrative Applications Division Silver Anniversary Award, and the Inspection Division Gold Medal Award. In 1996, he received the ASQC's Lancaster Award in recognition for his international activities. In 2001, he received the Magnolia Award in recognition for the many contributions he has made in improving quality in China. In 2002, Harrington was selected by the European Literati Club to receive a lifetime achievement award at the Literati Award for Excellence ceremony in London. The award was given to honor his excellent literature contributions to the advancement of quality and organizational performance. Also, in 2002, Harrington was awarded the International Academy of Quality President's Award in recognition for outstanding global leadership in quality and competitiveness, and contributions to IAQ as Nominations Committee Chair, Vice President, and Chairman. In 2003, Harrington received the Edwards Medal from the American Society for Quality (ASQ). The Edwards Medal is presented to the individual who has demonstrated the most outstanding leadership in the application of modern quality control methods, especially through the organization and administration of such work. In 2004, he received the Distinguished Service Award, which is ASQ's highest award for service granted by the Society. In 2008, Dr. Harrington was awarded the Sheikh Khalifa Excellence Award (UAE) in recognition of his superior performance as an original Quality and Excellence Guru who helped shape modern quality thinking. In 2009, Harrington was selected as the Professional of the Year (2009). Also, in 2009, he received the Hamdan Bin Mohammed e-University Medal. In 2010, the Asian Pacific Quality Organization (APQO) awarded Harrington the APQO President's Award for his "exemplary leadership." The Australian Organization of Quality NSW's Board recognized Harrington as "the Global Leader in Performance Improvement Initiatives" in 2010. In 2011, he was honored to receive the Shanghai Magnolia Special Contributions Award from the Shanghai Association for Quality in recognition of his 25 years of contributing to the advancement of quality in China. This was the first time that this award was given out. In 2012, Harrington received the ASQ Ishikawa Medal for his many contributions in promoting the understanding of process improvement and employee involvement on the human aspects of quality at the local, national, and international levels. Also, in 2012, he was awarded the Jack Grayson Award. This award recognizes individuals who have demonstrated outstanding leadership in the application of quality philosophy, methods and tools in education, healthcare, public service, and not-for-profit organizations. Harrington also received the A.C. Rosander Award in 2012. This is ASQ Service Quality Division's highest honor. It is given in recognition of outstanding long-term service and leadership resulting in substantial progress toward the fulfillment of the Division's programs and goals. Additionally, in 2012, Harrington was honored by the Asia Pacific Quality Organization by being awarded the Armand V. Feigenbaum Lifetime Achievement Medal. This award is given annually to an individual whose relentless pursuit of performance improvement over a minimum of 25 years has distinguished himself or herself for the candidate's work in promoting the use of quality methodologies and principles within and outside of the organization he or she is part of. In 2018, Harrington received the Lifetime Achievement Award from the Asia Pacific Quality Organization. This award recognizes worthy role models and committed APQO Leaders who have made significant contribution to the betterment of APQO.

## CONTACT INFORMATION

Dr. Harrington is a very prolific author, publishing hundreds of technical reports and magazine articles. For the past 8 years, he has published a monthly column in *Quality Digest Magazine* and is syndicated in five other publications. He has authored 55 books and 10 software packages.

You may contact Dr. Harrington at the following address:
15559 Union Avenue #187, Los Gatos, California, 95032.
Phone: (408) 358-2476
Email: hjh@svinet.com

**Frank Voehl, President, Strategy Associates**

## PRESENT RESPONSIBILITIES

Frank Voehl now serves as the Chairman and President of Strategy Associates, Inc. and as a Senior Consultant and Chancellor for the Harrington Management Systems. He also serves as the Chairman of the Board for a number of businesses and as a Grand Master Black Belt Instructor and Technology Advisor at the University of Central Florida in Orlando, Florida. He is recognized as one of the world leaders in applying quality measurement and Lean Six Sigma methodologies to business processes.

## PREVIOUS EXPERIENCE

Frank Voehl has extensive knowledge of NRC, FDA, GMP, and NASA quality system requirements. He is an expert in ISO-9000, QS-9000/14000/18000, and integrated Lean Six Sigma Quality System Standards and processes. He has degrees from St. John's University and advanced studies at NYU, as well as an Honorary Doctor of Divinity degree. Since 1986, he has been responsible for overseeing the implementation of Quality Management systems with organizations in such diverse industries as telecommunications and utilities, federal, state and local government agencies, public administration and safety, pharmaceuticals, insurance/banking, manufacturing, and institutes of higher learning. In 2002, he joined The Harrington Group as the Chief Operating Officer and Executive Vice President. Has held executive management positions with Florida Power and Light and FPL Group, where he was the Founding General Manager and COO of QualTec Quality Services for seven years. He has written and published/co-published over 35 books and hundreds of technical papers on business management, quality improvement, change management, knowledge management, logistics and teambuilding, and has received numerous awards for community leadership, service to the third world countries, and student mentoring.

## CREDENTIALS

The Bahamas National Quality Award was developed in 1991 by Voehl to recognize the many contributions of companies in the Caribbean region, and he is an honorary member of its Board of Judges. In 1980, the City of Yonkers, New York, declared March 7th as "Frank Voehl Day," honoring him for his many contributions on behalf of thousands of youth in the city where he lived, performed volunteer work, and served as Athletic Director and Coach of the Yonkers-Pelton Basketball Association. In 1985, he was named "Father of the Year" in Broward County, Florida. He also serves as President of the Miami Archdiocesan Council of the St. Vincent de Paul Society, whose mission is to serve the poor and needy throughout South Florida and the world.

# Contributors

### Billy Arcement

Billy Arcement, Med – *The Candid Cajun*, is a speaker, consultant, and executive coach on leadership strategies. He is a former elected official and author of 5 books and over 300 published articles on organizational and personal leadership topics. His website is www.SearchingForSuccess.com.

### Sid Ahmed Benraouane, PhD

Sid Ahmed Benraouane is a senior lecturer at Carlson School of Management, University of Minnesota (USA). He is the Chair of the United States ISO Innovation Management System Working Group. He also advises Dubai Police (United Arab Emirates) and MENA Governments on innovation and foresight.

### Dr. Sorin Cohn

Dr. Sorin Cohn has 40 years' experience managing all aspects of innovation. He is an ISO expert developing ISO 56000 innovation management standards. Sorin was Chairman of Startup Canada, the leader on *Innovation Management and Metrics* at the Conference Board of Canada. He lectures in USA, Europe, Canada, and SE Asia.

## Bill Copeland

Bill Copeland, Vice President – Sales and Marketing, EDGE Software Inc. An entrepreneur and longtime marketing and sales professional obsessed with identifying and satisfying customer needs. Returned Peace Corps Volunteer and co-founder/president of the Family Copeland Foundation (501 C 3 Charitable Foundation) providing academic scholarships for Ugandan women to become midwives.

## Ricardo R. Fernandez

Rick Fernandez has over 30 years' experience leading innovation efforts in the Manufacturing, Service, and Government sectors. Currently, he is serving as the Vice-Chairman for the U.S. team that is developing the new *Innovation Management System Standard Series ISO 56000*. Recently, he co-authored the book titled *The Framework for Innovation*. He is a former Examiner for the Malcolm Baldrige National Quality and Performance Excellence Award.

## Laszlo Gyorffy

Laszlo Gyorffy, MS, is President of the Enterprise Development Group, an international consulting and training firm headquartered in Silicon Valley. For over 25 years, he has worked with organizations around the globe to expand the possible; helping them refocus, redesign, and reenergize their business strategies and innovation practices.

## Jane Keathley

Jane Keathley, MS, PMP, helps organizations at the intersection of quality and innovation management. She was a founding member of the ASQ Innovation Division and currently sits on the ASQ Board of Directors. Her career spans medical device software, clinical research, biopharma manufacturing, and diagnostic microbiology. Jane holds degrees Medical Microbiology (MS) and Medical Technology (BS).

## Dana Landry, PhD

Innovation Consultant – Medical Device Executive – Business and Individual Transformation Leadership – Educator. President and Founder of ArtSci Innovation Consulting, LLC. Adjunct professor at NYU Polytechnic School of Engineering. Vice President of Certification Programs at International Association of Innovation Professionals (IAOIP).

## Mitchell W. Manning, Jr

Mitchell W. Manning, Jr. is the Advanced Manufacturing Systems Engineer at DSM Dyneema LLC in Greenville, NC; holds a BS and an MS from East Carolina University. His analytical problem-solving expertise provides sustainable improvements in areas of Logistics, DSCM, Operations, Engineering, and Information Technology using Lean Six Sigma methodologies.

## Mitchell W. Manning, Sr.

Mitchell W. Manning, Sr. is retired from Burroughs-Wellcome (GlaxoSmithKline). He was a member of the founding criteria committee for the Malcolm Baldridge National Quality Award. He has a BSBA in Management Science from East Carolina University.

## Chuck Mignosa

Chuck Mignosa is President of Business Systems Architects LLC, which is a training and consulting company, specializing in training and consulting with businesses to continually improve their business.

He holds patents in solid lubricants and has served as Director and Vice President of quality in biomedical devices, telecommunication, and other high-tech companies.

Mr. Mignosa has published two books on quality and contributed to four other books.

He can be reached by email at CHUCKM@ISOSYS.COM

## Langdon Morris

Langdon Morris is an award-winning innovator, world-renowned innovation consultant, best-selling author, and acclaimed keynote speaker.

He is Senior Partner at Innovation Labs LLC, where he leads the firm's global innovation consulting practice.

The breakthrough project he led for UNICEF was honored as a finalist in the Innovation Leader Impact Awards for 2018.

## Doug Nelson, MBA, PMP

Doug Nelson is a Lean Six Sigma Master Black Belt/Process Excellence consultant with a 25-year background of success in strategic planning, process management, product management, and development of sustainable management solutions.

He is a Past President of APICS, Portland Chapter and a Certified Fellow in Production and Inventory Management.

## William S. Ruggles

William S. Ruggles is Chief Operating Officer of Ruggles & Ruggles, LLC and an Adjunct Professor of Management, specializing in Projects, Programs, and Portfolios at Montclair State University, Montclair, in Northern New Jersey. His most-recent book (2018), co-authored with Dr. Harrington, is titled *Project Management for Performance Improvement Teams*.

## Chris Voehl

Christopher F. Voehl is the founder of Seven Sigma Solutions, a Tallahassee, Florida-based company focused on systems deployment, project management, and continuous improvement services in a variety of industries. Chris specializes in systems analysis, process optimization, and software test automation for business services, human capital consulting firms, nonprofits, and government agencies.

# Foreword: The Imperative for Innovation

*By Langdon Morris*

Thirty years of experience in the innovation field has revealed that innovation is best thought of as an organizational effort undertaken in service to an organization's strategy. But 30 hours would probably be sufficient as well, as by now it should be clear to everyone that we seek innovations because they are important for the achievement of an organization's strategic objectives. Hence, the context in which innovation efforts take place is the broader strategic context in which organizations function, the big picture as seen from outside. And so we start our discussion of TIME with a brief summary of the overall global context for innovation.

And what we observe is that the overall rate of change throughout the economy continues to accelerate, which is putting increasing pressure on all organizations. Technologies, customers, competitors, and markets are all evolving rapidly, which creates a compelling strategic situation. This is the reality that we have to cope with. Clearly, the days in which any company could set its strategy in place and then merely execute it over the subsequent months and years are long past. Instead, constant adaptation and response are necessary, because the strategic situation is constantly and rapidly evolving.

What this inevitably requires of organizations is renewed attention to innovation. But not just any approach to innovation is going to be sufficient.

Instead, what's mandatory is innovation that is strategically aligned, systematic, and in the end extraordinarily effective. Hence, we require a shift from the relatively random innovation efforts of the past, wherein we "hoped" that we'd come up with good, new ideas, to the determined and disciplined pursuit of brilliant insights across a wide range of operational domains that will confidently seed the development of our future. This is what "TIME" is all about.

This new form of systematic innovation has a number of key elements.

(1) As it is proactive rather than reactive, it is undertaken from the outset in alignment with and in support to an organization's overall strategy. Strategy thus defines the context in which innovation is pursued, and provides the primary targets toward which the search for innovation is directed.

(2) As it is pursued with great awareness of the rate at which new technologies are being discovered and developed, maturing, and impacting the market, it takes a broad view of the emerging technology landscape and seeks to understand future possibilities thoughtfully and comprehensively. The capacity to anticipate market's shifts thus becomes a distinct competitive advantage for any organization.

(3) And yet, paradoxically, this effort must not be guided by specific predictions about the medium- and long-term futures. Instead, given the acceleration of the change we take the view that all predictions are likely to be wrong. So what is our approach then? Instead of predicting the future, we model *alternative futures*, shifting from "prediction thinking" to "possibility thinking," and thereby broadening our innovation horizon to encompass these possibilities. When we recognize what could happen, we are much better prepared to recognize the new things that are happening, and to act quickly. We can also use this knowledge to be the drivers of change by harnessing trends and shaping market outcomes. This is of course the great advantage that innovation brings.

(4) As it is clear that great ideas may emerge from anyone, anywhere, at any time, innovation leaders actively encourage broad participation in the innovation effort. Indeed, innovation is understood to be the product of not an organization, but of an entire ecosystem, which may consist of individuals, organizations, clients, partners, and researchers. Hence, the role of innovation managers is to bring the entire ecosystem into alignment as co-participants in the innovation process. Innovation casts a very wide net, and by defining an inspiring and compelling process of inquiry seeks to engage people as co-explorers and co-creators.

(5) The innovation process itself is carefully managed to balance the broad early-stage learning and investigation with the mid-stage definition of possibilities and with the end-stage execution and delivery of value.

(6) Systematic innovation is also pursued with an acute awareness of risk. But risk in innovation occurs simultaneously across multiple dimensions, so risk management is a multi-faceted effort. For example, there is significant risk in pursuing only the sure bets, which drives us toward incremental thinking and sets us up to be blindsided by the big changes. Conversely, there is also risk in pursuing only the big bets and overlooking thereby the easy wins that could help sustain market share. So there is risk in being too broad, and also in being too narrow. Innovation management is always focused on finding the balance, and cognizance of this is also how we manage the inherent risks through the critical technique of innovation portfolio management.

(7) In contrast to common perception, innovation is not all about creative game-playing, toothpick towers, and Legos. While creativity is of course essential, so are disciplined development of and selection between options, tracking of schedules and deadlines, mapping technologies and new competitors, careful governance, and rigorous investment management.

You will find all these themes described throughout the book, and while there may be many additional dimensions of the disciplined innovation practice that we could mention here, hopefully the point is clear that innovation is a complex business process that requires focused and well-prepared management. Certainly it can and should be mastered, and doing so isn't random, it's entirely purposeful. Innovation is now a critical business discipline.

We also know that this is case by observing the behavior of the broader market, where it's obvious that a small number of firms are effective innovators, but most are not good at it at all. Why are the good one's good? Because they approach innovation in a disciplined and comprehensive manner. And why are the others not so good? It's obvious – they lack the necessary structures and rigor.

This, then, tells us clearly about the purpose of this book – to describe those structures and to define what it is that constitutes rigor in innovation.

Which, by the way, has some subtleties. After all, "rigorous innovation" must balance the art of inquiry and open-ended discovery with the science of project management. It must also balance the investment of time and money in the search for the new and the inevitable possibility – no, the likelihood – of failure, with the need for Return on Investment and solid financial gains. After all, companies invest in innovation to make money in the future, and yet they know that losses are necessary along the way.

The fact that all this lies so far outside of the norm for the execution-minded corporate management goes a long way to explain why innovation tends to be the exception among major corporations, and why most companies are better characterized by their lack of innovations than by their innovation achievements.

So this is the domain into which the would-be corporate innovators enter, the burdens and habits they must overcome, and the challenges they face.

But there are other challenges as well, and they deserve to be looked at more closely. Above I mentioned the acceleration of change, and as this defines the urgency of innovation, it's worth taking a deeper look at what this entails.

## THE ACCELERATION OF HISTORY, OR, YOU AIN'T SEEN NOTHIN' YET

Broadly, we can assert with confidence that society is entering into a new phase that we could readily describe as "you ain't seen nothin' yet ... ." And what is it that we ain't seen? It's change on a massive, global scale as it is occurring today. Furthermore, we ain't seen change like we're about to see it. In a recent book entitled *The Big Shift*, I inventoried 83 major changes that are happening simultaneously around the world, changes in technology, demographic patterns, urbanization, and climate, all of which are converging upon us, and all of which will require of us great insight and a profound willingness to do something different, better, in order for our organizations to survive. In the face of this acceleration of history, we must innovate.

Let us briefly look back at the pattern of recent changes. In the pre-industrial year of 1700, the most powerful nation in the European world was Spain; its enormous wealth derived from mountains of gold and silver torn from its New World colonies, the practice of *Extractive Colonial Capitalism*. One-hundred-thirty million Native Americans perished under Spanish rule, the worst genocide in history, but the riches were squandered in trivialities and the failed conquest of Great Britain, which ended with the sinking of the great Spanish Armada.

In 1800, the World's most powerful nation was France, which had thrown off its monarchy in favor of a republic, and which had found in Napoleon the most capable European general of his generation, or perhaps any generation since Alexander. Napoleon's triumphant armies subdued Europe for two decades and the wealth flowed back to Paris, until he met his match at Waterloo in 1815. It's said that during that last great battle, Napoleon watched the British army maneuvers from a nearby hillside in admiration. "They're learning!" he cried. They learned well, won the battle and also the war, and so Napoleon's reign of *Militaristic Capitalism* came to an abrupt end.

By 1900, the world's leading power was Great Britain, as Queen Victoria surveyed from London the largest mass of humanity and the greatest expanse of territory ever assembled into one empire. Britain's *Mercantilist Capitalism* enriched Londoners but impoverished the unfortunates in the colonies. A heavy blow to the empire was inflicted by World War I, and the fatal blow twenty-five years later with World War II; the empire was disbanded, leaving a small but proud island nation with rich memories of former glory.

A century later, in 2000, *Industrial Capitalism* had carried the United States to the world's economic and military pinnacle, but was that the peak? It's possible that greatness began slipping away as trillions of dollars were squandered in the failed attempt to remake the Middle East, followed by the debt-induced 2008 collapse, and capped off by the election of 2016 and the antagonistic social and political climate that it both reflected and exacerbated. The America of today does not project self-confidence nor does it convey a vision for the future.

So which nation will dominate in 2100? Will it be China? That's possible but unlikely, given the combination of massive debt and a demographic imbalance that will arise by mid-century, at which point China will likely follow Japan's path, a booming elderly population and economic malaise.

Perhaps instead the great power of 2100 will be a new nation, one that we don't know today. It could be *Blockchainistan*, a haven founded to escape the reach of national laws and currencies. Perhaps it will be *Digialmania* or *Robotopia*, owned and run by silicon intelligence rather than biological. If Ray Kurzweil is correct and the robot singularity arrives by 2045, then by 2100 robots should be fully in control. It could also be the *United Republics of Outer Space*.

These are fanciful ideas, but not implausible. The point, of course, is that we often assume that the way things are now is how they will remain, which is certainly a false confidence. Change is the norm, the Big Shift has arrived.

- Climate Shift is already changing our lives and its impacts will enormously worsen if more food-growing regions turn to deserts and if the glaciers melt and flood the urbanized coasts, casting billions into homelessness.
- Robot Shift is here already, 50,000 of them laboring at Amazon.com alone, and more arriving daily. If the forecasts are correct, then the sheer number of robots will dwarf the human labor force within a decade, and if the forecast robot singularity is correct, then by mid-century the ratio of human intelligence to robot intelligence will shift irreversibly in the favor of the robots, and no one knows what happens then. (That's why it's a 'singularity,' because all the known rules break down at that point.)
- Urbanization is driving a massive population shift from rural to urban, which marks the beginning of a population contraction that could last centuries. That's right, the population explosion is ending, shifting now to a population implosion. But since the success of the industrial economy depended on an ever-expanding pool of laborer–consumers, population implosion portends the demise of industrial consumerism, while the booming population of the aged will severely stress national health care systems and budgets.
- But maybe that doesn't really matter, because massive indebtedness and the financialization of the economy tell us that we're already living in a post-industrial system anyway. Today the combined wealth of the world's 2200 billionaires is $9 trillion, greater than the wealth of the poorest 3.7 billion people *combined* (half the world's population). Each billionaire is thus worth the equivalent of about 1.6 million of the much less fortunate, showing

us that the system is nicely enriching some, but largely at the expense of the many.

Yes, it's chaos out there.

If one or even a few of the key factors that shape a society and its economy are undergoing fundamental change, then we naturally expect some impact on the overall structure of the economy. If many of the essentials change, then we know something big is up. But today we see that *all* the factors are now experiencing fundamental change, and thus there is simply no escaping the fact that the entire social and economic system of human civilization absolutely must change. It is changing, irrevocably.

Among all the possibilities for the future, the idea that the next economy will be a digital one seems quite plausible given the total takeover that digital technology is already imposing across today's entire global economy, not only by robots but also by genetic engineering, big data, VR and AR, artificial intelligence, and of course in the financialization of the whole shebang, all expressions of and dependent upon digitalization.

Looking back, then, we see that industrialization and cities grew together as science expanded, technology advanced, education improved, and then modern life came into being. Modernity was an invention and by-product of the amazing industrial economic system.

And now due to the brilliant successes of industrialism, a new and different economy is emerging, not by plan or design, but because of incremental step, by incremental step we have found our way into the digital revolution. Because of the fast cycles of positive feedback, technology gets better and better every day, enabling still more progress in technology, a process that appears to have no end-point.

It would require thousands of pages of detailed analysis to fully grasp all the important things that are happening, but even then the most important parts of the story could still not be told, because they have not yet occurred. We have thus arrived at a situation in which the uncertainties of the future overwhelm the certainties of present and past. And so once again it's clear that strategically focused innovation is simply no longer an option; if your organization is going to survive all this upheaval, you'd better get good at innovation, and you'd better do it fast.

## THE INVALUABLE BENEFITS OF STRATEGIC INNOVATION

Innovation is a strategic response to the complex and demanding set of conditions that we see in the world all around us. And although it may be difficult to achieve, it does bring notable benefits.

(1) Innovators gain considerable benefit for their brands, demonstrating their commitment to the future success of their customers by innovating with and for them.

(2) Innovators enhance their own corporate cultures through broad engagement in innovation efforts that provoke thoughtfulness and provide inspiration by people working throughout the firm.

(3) Innovators achieve demonstrable improvements in their operational results, as measured through innovation-related performance metrics.

(4) Innovators utilize effective forums for collaboration between their staff, partners, and customers, focused around delivering solid innovation results to benefit customers inside and outside.

(5) Innovators learn and apply the best techniques for enhancing and accelerating creativity and innovation, such as "agile innovation" and "design thinking."

(6) Innovators help to prepare their organizations for coming disruptions which will come (or are already coming) from new technologies such as AI, robotics, predictive analytics, blockchain, etc., etc., etc. (It's an endless list … )

Is it true what they're saying these days, "Innovate or die?" The obvious option is to innovate, and then you won't have to find out for yourself … ! The benefits of successful innovation are immense, long-lasting, and in today's environment, entirely mandatory. Dig into this book written by experts in the field to learn more about how your organization can apply the best and most recent thinking and practices in innovation to become an innovator too.

## REFERENCES

Praveen Gupta, Brett Trusko et al. (2013) *Global Innovation Science Handbook*. McGraw Hill.

Ray Kurzweil. (2006) *The Singularity Is Near: When Humans Transcend Biology*. Penguin Books.

Langdon Morris. (2016) *Foresight and Extreme Creativity: Strategy for the 21st Century*. FutureLab Press.

Langdon Morris. (2018) *The Big Shift: The 83 Most Important Changes That Everyone Should Know about, and the Big Shift that Changes Everything*. FutureLab Press.

Langdon Morris and Moses Ma. (2018) *Blockchain City: Community, Technology, and Meaning*. FutureLab Press.

Gerald Piel. (1972) *The Acceleration of History*. Knopf.

# Introduction to Total Innovation Management Excellence

## H. James Harrington
CEO of Harrington Management Systems

## CONTENTS

> Stop worrying about quality, productivity, cost, and cycle time. Focus your energy on organizational innovative performance improvement and all the rest will follow.
>
> **H. James Harrington**

## INTRODUCTION

The abbreviation "TIME" stands for *Total Innovation Management Excellence*. It defines the system and culture that thrives because everyone realizes the importance of creativity and innovation and actively participates in contributing to it as it applies to the organization. It is specially designed for organizations producing products and/or delivering services.

We are fortunate enough to live in good old USA. That's just the problem. We have grown accustomed to accept old, sluggish and comfortable way things are done now. We have put that young vibrant, enthusiastic, energetic, and risk-taking pride out of our lives and replaced it with a soft reclining chair in front of a 60 inch television. We hire an illegal immigrant to mow our lawns and then go out to play golf because we don't get enough exercise. Playing golf is some exercise but to get the exercise we need, we should be pulling golf carts around the course rather than riding in them.

Thank the Lord that there are still some young entrepreneurs who are willing to risk their life savings to fund a new organization that they hope will add real value to their customers and their investors. We are living in the lap of luxury today thinking that when tomorrow comes, we will worry about it then. That's the old "Gone with the Wind" syndrome.

We just went through a cycle where many American families bought homes that they could not afford and needed to sell them because they could not keep up with their house payments. However, they couldn't sell the home because the value of the home had dropped to the point that its value was less than the outstanding mortgage against the property. For example, I helped a family member back in New York, who had $250,000 mortgage on his house at 10% interest rate, although his house was currently assessed at only $160,000. To add to this problem, many families had already topped out the maximum limit on most of their credit cards. This spiraling debt whirlpool is swallowing up even the strongest marriages. More divorces occur over money problems than over adultery. A large percentage of our population is nearing retirement age with little or nothing in the bank and a large amount of debt hanging over their heads.

Every one of us has a choice to make. You can be the bandleader out in front of the parade coming up with innovative creative ideas or stay sitting in our easy chairs and end up at the end of the parade sweeping up the horse droppings.

We are playing in a World Series – U.S. businesses versus the rest of the world. The score is U.S. "1" to World "6." (See Table I.1)

In the second inning, the World scored twice by capturing the clothing and steel industry. In the third inning, World scored again by taking over the shipping industry. In the fifth inning, World scored twice with the auto and commercial electronics industries. In the sixth inning, World scored again with the semiconductor industry. The U.S. went hitless for the first five innings but in the sixth inning we had a homerun from the biomedical industry (with no one on base.) When and how will the World score next? Will it be banking, healthcare, or aircraft? All of them have opened the market to foreign competition and unless we become more competitive than we have been to date, other countries will walk away with these markets also. China has already focused vast amounts of resources to become the AI (Artificial Intelligence) innovator leader in the world. At the present time, the United States is winning the innovation world series.

**TABLE I.1**

World Series for Business Scoreboard

|       | 1 | 2 | 3 | 4 | 5 | 6 | 7 | 8 | 9 | Total |
|-------|---|---|---|---|---|---|---|---|---|-------|
| World | 0 | 2 | 1 | 0 | 2 | 1 | 0 |   |   | 6     |
| U.S.  | 0 | 0 | 0 | 0 | 0 | 1 | 0 |   |   | 1     |

- 59% of the Engineering PhDs in the U.S. are foreign nationals
- Japan, with less than 50% of U.S. population, produces more engineers every year
- U.S. Engineering and Science faculty members are being replaced by foreign nationals
- Patents filed in Japan outnumber those filed in the U.S., 5-1 on a per capita basis
- Half of the U.S. university professor assignments are filed by foreigners

It is TIME to send our best team into the game with orders to score a minimum of 6 points during the last 3 innings.

## THE SIXTEEN GOLDEN TRAITS

It seems obvious that the key to productivity and survival is more than just improving efficiency and effectiveness, decreasing waste or having processes that are at the Six Sigma level. You must have every employee committed to following 16 Golden Traits until they are using them more efficiently than your competition.

I recently was researching to find a specific quote from a past IBM president that I wanted to use to make a point in a new book I was writing. In trying to find the quote, I pulled out the book, *The Quality/ Profit Connection*, which I had written 30 years ago. The book included a series of interviews with the CEOs/Presidents of Ford, General Motors, Avon, Corning Glass, General Dynamics, AT&T, HP, IBM, Motorola, 3M, and North American Tool and Die. These were the companies that had the best reputation for efficiency and effectiveness in the United States. In this book after reviewing the comments of these leaders in American organizations, on page 14, I summarized the traits of a successful company, which I called "The Sixteen Golden Traits." Looking back on this list now 30 years later, it's very interesting to me how little things in the business world have changed related to quality and performance improvement. I would like to share them again with you. It is important to remember that these conclusions describe the important trends that developed in the companies who had been recognized as successfully implementing performance improvement approaches around the world in the 1980s.

Rate your organization on a 1 to 10 scale (with 1 being low and 10 being far exceeds the traits statement) on how well you are performing related to each of the traits. Add up the 16 ratings and see how close you come to 160 credits. The following converts a total point score into a verbal rating.

- 0–34 = very poor
- 35–69 = poor
- 70–104 – average
- 105–139 = above average
- 140–160 = good but don't get overconfident.

The Sixteen Golden Traits

(1) *Close customer relationships.* They maintain close personal contact with their customers to ensure understanding of the customers' changing needs and expectations. When problems arise, they react quickly, pouring oil over the troubled waters.

(2) *Concern for the individual employee.* They respect the individual's rights and dignity, realizing that the company succeeds only to the degree that the individual succeeds. They respect the individual's thoughts and ideas, realizing that he or she has more to contribute to the company than just physical labor. They not only encourage the participation of the employee, they require it. They look at the individual as part of the solution to their problems, not as the problem.

(3) *Top management leadership of the quality process.* Members of top management in the company have accepted their role in leading the quality activities of the company. Support groups such as quality assurance provide advice, research problems, and data. But the company president sets the direction and establishes the standards. These company presidents realize that their company is an image of themselves, and they understand that they must set the personal quality example.

(4) *High standards.* These companies set extremely high standards for their managers, products, services, and people. They strive to

set the standard for their industry and are dissatisfied if they are not number one.

(5) *Understanding the importance of the team.* They use teams to unite the company, improve working relationships, and improve morale. They understand that only management can solve 85% of the problems and that the employee teams are required to attack the other 15%.

(6) *Effort to meet and exceed customer expectations.* They are not satisfied with the *state of the art* and are always trying to provide better products and services to their customers and at lower cost. They understand their customers' needs and go beyond them to fulfill their expectations, realizing that just fulfilling the customers' needs will not capture future sales. They want their output to be valued by their customers.

(7) *Belief that quality is first priority.* When a compromise between quality, cost, or schedule must be made, quality is never compromised. They realize that poor quality causes most of their cost and schedule problems and that if they focus their attention on the quality problems, their cost and schedule problems will take care of themselves. They also realize that the quality personality of the company is extremely fragile, particularly during the change period, and that even the smallest compromise in quality can set back progress many years.

(8) *View of organization for the long term.* Top management realizes that the important objectives are directed at the long-term survival and prosperity of the company. They give priority to the long-range plans that will build a product and customer base, paying secondary attention to quarterly and yearly reports. They measure their success by their company's long-term growth, not by short-term fluctuations over which they often have little or no control.

(9) *Sharing of prosperity with the employees.* They look at the employees as partners and establish programs that directly relate the success of the company to the employees' earnings and their contributions. Programs such as gain sharing, suggestion, and pay-for-performance are key parts of the employee benefit package.

(10) *Management and employee education.* They realize that education is not expensive; it is ignorance that is costly. These companies have realized that everyone is responsible for quality and that

everyone needs education related to the quality tools if they are to meet this responsibility. As a result, heavy focus on quality education has been directed at the management team and key professionals. At the employee level, education has been directed at problem-solving methods and job training.

(11) *Management leadership rather than supervision.* They realize that management must be leaders of the employees rather than dictators. It is much easier to pull a string in the desired direction than to push it. For management to assume the leadership role has not been easy, and many of the companies are still working on this change in their company personality. After all, for the past 40 years, we have trained our managers to be attack dogs, and now we want them to be purring kittens.

(12) *Investment in the future.* Research and development means investing in the future of the company. It ensures a steady flow of products and ideas needed to meet the expectations of the future market. Along with the need for research, a parallel need is to provide the employees with equipment that pushes the state of the art and allows them to perform at their very best. Companies that realize this have prospered; those that have not, failed or will eventually fail. Every organizational member should be created and hopefully innovative.

(13) *Focus on the business system.* They realize that the only way to prevent errors from occurring is by correcting the business system that controls the company activities. Employees work *in* the business system, while managers must work *on* the system.

(14) *Recognition systems.* These companies realize that recognition takes many forms – financial, personal, and public. They have established a recognition system with many options to ensure that it meets the total needs of employees and management. A pat on the back is good, but sometimes a pat on the wallet is better and more appropriate. On other occasions, a personal letter sent to the employee's home is the best action.

(15) *Employee involvement.* These companies go out of their way to make all the employees feel that they are part of the organization and that their contributions are important. They take time to involve the employees in their long-range plans and report progress back to them periodically. They make them part of the company by providing such things as a stock-purchase plan or gain sharing. They

provide the employees with opportunities to meet and understand customers, the ones who receive their output. Sometimes a customer is outside the company, but more often it is another company employee. It is not easy to care about customers when you never see or hear from them, but if the customer is the person who sits behind you or in the next office, the whole concept of customer satisfaction becomes a much more personal issue.

(16) *Decreased bureaucracy.* Management continuously works at making all decisions at the lowest level. Maximum authority is given to each level of management. Checks and balances are used, but only when absolutely necessary. Management realizes that bureaucracy has a tendency to work its way into the business systems, and they are continuously vigilant to minimize its impact.

## THE INNOVATION SYSTEMS CYCLE (ISC)

We have talked a lot about how things have changed, but in truth, the basic things that make for a successful organization, country or people, for that matter, have not changed. The fundamental things such as respect for the individual, doing our best all the time, understanding our customer, investing in our people, being honest, and finding win-win solutions are as important today as they were in the 1980s, or maybe even more important today. Yes, things may be moving faster. We may have more competition, but we also have more opportunities. We just can't let the rush of today set aside these very important basic values or we all will fail.

Extensive research has proven that improved perceived product quality and innovation is the most effective way to increase profits and the most important factor in the long-term profitability of a company. Organizations around the world are beginning to believe in the value of quality and to back its belief with action. It is a first step down that long road to excellence. The current challenge is how to keep ahead of our competition with high-quality innovative products. It is a race to satisfy expectations of customers around the world. You need high-quality innovative products and services that provide added value to success-fully compete in today's very competitive market.

- Customers initially buy products based upon its quality.
- They come back again and buy based upon the robustness and reliability that has been designed into the product.

The marrying together of high-quality output and creative innovative products that outperform the competition will provide your company with the competitive edge to put it ahead of the pack. Don't be left at the starting gate. The only way we succeed is by working together and never being satisfied with how good we are or the innovative products we put out yesterday. The race is not over yet. Remember, you can't win today's race with last week's press clippings.

With short product-cycle times, all the problems and potential problems should have been addressed and corrected during the product-development cycle. This requires a major shift in the performance-improvement activities from the production line to the research and development laboratory. There is just not enough time to recognize a problem after you start shipping products to consumers because by the time the problem is corrected, the competition has walked away with the market. It all depends upon how you use all of our resources to improve the quality, and innovation of your outputs, the productivity of our operations, and how we integrate technologies into our products while making the optimum use of the capital and facility available to the organization. Yes, to bring about optimum performance in an organization, the following must be in balance and in harmony to ensure that all of the stakeholders' needs and expectations are met.

- Innovation and Creativity
- Quality
- Reliability
- Adaptability
- Technology
- Productivity
- Costs

J. Jackson Grayson, Chairman of the American Productivity and Quality Center, put it this way, "We need to be lean and hungry, quick, dedicated to excellence, oriented towards inventive action – meaner than the junkyard dog, smarter than the barnyard cat."

We need to have an agile organization in all respects in order to be able to quickly react to the changing markets and customers' expectations around the world.

The ISC covers all activities related to an opportunity from the time it is recognized until the time the customer has a chance to evaluate his/her level of satisfaction or dissatisfaction. It is a complex system made up of many individual processes that go across the organization which almost penetrate every part of the organization. Many of the processes are closely linked together and others are completely separate from the other processes. The innovation system in most organizations is so complex and made up of so many processes that it is impractical to provide a breakdown to the individual process level in this book. To give you some idea of its complexity, the International Association of Innovative Professionals (IAOIP) developed the spider diagram in Figure I.1.

Because it may be difficult to read each box, we have listed below the major headings of each of the individual 10 spider web branches.

(1) Opportunity Identification
(2) Innovation Architecture
(3) Idea Generation
(4) Value Creation
(5) Innovation Concepts
(6) Business Essentials
(7) Project Development
(8) Methodologies and Tools
(9) Deployment
(10) Measurement

It has been estimated that 58% of all the breakthrough improvements are never capitalized due to lack of follow-through in the implementation areas. It's often more difficult to identify and quantify an improvement opportunity than it is to design the product or process that takes advantage of the improvement opportunity. Truly, there is a general process required to take advantage of an improvement opportunity. Red Skelton, the famous comedian from the 20th century, created what he called "The Mean Widdle Kid." *The Mean Widdle Kid* would look at the situation that might get him into trouble and debate whether he should do it or not. In each case he ends up saying, "I dude it." The following applies the "I dude it" approach to the way we manage our organizations.

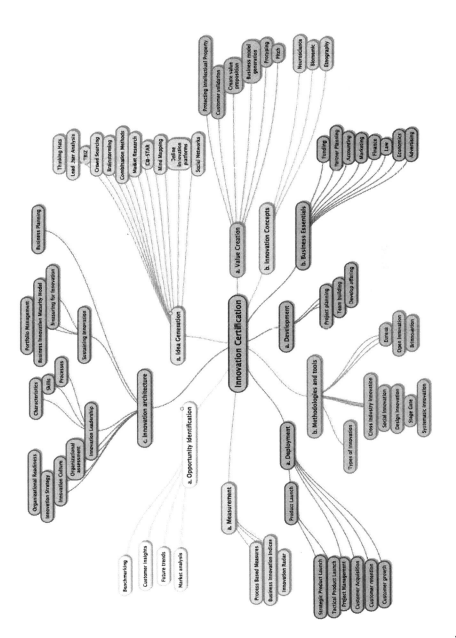

**FIGURE I.1**

Spider diagram of the innovation methodologies.

The Mean Widdle Kids are:

- The dream (identifying the opportunity) – Should *I dude* it?
- The vision – *Will I dude* it?
- The strategic plan – How *I will dude* it?
- The installation – *I am duding* it.
- The evaluation – Should *I have duded* it?

(Unknown author)

Another key concept in the TIME methodology is the belief that innovation is a process that starts when an opportunity for improvement is identified and ends when the added value is measured. We call this process –ISC. The following is a general breakdown of the major process activities that go on with a typical ISC. (See Table I.2).

When it comes to improving innovation in a specific product or part of an organization, that is, Research and Development, Sales and Marketing, Artificial Intelligence, and so on, the ISC provides an excellent tool to guide the organization through an individual innovation cycle. We have been criticized because we did not picture the cycle as a closed loop where once you've completed the transition, you go

**TABLE I.2**

The Innovation Systems Cycle

---

Phase I. Creation

- Process Grouping 1. Opportunity Identification
- Process Grouping 2. Opportunity Development
- Process Grouping 3. Value Proposition
- Process Grouping 4. Concept Validation

Phase II. Preparation and Production

- Process Grouping 5. Business Case Analysis
- Process Grouping 6. Resource Management
- Process Grouping 7. Documentation
- Process Grouping 8. Production

Phase III. Delivery

- Process Grouping 9. Marketing, Sales, and Delivery
- Process Grouping 10. After-Sales Services
- Process Grouping 11. Performance Analysis
- Process Grouping 12. Transformation

---

back and identify another improvement opportunity. We believe that you cannot wait until you have made the transformation before you can start another improvement opportunity. In most organizations there are many innovative opportunities being pursued at the same time. It would be extremely dangerous for most organizations to wait for a project to be completed before a worthwhile improvement opportunity is started. Typically an improvement opportunity is a project and by definition a project has a starting and endpoint. In addition, many of the individuals who are working on an improvement opportunity will not be assigned to another improvement opportunity until the one they are working on has been completed.

The following is a high-level view of the 3 phases and 12 process groupings that make up the innovative process. They are as follows:

- Phase I. Creation – This phase covers all the activities required to recognize potential improvement opportunities/problems, to creating a potential solution, and validating that the potential solution will address the opportunities/problems.

  Process Grouping 1. Opportunity Identification

  This is where an individual or group view the same old situation and see it in a different light than had been reviewed before. It's where an individual or group states, "We should be able to do it differently bringing additional value to the organization." At this point the individual or group usually does not know how to make the improvement but they are committed to come up with an innovative/creative solution. Frequently this ends up with a mission statement being approved.

  Process Grouping 2. Opportunity Development

  Also, during this activity, steps a number of potential problem solutions and/or opportunity improvement approaches will be identified, analyzed, and prioritized. Also during this, activity steps are actually taken to protect intellectual capital (patent new and unique concepts and/or check to see that there are no patent infringements).

  Process Grouping 3. Value proposition

  During this activity, the return-on-investment for the high-priority changes will be calculated. It is important that both the positive and negative impacts that the individual change would have on the organization are defined and analyzed. Take time to develop, refine, implement, and maintain, then compare this to the value-added content that the changes will bring about. Based upon this analysis, the changes that have the biggest impact, both real and imaginary, on the organization will be prioritized. For a more thorough understanding of developing a value proposition, we recommend reading the book entitled, "Maximizing Value Propositions to Increase Project Success Rate" published by CRC Press, 2014.

Process Grouping 4. Concept validation

During this activity, the proposed change is modeled allowing new performance data to be collected. Modeling can be accomplished by building an engineering model of the change and submitting it to a number of conditions (for example, temperature, humidity, vibration, electronic delays, and so on). The results can be used to project failure rates and/or reliability. Simulation models are also frequently used to validate the engineering and financial estimates.

- Phase II. Production – During this phase, the proposed changes are analyzed to determine if they should be included as part of the organization's portfolio of active projects. Once the change becomes part of the organization's portfolio of projects, resources are set aside to support the change process, to create the necessary engineering and manufacturing documentation, to validate the acceptability of the production outputs through a series of manufacturing process model evaluations, and start shipping to an external customer/consumer.

Process Grouping 5. Business Case Analysis

During this activity, an independent analysis is conducted to estimate the value-added content the particular project would have and compare it to other active and proposed opportunities to determine how the organization's resources should best be utilized. Approved projects should have detailed project management packages prepared for them. Projects that successfully complete this analysis are usually funded through first customer ship and become part of the organization's portfolio of active projects. To get a better understanding of the business plan analysis activity, we recommend reading "Effective Portfolio Management Systems" published by CRC Press, 2015.

Process Grouping 6. Resourcing

During this activity, the resources that are required for the approved project are put in place. In small and startup companies, financing usually becomes a major problem. Initially personal funding is used, then family funding, angel funding, and borrowing from banks are all legitimate sources.

People resources also present a problem for both the small and large companies. Although there are sufficient people out of work today to fill all the available jobs, there's big shortage in fields such as product engineering, programming, and manufacturing engineering. Finding the right suppliers at the right price that can produce the correct item, and do it on schedule in small lots is another problem that an organization faces during this activity. The last major item addressed in this activity is facilities. Not having the right equipment and/or the floor space required to support the output is a problem that is stressed during this activity.

Process Grouping 7. Documentation

During this activity, the engineering documentation, maintenance manuals, production routings, and job instructions are prepared and operators are trained on how to use them. Packaging and shipping containers are evaluated to ensure that they provide adequate protection for the product. The information collection system is defined and put in place. The project management data system generates frequent status reports to keep the management team aware of the status and point out activities where they need to be involved in.

Process Grouping 8. Production

As soon as the product is approved for shipment to the customer/consumer, the manufacturing floodgate is opened. The documentation and estimates are put under stress to meet the initial output demands that occur at start. The information collection system is initialized and status reports are generated.

• Phase III. Delivery – During this phase, the output from the process is transformed from items into dollars and cents. It also includes a performance analysis to compare actual results to projected value-added stakeholders.

Process Grouping 9. Sales and Delivery

Here we have entered a different world. Somehow the sales and marketing activities and culture are uniquely different than the culture in other parts of the organization. During this activity, promotional and advertising campaigns are developed and implemented. Sales strategy and quote approaches are prepared and the motivational compensation packages are designed.

Process Grouping 10. After-Sales Services

After-sales service includes individuals that man the control center, handle customer complaints, customer questions, and provide a line interface between the organization and its clientele. Another key part of after-sales service is a repair center. These two areas have to have the "patience of Job" since they are continuously faced with unhappy customers who just need someone to be mad at. Empowerment is the most useful weapon you can give these people.

Process Grouping 11. Performance analysis

During this activity, data are collected to determine whether the actual results meet or exceed the commitments at the business plan analysis stage. A post postmortem should be conducted before the project is closed out. This will provide input both positive and negative into the knowledge management system to help optimize future projects. Usually based upon this analysis, individuals doing outstanding work are rewarded and/or recognized.

Process Grouping 12. Transition

Usually the project team is disbanded after the Process Grouping 11 is completed but that's only the beginning of the project story. The real test of the project occurs over the next year or two when the approaches are often reset to the original habit patterns. For successful innovative projects, changes have to become part of the organization's culture and habit patterns. This is where the real impact of the project is evaluated.

## ISC Summary

The ISC is a continuous flow activity with a number of loops to take advantage of additional data that becomes available. Treat it like a process and it will behave well; treat it like a lot of little pieces and it will bite you every time. Like any process, it has to have a start and finish. The starting point for the ISC is the search for an opportunity to apply your creative powers to bring about a new and unique answer to a previously unanswered situation. It ends when output from the process delights the projected user.

## THE 12 STEPS IN THE INNOVATIVE WIN-WIN SQUARE

The effective use of a TIME process provides a "Win-Win" scenario for all the organization's stakeholders. Organizations that are serious about improving march around the 12 steps in the Innovative Win-Win Square. (See Figure I.2)

- Step 1. Increase dedication to innovation.
- Step 2. Increase innovation investment
- Step 3. Increase management attention
- Step 4. Improve processes
- Step 5. Increase employee involvement
- Step 6. Increase trust
- Step 7. Increase cooperation
- Step 8. Better products and services
- Step 9. Fewer customer complaints

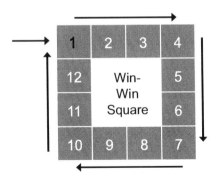

**FIGURE I.2**
Going around the Win-Win Square.

- Step 10. Increase customer loyalty
- Step 11. Increase growth and profit
- Step 12. Increase owner returns

---

## THE ELEVEN GUIDING RULES FOR PROGRESS

In Harrington's 1991 book entitled "Business Process Improvement," he provided his 10 guiding rules plus one new one for progress. These rules are as good today as they were 25 years ago. How you implement these rules will make the difference between success and failure of your innovative improvement initiative.

(1) The organization must believe that change is important and valuable to its future.
(2) There has to be a vision that paints a picture of the desired future state that everyone sees and understands.
(3) Existing and potential barriers must be identified and removed.
(4) The total organization must be behind the strategy to achieve the vision.
(5) The leaders of the organization need to model the process and set the example.
(6) Training must be provided for the required new skills.
(7) Provide an excellent design of product and process. The output can never be better than the design.
(8) Measurement system should be established so that results can be quantified.
(9) Continuous feedback should be provided to everyone.
(10) Coaching must be provided to correct undesirable behaviors.
(11) Recognition and rewards systems must be established to effectively reinforce desired behaviors.

Although there are differences between the innovation methodologies that are presently being used, they basically are all directed to achieve the same end result. I will admit that some of these methodologies are more effective than others. The big differential is not the methodologies, but the way these methodologies are implemented and used. I'm not going to try to convince you that our TIME methodology is the best. The one that you select should match your organization's culture and customers' expectations the best.

## NEVER-ENDING LEARNING EXPERIENCE

We understand that radical change can bring about massive resistance throughout the organization. People are comfortable with the current state and afraid of how they will be impacted by any change. But when the radical change will be affecting the culture within the organization, resistance increases by a factor of 10. We just completed a 20-year cycle where we embedded into our basic culture a Six Sigma philosophy. In the Six Sigma culture, the desirable performance standards were fewer than 3 errors per million opportunities. Major errors were treated as a cause for dismissal. Now as we enter the next phase of our organizational improvement effort we're looking at becoming more and more creative and innovative. One of the basic fundamental concepts with the innovative methodology is that errors will occur and are acceptable or at least forgivable. With innovation, errors are considered a learning experience rather than failures.

### The CEO Story

I remember a discussion I once had with a CEO of a major automobile company. He told me a story about one of his experiences as a young manager. This story went something like this:

*I had been working for 2 years on developing a new carburetor. Our company had invested millions of dollars in this project. The basic idea was a good idea, but we were never able to make it reliable enough to be used in production. As a result, the project was dropped and my team was reassigned. I was sitting in my office wondering what my next assignment would be when my secretary got a phone call from the president's office scheduling me for a 2 p.m. meeting that afternoon. It was obvious to me that I was on my way out and I spent the rest of the morning thinking about where I would look for another job. At 1:50 PM I came out of my office waved goodbye to my secretary and headed for the president's office.*

*As I walked up to the president's secretary, she said, "Walk right in. He's waiting for you."*

*As I walked into the president's office, I said, 'I realize I am fired. I have enjoyed working here and being able to work with you.'*

*He replied, 'Fired? No way. I just invested $2 million in you. I have a new assignment for you to start right away. And by the way, don't make the same mistake you did on the last assignment.*

## To Error Is Human

In any innovative methodology a degree of failure is acceptable. Just don't repeat the same mistake twice as that may be dangerous to your health (job assignment).

H. James Harrington

For the last 20 years, we have been preaching the benefits of the Six Sigma methodology. It was based upon the concept that anything less than 3 errors per million opportunities was unacceptable and needed to be improved. This resulted in a concentrated effort to improve employees' process and problem-solving skills. The American professional has become one of the best problem solvers in the world. That's because we have more problems than other countries. Our standards and methodologies have focused heavily on prevention of errors and failures but our classes were primarily directed at corrective action and problem solving.

To err may be human, but to be paid for it is divine.

H. James Harrington

Now our standards have replaced prevention with risk analysis. We now are thinking about what risks we can live with rather than how can we prevent them. Everyone makes errors; it doesn't matter if you are the floor sweeper or the executive in the 5th story of the head-quarters building. Everyone does something wrong once in a while. In fact, the higher you move up in the organizational structure, the greater impact your errors have on the organization and the more errors you make.

All individuals make errors. Some people learn from their errors and other people just go on repeating the same mistakes. It doesn't matter if you're the President of the United States or a clerk at McDonald's. (See Table I.3.) Abraham Lincoln is a good example of a person who failed many times but in the long run was very successful in freeing the slaves and keeping the United States together.

**TABLE I.3**

Abraham Lincoln's Failures and Successes

| Abraham Lincoln past President of the United States | Age |
|---|---|
| Failed in business | 22 |
| Ran for legislature – defeated | 23 |
| Again failed in business | 24 |
| Elected to legislature | 25 |
| Sweetheart died | 26 |
| Had a nervous breakdown | 27 |
| Defeated for Speaker | 29 |
| Defeated for Elector | 31 |
| Defeated for Congress | 34 |
| Elected to Congress | 39 |
| Defeated for Senate | 46 |
| Defeat for Vice President | 47 |
| Defeat for Senate | 49 |
| Elected President of the United States | 51 |

You will note that Abraham Lincoln failed many more times than he succeeded, but each time he failed or was disappointed in life, he came back a little wiser and a lot more committed to succeed.

## The World in a Whirl

Innovation is changing the world so fast today that it's hard to keep up with the latest technologies and products. By the time I get all my apps and names added to my new telephone (telephone seems like an obsolete name; it would be better off calling it a technaphone), it's obsolete and a new telephone that does a great deal more and does it faster is in the market. It wasn't long ago that Dick Tracy's telephone watch was just a cartoon artist's fantasy. Today many of us are wearing watches that allow us to make telephone calls. Since the turn-of-the-century, innovation has caused the earth to change so fast you can't keep up with it even if you study 24 hours a day. As we look ahead, technology and innovation are going to drive change at a much faster rate than it ever has been driven before. It's almost like we will have to implement the old song lyrics, "I'm going to change my way of walking, my talk and my name. Nothing about me is going to be the same." Innovation is now going at supersonic speed making it more and more difficult for any individual to stay well informed and up-to-date.

It's scary to think of what can be done with artificial intelligence and cloning. Just think what will happen when we have direct brain stimulation? Anyone will be able to put on their thinking cap and in a matter of a few minutes they will have completed the 4-year college curriculum. Basically, our whole education system will undergo a radical innovation change. Within the last 10 years, the online university programs have given anyone in the world the opportunity to graduate from a recognized university at a much lower expense and do all of this without ever leaving home. It provides us with the advantage of studying at our own pace and going to class on our own schedule without being away from home or traveling long distances to get to the University. The University of Phoenix is a prime example of a very successful online training program.

Practically the more minds you have thinking about improvement, opportunities will result in a higher level of innovation. Today China has more engineers available in the work force and far more engineers in the University that we have in the United States. In the 1980s and 90s, China was a copycat country. They relied heavily on other countries doing the design development work and they specialized in producing the product faster and less expensive. But things are changing rapidly in China; they now have the world's fastest computers and have now focused on shifting away from putting another country's trademark on the product that they produce. Today their goal is to develop their own brand reputation. Trademarks like Good Baby's are readily recognized around the world. This company produces 90% of the children's car seats. After giving a speech at their headquarters, they sent me a children's motorized replica of the 300 SL Mercedes that I used to drive and still love.

China is being driven into a new industrial revolution as they concentrate on bringing out their own innovative products. This focus is on products from the very low end all the way up to artificial intelligence. Watch out Silicon Valley – China has its product bomb sites on you. Admittedly you are now the leading developer of artificial intelligence but unless you increase your innovation activities significantly, you are going to go the same way that Ford, General Motors and IBM went. For many years China has been the biggest and now their goal is to be the biggest and best. Their goal is to do everything better than anyone else. Just look at the show they put on at the closing of the last Olympics.

Star Trek, one of my all-time favorite TV programs, has opened up the cobwebs in our mind presenting impossible things such as laser guns and teleportation. Today laser guns are a reality and who knows how soon we will be able to teleport material with beams of light. When this occurs, the car and airplane will be as obsolete as the horse and wagon are today. Sure there will still be some people driving or flying in them on the weekend much as there are people driving model T Fords today. Collecting the old things is a good hobby but not the reality.

Here is a recent personal example of how innovation is changing our world. A few months ago I was stopped at a red light (I usually stop for red lights) in Santa Clara, California when a small blue car pulled up beside me. I casually glanced at the car and my focus went back at the red light. My mind quickly came back to me saying, "Did you see what I thought I saw?? There was no one driving **that blue car!**" My head quickly swung 90° to the right. My first impression was right; there was no one in the car. I then remembered there was work going on in Silicon Valley to develop a driverless car. This was one of these models. When the light turned green, my foot pushed the accelerator all the way to the floor, my wheels spun for a few seconds and off I took like a bat out of hell. I made sure I was well ahead of that blue car for the next 5 blocks when it turned off in a different direction. A driverless car is a technical reality using today's technology.

## Different Functions Improvement Approaches

James Kirk from Star Trek would define today's organizations as a no-win scenario. TQM, Lean, CRM, BPI, TRIZ and other best practices – the list of these methodologies goes on and on. The champions of each of these methodologies often report into different parts of the organization. Each of these functions considers their "favorite" as the priority activity that needs to be improved. In order to improve the organization's performance management searched for the silver bullet, they flow from one improvement approach to another in an effort to get better results. These methodologies typically focus on one or more of the following: innovation, quality, productivity, creativity, profits, supply chain management, return on investment, market share, and so on. Each function has their own favorite methodology to promote:

- Finance wants management to invest heavily in cost reduction methods such as Activity-Based Costing.
- Manufacturing engineering wants management to invest heavily in automation and mechanization.
- Product engineering wants management to spend more money on basic research.
- Sales and marketing wants products that are far more innovative than the competition has.
- Human factors believe that the secret to profitability is investing in our employees training so they have better skills.
- Field services want products that are much more reliable.
- The investor wants increased stock prices and dividends.
- The employee wants increased pay for less work along with job security.
- The consumer wants products and services to be much less expensive but function better than the more expensive products and services they are getting today.
- The consumers constantly threaten to go to our competitor if your organization doesn't meet their needs.
- Quality engineering wants – they want everything.

All of these functions want the executive team to devote all of their time to their favorite improvement approach. However, the CEO knows that between 85% and 90% of his budget is already committed to things such as taxes, maintenance, payroll, and materials. These are the day-to-day things that are absolutely essential to keeping the organization functioning. As a result, there is only 10–15% of the budget that could be considered discretionary spending. Every function within the organization is competing for this part of the organization's budget and a 100% of the CEOs time. Each of these functions promises mouthwatering results. (See Table I.4)

If these figures are correct, the CEO could invest in just three of them and make a profit without producing a product. Obviously this is a ridiculous conclusion. As a result, there is strong competition between the individual functions to have the discretionary spending assigned to their project.

**TABLE I.4**

Typical Promised (Projected) Savings

| Function | Methodology | Budget Savings | Increased Profit |
|----------|-------------|----------------|------------------|
| Finance | Activity-Based Costing | 20% | |
| Manufacturing Engineering | Automation | 25% | |
| Human Factors | Total Resource Management | 30% | |
| Product Engineering | Innovation to expanded product lines | | 45% |
| Information Technology | New software packages | 20% | |
| Quality Assurance | TQM | Cycle time/costs reduction | |

## WHAT IS TIME?

Where the ISC methodology is designed to focus on individual parts or products of an organization, TIME is designed to change the organization's culture. Some of the more innovation-aggressive organizations are using both of these in parallel as the ISC methodology focuses on the immediate future and TIME provides for a long-term across-the-board improvement in innovation and creativity.

Well, it's about time for TIME (Total Innovation Management Excellence). TIME is a methodology that is designed to take advantage of the most positive aspects of each of the best practices that the various functions within the organization are promoting. TIME blends together key parts of these methodologies in a manner that demonstrates to the individual stakeholders that the culture of the organization is primarily focused on improving performance and value-added to each of the stakeholders. The six tiers of the innovation pyramid are as follows: (see Figure I.3)

- Tier I – Value-added to Stakeholders (the Foundation)
- Tier II – Setting the direction
- Tier III – Basic Concepts
- Tier IV – Delivery Processes
- Tier V – Organizational Impact
- Tier VI – Shared Value

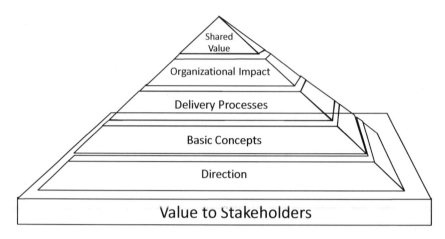

**FIGURE I.3**
The six tiers of the Total Innovation Management Excellence pyramid.

To accomplish this, TIME uses 16 key building blocks to construct an organizational profile designed to consider all of the individual stakeholder desires. These building blocks are strategically aligned with each other to increase the organization's innovation, creativity, efficiency, effectiveness, and adaptability. (See Figure I.4.) This combination of building blocks makes up a pyramid that is commonly known as the TIME pyramid.

## Tier I – Value-Added to Stakeholders

Tier I is the foundation that is designed to support the pyramid whose objective is to provide added values to the stakeholder. The bottom tier contains only one Building Block – BB1 – value-added to stakeholders, which is the foundation of the pyramid. This foundation is setting firmly on a bedrock of the investors', employees', and customers/ consumers' confidence in trust thereby establishing a platform for the other 15 building blocks.

### *BB 1: The Foundation*

This foundation is built on bedrock to provide maximum stability to the pyramid as mounted upon. It provides assurance to the stakeholders that the organization that its activities are stable and well constructed.

**Total Innovation Management Excellence**

**FIGURE I.4**
The TIME pyramid.

Without a good foundation, no matter how elaborate the construction is, the organization is doomed for failure. Too many of the present technologies are built on a "sand" base. As such, they looked beautiful for a period of time and then slowly decayed taking the organization's culture, investors' money, and employees' jobs with it. It is absolutely essential that you invest heavily in building the foundation that is capable of supporting the weight of the structure that will be placed upon it when it's subjected to time and environmental conditions (hurricanes tornadoes, earthquakes, sandstorms, floods, and so on). The tallest skyscraper in San Francisco (The Millennium) is slowly tilting to one side because the foundation was not built on bedrock. It was the pride and joy to its San Francisco residents until it turned into San Francisco's Leaning Tower of Pisa. Literally millions of dollars will be required to correct the foundation that the building was built upon. As of this date, no one knows how to correct the situation other than tearing down the upper stories of the building to reduce the weight on the foundation. I realize that investing money in the foundation looks like a waste of time and resources but let me assure you, the biggest wastes occur when you don't provide a stable foundation. The culture within your organization rests heavily on what it is supported by.

## Tier II – Setting the Direction

The second tier in the pyramid is used to set the innovative direction of the organization's performance strategy. It consists of five building blocks, which are as follows:

- BB2 – Innovative Organizational Assessment
- BB3 – Innovative Executive Leadership
- BB4 –Performance and Cultural Change Management Plan
- BB5 – Meeting Stakeholders' Expectations
- BB6 – Project Management Systems

### *BB2: Innovative Organizational Assessment*

It is not practical to start any type of innovative improvement effort without establishing what your present situation is including as its strengths and weaknesses. One of the major mistakes many organizations make is thinking that the executive team has an excellent understanding of what problems the workforce is facing. We often find out that the executive team frequently has a more positive view of the organization's operations and the employees have very different opinion.

### *BB3: Innovative Executive Leadership*

"If you're going to sweep the stairs, always start at the top." My grandmother.

There is a big difference between executive leadership and management involvement. Leadership requires the executive management team to be out in front. The first one out of the trenches leads the charge to reduce project failure rate and deliver an increased number of new products that are considered innovative by the consumer. His/her actions inspire the total organization to want to be more innovative. If you want to be an innovation executive leader, ask yourself if you know more about the status of new projects than you know about the status of last week's shipments. Management involvement is how the executive performs when the spotlight is not on him or her.

Here are some key definitions

- *Definition of executive*: Person or group appointed and given the responsibility to manage the affairs of an organization and the authority to make decisions.
- *Definition of leadership*: Leadership is the art of motivating a group of people to act toward achieving a common goal. He or she is the person in the group that possesses the combination of personality and leadership skills that makes others want to follow his or her direction. Leadership consists of the interlocking functions of creating corporate policy and organizing, planning, controlling, and directing an organization's resources in order to achieve the objectives of that policy.
- *Definition of management*: Management is defined as being responsible for organization and coordination of the activities of an organization in order to achieve defined objectives. Innovation management can include establishing an innovation vision, innovation process, structure, roles and responsibilities, and innovation support to achieve the objectives through innovation planning, innovation operations, performance, evaluation, improvement, and other activities.
- *Definition of involvement*: involvement is the act or process of taking part in something: the state of being included in an activity:

Top/executive management must do more than just support TIME. We like to start our innovation improvement initiative with the Board of Directors. The primary responsibility of the CEO of an organization is to meet the requirements of the Board of Directors. His/her performance is based upon what the Board of Directors say and how they measure the organization's performance. All too often the Board of Directors are not familiar with the goals and objectives related to innovation initiative and have other higher priorities with better measurement systems that are used to direct the organization's activities. Of course, the total executive team must be part of the process, participate in designing the process, assign resources, and give freely of their personal time. The start of any improvement process is the total executive team belief and leadership to make it successful. A typical way the executive team can demonstrate their leadership is to be among the first individuals who attend an innovative training program.

The executive team must do more than just support innovation. They must be part of the process, participating in designing the process, assign resources, and give freely of their personal time. The start of any improvement process is top management leadership.

I cannot over emphasize the importance of BB3 – Innovative Executive Leadership. Changing the culture of an organization to make it more innovative doesn't happen by chance; it happens because it is a major shift in the organization's behavioral and thinking patterns. Every day we are faced with a number of improvement opportunities that would drive the organization forward. It has been said that, "Every human being in the United States at least once in their life has defined an improvement opportunity that would make them a millionaire. Unfortunately most people do not take advantage of the opportunity." One of the most important contributions the executive team can make is to help their team members to recognize improvement opportunities and then have the skills and motivation to creatively develop a means to take advantage of these opportunities.

Unfortunately, too many executives think that they can improve innovation simply by putting out an executive order, "Every employee within the organization must become more innovative." From the employee's standpoint they think, "I am already very creative. What does the CEO want from me? This can't apply to me; it applies to everyone else."

As Dana Landry so wisely pointed out in BB3 – Executive Leadership that one approaches will not fit all types of organizations. The one most common thread in most profit-making organizations is the major groups that they need to satisfy in order to be successful. They are:

(1)  The Investor (The Board of Directors)
(2)  The External Customer
(3)  The Executive Team
(4)  The Employees
(5)  The Suppliers

These five major groups are the main impact areas. It's absolutely imperative that the system designer and the executive team understand how each of these major groups would view the organization as becoming more innovative. Unfortunately most of the individuals in each of these five major groups look to the people in other organizations to drive innovation. It is the executive team's responsibility to make innovation important to the individual dumping the waste paper basket and to the individual who is using artificial intelligence to transfer a pile of old steel into a robot that can simulate and/or duplicate any activity performed by a human being. To accomplish this, highly motivated speeches need to be transferred into firm visible action directed at meeting the needs of each of the five major groups.

Of the hundreds of different things the executive and the executive team could do to increase emphasis and results of the innovative activity. The following are 22 typical ones that you might be considering:

(1) Organize the Board of Directors ensuring that there is more representation of highly skilled technical people compared to people interested in financial accomplishment.

(2) Understand your customers to the point that you can predict what they are going to want in the future and have it ready when they need it.

(3) Establish a no-layoff policy where no one will be laid off as a result of innovative initiative. Example automation, robotics, and artificial intelligence).

(4) Develop a new product strategy that has one group focusing on continuous improvement ideas and second group focusing on major improvement ideas.

(5) Set up a Knowledge Management System that provides screen-proven information related to the technologies that the organization is using and future projections of how it will change.

(6) Ensure that your rewards and recognition system puts a new level of emphasis on creativity and innovation.

(7) Establish an innovative measurement system that is as complete as a financial measurement system.

(8) Don't just talk the talk, but also walk the talk. The executive team needs to show how innovative they are. They need to set a good example for the employees. Do it; don't just talk about doing it.

(9) Review the job descriptions ensuring that creativity/innovation is part of everyone's job description. In many organizations asking the employees to be more creative is better accepted than asking them to be more innovative.

(10) Hire people who are smarter than you so that they will challenge your decisions based upon knowledge and facts rather than being

yes men/women. It is the individual that challenges your thinking who is a real valuable asset.

(11) Define and measure your personal contributions to innovation and creativity. Set goals for yourself and measure to determine if the goals were met.

(12) Develop a personal communication plan related to innovation and creativity

(13) Provide the required resources.

(14) Releasing and enforcing pertinent directives, policies, and procedures.

(15) Set the example for organizational change.

(16) Develop a new product cycle with appropriate checks and balances and told gates in place

(17) Restructuring the organization to focus on innovation.

(18) Tie their compensation into the innovation measurements.

(19) Set very stringent controls on approving innovative value propositions and business case analysis. The best time to stop an unsuccessful innovation project is before starts.

(20) Becoming skilled in risk management analysis as you are in financial management analysis.

(21) Ensure anyone that is going to manage a project has been trained in project management.

(22) Accept failures as learning experiences rather than negative outcome.

Number 22 was the hardest one for me and for most experienced managers to accept. For years we've been taught two to three defects per million opportunities was the standard for acceptable output. In addition, error prevention was a key part of everyone's job description. Now all of a sudden with innovation projects we are encouraged to take bigger and bigger risks and that failure is acceptable. Now with the innovation methodology, risk taking is encouraged and failure is just a learning experience.

> If my employees learn from failure, I'm going to go bankrupt educating them.
>
> H. J. Harrington

The Board of Directors are the check and balance on the executive team. To do this job correctly and not just be a rubberstamp for the executives, requires a very special type of person. At least 60% of the Board of

Directors should not be officers in the organization. For example, 14 of the 17 members of GM Board of Directors are not GM employees. The Board should be made up of some technical people who understand the technology the organization is involved in, consumers of the product and service that the organization provides, people who have had an excellent understanding of the innovation improvement process, and financially oriented people. Unfortunately, most Boards have members who truly understand the innovation process. This is a situation that should be quickly corrected at the start of the innovation improvement process.

### BB4: Performance and Cultural Change Management Plan

All employees need to understand why the organization is in existence, what the behavioral rules are, and where the organization is going. This direction must be well communicated to the stakeholders, and there needs to be an agreed-to plan on how the organization wants to change and where it wants to stay the same. That is what a business plan does for an organization. It sets the direction of the business, what products are going to be provided, what markets are going to be serviced, and what goals need to be reached in the future. Without an agreed-to, well-understood business plan that is implemented effectively, the organization has no direction so it meets its goal of going no-where.

> A business plan setting on someone's desk is no plan at all.
>
> H James Harrington

Most changes in an organization's operation and/or products meet a natural resistance by the individuals who need to undergo the change. This resistance can have a major impact upon the organization's performance. Part of an organization's business plan should be a change management plan that prepares the individuals affected to accept the new concepts and procedures. Without this a high percentage of the new project will fail due to lack of acceptance by the impacted individuals.

### BB5: Meeting Stakeholders' Expectations

Every organization has an obligation to the individuals who are impacted by the organization's activities. This includes investors, management, employees, suppliers, customers, consumers, the community, interested parties, and the employee's family. Often what one stakeholder expects from the organization is detrimental to another stakeholder. For example, the employees typically want increased benefits including salary. The investor wants decreased cost so that bigger dividends to be paid. One of the biggest problems top management faces is how to balance the activities within the organization so that all the stakeholders have a win-win impression of the way the organization is managed.

### BB6: Project Management Systems

One of the fastest growing professional societies in the world is Project Management Institute with headquarters in North America. They have just issued an updated version of their standard called "PMBOK." It is a well-prepared comprehensive document that provides detailed guidance to the professional project manager. Its contents also apply to projects that are too small to have a project manager assigned to them or are considered as not requiring the project manager level of support. I will not try to condense it down in this technical report and I strongly recommend that you obtain a copy of the PMBOK. It is sufficient to say that any project that addresses the organization's culture should have a professional project manager coordinating it. When the culture of an organization is being changed, the risk of rejecting the concept is so high that the organization must take every precaution to ensure the project runs smoothly. Project management and change management are a critical part of this risk avoidance. To decrease the number of project failures, I recommend reading "Effective Portfolio Management Systems" (CRC Press 2015).

## Tier III – Basic Concepts

The third tier in the pyramid is directed at integrating the basic innovative concepts into the organization. It consists of four building blocks. They are as follows:

- BB7 – Management Participation
- BB8 – Innovative Team Development
- BB9 – Individual Innovation, Creativity, and Excellence
- BB10 – Innovative Supply Chain Management

### *BB7: Management Participation*

There is a huge difference between leadership and participation. The coach of a football team provides leadership to the team. We are participating in the game if we are out on the field blocking, catching passes, being tackled, pushing and shoving to get that extra inch. We have bystanders in the football stands. They stand up and yell at the top of the lungs instructing the quarterback that he must throw a pass, complain when the coach calls a play they did not like, or when the guard misses a tackle. None of the players arc working as hard as they could according to the bystanders in the stands. These are the fans who are out of breath just walking up the stairs to their seat. They are the type of person who seems to always sit beside me and spill mustard from his hot dog all over my pants.

Our management team has to do much more than just provide leadership; they have to be actively participating in the operation of the organization. I'm not talking about micromanaging their employees. I'm talking about micromanaging their value-added content to the organization's performance. They need to answer the question, "In what creative way have I changed my operating mode in the last year to add more value to the organization?" They need to answer questions like, "How much has morale changed within my organization and is it up or down?", "Have my actions increased my employees trust in the organization?", "Am I truly living up to the organization's values statements and my personal values statements?" Each manager annually should have a documented personal improvement plan that prevents them from micromanaging and transforms them into an active supporter of innovation and the associated changes. In the past, management has served as devil's advocate related to changes in the organization. They should change to become angel advocates of innovation and change activity.

This building block is designed to get all levels of management actively participating (out on the playing field) in the transformation activity and improvement effort. Having management feel comfortable in a leadership role is essential to the success of the total process. It is important that you bring about the proper change in top, middle, and first-line managers and supervisors before the concepts are introduced to the employees. Most organizations have done a poor job of preparing management for their new leadership role. All too often the management rule is, "Do what I say – not what I do."

### BB8: Innovative Team Development

What is a team? Why should I be on a team? Will someone else get credit for my good ideas? Do you have a charge number for the time I spend with the team? Can I decide which team I want to be on? What part of my job will be relieved so that I can participate on the team? At what bowling alley will a team meeting be held?

These are all good questions that management has to be prepared to answer based upon their activities in BB7. No, this is not an athletic team; it's a performance improvement team so do not bother to bring your bowling ball.

The organization needs to take advantage of manager teams and employee teams in order to take maximum advantage of the improvement opportunities. Everyone involved in the organization's change process is a key ingredient in today's competitive business environment. This building block develops team concepts as part of the management process and prepares all employees for participating in a team environment. The team usually uses a set of standard problem-solving tools selected to meet the specific requirements of the organization and serve as a standard idea generating approach that everyone in the organization is trying to use.

One of the prime outputs from the team environment is a sense of being a member of the organization and a feeling of cooperation between the individuals within the organization. It will develop a team environment that will have a big impact on employee morale, efficiency, and effectiveness. It has a tendency to eliminate comments like, "I knew she was doing it wrong but it is not my job to train her."

It is often been said that in teams 1+1=3 that can be true. Even the Bible points out the importance of working together so that when one individual falls, there is someone else there to help pick them up. But if teams are not managed properly I have often seen 1+1= −0.5, as good ideas are compromised to get consensus within the team.

### BB9: Individual Innovation, Creativity, and Excellence

Management must provide the environment, as well as the tools, that will allow and encourage employees to excel, take pride in their work, and then reward them based on their accomplishments. This is another key ingredient in every winning organization's strategy. You can have a *good* organization using teams, but you will have a *great* organization only when each employee excels in all jobs he/she is performing. Care must be taken to have a good balance between team cooperation and individuals who strive for excellence in all their endeavors. The two concepts need to work in tandem, not compete with each other.

Can you imagine calling into Apples' help desk because your computer won't turn on and being told, "That's an interesting problem. I will bring it up at our weekly team meeting and get back to you when they come up with an answer."

But exceling at your job is only part of your responsibility. Individuals are hired into an organization based upon their ability to define and take advantage of creative improvement opportunities. Employees are hired not only for their physical capabilities but also for their mental capabilities. No one should follow or implement obsolete or wrong procedures. The individual who identifies the obsolete or wrong procedure is responsible for getting it corrected prior to using it. But that is not enough; it's everyone's responsibility to look for ways that can improve what is acceptable today so we can be better tomorrow. All too many employees hang up their brains as they ring in on the time card.

There's a story about a man driving past an insane asylum when he had a blowout. As he started to change the tire, one of the inmates stopped on the other side of a tall steel fence to watch the process. As the driver removed the five bolts that hold the tire onto the car, he carefully put each one into the hubcap cover to be sure he didn't lose one. As he rolled the tire back to the trunk, he accidentally hit the hubcap cover flipping it over and the five bolts went flying into a nearby drain. The driver tried unsuccessfully to reach through the cover in the drain so that he could rescue the bolts. This proved to be an unsuccessful endeavor because either his hand was too big or the holes in the manhole cover were too small. The driver was now faced with an unsurmountable problem. After thinking about his problem for a while, he decided it was best to call AAA and have them buy five new nuts for him and change the tire. Searching for a phone or help, he went over and asked the inmate to get a guard for him. The driver explained to the inmate that he needed someone to make a telephone call for him because he lost the nuts that hold the tire onto the car. The inmate replied, "Why don't you take one nut off from each of the other three tires and use them to hold the fourth tire in place?"

The driver thought for a minute and replied, "That's an excellent idea. How come they have you locked up here in the insane asylum?"

The inmate replied, "I may be insane, but I'm not dumb."

Everybody has the capability to come up with a new idea that would never be thought of by a PhD.

### BB10: Innovative Supply Chain Management

Winning organizations have winning suppliers. The destiny of both organizations is inevitably linked. Once the innovative improvement process has started to take hold within the organization, it is time to start to work with your suppliers. The objective of this partnership is to help them improve the performance of their output and increase their profits, while reducing the cost of their product and/or service to you. It's a search for that win-win situation that benefits both you and your suppliers.

## Tier IV – The Delivery Processes

The fourth tier is the Delivery Processes Level. This tier of the pyramid focuses on the organization's processes and the output that the customer/consumer receives. It consists of three building blocks. They are as follows:

- BB11 – Innovative Designs
- BB12 – Innovative Robotics/Artificial Intelligence
- BB13 – Knowledge Assets Management

Tier IV is one of the most important tiers in the pyramid.

### BB11: Innovative Designs

An innovative design is not one that gradually changes even though the change is in the positive direction. An innovative design is one that jumps forward in the march of progress, rather than a step forward. From the consumer standpoint, an innovative design has to be one that is significantly better than any other one that's available. From the organization's standpoint it needs to bring in more value-added than the cost to develop, produce, sell, and maintain it through the warranty period. Over a short time period, an innovative design is no longer innovative as it is no longer significantly better than what is available from other sources. The first time a man cooked meat to eat over a fire was innovative; having a barbecue out in the backyard is not innovative.

After 70 years where the biggest percentage of my time was spent doing problem-solving, I realize that in most cases poor design of products, processes, organizational structures, and methods were the real root causes of the problem and we were focusing on correcting symptoms, rather than preventing a repeat of the same problem in the next product cycle. An innovative designer delivers a design that is efficient, effective, and adaptable in addition to meeting customer expectations. The current trend of focusing on minimizing risk needs to give way to preventing errors from occurring. To accomplish this, tools such as Design for X needs to be incorporated in a design methodology and design evaluation. Typical Design for X techniques are

- Design for manufacturability
- Design for reliability
- Design for repair ability
- Design for safety
- Design for costs

Increased emphasis needs to be placed upon knowledge management. Most designs are reviewed by a number of functions so that the individual function is not held accountable for finding errors. All errors that occur after a design review should be charged to the organizations being paid to do the design review, not to the design department.

Unfortunately we have all become accustomed to using our customers as the final testers. It's fast, quick, and sloppy. To offset this trend, you need to improve the effectiveness tools like Business Process Improvement, Total Quality Management, Activity-Based Costing, and Lean. With today's short product cycle times, it's too late to correct any problem once the manufacturing processes have started. By the time you find and correct a problem in manufacturing, the product cycle is over and the organization is just left with an extensive recall. It means that we need to develop innovative ways to evaluate potential and improvement opportunities.

### *BB12: Innovative Robotics/Artificial Intelligence*

This building block focuses on how to design and maintain product and services delivery processes so that they consistently satisfy external and/or internal customers and the people who consume the end product. It is directed at the product and services design activities process. All organizations, whether they are classified as service or product related, rely on process to produce their output and control the organization's operations. The delivery processes for products and services are very different. These differences make it necessary to apply different improvement methods and common methods in different ways in the delivery of service. This building block focuses on how to design, implement, and improve the service and production delivery process in the service and product industries.

Innovative use of technology, automation, and artificial intelligence has drastically changed the way our processes are designed and function. Automation has made concepts like Six Sigma practical in our manufacturing processes. Technology provided us with new products almost on a monthly basis. Artificial intelligence provides the capacity for a computer to perform operations analogous to learning and decision-making in humans, as by an expert system, a program for CAD or CAM, or a program for the perception and recognition of shapes in computer vision systems. In many applications it is impossible for humans to make decisions as fast or as correctly as artificial intelligence can. The combination of innovative personnel using technology, automation, and artificial intelligence is bringing us closer and closer every day to the ultimate factory of the future. It will need only one person to come in to turn on the organization daily and a dog to keep him awake. His job is to turn the switch that sets the total factory into motion and turns it off at the end of the day. For accuracy, repeatability, dependability, and precision are not in the hands of a human but in the programming in the new computerized environment.

In this building block, we will show you how automation, technology, and artificial intelligence can be used to reduce costs, assist in creating new products, reduce cycle time, while improving the quality of the delivered product and increasing customer satisfaction.

### BB13: Knowledge Assets Management

Today more than ever before, knowledge is the key to organizational success. To fulfill this need, the Internet and other information technology and provided all of us with more information than we can ever consume. Instead of having one or two resources of information, the Internet provides us with hundreds of them, if not thousands, of inputs, all of which must be researched for the key nuggets of information. We are overwhelmed with so much information that we don't have time to absorb it.

To make matters worse, most of the organization's knowledge is still undocumented. It rest in the minds and experiences of its employees. This knowledge disappears from the organization's knowledge base whenever an individual is reassigned or leaves the organization. This individual storehouse of knowledge is often not made available to the rest of the organization. In many organizations today, their knowledge assets are of more value than all of the facility, equipment, and unsold inventory.

An organization's first challenge is how to collect the undocumented knowledge that rests in the minds of its employees. A second challenge is, "How do you prevent outside sources including competition from capturing the same knowledge base?" Unfortunately much of the information available on the Internet today was based upon a small sample size to provide meaningful results. Fact and fiction needs to be separated and only the facts included in our knowledge management system. Typical excellent knowledge management systems are Interpol and the World Bank.

## Tier V – Organizational Impact

The fifth tier of the pyramid is the Organizational Impact Level. By now, the innovative performance improvement process is well underway within the organization and it will soon start to impact the organization's structure as well as its measurements system. This tier consists of two building blocks. They are as follows:

- BB14 – Comprehensive Measurement Systems
- BB15 – Innovative Organizational Structure

### BB14: Comprehensive Measurement Systems

This building block highlights the importance of a comprehensive measurement plan in all improvement processes. It helps the organization develop a balanced measurement system that demonstrates how interactive measurements such as quality, productivity, market share, cost and profit can either detract from or complement each other. Only when the improvement process documents positive measurable results can we expect management to embrace the methodology as a way of life. A good measurement plan converts the skeptic into a believer. As the process develops, the measurement system should change. When you start the improvement process, you measure activities. About six months into the process, you start to measure improvement results, and about 18 months into the process, the normal business measurement should start to be impacted. Management has continued to criticize methodologies and consulting organizations whose activity has not impacted the bottom line in a positive manner.

### BB15: Innovative Organizational Structure

As the smokestack functional thinking and measurement systems begin to change to a process or product view of the organization, bureaucracy is removed from the processes and decisions are made at lower levels. In this new environment, employees are empowered to do their jobs and are held accountable for their actions. With these changes, large organizations need to give way to small business units that can react quickly and effectively to changing customer requirements and the changing business environment. Functions such as Quality Assurance and Finance take on new roles. The organization as a whole becomes more process-driven rather than functional organization-driven. In this environment, the organization needs to become flatter and decentralized, requiring major changes to the organizational structure. This building block helps an organization develop an organizational structure that meets today's needs and tomorrow's challenges. The new structure is designed so that its activities are customer centric.

In one organization we worked with, we were able to reduce two layers of management and eliminate 32 management positions. To accomplish this, we established a dual ladder for management and technical people, which was equivalently rewarding.

## Tier VI – Shared Value

Shared value is at the very top of the pyramid as it provides the mortar that holds the individual building blocks together. Without enough innovative mortar, it can cause the pyramid to shift and decay. As the individual building blocks shift around, it causes large cracks and voids to weaken the pyramid until the pyramid is unstable and often collapsed into bankruptcy.

The TIME pyramid is created to provide additional value to all the stakeholders. It is absolutely imperative that the added-value content and results are shared with the relevant stakeholders. You cannot expect an employee to suggest efficiency improvements if he or one of his friends is going to be laid off as a result of the suggestion. If you start a continuous improvement process and you have layoffs, what you will end up with are continuous sabotage activities. We like to see the organization release a no layoff policy. For example:

> No employee will be laid off because of improvements made as a result of the TIME methodology. People whose jobs are eliminated will be retrained for an equivalent or more responsible job. This does not mean that it may not be necessary to lay off employees because of a business downturn.

The organization's dollars and cents savings should be shared with following four groups:

(1) with the customer/consumer
(2) with the employee
(3) with the investors
(4) with management

Should everyone be recognized in the same way and equivalent value rewards? No!! All rewards and recognition systems should be capable of adjusting its output based upon the contribution that the individual or team made to the organization's overall performance. It is a good practice to document why an individual is being given an award or recognition. This keeps the award system and balance throughout the organization and in line with the employee's job descriptions.

Tier VI is made up of one building block. It is BB –16 Rewards and Recognition.

### BB16: Rewards and Recognition

The Rewards and Recognition process should be designed to pull together the total pyramid. It needs to reinforce everyone's organization's desired behavior that includes creativity and innovation. It also needs to be very comprehensive, for everyone hears "Thank You" in a different way. If you want everyone to take an active role in your improvement process, you must be able to thank each individual in a way that is meaningful to him or her. There is a time for a "pat on the back" and a time for a "pat on the wallet." Your rewards and recognition process should include both.

> There is time where a pat on the back is sufficient and other times where ten $100 bills is not enough.
>
> H. James Harrington

## SUMMARY

There is no doubt about it. The United States is the blue-ribbon country of the world – the best place to live, work, and raise a family. We are more productive and have the best standard of living than any place in the world. People are more satisfied with their jobs in the United States than in Canada, Europe, or Japan.

- U.S. Index 40
- Canadian Index 39
- European Index 29
- Japan Index 16

Money magazine evaluated the standard of living in the 16 wealthiest nations. It compared them in five areas: health, solid job prospects, comfortable income, upward mobility, and adequate leisure time. The United States ranked #1; Japan, #7; Germany, #8; and the United Kingdom, #15. We are the envy of the rest of the world, and when you are #1, everyone is using you as a benchmark to beat. As a result of the gap between the United States and other countries around the world, everyone has targeted the United States as the gold standard.

I hate to complain about the United States of America, as we are extremely lucky to live in the best country in the world. But it is up to us and the next generation to creatively and innovatively improve the U.S. living standards keeping us as the benchmark country. It's up to you and me so let's make a commitment to be more creative and innovative related to our personal life and our work environment making the good old USA even better for our children.

> There is not a TIME for planning, a time for sleeping, but now is the TIME for innovative action.
> – H. James Harrington

> You make your future today. You live it tomorrow.
> – H. James Harrington

# BB1

## Value-Added to Stakeholders: The Foundation

*H. James Harrington*

### CONTENTS

### INTRODUCTION

There are many approaches to bringing about improvement within the organization. Some work better than others. Some do not work at all. Others are unproven theoretical concepts of the ideal situation. Some of the more popular ones are Six Sigma, Activity-Based Costing, Lean, Automation and Mechanization, Human Resource Management, Suggestion Programs, Design for Manufacturability, Process Redesign, Process Reengineering, Strategic Planning, Knowledge Management, Organizational Change Management, ISO 9000, Reverse Engineering, etc. We have seen examples where each of these has been very effective at adding value to parts of an organization and the same ones that have had a negative impact upon the organization's total performance. What are the right ones for you? That all depends upon the situation the organization is involved in. Some of the key conditions that drive the selection of improvement methodologies are:

- Type of output you are producing.
- The organization's financial conditions.
- The type of defects that the organization is experiencing.
- Where the process errors occurred and the frequency of occurrence.
- The skill level that the employees need to produce the output efficiently and effectively.
- The performance that the output needs to have.
- The skill level that the producers of the output need to have.
- Changes in the technology that you're using.
- Past history of implementing changes.
- Pressure from interested parties.
- Pressure from the labor union.
- What the competition is doing.
- What the consumer/customer needs are.
- What the consumer/customer would like to have.
- What's happening to the stock price.
- The type of equipment that the organization has.
- Where the organization's product is on the S-curve.
- Government regulations and changes to regulations.

This list could go on and on as many different conditions impact the type of improvement approaches/methodologies that will produce the best results for the organization.

## THE BALANCE BETWEEN USEFUL AND HARMFUL

In BB1 – Value-Added to Stakeholders: The Foundation, our efforts will be focused on defining the stakeholders for your organization and providing a means to weigh the importance of each of the stakeholders. We have seen time after time where the side effects of this seemingly excellent solution have a negative impact on value to other stakeholders.

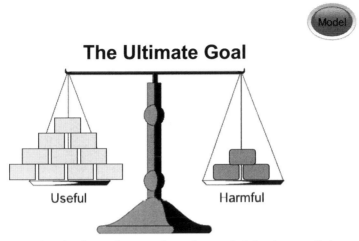

**FIGURE BB1.1**
The balance between useful and harmful changes.

The problem that the organization is facing is how to tip the scales in favor of the positive impact (Value-Added or useful changes) compared to the negative impact (Negative Value-Added or harmful changes). (See Figure BB1.1)

In Figure BB1.1 the useful and harmful changes are of equal weight. In this case there is no advantage in refining the proposed change unless the useful changes far outweigh the harmful changes. Useful changes far outweighing the harmful changes are the unmined gold. The benefits that the organization get are only equal to the difference between the useful changes and the harmful changes. Unfortunately the majority of the change initiatives have focused on the useful changes (value additions) and spent little time understanding the harmful changes that result from an improvement project to an organization.

Newton's third law states that all forces between two objects exist in equal magnitude and opposite direction: if one object A exerts a force $F_A$ on a second object B, then B simultaneously exerts a force $F_B$ on A, and the two forces are equal in magnitude and opposite in direction: $F_A = -F_B$. Simply put – for every positive impact there is an offsetting negative impact that may be of greater or lesser magnitude.

Theoretically that sounds like a very fine approach. Unfortunately there is a big difference between theory and practice. Most organizations talk about providing value-additions to the stakeholders. For years it is been all talk and no steak and potatoes put on the table. Most decisions that are made in the Board of Directors and by the executive committee are based upon optimizing return on investment or changes in the market share. For example: if the organization can outsource a number of machining operation at US $2 million are paying for when it's done in-house and it would mean laying off 10 workers. In your organization would the project be dropped or approved to outsource the activity? In most of the organizations we have worked with it would have been approved without looking at the negative aspects of approving the projects like fixed overhead costs, retraining costs, replacement costs, etc. To put it another way, do you care more about making a profit than about your employees and customers? I have worked for 40 years for IBM; at one point in my career I tried to get the ideas of installing a poor-quality cost system that would consider the customer-incurred cost when the computer broke down. At that point in time much of our equipment was rented instead of owned by the customer. To me it was obvious that we should consider the cost to the customer whenever the computer was not functioning as a result of an IBM problem. In our analysis we suggested that the rental rate per hour became part of the equation. The best I could get our executive team to agree on was one dollar for customer inconvenience for each time the computer broke down.

Another example is my son and I worked six hours to get a defective alternator out of his car and putting a new one that didn't work (12 hours of lost work time). We had already spent an hour and a half going down to the Ford garage and picking up a new alternator (three hours of work time lost). A second trip to the Ford garage to return the defective alternator lost us an additional three hours. It took additional three hours working together to install the new alternator. That's a total of over 20 hours due to the first alternator being defective. That's half a week's work at US $1,500 per week; that is, consumer incurred an additional cost of US $750. That does not include the cost of traveling to the Ford garage to take back the defective alternator. In addition the car was out of service for an extra two days. It makes a big difference when you include customer-incurred costs into your model.

Likewise when the individual is laid off, the value-added to the stakeholders is often **negative value-added** in many cases. The impact to the employee is not only the salary, it is the impact of how the employee was to spend the income. The only impact on the customer is if the purchase price has been reduced.

## WHO ARE THE STAKEHOLDERS?

From our standpoint it means that we need to understand the positive or negative value-added to each of the organization's stakeholders before we can make a decision if the change is positive value added. This is far simpler to state than it is to accomplish. To get started in this direction the following is a list of potential stakeholders within an organization.

1. Customers.
2. Consumers.
3. Management.
4. Investor.
5. Suppliers.
6. Employees.
7. Employee's family.
8. Government.
9. Special-interest groups.
10. Service providers.
11. The community/mankind.

The stakeholder is any individual or group of individuals impacted by an organization's products or processes. It is becoming more and more accepted that all organizations need to consider all of their stakeholders in every decision that is made. If you accept the premise, it is easy to see that your improvement process must consider more than just the end consumer. Certainly it is easier and less complicated if you can direct your efforts at maximizing the potential impact on just one or two stakeholders (usually the investor and the external customer). But that is not possible for most organizations today, since most organizations have at least six different stakeholders with very different priorities.

Although all stakeholders are important, the ones who have the biggest impact upon government and functioning organizations are:

- Its investors.
- Its management.
- Its external customers.
- Its suppliers.
- Its employees.
- Its community/mankind.

These six stakeholders have very different needs and expectations. Trying to satisfy six different stakeholders with such different needs is a very significant challenge to any management team. For what is good for one, maybe bad for another. For example, it would be good for the investor and management to reduce costs by having less benefits and lower salaries by moving the operations from the United States to Mexico. However, for obvious reasons, this change is not advantageous for the employee's and the communities' standpoint. It could also increase the pollution in Mexico.

## Management's Prioritization of Stakeholders

To live with this dilemma, management teams have prioritized the importance of improvement on individual stakeholders. Typically the way management considers priorities for the six stakeholders is shown below.

- Priority 1 – Investors.
- Priority 2 – Management.
- Priority 3 – External customers.
- Priority 4 – Their employees.
- Priority 5 – Their suppliers.
- Priority 6 – The community/mankind.

In this case investors are the top priority with the community at the lowest priority. This unwritten prioritization has resulted in our government passing laws to protect the general public, the environment, and employees.

## Top Five Positive/Negative Innovation Change Impacts

In order to understand the complexity of trying to satisfy all stakeholders, we need to understand each stakeholder's priorities. The following table lists the six stakeholders and their top five priorities and their top five negative change impacts.

List 1.1 – Investors Measure of the Improvement in Priority Order.
1. Return on investment.
2. Stock prices.
3. Return on assets.
4. Market share.
5. Successful new products.

List 1.1.1 – Investors Measure of Negative Change Impacts in Priority Order.
1. Reduce stock prices.
2. Reduce dividends.
3. Lower profit levels.
4. Reduce market share.
5. Failure of new products.

List 1.2 – Management Measure of the Improvement in Priority Order.
1. Return on assets.
2. Value-added per employee.
3. Stock prices.
4. Market share.
5. Reduced operating expenses.

List 1.2.1 – Management Measure of Negative Change Impacts in Priority Order.
1. Increased operating costs.
2. Reduce market share.
3. Lower customer satisfaction levels.
4. Failure of new products.
5. Longer cycle times.

List 1.3 – External Customer Measure of the Improvement in Priority Order.
1. Reduce costs.
2. New or expanded capabilities.

3. Improved performance/reliability.
4. Ease to use.
5. Improved responsiveness.

List 1.3.1 – External Customer Measure of Negative Change Impacts in Priority Order.

1. Increase purchase costs.
2. Decreased reliability.
3. Fewer capabilities than competition.
4. Poor customer service.
5. Increased difficulty to use.

List 1.4 – Their Employees Measure of the Improvement in Priority Order.

1. Increase job security.
2. Increased compensation.
3. Improved personal growth potential.
4. Improve job satisfaction.
5. Improve management.

List 1.4.1 – Employee Measure of Negative Change Impacts in Priority Order.

1. Layoffs.
2. Decreased benefits.
3. Salaries not keeping pace with cost-of-living.
4. Poor management.
5. Decreased skills required to do the job (boarding work).

List 1.5 – Suppliers Measure of the Improvement in Priority Order.

1. Increased return on investment (supplier).
2. Improved communications/fewer interfaces.
3. Simplify requirements/fewer changes.
4. Long-term contracts.
5. Longer cycle times.

List 1.5.1 – Suppliers Measure of Negative Change Impacts in Priority Order.

1. Loss of contract.
2. Shorter order cycles.
3. Increased competition.
4. Imposing new standards.
5. longer Accounts Payable cycle times.

List 1.6. – Community Measure of the Improvement in Priority Order.
1. Increasing employment of people.
2. Increased tax base.
3. Reduce pollution.
4. Support of community activities.
5. Safety for employees.

List 1.6.1 – Community Measure of Negative Change Impacts in Priority Order.
1. Moving work overseas.
2. Decreasing the number of employees.
3. Decreased facility resulting in lower taxes.
4. Unsafe working conditions.
5. Increase pollution of the environment (Increase in toxic gases and materials).

We agree that improvement impacts and negative change impacts can be different and/or rearranged based upon the type of products that are being provided, the culture of the organization, and where the organization is in its development cycle. They can be different for nonprofit-making organizations like the government and there is some variation depending upon the country/state that they are located in. However the way they are presented represents our research related to a variety of industries from the United States to China and other countries along the way.

The ideal improvement process would improve the organization's performance in all the stakeholders' priorities issues with lesser impact upon the negative change impacts. In these tables the most frequent impact was noted, but sometimes one methodology can have more than one impact, depending upon the circumstances. For example, Total Quality Management (TQM) can have a positive or negative impact on job security. If improving the product increases the organization's market share resulting in an increased workload, job security is improved. But if TQM results in waste reduction, thereby improving productivity, but does not increase market share to the point that it offsets the productivity gain, employees can be laid off. This results in a negative impact upon job security.

It's easy to see that if an organization is a nuclear power plant, safety would be the number 1 priority for the management, community and the employees.

## THE TIME METHODOLOGY IMPROVEMENT TYPE

The TIME methodology when implemented correctly can have positive impacts on the organization as noted below:

- Increased market share.
- Increased return on investment.
- Increase value-added per employee.
- Increased stock prices.
- Improved morale.
- Improved customer satisfaction.
- Improved competitive position.
- Improved productivity.
- Improved adaptability.
- Improved reliability.
- Improved maintainability.
- Improved safety.
- Increased number of employees.
- Increased profits.
- Decreased waste.
- Decreased overhand.
- Decreased inventory.
- Decreased or eliminate layoffs.

## RETURN ON INVESTMENT

Every year millions of dollars are spent on training that is not put to good use. I estimate that 5 to 10% of organizations do a very poor job of implementing the innovative improvement process and receive little or no return on the huge investment. Additionally I estimate that about 10 to 20% of organizations successfully implement their innovative improvement process very effectively and can document a return on their investment of as much as 40 to 1. For example, Globe Methodological, Inc. has documented a 40 to 1 return on improvement effort. And somewhere between 70% and 85% of organizations implement an improvement initiative fall someplace in the middle. They improve about 5% per year making it worthwhile, but these organizations do not obtain the results that they should be getting. Many of the same organizations are not seeing their market share grow even though they reduced waste, cut defect levels between 15% and 20%, and came out with new products and cut cycle time. Why? Because the savings are not passed on to the external customer but are absorbed in increased bonuses for the executive team. As a result, there is no impact to the bottom line. Other times the savings are just absorbed into the process resulting in no tangible savings. For example, all too often improvement activities reduce the time to perform a specific task from 8 hours to 7 hours. If there are 20 people who are performing the specific job that's a savings of 20 employee hours per week or a savings of 1,000 employee hours per year. The employees pay plus overhand is US $52 per hour, which is a total savings of US $52,000 per year.

However, if the employees are not assigned a different value-added job they adjust their work pattern to accommodate an eight-hour day. The old saying "Work expands to meet the defined work hours." In these cases employees' breaks are extended a little longer, actual work begins a little later and everyone can slow down to talk to their neighbor about last night's TV program.

When a change in a product or a process occurs, it reduces the time required to perform a specific task and the individuals who are now surplus should be defined and placed on the surplus list. Before any new job can be filled, Human Relations and the requesting manager needs to look at the surplus list to be sure that none of the employees can be trained to do the value-added job. All too often we hide surplus people by assigning them to jobs that didn't need to be done before because they were not cost-effectively justified. If it didn't need to be done before, it probably does not need to be done now.

One of the reasons for the lack of bottom line results is that these organizations are improving exponentially, but the competition is also implementing the same innovative improvement processes at the same time, causing these organizations to stay in a par with their competitors. As a result, their market share does not increase. In some cases the competition that is utilizing the improvement activities are even losing market share. This usually occurs when organizations observe that their competition is implementing an improvement activity and they decide to copy it.

You just learned innovation Rule number 1: You cannot copy your competition. For when you get to where you want to be, they will be far ahead of you. You must improve at a much higher rate than your competition in order to be competitive.

Here is Rule number 2: Do not go to your competition and give them all your Innovation strategies. They may listen to you.

## WHY ORGANIZATION INNOVATION FAILURES OCCUR

Organizations that are unhappy with their progress have many things in common. The following are the primary reasons why an organization is disappointed with the progress of their improvement efforts:

1. Change is top management (new top management).
2. Management thought the employees with the problem not themselves.
3. Management was unwilling to change but they want others change.
4. Change to top management's priorities and/or direction.
5. Differences in priority between management and the employees.
6. The theory has been taught in class but not put into practice.
7. Use of theoretical concepts rather than proven methods.
8. Using consultants that where it's not skilled in the methodology.
9. Downturns of the economy caused them to discontinue their efforts.
10. Middle-management did not buy into the change.
11. No results after first six months.
12. Other higher priorities within the organization kept it from being affected.
13. The consultants they hired did not understand their business.
14. They are not improving fast enough to keep pace with the competition.
15. Lack of hands-on, measurable results. There is a need to show management needs return on investment.
16. The changes are not selling meaningful problems.
17. The change activity is interfering with getting the job done.
18. Lack of focus strategy to integrate all efforts.
19. The innovative effort is not reflected in the bottom line.
20. Lack of organized labor support.
21. The methodology did not work.
22. Layoffs killed the activities.
23. High project failure rates.
24. Insufficient support for the initiative.

25. The innovative activity was poorly timed.
26. All the creative activities were assigned to product engineering and development.

These are all symptoms, not root causes. The real causes of these failures are:

ROOT CAUSE 1: Upper management did not believe that they needed to change.

ROOT CAUSE 2: Lack of trust between management and the employees is the biggest single cause of innovation failures.

ROOT CAUSE 3: The organization's innovative champion can be the third major cause of failure. The champion or Czar is the person within the organization selected to lead the innovative initiative. And in many cases he or she was not qualified. Attending one class does not qualify a person to teach and certainly not to lead innovation improvement activities.

ROOT CAUSE 4: Both the successful and unsuccessful organizations based there innovative initiative on a consultant's methodology. Often their implementation was based upon a book written by a consultant. The methodology that is used needs to be flexible enough to adjust to the individual circumstance.

ROOT CAUSE 5: Forgot Middle Management – Of all the people who have been impacted the most by improvement efforts is the middle management. Middle managers are the ones who have felt the pinch of all layoffs and flattening organizations more than anyone else.

## WHY BUY FROM YOU

After World War II, our production capabilities were the only ones that were not out-of-date or bombed out, ensuring us immediate success. As a result, we gained a false sense of confidence. We began to believe it was our management style that set us apart, not because the war was not fought on our soil. In Europe an MBA degree began to stand for a Manager who had Been to America. The rest of the world was quick to learn from the United States. People around the world set a personal objective to exchange their rice and potatoes for the steak that was on our plates.

As a result, we slept through the 1960s and 1970s. The alarm clock rang in the 1980s but we rolled over and turned it off. In the 1990s we woke up, showered, shaved, dressed, and drove to work. It wasn't until the 2000s that we rolled up our shirt-sleeves and we were committed to not losing more ground. This new, leaner America is transforming itself from a sleeping giant into a customer-related team that will do anything to satisfy its customers.

International customers are attracted to your organization for four reasons, in the following order:

- Customers Are Won Because of:
  1. Capabilities.
  2. Trust.
  3. Price.
  4. Quality.

- Customers Are Lost Because of:
  1. Trust.
  2. Quality.
  3. Capabilities.
  4. Price.

Product and service capability is driven by using the latest technology and/or using present technology in a more creative ways. Trust is based upon experience and reputation. It reflects the faith that the customer has in your ability to meet your cost, schedule, and performance commitments. Price today is tied directly with value. Customers are looking at getting the best performance at the least cost. Quality reflects more than just the internal view of the product and/or service purchase. It reflects the quality of the total organization, the reliability of the product, and the capability of its sales and service personnel. You lose customers for the same four reasons that you attract them, but in a different order.

For an organization to survive in today's competitive international environment, there must be innovative improvement efforts using both the continuous and breakthrough improvement methodologies. Management needs to make the correct business decisions so that the correct products are available at the time they are needed, while making the most of everyone's efforts. There needs to be a high level of cooperation between government, business, labor, and academia. Each must improve the value of the product and/or service as viewed by its customers. This means that all functions in an organization must use the most appropriate technology to improve their efficiency, effectiveness, and adaptability. In addition all organizations need to have a well communicated agreed-to plan that merges together the many improvement methodologies to provide the greatest value to all the stakeholders.

## PROVIDING VALUE TO STAKEHOLDERS

The purpose of any progressive, long-lasting organization is to provide products and services to its customers that have more value, better quality, and are less costly than what other organization's offer. But it also has an obligation to all its stakeholders, which include investors, management, employees, suppliers, and the community. Truly great organizations provide ongoing security and value to all of their stakeholders, not just their customers. TIME is based upon establishing strong stakeholder partnerships with the organization using the innovative improvement approaches. The word "partnership" infers that all parties involved will mutually benefit from the innovative improvement activities.

Without building a strong stakeholder foundation your innovative improvement process cannot sustain itself. It is like building your house on sand close to the ocean. No matter how well you put the building blocks together on top of a bad foundation, sooner or later the sand will shift and your house will come tumbling down. One of the most difficult jobs all organizations face is to balance the needs of all its stakeholders so that the organization is perceived as value-added to all of the stakeholders.

### Determining Value-Added for All Stakeholders

I suggest that you start the evaluation by making a check sheet for your most important stakeholders. Typically these are the investors, the external customers, management, employees, the community/mankind, and suppliers. For each of these stakeholders you should define the top positive value-added outcomes and a second list of the negative value-added outcomes that would result from implementing a project, program, or change.

Samples of these lists can be found in List 1. 1 through 1.6.1. Due to the variety of organizations, cultures, outputs, and operations conditions you may find it necessary to modify the list to accommodate your specific organization's specific environment. The information in the above-mentioned lists represent the information that we would include in a typical engineering and production-type organization.

For each of the 10 outcomes per stakeholder you should determine if you agree or disagree with the statement. We use a "10" to indicate a strong agreement with the statement and a "0" to indicate a strong disagreement with the statement. This will provide you with an understanding of which major stakeholder change activities are positive value-added and which have no value ("5" rating) or negative value-added for the change. Periodically the changes that have or are being implemented should have this checklist reviewed and combined to identify major stakeholders that are receiving no or negative value-added improvements in all 10 outcomes per each major stakeholder. When this occurs, your organization should consider some change activity that will result in positive value to that stakeholder.

## Determining Value-Added for Individual Changed or New Activities

Determining what stakeholders are being served by the organization's change or new initiatives is much easier to define. The difficulty occurs when we start to justify a potentially innovative change initiative. Usually organizations focus their analysis on the organizational key measurements like return on investment, value-added per employee, reduce cycle time, and increased customer satisfaction. Typical types of data that need to be assembled are:

- Cost to produce the output – Finance, Manufacturing Engineering, Sales, and Marketing.
- Average employee costs including variables overhead – Finance.
- Sales forecast by month for first year by quarter year next two years – Sales and Marketing.
- Additional equipment requirements estimated price– Manufacturing Engineering and Information Technology.
- Supplier projected cost – Procurement.
- New employee acquisition costs – Human Relations.
- Projected cycle time – Product Engineering.

Some key tips to remember:

- Whenever your innovative change value-added results from eliminating or simplifying work activities, there is no savings unless individuals are assigned to do different value-added activities. These cannot be activities that were not being done before because they could not be justified. For example, if you change an 8.0-hour per day operation that individual is performing so that it can be done in 7.8 hours a day, the employee must adjust his work rhythm to fill up the rest of the 0.2 hours. This in reality is not value-added. Example 2: if an innovative improvement effort resulted in savings of 80 hours per week and no one is assigned to another activity, there is no work hour savings involved in the project. If 80 hours is assigned to other or new activities, the savings from the initial project is equal to the additional value-added as a result of applying the 80 hours to a different assignment. You cannot claim work hours saved unless the savings is applied to a different assignment, to a newly created assignment, or employees are released from the organization as a result of the innovative performance improvement activity. Value-added when a job is eliminated, there is a savings of the employee's salary plus the variables overhead costs. The fixed overhead cost cannot be considered.
- The cost of the person laid off is immediately reflected as a decrease in cost but you must consider the replacement cost to your organization. We like to use the replacement cost for an individual as a negative value-added to the innovative change. The average replacement cost runs between 50% and 150% of the employee's annual salary. That means that for an employee whose salary is US $60,000, it will cost the company anywhere from US $30,000 to US $45,000 to hire and train a replacement.
- The first type of cost that results from separating an individual from the organization is direct costs. This category includes:
    - Separation costs such as exit interviews, severance pay, and higher unemployment taxes.
    - Replacement costs advertising, search, agency fees, etc.
    - Temporary staffing.
    - Training costs.

- Personal purchase items like uniforms, and informational literature.
- Reduce productivity due to learning curve.

Indirect costs. This includes:

- Lost productivity for the departing employee.
- Lost clients and lost organizational knowledge.
- Reduced morale.
- Hiring temporary employees.
- Additional work to other employees.
- New employee learning his or her job.

These costs vary greatly from country to country and type of output. The following are typical replacement costs for a manufacturing-type organization in the United States.

- Heavy manufacturing plant employee US $760.
- Registered nurse US $1,200.
- Financial professional US $8,500 to US $13,000.
- Senior manager at a residential construction company US $80,000 to US $90,000.
- Middle manager at a consumer products company (making US $50–125k) US $98,000 to US $117,000.
- Lower-level executive at a consumer products company (making US $125k) US $185,000.
- Senior-level executive at a consumer products company (making US $200k) US $300,000.

When you reduce inventory, you only save the interest on the value of the inventory that was reduced. Typically this is about 3% of its value. By reducing inventory, this frees up additional space that can be used for something other than inventory. In this case additional space can be considered as positive value-added savings at a rate in keeping with renting a similar area.

The cumulative positive or negative value-added should be included in the Value Proposition and the Business Systems Analysis. It should be used as an initial projection that justified making the project of the organization's portfolio of activities.

## SUMMARY

The importance of having a solid foundation for your TIME initiative cannot be overstated. All too often organizations march blindly into new initiatives without establishing a firm base to build the new culture on. Obviously ideas discussed in BB1 needs to be established early in the transformation initiative. As a result much of this activity has to be based upon good judgment, acquired knowledge, and experience. When you design your foundation there are two things that you need to consider. They are:

1. The materials that will be used in the foundation including the steel rods that holds it together and reinforces the foundation.
2. The materials that the foundation sets on. If the material that the foundation is sitting on shifts, it can weaken and/or destroy the best-designed foundation and everything that the foundation supports. Ideally the foundation is constructed on bedrock that is firmly based in the organization's mission and values. If this is not the case, support columns need to be designed to penetrate the sand until there can be no movement in the materials that the foundation is resting on.

You need to build your foundation in a manner that will support the present activities and continue to support your activities if the organization grows by 100%. Given a sound foundation the organization can extend upward without jeopardizing any of its strengths and advantages.

> Building a temple on the foundation that was designed for a bungalow is a sure combination for failure.
>
> H. James Harrington

# BB2

## *Innovative Organizational Assessment*

*Laszlo Gyorffy and H. James Harrington*

## CONTENTS

> One accurate measurement is worth a thousand expert opinions.
>
> **~ Grace Hopper**

## INTRODUCTION

It is not practical to begin any type of innovation improvement effort without determining a baseline and understanding the organization's current strengths and weaknesses. It is helpful to know, "How are we doing?" before proceeding with well-intentioned interventions. Your doctor would not prescribe surgery without first giving you a thorough physical check-up. Obtaining valid information about the health of the organization's performance with regard to innovation and the factors that affect performance is a sound place to start.

To answer the question, "How are we doing?" we explore a variety of assessment tools and methods and offer tips to help you succeed. You can use off-the-shelf surveys, create one from scratch, conduct in-person assessments, or take advantage of online tools to survey people at scale. For example, you might gather the executive team for a two-hour meeting to get a quick snapshot of their perspective on innovation. You could have them consider their enterprise's effectiveness in executing these foundational innovation tasks.

1. *Strategizing*: Setting direction and priorities for innovation
2. *Exploring*: Uncovering unmet needs and significant opportunities
3. *Generating*: Creating many high potential ideas
4. *Optimizing*: Iterating and improving the value of ideas
5. *Selecting*: Making good choices among new ideas
6. *Developing*: Designing, building, and testing operational improvements as well as new products and services
7. *Implementing*: Delivering innovative solutions on time and within budget
8. *Commercializing*: Launching and scaling up new businesses or offerings
9. *Competing*: Beating the competition with new or enhanced offerings
10. *Profiting*: Generating sufficient returns from operational improvements as well as new offerings

The process is straightforward. Ask each leader to write on a post-it note their "effectiveness" rating (very low 1–10 very high) for the organization. The notes are collected and posted for all the leaders to see how the group evaluated the innovation tasks. Each task is discussed and then the group is asked to step back and consider the overall picture and the implications for their enterprise. Through this process, they discover what their colleagues think about the enterprise's innovation strengths and weakness as well as where they have consensus and where their opinions differ. The exercise also raises questions about what they don't know. Self-discovery is the best discovery, and this two-hour meeting may prove to be a tipping point for the leadership team and your innovation improvement effort.

Activities like these offer helpful insights and often provoke leaders into action, one of which is to authorize the innovation team to conduct a more comprehensive assessment of the organization. This is particularly important because one of the major mistakes many organizations make is to believe that the executive team has an accurate understanding of the problems the workforce is facing. We often discover the executive team has a more positive view of the organization's operations and innovation practices than their employees. (See Figure BB2.1.)

This dynamic surfaces when we ask individuals taking one of our organizational surveys to list the top 10 activities needing the most improvement within the company and then to list the activities that need the least improvement. Typically, the survey is completed by the executive team and a sample of management and employees. One of the questions that is evaluated is, "How much trust and confidence do you have in the upper management team?" Almost without exception, this question is rated on the executive's list of ten things that has little need of improving. It is an

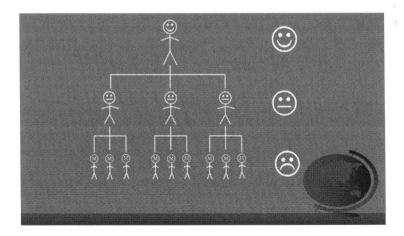

**FIGURE BB2.1**
The view of the organization based upon position within the organization.

exception to find it not on the top 10 needs-improvement list for middle management and employees. It is absolutely essential that any assessment of an organization collects information related to the needs, expectations, and desires of the executive team, middle management, and the employee. Once this is done, the stakeholders are in a position to compare the organization's strengths and weaknesses as viewed from these three separate levels. (Note: It is a rare organization where a single survey and/or assessment is adequate to characterize the culture of the organization and identify opportunities for major improvement.)

This chapter will show you how to overcome issues like "executive team bias" as well as introduce a set of innovation assessments and question formats for your consideration.

1. **Innovation Fitness Survey** – This survey takes a systems' perspective to gather employee views on the key innovation factors driving the organization's overall innovation performance.[1]
2. **Is-Should Be Analysis** – Focus groups are run for stakeholders at all levels (e.g., employees, first-line managers, middle managers, executives, and key staff personnel) and the results are analyzed related to where the organization is today, where it should be in 3 years, and how important is it to reaching the objectives.
3. **The 7S Survey** – This survey is directed at management and explores the organization's *Hard Elements* (i.e., Strategy, Structure, Systems) and *Soft Elements* (i.e., Shared Values, Skills, Staff Style). The model is based on the theory that for an organization to perform well, these seven elements need to be aligned and mutually reinforcing.[2]
4. **Historical Trend Analysis** – Past performance is an effective way of projecting future performance. An individual's attitude is usually based upon their past experience in implementing changes within the organization. The survey is designed to define potential roadblocks to the change in an innovative culture.
5. **Customer Focus Groups** – These focus groups are designed to develop an understanding of how the organization's innovation activity is perceived by the customer. The feedback is used to identify ways that the customer's perception of the organization and how it innovates can be improved.
6. **Magazine Innovation Analysis** – A number of major magazines (e.g., *Fortune*, *Fast Company*) have developed comprehensive strategies for rating and then ranking the innovation level of the top

100 companies.[3] If you're not in the top 100, the rankings can provide an excellent target goal for the organization. The strategies and analysis can be applied to your organization, providing deep insight and a path toward improved innovation.

7. **General Employee Opinion Surveys** – One benefit of conducting an employee opinion survey is that it provides feedback on a wide variety of management issues. From an innovation standpoint, it allows the questions targeting innovation to be intermixed with other probing questions on different topics eliminating a tendency to provide positive feedback on any single issue. We have seen instances when a survey directed toward innovation got an overall rating of 82% above average. When it was mixed in with an employee opinion survey, the innovation rating was only 46% above average.

8. **Do It Yourself (DIY) Survey** – Creating your own online innovation survey allows for easy targeting and tailoring of questions, provides cost savings, and is convenient in terms of distribution and gaining audience participation.

The surveys have their differences, but they are all tools intended to help you efficiently and effectively collect high-quality data about your current innovation capabilities, generate actionable insights, and develop a sound strategy for moving forward. Examine the surveys carefully and take time to think about how you might apply them to your situation. You may use all or part of the surveys or find another one better suited to your needs or create a customized assessment tool from scratch. Constructing your own survey has now become much easier with the growth of online survey providers like QuestionPro. The chapter will conclude with tips on how to build your own assessment tools using these vendors.

## CONDUCTING ORGANIZATIONAL ASSESSMENTS

By taking a well-planned approach, you can efficiently gain many insights from conducting organizational assessments. The benefits are multiple: greater insight for leaders, employees who feel their voices are heard, and improved strategy and focus when implementing enhancements to innovation within the enterprise. They also provide a benchmark to measure continued improvement. Unfortunately, many organizational assessments are not well designed, executed, or acted upon. A lack of leadership support and timely communication can result in lower morale and increased frustration for employees. For these reasons we recommend following a proven 4-step approach. (See Figure BB2.2.).

### Prepare with Purpose

For an organizational assessment to be successful, it must serve a specific purpose. Assessments designed without clarity regarding the *who, what, where, when, how,* and most importantly *why,* typically produce poor results. It may seem obvious, but identifying the reason you are conducting an innovation assessment is critical: What do you want to know? What has prompted the need for the assessment? What areas of the organization need improvement or change? What information would help you to make better decisions? Identifying what you want to know makes it easier to determine the design, content, scope, and tone of your organizational assessment.

If innovation is falling below expectations, use the assessment to determine what is needed for employees to innovate and collaborate effectively or what leadership support should be put in place. A sound "form follows function" guiding principle is to select an assessment methodology to fit your informational and organizational needs.

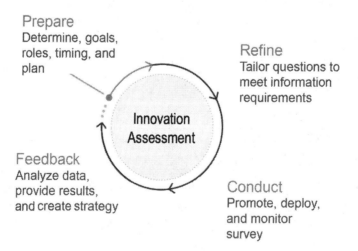

**FIGURE BB2.2**
Four-step assessment process.

In addition to figuring out who should be included in the assessment, what the timeline is, and when it should be distributed, you will need to determine two key roles. You must settle on who will be the project manager for the assessment and who will conduct the assessment. Finding a good project manager is vital. Ideally you select someone who is not only effective at developing and implementing a plan, but also has the respect of organizational stakeholders. The second key role is often determined by whether or not you have the in-house expertise to conduct the assessment. If not, the assessment process will likely require the services of an external expert.

- **In-house Resources**: Conducting assessments with internal resources provides some advantages. The staff take greater owner-ship of the process and the assessment tends to be more informal, more economical, and can be better suited to certain situations. For example, leaders may want to know how employees in a specific division or region view innovation. A small-scale in-house innovation survey, for example, can yield results quickly and economically.
- **External Resources**: For more complex assessments at a bigger scale, you may want to hire an external firm to guide you through designing and conducting your employee survey. These firms save their clients' time and effort while offering assessment expertise that can be helpful in designing the questions, summarizing responses, and segmenting the assessment results based on the location or type of respondents. There are other benefits to employing a third-party provider that can have a significant impact. The two biggest are confidentiality and unbiased results. For example, if you use a third party to conduct the survey, you'll likely generate greater response rates due to increased employee confidence in anonymity. There is also a sense that a third party will be more objective when writing the report and/or sharing the results. If assured of confidentiality and an unbiased perspective, employees tend to be more willing to participate and be more candid in their responses.

Whether you conduct the assessment with external, internal, or a mix of both resources, the project manager and team should have the knowl-edge, skills, and abilities to do the job. Specifically, ensure they possess the necessary credibility, assessment know-how, communication skills, and of course, availability. Nothing is more frustrating than running a team where people are inaccessible, slow to respond, and don't complete their assignments on time. The credibility and communication skills are especially valuable upfront when you are not only encouraging people to participate in the assessment, but also are at the end of the process when you may have to share sensitive data in a manner easily understood by all parties.

If you are going to use a survey, consider the benefits of both online surveys and paper-based questionnaires. Online surveys save money, responses are collected quickly, and reports are much easier to produce. Paper surveys, however, are helpful when engaging hard-to-reach groups who don't have internet access. As you read in the opening of this chapter, paper surveys (as simple as post-it) can also be used to facilitate in-person data collection and analysis.

## Refine

Since most organizational assessments are done via survey, my tips and techniques are targeted in that direction. The design of your survey and the questions you ask can make all the difference in the quality of the responses you gather. Consider the following factors when creating your innovation survey

- What type of survey? As we noted, surveys come in many forms. They can be interviews (in-person or by telephone), paper-based, or digital (either by email or online).
- What types of questions should be included? You have many options, including rankings, scale ratings, forced choice, or open-ended questions that encourage employees to comment. Most innovation surveys incorporate a combination of the question types.
- What demographic information do you want to collect? You may choose to gather demographic data such as tenure (years with the company), functional area, or job classification. This can be very helpful when analyzing the survey responses, especially if the assessment covers many different groups and regions.
- What type of language should be used in the survey? Avoid using acronyms or terminology where respondents may be unfamiliar. Don't use leading language that might sway survey responses in a particular

direction. Decide if the survey will all be in English, for example, or will be in the native tongue of the regions you are assessing. If you are creating the questions, a best practice is to have someone else review them to ensure they are understandable. If you are using a third party, you or a fellow employee should do a review of the survey questions as well to ensure they will resonate within the organization.

- What level of participation will you require? Are you going to demand full participation or will you be able to gather sufficient information from a sample of employees? Typically, the type of innovation surveys we are describing are voluntary.

- What is the timing and timeline? Are employees able to complete the survey during work hours or must they do it on their own time? Given everyone's limited bandwidth, we recommend allowing them to do it during work. This usually provides a positive boost to participation rates. In addition, consider the timing of the survey, avoid sending it out during peak business periods (e.g., just before the release of a new product) or during the holidays. And make sure to allow adequate time for all participants to respond.

Once you have completed designing or selecting an off-the-shelf the survey, we recommend running a pre-test with a small group of employees. Gather feedback on the survey questions, the survey length, and explore any other questions and concerns that might arise.

## Conduct

We recommend you develop a series of communications in advance so you are ready to promote the survey. Typically, this is done through email notification, a notice on communal bulletin boards, or on the organization's intranet. You want to avoid distributing your innovation survey without adequately explaining the purpose of the survey, what will happen with the results and what actions the leaders might take based on the data that is gathered. Participation as well the quality of the survey responses can be increased by being clear about why you are asking the questions. Include messaging about data anonymity and the confidentiality of results to increase the likelihood that employees will provide honest and accurate feedback. And finally, it helps elevate response rates if a member of the executive team or someone with organizational clout authors the initial invitation to participate in the survey.

The series of communications begins with an invitation, but then moves on to messages reinforcing the timeline and reminds employees to complete the survey. We have provided examples of these communications for your review.

1. Subject: Innovation Survey – We need your input

   As you know, one of our Vital Few initiatives for this year is ***Innovate for Sustained Revenue Growth***. To accomplish this goal, we are using a survey to gather feedback from everyone. Data from this baseline survey will help us determine how we can improve our processes, develop new and profitable products, and continue to meet the needs of our customers in the future.

   **How Long Does It Take?** The survey has 40 questions and should take no longer than 20 minutes to complete. The survey assumes we all have the ability to come up with new and innovative ideas. New products, new services, new business models, new cost-saving ideas, process improvements, etc., are part of what we are trying to address with this initiative. We would like to use this survey as a first step.

   We are working with a consulting firm, EDGE Software Inc., to administer the on-line innovation survey. They possess deep expertise in the field of innovation and will assist us with the compilation and analysis of the data. Individual responses will be kept completely confidential. This is an online survey that will immediately provide you with an analyzed report related to your view of the organization's innovative system. Only aggregate tabulations of groups or functions will be reported so I would like to encourage you to be open and honest with your responses. We will make an executive overview available to all who contribute to the survey.

   You have two weeks to finish the survey. The survey must be completed by March 25th at 5:00pm PST.

   Survey URL: https://Go.EDGESoftware.cloud/InnovationTIME

   Let me take the opportunity to thank you in advance for your time. Again, your feedback is critical information for us in determining our innovation strategy going forward. If you have any questions, don't hesitate to contact me.

   Thanks,
   Robert

2. Subject: Innovation Survey – Reminder

   There are only two days left to complete the innovation survey. The deadline is March 25th at 5:00pm PST. If you have already completed the survey, I want to thank you for your participation. If you have not yet had a chance to take the survey, I would like to encourage you to do so.

   It is our belief that surveys such as this one offer an objective way of assessing how we "measure up" in terms of innovation. The data generated can confirm what we are doing well and also help us respond to problems. It is important that we hear from everyone so we get an accurate picture of our current innovation capabilities.

   Survey URL: https://Go.EDGESoftware.cloud/InnovationTIME

   If you have any questions, please don't hesitate to contact me.

   Thanks,
   Robert

3. Subject: Innovation Survey – Thank you for completing the survey

   I want to personally thank you for taking time to complete the baseline innovation survey. It is one of our first steps to achieving the Vital Few: Innovate for Sustained Revenue Growth. Your feedback is a key factor in starting the process. Expect more communication from the Innovation Team as we move forward.

   Thanks,
   Robert

## Feedback

Compile the survey results and begin your analysis. Review results for each question and get comfortable with all the rankings, averages, percentages, and open-ended comments. Identify the overall highs and lows, the surprises and the expected, the strengths and weaknesses. Look for recurring themes in open-ended questions and underscore any responses that reflect important issues or ideas. Drill down into the data using demographics to analyze the results at a more granular level. Identify key differences and commonalities that exist between groups. Take advantage of advanced statistics if you have them (e.g., correlations, standard deviations). Determine the critical highlights and clarify the overarching narrative emerging from the results. For example, Figures BB2.3 and BB2.4 are actual graphs from an individual survey,

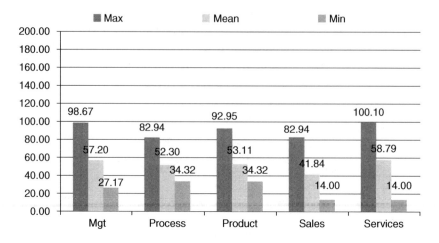

**FIGURE BB2.3**

Maximum value is 200 for each of the 5 major categories for a total of 1000 points. The results are consistently low across the 5 categories (overall mean of 52.5). The lowest mean rating belonged to Sales and the widest gap among opinions (Max – Min) involves the Services category.

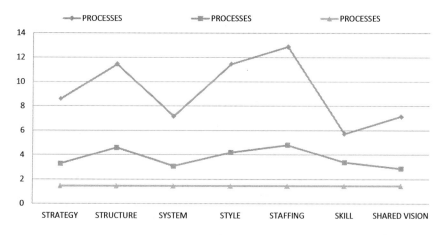

**FIGURE BB2.4**

Survey results show the areas that need attention. In this organization, management staffing is the major negative influence on innovation.

which represent typical survey output. The results are from an online 7s maturity analysis for one specific organization.

We also find that if there are enough people that took the survey, it is advantageous to subdivide the survey results down to the individual work area. There often is a great deal of variance in performance and opportunity between work areas. We made it a point not to break out any work area that has less than 8 people involved in inputting into the survey from the specific work area (typical work areas with the organization like development engineering, product engineering, marketing, sales, production, etc.).

## PRESENTING RESULTS

Now that you have a good feel for the results, the next step in the survey process is to present the feedback to decision-makers and other stakeholders. Decide how best to engage these audiences and properly introduce the results: Will you provide information on each question or will you present the responses in aggregate? Will you share the results in person, our preferred method, or simply distribute a report? Will you use slides or a more formal written report or both? The goal is to inform decision-makers and stakeholders on the current state of innovation, to collectively agree on the issues and opportunities, to reinforce the need for change, and to determine how to bridge the organizational gaps. The outcome of your feedback should be a deep understanding of the results and recommendations, and alignment around the steps needs to achieve the TIME goals.

If you decide to create an Innovation Assessment report, consider this structure:

1. Title Page
   - Author(s)' names and affiliation are identified
   - Date of preparation is included
   - Name of report (Innovation Organizational Assessment for ...)
2. Executive Summary
   - Description of organization and areas that were assessed
   - Purpose of the innovation assessment
   - Brief description of assessment methods and analytical strategy

- Summary of and implications main findings
- Recommendations, if appropriate

3. Table of Contents
4. Introduction and background
   - Overview of TIME
   - Summary of the purpose for the assessment
   - Description of the organization and employees and stake-holders surveyed
5. Methodology
   - List of the assessment objectives
   - Description of the approach to the organizational assessment
   - Introduction to survey or framework being used, as well as rationale for the survey or framework
   - Description of data collection, sources of information and data, and any relevant limitations (e.g., limitations related to methods, potential sources of bias, etc.)
6. Findings
   - Details of the results for each section of the assessment are clearly and logically described with appropriate charts, tables, and graphs
   - Brief analysis of each section highlighting significant findings (analysis is objective and includes both negative and positive findings)
7. Conclusion
   - Summary and interpretation of overall findings
   - Recommendations are included to address key findings
8. References and Appendices

---

## FROM REPORTS TO RESULTS

It is not enough to conduct an organizational assessment. The management and/or the innovation team needs to make sure they act on the survey results and communicate their commitments to employees. A positive plan of action needs to be created and implemented to fulfill the goals of the TIME initiative. Typically, the feedback session includes a review of initial recommendations. Others recommendations may emerge during the feedback session as the data is shared and new insights emerge. It is helpful to document these recommendations and use them as the foundation for the action plan. We offer a simple format for capturing the Innovation Action Plan (Table BB2.1) and for monitoring its execution going forward.

Whether positive or negative, it is important to share the results of the assessment with everyone who participated. It may be advantageous to communicate the results and commitments with all employees. This way everyone knows what is going on and why, even if they weren't invited to complete a survey. Inform people quickly to show management is being serious and to convey that their feedback is important to the organization. The Innovation Action Plan can be a helpful resource for these communications. Provide employees with progress updates, linking the various TIME projects to the survey results. These communications are vital to the success of future assessments. Employees will feel their input was valued, strengthening their trust and commitment to the organization and the TIME initiative, and will be more willing to participate in the future.

4). Subject: INNOVATION SURVEY – Going Forward

Thanks again for your thoughtful responses to the innovation survey. Based on the survey results and our executive strategy session, a number of priorities were identified and we have begun putting plans in place to build a Total Innovation Management Excellence (TIME) program.

We are proceeding with the Individual Innovation, Creativity, and Excellence track to nurture an entrepreneurial mindset and establish common innovation language, concepts, and practices across Europe, Asia, and the US regions. Over the next 18 months, everyone will learn how to:

**TABLE BB2.1**

Innovation Action Plan

| Recommendation (Based on results of the Innovation Assessment) | Decision (Accept/ do not accept and Why?) | Commitments (What actions are going to be taken? What are the organizational implications?) | Responsibility (Who will do it?) | Target Completion date (By when?) |
|---|---|---|---|---|
| 1 ... | | | | |
| 2 ... | | | | |
| 3 ... | | | | |

- Identify significant innovation opportunities
- Generate creative solutions
- Develop strong value propositions
- Communicate ideas in a clear and compelling manner
- Create cost effective prototypes of their ideas
- Collaborate effectively with colleagues to rapidly improve ideas

Collectively, these skills are the cornerstone for establishing a discipline of innovation. When spread across our entire enterprise, they will provide a multiplying effect that boosts speed and impact, and allows our organization's scale and diversity to work as an enabler rather than a barrier. The skill building will be carried out through a mix of Onboarding (for new hires), Bootcamps, Project Launches, Management Training, and Online Learning.

We are working out the details and timeline. Be on the lookout for training opportunities taking place in your region.

Sincerely,

Robert

Follow these four steps to conducting organizational assessments and you will be sure to gather the information you need while preparing your organization to achieve innovation excellence.

## SAMPLE SURVEYS AND FORMATS

### The Innovation Fitness Survey

Based on our work with pioneering enterprises around the world (e.g., BBC, Panera Bread, IBM, Toyota, Swisscom, Phillips, Stanford University, Kaiser Permanente), we have learned a great deal about what makes innovation successful. It is clear that measurement is foundational to building innovation excellence. The question becomes, what should be measured when it comes to innovation. Most organizations track business KPIs (Key Performance Indicators) and can tell if a given percentage of their revenue comes from products and services developed in the past 3 years. Many others introduce innovation spaces, create skunkworks teams, hold innovation competitions, and track participation levels and output. Some conduct corporate culture assessments to get a feel for the emotional health of the workforce and their enthusiasm for innovation. Such insights are important, but not sufficient. They add clarity and texture to the story, but none provides a comprehensive picture of the organization's innovation capabilities.

### STEP – Systematic Measurement Of Key Dimensions Of Innovation Of The Enterprise

To gauge the sum total of innovation fitness level of an enterprise, it is helpful to apply a systematic method for assessing the quality of, and the relationship between the various and distinct dimensions that drive all functions in the enterprise. Like a team, simply having talent does not ensure success. It is the quality of the team work which ultimately elevates or hinders the level of their play.

STEP stands for **S**tructure, **T**ask, **E**nvironments (both internal and external), and **P**eople. The model articulates the fundamentals of a working enterprise system: the **tasks** (products and services) of a business are supported by **structures** that allow **people** to work in service of **external** (market) demands while being guided by the mission and values advocated in the **internal environment.**

These fundamental elements act as an interconnected system where a change in one element will impact all others. For example, if the task of your innovation effort expands from internal improvement initiatives to **external** venturing, you may decide to create an outpost **structure** with investment funds, which requires **people** with startup scouting skills, and find a way to bridge their entrepreneurial spirit with your own **internal environment's** focus on operational excellence. You can measure the performance of this new capability and see how it is impacting the rest of the organization. If adjustments are not made, the system will soon be out of alignment and begin underperforming.

If not measured and properly aligned within the realities of the overall enterprise system, innovation initiatives may offer a temporary boost, but are generally not sustainable. Innovation becomes an add-on that is not woven into the collective mindset, skills and fabric of the company's culture. Ideally, unimpeded by structural obstacles and instead fully supported by a well-integrated innovation system, everyone, everywhere, will be able to take responsibility for innovation everyday – whether as an idea generator, mentor, sponsor, facilitator or team member.

## A STEP Assessment

A STEP assessment measures the efficacy of each element of the enterprise system as well as the flow across all elements, and in this way can also track the quality of innovation within the system, top down, bottom up, outside in and inside out. Innovation practices are evaluated as well as the experience employees and stakeholders are having in using them. The assessment highlights innovation effectiveness related to:

**Environment (External)**: Understanding of customer needs, market trends, and disruptive technologies.

**Task**: Methods (i.e., common concepts, practices, and tools) for enhancing the core business, and creating new or improved products, services, and lines of business.

**Structure**: All functions including finance, information technology, human resources, legal, facilities, etc. are organized to support innovation efforts.

For example, many innovators view their legal department as the group that tells them why they can't try something new, when in fact, legal departments can add a great deal of value for innovators. Legal advisors can help to create agreements with partners, suppliers, or external funders that enable groups to innovate across boundaries. They can guide innovators through the process of checking patents or trademarks, and to secure intellectual property created. Legal teams can also provide the basic agreements needed in large open innovation networks or communities, to help these groups create ownership or reward arrangements that work for all involved.

**People**: The expertise and passion needed to identify opportunities, and successfully generate and champion high potential ideas.

The People portion of the assessment will also provide insights into employee engagement, which has a direct impact on innovation and other organizational performance outcomes. Many studies have shown relationships to outcomes, such as voluntary turnover, employee productivity, and customer satisfaction–all of which can ultimately affect the bottom line.

**Environment (Internal)**: The quality and values of the culture, that is, one that promotes courage, creativity, and collaboration and a willingness to experiment and adopt new ideas.

Having a systematic evaluation of innovation within an enterprise provides understanding of the strengths, and actionable insights into the weaknesses and misalignments that are impacting performance. The Value STEP Survey allows leaders and innovation teams to:

- Understand what is required to achieve innovation excellence in their enterprise, for example, specific areas of focus for improving the speed, quantity, and quality of innovation,
- Create targeted plans for enhancing existing innovation capabilities,
- Generate buy-in for innovation and unlock employee enthusiasm and imagination,
- Track progress and ensure goals are attained.

### Innovation Fitness Survey Questions

The survey is tailored for each client to reflect the nuances of their organization and industry. It typically begins with demographic questions, overall innovation questions, and finally focuses on the sixteen innovation success factors (market insights, leadership, metrics, culture, etc.) that separate the peak performers from these serendipitous innovators.

*Examples of Demographic Questions*

What is your **tenure** at the organization?
  < 1 Year 1–5 Years 5–10 Years 10+ Years
  Where is your primary **location?**
  USA Asia Canada Australia

*Examples of Overall Innovation Questions*

**5 Point Likert Scale**: Please rate the effectiveness of your organization's ability to innovate in the following areas:

- **Technological Innovation**: Coming up with breakthrough technologies.
- **Products/Services Innovation**: Developing new offerings, or improvements to offerings for clients.
- **Business Model Innovation**: Creating new ways to do business with partners, clients, others.

- **Operational Innovation**: Improving the effectiveness and efficiency of current processes.
- **Overall Innovation**: Effectively innovate across all areas of the organization.
- **Open Ended Questions**: What are the biggest barriers to innovation in your organization?

*Examples of STEP Questions*

*Section 1: External Environment*   Please rate your agreement with the following statements regarding the external environment in which your organization operates.

**End User Customers**

- We have close relationships with our customers, and have a clear understanding of their needs and preferences.
- Our customers would describe us as "innovative."

**Suppliers/Vendors**

- We have close relationships with our suppliers/venders, and clearly understand their needs and preferences.
- Our suppliers/venders are seen as a source of new ideas and help our organization come up with innovative solutions.

**Competitors**

Are we ahead of, even with, or behind our competitors in innovation effectiveness?

- Today?
- Where were we 3 years ago?
- Where do you anticipate us being 3 years from now?

**Other external groups and forces:**

- **Government Agencies/Regulations**: We have close relationships with the government agencies that impact our business, have a good handle on upcoming regulations, and are well positioned for the future.

- **Science & Technology**: We are well aware of the rapid changes in science and technology and the potential impact on the future of our business, and are well positioned to take advantage of these changes.
- **Social & Environmental**: We are well aware as an organization of the social and environmental trends that might impact our business, and are well positioned to meet these changing needs.

*Section 2: Business Activities* Please rate your agreement with the following statements about your organization's business practices.

### Vision/Strategy

- My organization's strategy inspires and guides my innovation/improvement efforts.
- We set clearly defined stretch goals/ambitious performance targets that demand innovative solutions.
- Innovation is expressed by our management as a core corporate value and this is translated into practice through frequent communications.

### Customer Focus

- We consistently make key decisions based on customer needs as opposed to internal convenience and politics.
- We are good at responding to changes in customer requirements.
- We actively involve customers (open dialog at idea stage, focus groups, prototype testing, pilots, etc.) in our innovation process.

### Product/Service Offering

- Overall, our end users are delighted with our current products.
- Our products are very competitive in the market today.
- I am confident that our pipeline of innovative ideas will secure our organization's future.

### Innovation Process

- Our organization has a disciplined end-to-end innovation process that facilitates idea generation all the way to new product/service deployment.

- Everyone in our organization relies on a common set of concepts, language, and tools to quickly articulate, evaluate, and develop the value in their ideas.
- The best ideas in our organization usually end up in practice within a reasonable amount of time because our innovation process helps support and develop them into winning products and services.

*Section 3: Organizational Structure*   Please rate your agreement with the following statements about your organization's structure and systems.

## Organizational Design

- Our organizational structure is transparent: it is easy to get access to the people and information needed for new ideas.
- Our structure supports communication, collaboration, and the flow of innovation across organizational boundaries (e.g., functions, units, disciplines, product lines, geography).
- Our organization has effective means for forming temporary units/ project teams (e.g., incubation, skunk works) to develop fledgling ideas into new products/services.

## Incentives (Rewards and Recognition)

- Employees are acknowledged and/or rewarded (e.g., promoted, given bonus, celebration) for contributing to innovation.
- Rather than punish failed innovations and risk takers, we seek to learn from our mistakes.
- Resources (e.g., time and money) are made available to encourage and seed innovation projects.

## Measures

- Current performance metrics balance the short-term needs of the business with our long-term strategic objectives.
- We know what our customers value most, and monitor and report their levels of satisfaction regularly.
- We continuously monitor and seek to improve both the efficiency of our innovation process (e.g., development costs, time to market) as well as the results (e.g., sales, brand loyalty).

**Systems/Technology**

- Our organization is effective at capturing and sharing lessons learned and best practices.
- We have sufficient infrastructure and technology platforms to support our innovation efforts.
- Our financial systems and procedures make it easy to allocate funds to high potential innovation projects, tools, and people.

*Section 4: People* Please rate your agreement with the following statements about your organization's people and their innovation practices.

**Innovators**

- We have enough people willing to be hands-on leaders of innovation, who self-select to champion new ideas.
- People with innovative ideas are able to get the tools, resources and training they need to be successful.
- People with innovative ideas are encouraged to see their idea through and not simply to hand it off to others.

**Teams**

- Teams are seen as a necessary part of our innovation process (as opposed to a reliance on the lone genius).
- We are good at forming and managing cross-disciplinary teams to solve complex problems.
- Effective communication and collaboration between departments/business units allows teams to operate across organizational boundaries easily.

**Sponsors/Mentors**

- Sponsors see innovation/improvement projects as opportunities to develop their people's skills and careers.
- Being a good sponsor is a valuable part of being a good leader in our organization.

- It is easy for people with innovative ideas to find sponsors with the necessary skills, power, and commitment to actively improve their ideas, remove barriers, and steer them in the right direction.

## Talent

- Our organization has the internal expertise needed to succeed (the right people with the right skills).
- We have access to a rich and active network of the best people in and around our industry.
- We have a great reputation and are considered by people in our industry to be innovators.

*Section 5: Internal Environment* Please rate your agreement with the following statements about your organization's internal environment.

## Climate

- There is a real sense of trust and community in our organization; a feeling that we are all in this together.
- We work in a stimulating environment filled with creativity and experimentation.
- Our employees enjoy a high level of job satisfaction.

## Culture

- We have a collaborative culture where people naturally invite and respect each other's opinions.
- We have an entrepreneurial spirit where people take the initiative and act and feel like owners of the business.
- Everyone in our organization, not just R&D or marketing for example, actively contributes to developing innovative ideas.

## Change

1. We are quick to recognize and adopt new ideas.
2. We have high standards and continuously strive to be the best.
3. We are capable of breakthrough innovations, and not just incremental improvements.

**Leadership**

- Our leaders treat innovation as a strategic priority, consistently demonstrating their commitment by providing the time and resources needed to ensure success.
- Leadership encourages decision-making about innovative ideas to take place at the appropriate level by those with the greatest knowledge.

**Conclude Survey with Open-Ended Question**: What suggestions do you have for improving innovation in our organization?

## The Is/Should Be Analysis Format

As we indicated earlier, there are many different assessments that can provide different viewpoints related to improving innovation. The Is/Should Be survey has a unique format. Each statement is looked at from 3 different points of view.

1. How is it performing today?
2. Where should it be 3 years in the future?
3. How important is it that the change takes place?

The following is a typical question …

1. To what degree does your COMPANY focus on preventing errors?

| Is | 1 | 2 | 3 | 4 | 5 | 6 | 7 |
|---|---|---|---|---|---|---|---|
| Should Be | 1 | 2 | 3 | 4 | 5 | 6 | 7 |
| Priority | 1 | 2 | 3 | 4 | 5 | 6 | 7 |

## The Change Resistance Survey Format

This survey is designed to predict the amount of resistance that an innovation initiative will encounter during implementation. It taps into people history with innovation and change. People who have been a part of unsuccessful change efforts and/or struggled with innovation in the past, are likely to have greater resistance to the proposed initiative than those who have had positive experiences.

1. Do You Understand The Purpose Of The xyz Initiative?

   When people lack a full understanding of why a change is being implemented, anxiety, and suspicion often fill the information vacuum.
   The purpose of the initiative is clear. The purpose of the initiative is unclear.

   | 1 | 2 | 3 | 4 | 5 | 6 | 7 | 8 | 9 | 10 |
   |---|---|---|---|---|---|---|---|---|----|

2. Do You Believe That This Change Is Really Needed?

   Even if people fully understand the organization's rationale for a change, they may have different perspectives than that of the initiative's sponsor and may not agree that a change is truly necessary.
   I believe the initiative is needed. I believe the initiative is not needed.

   | 1 | 2 | 3 | 4 | 5 | 6 | 7 | 8 | 9 | 10 |
   |---|---|---|---|---|---|---|---|---|----|

## Do It Yourself (DIY) Survey

Creating an online innovation survey has become much easier – many great providers like QuestionPro, SurveyMonkey, Typeform, etc., offer advanced yet simple survey software platforms that enable you to construct highly customized assessments. You can start from scratch or choose from already existing free online survey templates. You also have the choice to go the paid route or start with free and upgrade to pay if necessary. For a quick and simple assessments, free surveys should work just fine. The paid versions typically offer added capabilities, like exporting the data, customizing the user interface (e.g., add your own logo), and incorporating more question types (e.g., selecting multiple options in a dropdown or using star rankings).

## 10 TIPS FOR WRITING GREAT QUESTIONS

To take advantage of the speed, cost-effectiveness, customization, real-time analysis and all the other benefits of an online survey, you will need to design a good one. For those of you who want to Do It Yourself, the challenge of question writing is usually people's biggest concern. We have all heard the refrain, "garbage in, garbage out." The tips that follow will help ensure you are asking the right question in the right way in order to get the information you want.

1. **Avoid unnecessary questions**: When building a survey to collect important insights about your organization's innovation capabilities, every question in the survey should be there for a reason. It is a good idea to design your survey by identifying the data outcomes you desire, then determining what questions need to be asked.

2. **Avoid misplaced or out of context questions**. In general, a funnel approach is advised. Broad and general questions at the beginning of the survey act as a helpful warm-up. Engage the respondent with more detailed or specific questions once a flow and proper context has been established. Respondents may get irritated and be less likely to complete the survey if you don't follow a logical order and bounce back and forth among topics.

3. **Avoid loaded or leading words or questions**: Slight wording changes can produce great differences in results. "Could," "Should," "Might" sound almost the same, but may produce a 20% difference in agreement to a question (The executive team could … should … might … have forced retailers to sell our new products). Strong words that represent control or action, such as "prohibit" produces similar results (Do you believe the executive team should prohibit our southern regions from participating in company innovation events?) Sometimes wording is just biased: You wouldn't want to go to the company's hackathon would you? Once you have finished a draft of your survey, review the questions for unintended bias. Ask others to review it as well.

4. **Avoid mutually nonexclusive response categories**: Multiple choice response categories should be mutually exclusive so that clear choices can be made. Nonexclusive answers frustrate the respondent and make interpretation difficult at best.

5. **Avoid nonspecific questions**: Do you like innovation? This is a very vague question. The person taking the survey will be unclear … do I like what? Ideating, collaborating, prototyping, pitching? Be specific in what you want to know about. Do you think up new ideas regularly? (What is regularly?).

6. **Avoid confusing or unfamiliar words**: Asking about MVPs, "colla-boratories," ROI, and other innovation specific jargon and acronyms are confusing. Make sure your audience understands your language level, terminology and above all, what you are asking.

7. **Avoid forcing answers**: Respondents may not want, or may not be able to provide the information requested. Privacy is an important issue to most people. Questions that could easily identify the person (if there are only one or two people in the company with a specific job title) or questions that are very personal (political, religious) can be too intrusive and rejected by the respondent.

8. **Avoid dichotomous questions**: Make sure answers are independent. For example, the question "Do you think innovation is about being creative or implementing new ideas?" Some believe "yes," that innovation is both.

9. **Avoid double-barreled questions**: For example, "What is the most confidential and convenient way to share new ideas for you?" Unfortunately for the persons responding, the most confidential, may not be private or anonymous. Two questions should be asked rather than having the topics combined.

10. **Avoid the drawn out overly long mega survey**: Surveys with lots of questions can be problematic. If they are perceived as too lengthy, respondents may lose interest half way through the survey. Incomplete surveys may compromise the results. Or respondents may avoid taking the survey all together, because they feel they don't have the time to spare. Whenever possible, keep it short and simple.

You will also have to decide if you want to use open-ended questions or closed-ended questions. There are trade-offs between the two. The trick is to leverage the benefits of both types of questions. Assuming it aligns with the intent of your assessment, try and include descriptive questions ("What are the barriers to innovation you see in our organization?") and objective questions to balance the survey. Keep in mind the insights gleaned from open ended questions, and the power they provide when you get to read how people respond in their own words, must be weighed against the extra effort it takes to compile and review them. Question types should be carefully considered as it impacts the tone and intent of the survey.

Do It Yourself survey creators should pre-test the survey with a focus group of colleagues during the development process to get a better understanding of how employees may respond. As you can see from the top 10 list, your questioning can go array. Your colleagues may surface issues, identify areas or confusion, and offer improvement suggestions. You can also use the test to gather specific survey content from the group. For example, you want to avoid questions that will generate non-exhaustive listings. In other words, "Do you have all of the options covered?" If you are unsure, use the pre-test with a question that includes an "Other (please specify) _____" option. Then, revise the question making to ensure you cover at least 90% of the respondent answers. Pre-testing is a good practice to see if your questions are on target and if any changes are required in order to deliver an excellent innovation survey.

## SUMMARY

> Every morning in Africa, a gazelle wakes up, it knows it must outrun the fastest lion or it will be killed. Every morning in Africa, a lion wakes up. It knows it must run faster than the slowest gazelle, or it will starve. It doesn't matter whether you're the lion or a gazelle-when the sun comes up, you'd better be running.
>
> ~ Christopher McDougall, Author of Born to Run

Building and maintaining peak innovation performance requires understanding your current innovation eco-system and how best to leverage it. If you want to improve your innovation efforts to optimize speed and creative output, it helps to measure and understand the strengths and weaknesses of your organization's capabilities (people, processes, practices, etc.). With the right metrics and analysis, you can manage these capabilities and effectively align them around solving operational issues or generating market strategies that drive new value creation. Without a sense of your collective capabilities and a plan to get your organization innovating at startup speed, you run the risk of becoming an out-of-shape bureaucracy that is unfit to compete for the future.

Use the survey tools we highlighted or select one of your own that better meets your needs, but don't miss the chance to find out "How are we doing?" Organizational assessments, and the insights and momentum they create, are a fundamental building block to the TIME Pyramid and for bringing an innovative direction to the organization's performance strategy.

## REFERENCES

1. Enterprise Development Group (2011). Innovation Fitness Survey. Available at http://enterprisedevelop.com
2. Peters, Tom (March 2011). A Brief History of the 7-S ("McKinsey 7-S") Model. Available at https://tompeters.com/2011/03/a-brief-history-of-the-7-s-mckinsey-7-s-model/
3. Fortune Magazine (2015). 50 Most Innovative Companies. Available at http://fortune.com/2015/12/02/50-most-innovative-companies/

# BB3

## Innovative Executive Leadership

*Dana Landry*

## CONTENTS

## INTRODUCTION

This chapter will discuss the TIME BB3 – Innovative Executive Leadership. Considering the many definitions available for the word "innovative," creating a clear and concise chapter useful to readers may prove difficult. For example, do you need an "innovative style" in executive management or do the regular time-proven methods work just as well? Is there something different in a start-up versus an ongoing enterprise of medium to large size that requires a "new and creative" approach to management? There are many types of executives, many types of organizations, and many types of leaders. We will attempt to bring together the most important and practical aspects of these factors and others under the umbrella of TIME.

The chapter will start with a discussion of the various ways to understand the term "Innovative Executive Leadership" in the current modern context. We will focus first on critical jobs the executive must perform in any effort to drive an organization to be more creative, more innovative, and hopefully more successful. All too often, executives use general platitudes toward innovation efforts only to see little change in their organizations. Executives make quick speeches, demand more innovation, and then drive their organizations focusing only on the same short-term financial results as they have been managing for all of their careers. Some may think, even today, that they can cut cost or achieve higher efficiencies and call that innovation. The future of organizational leadership requires a *new executive mind set* and the core of that new mind is creative problem solving and new, innovative management and leadership understanding. Only with this new mind set can it be said you demonstrate *innovative executive leadership*.

Before changing any organization, most executives will have to first change themselves. The critical function of executive self-development to enable leadership of innovation efforts is discussed. This is much more than changing a few lines in a few standard speeches given at predictable company meetings or other planned public appearances. It is how the executive acts in their daily interactions with their employees. The in-the-moment few words tell your employees just what you really believe about innovation.

We will touch on executive team development here but broader discussions of team and organizational development can be found in other chapters in this book.

## DEFINITIONS

*Creative Problem Solving*: a body of methodologies for solving often ill-defined problems or to help you search for possibilities and opportunities not readily apparent. It also includes methods to help you evolve your understanding of what the problem might be and what possible solutions may exist. Contrast this with linear problem solving consisting of rigid methodologies seeking the "correct" answer as practiced by most executives and their staffs today.

*Executive management of innovation*: the day-to-day tasks performed by executives to drive an organization to achieve their stated innovation goals.

*Innovation*: a word with many definitions. In this chapter, it will be defined as the output of a *conscious and purposeful effort* to create, be creative, identify, develop, and bring to the customer a new value proposition. (Note from the editor: This is not in agreement with the definition of innovation as used by ISO. Personally, I like it better and it is more descriptive.)

*Innovative executive leadership*: efforts by senior leaders of an organization to change themselves, the way they operate both individually and as the executive team in order to become more creative in their approaches to all areas of their organization. The type of executive leadership required to make the TIME framework a success.

*Incremental improvement*: a change to a product or service that creates a new value proposition to the customer above and beyond just a lower price for essentially the same product or service. Basically making something faster, smarter, better, or more efficient at doing what it has always been doing.

*Innovation content*: a reflection of the relative rations of the mixture of linear problem solving, uncertainty, and creativity required to achieve a given task(s). Some projects may require only small focused efforts toward creating and implementing innovations while some may require high levels of innovation content focused on finding/creating/inventing and delivering whole new businesses or business/life-changing products or services.

*Innovation Vision Statement*: the vision statement set by executive leadership to guide the whole or specific parts of the organization as they endeavor to develop new products or services or change the way the business operates. The statement is used to focus and direct efforts to achieve maximum effectiveness, and can be applied to whole organizations or specific projects or wherever a conscious decision has been made to develop something new.

*Linear Problem Solving*: any of the standard methods used to solve problems that have a correct or right answer. This is what we all did in school. We were given a problem, we applied the prescribe methodology for answering that type of problem, and then proceeded to churn out the answer the professor desired. (Questioning the question was rarely, if ever, allowed.)

## UNDERSTANDING KEY POINTS

### Managing for Results or Leading for Innovation?

There is a big difference between an executive whose focus is to manage for specific results and the executive who leads and manages for innovation. On the one hand, this can be directly surmised from the large body of literature that separates management and leadership as separate, if connected, topics. Some readers will undoubtedly feel that good managers really are just good leaders and vice versa. We will not say here that management or leadership is more important and indeed most business schools and authors drive home the point that successful executives need to do both. What we will contend in this chapter is that managing and leading efforts focusing on and containing innovation, especially those with high levels of *innovation content*, are very different from driving the organization to lower cost and/or higher levels of efficiency. The fact that innovation is hard to define is a leading cause for complicating the matter. In order to fully understand the manager versus leader components in the TIME context, we need to use some common concepts.

In the modern business world, executive leaders are those who set vision, create strategies, and communicate to the organization the importance of achieving the various specific goals/objectives they have set. How then does this occur if you cannot fully define what you are trying to achieve? This will be discussed at some length later in the chapter. For now, let's make the point that it's exactly because innovation is hard to define that a new *innovative executive leadership* is necessary. To be successful, a leadership style is required that can handle ambiguity, is willing to accept different forms – and sometimes higher – levels of risk, and has the open mind able to absorb new learning quickly so that they can *correct and redirect* their organization most effectively.

In much of the current literature, you will read that executives must set vision and inspire their organizations to achieve any level of innovation. This, of course, bestows on many executives a halo of grandness as they make bold proclamations in support of more innovation but then do little to actually achieve any real innovation activity. Instead they speak of change but go on to operate in the same manner as they always have, driving and rewarding their staff and the organization for doing pretty much what they have been successfully doing in the past. As Jim Collins wrote in his book *From Good to Great*, "good is the enemy of great." There is often little need to change until, as so many brick and mortar retailers have discovered, it is too late to change.

*Innovative Executive Leadership* is a building block in the TIME pyramid for a very good reason. For real change to occur, a new approach, a more inclusive and broad approach (such as the TIME framework) is needed to guide and inspire the very executives who themselves must go forth and inspire their organizations. But as one can readily see from the TIME pyramid, it is filled with straight-forward building blocks that require strong traditional management to drive the organization to success in its overall goals as well as its specific innovation goals. Most executives can effectively drive their organization to good financial results. The rest of this chapter focuses on how to help executives become the leaders of the innovation content their future organization, and their personal, success requires.

## What's Wrong with the Current View of Executive Leadership of Innovation?

Too many executives today hear the sirens call to *innovate or die* coming from business schools, solution providers, popular authors (some with questionable qualifications), consultants, and everyone else. One would almost think that change in business climate, new technology destroying old business, etc., was some new phenomena, perhaps a by-product of recent specific technological change. But executives have been faced with these challenges since business began. Joseph Schumpeter, in his classic work of economics titled *Capitalism,*

*Socialism and Democracy*, noted that one of the great strengths of American capitalism was what he termed "creative destruction"; that the society as whole constantly created and developed new products, destroying the old ones in the process. Clayton M. Christensen expanded on this idea in his book *The Innovator's Dilemma*, where he coined the now very popular term *"disruptive innovation,"* explaining the "how" behind how much of creative destruction actually occurs in today's world of modern technological advancements.

The reality is that executives today are facing many of the same problems their predecessors faced. The one big difference, and this is crucial, is that society is creating new products, services, business models, etc., at a rate and in a variety faster than ever before. Many executives are simply, even if they will not admit it, overwhelmed with the sheer magnitude of the situation. The situation is huge both in the problems it presents and the possible solutions that may exist. It's no longer a simple matter of Company A makes a product, then Company B makes one a little better or cheaper, and then Company A makes their original product a little better or cheaper than Company B. Today, while Company A and B are fighting the losing battle of profits through efficiency alone, Company C comes along and removes the need for the original product all together. This is further complicated by the simple, but overpowering fact, that many executives must still deliver expected quarterly results while trying to change their companies to meet new competition. It is not that the current executive leadership lives in a world filled with few options; it is more that organizations today exist in a world filled with too many options (some known and others just waiting to be discovered).

Some, perhaps too many, executives take the easy way out. For example, driven to be more innovative by their Board of Directors, stockholders or the now updated-by-the-minute business press per-form a review of their product/service portfolio, declare perhaps one or two of the more difficult projects as innovative, declare victory, and go about managing their organization as they always have. In other cases, they may appoint a "new" executive, like the Chief Innovation Officer, which is a popular choice, to drive their vision into real products and results. A good method, but only if the full executive staff has completed the process outlined below. Perhaps the executive creates what is popularly known as a "skunk works" after the model made famous by Lockheed and which turned Clarence

"Kelly" Johnson into a hero for engineers everywhere. Again, not a bad idea and one that can work, at least for a while, but the literature is becoming clear that most such efforts peter out in 3–5 years with little to show for the effort.

There is a better way for executives to be both *innovative executives* and be *executives that drive innovation* – the first and perhaps most important task for executives to define what innovation means to their organization. Then they embrace a system such as TIME to help them drive that understanding throughout their organization.

## THE KEY ROLE OF INNOVATIVE EXECUTIVE LEADERSHIP

A former tank commander, turned medical device executive, once told me a story, which is useful here. He was a bright newly minted Second Lieutenant assigned to a Logistics branch. The commanding general of this logistics branch apparently liked to play a little practical joke on all new officers. He would called his new officer into his office, tell him/her most energetically that he too is also new to logistics and he does not know what it really is. He then orders the young officer to bring him six pounds of logistics and have it on his desk by noon, then ordering him/her quickly from his office.

Now this story may be true or not but you can certainly imagine what a young officer in his or her first assignment would be feeling at that time. Pure fear and confusion. How on earth does anyone find six pounds of a concept and put it on the desk? After all, telling your commanding general he is lacking a certain level of knowledge certainly would not appear as the first useful option.

Unfortunately, unlike our befuddled new officer, executives do not have someone to come out and join the laughter as they explain the joke. No, achieving innovation is far too serious a matter. Yet, like this new officer, the innovative executive leader must find a way to drive innovation, that is both a process (the how to achieve the specific innovation content the organization needs) and a result (a product, service, policy, or new thing that creates a new customer value proposition). It is their job to envision, define, strategize, oversee tactics, measure results, kill bad performing projects, and support ones that may seem dangerously close to failure all while running everything else.

The good innovative executive will rarely, if ever, use the word "innovation" or "innovative" alone. They understand, instinctively if not from experience or education, that the vision for innovation must be clear enough to be directive and broad enough to allow for maximum creativity when needed. These terms are best used as an adjective or adverb to describe more specific things or actions. This does not mean simply saying "innovative product" or "innovative service." The executive will instead repeat the vision or strategy to the organization repeatedly and in many different ways to keep them focused. The following statements hold no real or useful meaning for the innovative executive:

> *We need to be more innovative!*
> *I want everyone to innovate!*
> *Innovation is everyone's responsibility!*
> *10% of all projects must be innovation!*

This is all like asking for six pounds of logistics! What the innovative executive must do, and provide leadership to achieve, is the definition and targeting of the *type* and *amount* of innovation the organization requires in the present and near future. Let's discuss what we mean by the type or the amount of innovation.

Innovation may be a word that is hard to define but we generally agree that it exist along a continuum. One can envision some innovations as being fundamental discoveries that form the basis for hundreds of uses, dozens of new companies, and thousands of products. One example I often use is the laser beam. This fundament discovery (the inventor of which was a subject of court cases for decades) has created a technology that we find in everything from laser weapons to medical devices to the simple presentation pointer.

At the other end of the continuum is the incremental improvement. Such improvements make things better, faster, stronger, cheaper, etc., but still provide the same basic functionality. Some incremental improvements can be very important as is shown by the development of the modern electronics industry and components became better, faster, more functional per unit weight, etc. We could hardly have made it to the moon using instruments filled with 1920s style vacuum tubes. Pacemakers, smartphones, and tablet computers would have been impossible with early chip technology. When incremental improvements are planned and executed over time with reliability and cost effectiveness, they can drive a business for generations. They can also lead the business to falsely assume they are invincible and firms such as IBM and GE may be examples to consider from their long history of success mixed with trial and tribulation. They may be considered as case studies in many business schools.

We can also combine here new uses for the same technology in closely adjacent fields and similar efforts. As many readers will know, this is the majority of what many executives will call innovation and claim the results to be innovations. This is not necessarily wrong but the innovative executive leading his or her organization to new heights must be honest and clear in what they are asking of their organization if they have any hopes of achieving their goal at acceptable levels of certainty. Some organizations can be very successful by consciously, consistently, and effectively exploiting the lower end of the innovation scale. It comes with risks but it is a valid strategy.

Since this is a continuum, there are infinite possibilities between the extremes. A possible way to look at this continuum is shown in Figure BB3.1.

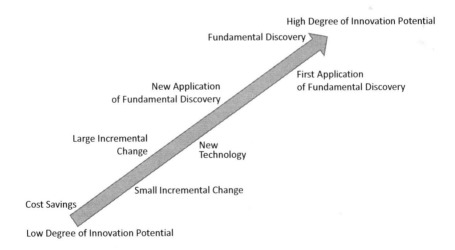

**FIGURE BB3.1**
Innovation Continuum.

In Figure BB3.1, we plot a continuum from low level of innovation content to high level of innovation content. Placed along the continuum is a view of the progressive growth of innovative focus within an average bedside organization. I am sure there are many other ways to view this as well as more complex ones but let's focus on this one example for now. On this view we see the most fundamental discoveries as being more likely to allow for higher levels of innovation and lower levels of technology changes as being more likely to yield lower levels of technology changes. This is by no means cast in stone and the variations are legend. For example, the first smart phone may well be considered to have been a collection of available technologies put together into a new format. (It was also not a very good phone, at least at first.)

I often caution executives and managers seeking to improve their *innovation content* that they may see a useful fundamental discovery once in their life time. Twice or more is rare. Yet when you ask people what they think of their own innovations, they often glow proudly and explain how it will change the world. The innovative executive must display the leadership that keeps the organization well-grounded in judging their place on the innovation continuum.

Now this is helpful to the innovative executive, but only half the story. The executive must know what is the state of their organization relative to its business environment, what level of risk can the organization sustain, and what are the needs of the organization, before he or she tries to determine what level, or levels, of *innovation content* they must lead their organizations to achieve. This is a complex issue since there are infinite potential combinations of large versus small organizations, profitable versus struggling, nonprofit versus for-profit, start-up versus multinational, public versus private, public sector versus government, etc. However, as complex as the problem appears in general discussion, it is often much simpler and certainly more focused to the specific executive trying to lead innovation efforts toward specific goals.

## HOW DO INNOVATIVE EXECUTIVE LEADERS SET INNOVATION GOALS?

Innovative executives start with their *innovation vision statement*. Simply put, it has to control who you are and that controls what you are allowing the organization to do. Set a vision that you will always be the innovation leader and you have created a vision as clear as a London city fog. Sounds good but leads everyone to go their own way according to their definitions and immediate constraints of time, people, and money.

The vision statement must be clear about what you are allowing your organization to excel. You may be a start-up and just beginning to exploit a new technology hoping to create a major innovation. Or perhaps a medium-size company feeling the pressure from new rivals who have incrementally improved their product or service and are taking market share. Do you try to one up them or do you search for a bigger leap in innovation content? You may be a multinational organization that is suddenly facing the obsolescence of your business and you need to reinvent yourself as IBM successfully did by becoming a services company in place of a hardware provider. Only the executive leadership can make this determination and then drive this understanding into a vision and then a strategy. If you are struggling, the one thing you do know is that you cannot keep doing things the old way. That is a death sentence for the organization (or for some the definition of insanity).

## INNOVATIVE EXECUTIVE LEADERSHIP LEADS TO INNOVATIVE PORTFOLIOS

When you really think about this, setting "innovation goals" for an organization's portfolio sounds ridiculous especially given the lack of a firm definition for the concept of innovation. Yet there are more than enough authors, consultants, and solution providers who suggest such a practice. How can you tell a group that they must deliver 25% innovative projects? 25% or six pounds, whichever comes first! Most people today just take the current portfolio, call some percentage innovative, declare victory, and proceed right back to doing whatever it is they know best. The innovative executive will lead his or her organization to decide on the right level of innovation content for the needed area of the business and focus the efficiency and cost-saving efforts where they are appropriate. This should be a joint decision and consensus agreement by the entire senior staff.

Once decided and the portfolio understood, the gap analysis between current and future situations will let the staff know how much "newness" is going to be required. This is a term indicating how much organizations change in all the areas shown in the TIME pyramid that will have to be touched, altered, revised, completely changed, etc., depending on the specific situation. It may be necessary to bring some innovation content to many projects across the organization and this will almost assuredly require the executive leadership to drive new organizational capabilities in all areas shown in the TIME pyramid. It may require very specific innovation efforts in targeted business sectors while directing other sectors to drive differently.

Of course, all this sounds simple but it is usually difficult and occasionally results in executive personnel changes. Some executives are very good at making things lowest in cost or at squeezing out the next 1% of efficiency in performance. Such people are good, often brilliant, linear problem solvers. It is rare, very rare, to find executives who are equally good at all types of problem-solving and creative thinking. Real change requires organizational change.

---

## THE STRATEGIC PLANNING PROCESS

Innovation should not be left standing by itself. In order to be effective, it needs to be a key integral part of the organization's Strategic Plan. Let's start out by answering two questions. Rate these using a scale of 1 to 10 with one being extremely low and ten being extremely high.

1. How important is Strategic Planning to the organization? _____
2. Based up on actual performance, how effective have the Strategic Planning activities been to date? _____.

> Good fortune is what happens when opportunity meets with planning.
> – Thomas Edison

For most people, there is a major difference between the answers to #1 and #2. Ask yourself why there is a difference and take the time to make a list of why this might be true. The third question might be, "What part does innovation play in the organization's Master Plan?" Although it should not be the major part of the organization's Master Plan, it should be an important key part of the plan.

The Organization's Master Plan combines the five major management plans together into a homogeneous, agreed-to, focused approach to managing the organization's culture, business, and operations. (See Figure BB3.2.) These major management plans are:

- The Business Plan (BP)
- The Strategic Business Plan (SBP)
- The Strategic Improvement Plan (SIP)
- The Strategic Plan (SP), which is the prioritized integration of the Strategic Business Plan (SBP) and the Strategic Improvement Plan (SIP)
- Annual Operating Plan (AOP)

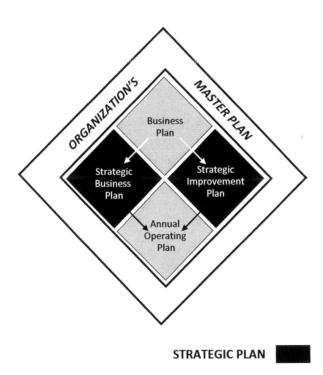

STRATEGIC PLAN ▮

**FIGURE BB3.2**
Five Parts of the Organization's Master Plan.

## Definition: Business Plan (BP)

A Business Plan is a formal statement of a set of business goals, the reasons why they are believed attainable, and the plan for reaching those goals. It also contains background information about the organization or team attempting to reach those goals.

## Definition: Strategic Business Plan (SBP)

The strategic business plan focuses on what the organization is going to do to grow its market. It is designed to answer the questions – What do we do? How can we beat or avoid competition? It is directed at the product and/or services that the organization provides as viewed by the outside world. When an organization is just being funded, this plan is often just called a Business Plan.

## Definition: Strategic Improvement Plan (SIP)

The Strategic Improvement Plan focuses on how to change the culture of the organization. It is designed to answer the questions – How do we excel? How can we increase value to all the stakeholders? It addresses how the controllable factors within the organization can be changed to improve the organization's reputation and performance.

## Definition: Strategic Plan (SP)

Strategic Plan is a document that is the result of Strategic Planning. It defines the organization's strategy and/or direction and makes decisions on the allocation of resources in pursuit of the organization's strategy including its capital and people. It focuses on the future of the organization and is the combination of the Strategic Business Plan and the Strategic Improvement Plan with each item prioritized to maximize the organization's performance. The Strategic Plan is the combination and prioritization of the Strategic Business Plan and the Strategic Improvement Plan individual strategies.

## Definition: The Annual Operating Plan (AOP)

The Annual Operating Plan is a formal statement of business short-range goals, the reasons they are believed to be attainable, the plans for reaching these goals, and the funding approved for each part of the organization (budget). It includes the implementation plan for the coming years (year 1–3) of the Strategic Plan. It may also contain background information about the organization or teams attempting to reach these goals. One of the end results are performance plans for each manager and employee who will be implementing the plan over the coming year. The Annual Operating Plan is often just referred to as the Operating Plan (OP).

### Definition: Strategic Management

Strategic management is the process of specifying the organization's mission, vision, and objectives, developing policies and plans, often in terms of projects and programs that are designed to achieve these objectives and then allocating resources to implementation of policies and plans, projects and programs.

The Organization's Master Plan must combine all of the major planning processes together and, at the same time, ensure they are customer focused. All of the plans must be based upon understanding the customer requirements and preferences, plus having an excellent understanding of what the competition is doing currently and in the future. Figure BB3.2 is a model of an Organization's Master Plan, indicating the five different parts of this plan: the Business Plan, the Strategic Business Plan, the Strategic Improvement Plan, the Strategic Plan, and the Annual Operating Plan. (The Strategic Plan is the prioritized combination of the Strategic Business Plan and the Strategic Improvement Plan and, in the model, it is represented by the combination of the two black diamonds.)

The Business Plan's primary objective is to inform external investors. It is prepared early in the organization's development cycle and it is often used to provide potential investors information related to the organization and its management. Information from it feeds directly into the Strategic Plan. While the Strategic Plan focuses on the future of the organization, the focus of the Annual Operating Plan is short range and addresses the current operations. You will also note that the Strategic Business Plan and the Annual Operating Plan define the direction that the organization wants to take and complement each other. On the other hand, the Strategic Improvement Plan is focused on the organization's operations (how things get done) and its culture.

The purpose of any planning process is threefold. First is to set direction, second is to define expectations, and third is to define actions that need to be taken to meet the commitments documented in 1 and 2. The connections between the 3 points are not unidirectional; it's a continuous flow back and forth to optimize total performance. (See Figure BB3.3.)

By viewing Figure BB3.4, you will note that the planning process starts with a vision that sets direction for the total organization. Normally all five direction outputs are prepared by the executive team with the Board of Directors approval. The two expectation outputs are typically prepared by middle-level managers with their immediate superior's agreement. The four action outputs are ideally prepared by first-level management and the employee. This approach has the

**The Three Purposes
of Business Planning**

**FIGURE BB3.3**
Three Purposes for Organizational Planning.

| PURPOSE | 11 OUTPUTS | TIME FRAME |
|---|---|---|
| Direction | Visions | 10 - 20 years |
| | Mission | Open-ended |
| | Values | Open-ended |
| | Strategic Focus | 5 years |
| | Critical Success Factors | 3 years |
| Expectations (measurements | Business Objectives | 5-10 years |
| | Performance Goals | 1-5 years |
| Actions | Strategies | 1-5 years |
| | Tactics | 1-3 years |
| | Budgets | 1-3 years |
| | Performance Plans | 3-12 months |

**FIGURE BB3.4**
Business Planning Elements and Timing.

advantage of tying the entire planning product together from the Board of Directors down to the individual employees committed performance plan and the budget required to support tech commitment.

## CREATE STRUCTURE AND REWARD SYSTEMS TO SUPPORT THE LEVEL OF INNOVATION REQUIRED

No one expects the innovative executive team to engage in every detail of every project to assure that the best type and level of innovation content is being applied. Experience has also shown it rarely helps to talk about it if speeches are all the executive team can offer. Much more effective is to reward those real-life examples that best fit the vision and specific requirements of the innovation content the innovative executive team has decided needs to occur. Regardless of the organization, its purpose (cost efficiency or major innovations), and despite what any executive says in hopes of creating inspiration, people will do what they are rewarded for doing. If you want small amounts of innovation over many projects, then reward that type of result. If a project needed a major innovation to be successful but only provided small incremental changes, you may have more of a learning opportunity to share with the organization.

There is a popular trend that is grossly misunderstood. Some people feel they need to reward failures. The truly innovative executive leadership team will know that this is fundamentally flawed. Failure is not a career path for anyone. Some failures will, if placed into the proper context, provide a real learning opportunity that can be communicated to the whole organization as a way of helping the organization develop their innovation skill set. But to reward real failure is not an option. Executives simply do not have the time and the majority do not have the talent to put a lot of failure into a positive context. Innovative executives understand the value of experimentation as a natural part of the trial and error that is key to creative problem solving. Experiments that provide information on what will not work when such a result is fully or reasonably expected is not failure, it is learning and should be managed in that way. The only true failure is where you have no idea how it happens, no idea how to prevent it from happening again, and no idea of its significance if any.

## PEOPLE DO WHAT YOU REWARD THEM TO DO, NOT WHAT YOU TELL THEM TO DO

It is useful and supportive to create reward programs that align clearly and simply with organizational requirements. When you have need for cost-savings and efficiency, reward that. You probably will need for moderate innovation reward that is for achieving its goal and share how it was done. On those rare occasions where the team and leadership recognized a long shot and nurtured it to success, quite possibly with high levels of problem solving and/or high innovation content, reward that and make clear what you are rewarding.

One thing is clear, if all the executive team states that they are rewarding the financial results, then all teams will work toward financial results and human nature will often send them down the path of least resistance. This can sometimes lead to less than lasting results and sometimes immediate discomfort when shortcuts show their "unexpected" outcomes such as poor reliability in products, services that fail to sustain customer satisfaction, or are easily duplicated and surpassed by your competition.

This area is also a great way innovative executive leadership shows itself. The concept of rewards can take many forms and executive leadership should direct appropriate amounts of their time to be creative, and develop and deliver creative reward options that support the innovation vision and specific innovation goals. Rewarding people for good ideas is great but unfortunately too many reward programs stop there. The innovative executive leadership team will take this task as a serious part of their personal workload to complete, manage, and constantly measure and review for improvements as well as continually search for new ways to reward the right behavior.

One caution here is not to fall into the trap of believing the often-made statement that money is not a motivator. Yes, there are many studies out there that seem to indicate that money does not motivate. What they really mean is that the money being offered does not motivate. Now here we must exclude those few who for truly altruistic motives perform work that pays little or seem not to be interested in money. Bless them all each and every one, but we are focused on the far greater number in everyday business environments.

Here is an illustration. Imaging you have two crowds of people waiting to run into a stadium to collect their rewards by giving them two choices.

They can run to the left and collect a nice plaque memorializing their accomplishments or they can run to right and collect $1 million each. Now decide which group you will lay down in front of. I have never had an executive tell me they will lay down in front of the money side. It's not that money does not motivate and it is not just that "everyone has their price." It's that the money offered has no impact upon the individual. It takes little research to read a corporate finance statement and see that the CEO and direct reports may well earn millions for what some may, with considerable justification (rightly or wrongfully), consider their creative accomplishments. It's not that money does not motivate; it's that unfairness is such a demotivating power.

So this is where the innovative executive team must look across the TIME structure and find ways to reward and motivate groups in new and exciting ways. This chosen method will need to be tailored across the originations, tied to the nature of the work being performed, distinguished between individual or team accomplishments, and, of course, be within the ability of the business or organization's ability to deliver. BB16 – Rewards and Recognition will discuss this subject much more thoroughly.

I like the fact that here in the United States our status is governed by how hard we work and how creative we are. The big money that is earned by the CEO could be motivating enough to have the CEO'S position as your goal and how you are structuring your career. An alternative path is going into your own business risking everything on being successful as the CEO of your own company. That requires some creativity, innovation, and takes risk but that the potential bigger paycheck may be worth it to you.

## DEVELOPING THE INNOVATIVE EXECUTIVE LEADERSHIP SKILL SET

Many executives probably think they have all the skills necessary to be a truly "innovative executive leader" right way. Many are already successful (as measured by current title and compensation), perhaps graduated from prestigious schools, or have some other past measurement to show they "have what it takes." Maybe they are right. Clearly, some people seem to have a natural talent for this type of executive leadership. For many, the late Steve Jobs comes to mind. But I would contend from years of experiences working for and with many such executives, they may have what it takes but probably not, and even if they do, they probably need to use their skills in whole news ways. They just don't know that part yet.

Many executives are good problem solvers and have strong analytical skills when presented with hard data and facts, but innovation and projects that require high levels of innovation content are different creatures. In school, one learns to solve problems, which are clearly stated and where available data is designed to allow one to solve the problem using readily available tools and methods. The case-study method, practiced still by prestigious schools, still overly use this method. The more ambiguous problems often require the executive to first define the problem for the organization and then work creatively to find possible solutions. It is defining the problem that trips up so many executive teams trying to be innovative executive leaders. They simply cannot define a problem in a way they cannot see the solution for themselves. The true innovative executive leadership team can define a problem in an ambiguous manner and comfortably move forward knowing that the clearer definition will come over time. Not the answer, mind you, just the definition that may well be something they had not been really considered.

Executives therefore must develop new skills in at least two areas if they wish to be successful in leading innovation efforts. One is creative problem solving and the other is in creative leadership. Creative problem solving is a recognized field with all the associated trimmings of associations, meetings, consultants, and universities promoting their programs in the subject. Creative leadership is a bit newer. While there are many theories about leadership, the concept of creative leadership as used here is that form of leadership that combines the best of creativity with the necessary facts, demand requirements, and daily chores of running a business of any kind.

A full discussion of either creative problem solving or creative leadership is beyond the scope of this book, much less this chapter. A brief summary is discussed here for basic clarification. Let's think of creative problem solving along a continuum as shown in the graph displayed in Figure BB3.5.

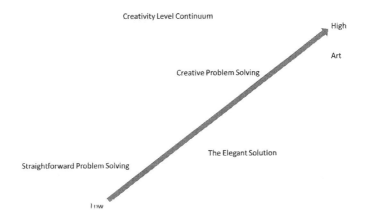

**FIGURE BB3.5**
Creativity Level Continuum.

At the lowest level (based on page position, after all some problems are huge and require tremendous intellectual capacity to solve), we have straight-forward linear problem solving meaning where executives can gather the necessary data and solve the problem where there is one right, or at least one very much desired, answer. Then we have what was once the highest compliment you could pay an engineer, designer, or scientist. That is, to call their solution "elegant." This means that not only was there a satisfactory, or correct, answer, but also that the answer itself or the method followed showed a certain level of creativity that others could appreciate.

At the next level is creative problem solving where executives will need to apply new methods and skills to help define, often re-define, the problem until they finally understand enough about their situation, even if nowhere near perfectly, to being searching for solutions. The techniques used by the innovative executive leader are focused more on learning about the problem than in immediately and linearly proceeding to the solution.

## THE INDIVIDUAL

The first step to becoming a leader in the process of *Innovative Executive Leadership* is to recognize that you must constantly review, learn, develop, practice, and reflect on the results of your skills and how they are applied by you as an individual. Very few, if any, senior executives, when asked to leave a company for poor performance of the organization, ever say "it was my fault." Mostly you hear a string of excuses; they move on to another firm and might even be highly successful if their unchanging skill set aligns with the specific needs of the next company to employ their abilities.

Now many of you will say "but of course that makes sense." You are supposed to hire the person able to solve the company's problems and grow the business. Unfortunately, the more narrow liner problem solving skills often yield only shorter term results. As Amazon has shown, the crushing losses in the brick and mortar retail sector of long-standing brand names, more of the same is rarely a long-term solution to survival in the face of innovative new approaches. Who tends to succeed? Those who employ both the problem solving and creative leadership to create and reinvent organizations to meet the current and near-future challenges.

The individual leading a commodity company will probably require different personal development from a start-up and different than a growing midsize, and also different from a large multinational. As a result, there is no one-size fit all-solution set no matter how much the university, consultant, or solution provider may tell you. Careful reflection on your own situation and the research on available training and other educational opportunities are the best start. And I think one new message with "do" mean just a start. For nothing is of value unless you implement it and carefully review what works or not.

There's an old story of a company president who was released because the organization was not meeting the investors' expectations. Being a good soldier, he agreed to overlap for two weeks with the new president. On his last day with the organization, he wrote three letters and gave them to the new president telling him, "Based upon my experience with this organization I prepared three letters that I hope will help you in doing the assignment. If you get into trouble, open the letter marked 1."

They said goodbye and the new manager tossed the three letters in his desk drawer not thinking much about them.

Just as predicted the new president found he was missing ship schedules in his second month in the assignment. Remembering the advice, his predecessor had given him, he went to his desk and opened letter #1. Inside was a one-page letter that said, "Blame it all on the terrible condition the organization was in when you took over. If after 2 months you're still having problems or have run into some new problems, open letter number 2." He followed this advice and the Board of Directors accepted his reasoning and understood he had the condition well under control now.

Things in the organization did not get better; in fact, they got worse. A number of key people resigned and sales dropped off significantly. As a result, he decided to open letter number #2. A single sheet of paper in letter read, "Blame it all on whole management team. If things still do not get better, open letter number #3."

Again the new manager followed the sage advice and again things got worse as two of their major customers decided to move the work to the Philippines. Now really unhappy with the way things were going, he decided to open letter #3 which simply read "Write 3 letters."

The simple lesson is "Don't blame things on someone else. It is you that makes the difference."

We can offer guidance in what a learning executive may be looking for in terms of new knowledge. The first and foremost would be developing skills in creative problem solving. Now this is a broad field and there is the *Creative Problem Solving Institute*, which is a good place to start. Like all institutes they may be someone parochial to their philosophy and seeking a broad range of seminars and course is always recommended.

There are some caveats on training in creative problem solving. It can be fun to take a course that brings out the plastic building blocks or uses art assignments to help you understand the value of reframing and thinking differently. But what you really need to find are those courses, seminars, and the like that focus on *applying* creative problem solving to real-world problems. You need to practice. As the great NFL coach Vince Lombardi is quoted, "Practice does not make perfect, perfect practice makes perfect." Many courses in subjects such as design thinking are quite good at this and should be considered regardless of your industry.

A second caveat is to avoid courses that state they will help you think "outside the box." There are now a number of books in publication about thinking inside the box. Based on research into what helps people actually think both creatively AND productively, it has been shown that most people are actually more creative when they have effective constraints (aka, a "box"). Those constraints that represent the Goldilocks area of not to rigid and not to lose tends to focus people and their creative minds in practical and useful directions. It is this box that is the major task for the innovative executive leadership team. (See Figure BB3.6.)

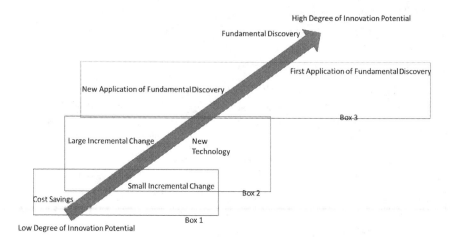

**FIGURE BB3.6**
Innovative Executive Leadership Sets the "Box".

In Figure BB3.6, we have three examples of "boxes" that innovative executive leadership could set. Let's discuss each one by citing a possible example. Each example is, of course, just one of what may be many possibilities.

### BOX 1   A COMMODITY COMPANY STRUGGLING TO OBTAIN A COMPETITIVE ADVANTAGE

The executive leadership in a commodity-type company may want to break out with some tremendous innovative leap forward but such a dream is hardly, if ever, realistic. The executive team needs to define for their organization the type and nature of innovation that best fits their business. They may set compensation and rewards systems that recognize those people who achieve "cost cutting" results but do so in different, more effective, and customer-pleasing ways. There may be further in-the-box limits that say such innovations should be compatible with some or all aspects of a sector of the current business operation. Some people will contend that Amazon is just such a company since they started out as a "book store on-line" in a world filled with bookstores.

## BOX 2    A TECHNOLOGY COMPANY NEEDS NEW TECHNOLOGY TO REGAIN MARKET LEADERSHIP

In such a case as this, many executives will use the buy-or-develop form of the problem to see if they have a technology ready or can they simply purchase something "new" to sell to customers. The innovative executive leadership team will more often start off with trying to better define what they mean by "regaining market leadership." They may well seek ways to redefine the business they are in and develop new products or services. It is always better to be the market leader of the new business just breaking the disruption line than the on-going, even currently rising busi ness that is still open to be overtaken by the upcoming disruption. Such analysis requires creative thought and imagination in combination with facts and figures.

## BOX 3    A NEW TECHNOLOGY COMPANY NEEDS FIRST OR NEW APPLICATIONS

In this box, the executive leadership needs to keep the organization focused and flexible as they learn about what the technology can do and not jump to the first application that comes to mind or simply the easiest one to implement with the least risk. This area can be very expensive to operate in and by nature is high in risk. The innovative executive leadership team will find ways to distribute the risk over the organization such that new and creative ways are identified through. Too often such firms as in this specific example are so focused on delivering the technology they do not plan ahead to the type of organization that will deliver and exploit it while continuing to develop the creative approaches to problem solving that gave them their first insights.

Of course, large multinationals with many individual companies may well have divisions with one, or all of the type of problems shown on the continuum. The innovative executive leadership teams must develop the agility to maintain balance between the level of innovation content and the specific requirements of the particular subdivision.

## SUMMARY

In this chapter, we looked at innovative executive leadership as a new way to manage the innovation content of your organization under the umbrella of an encompassing approach called TIME. Stressed in this chapter is that the innovative executive will display his or her leadership through a new approach to organization combining the best of creative problem solving, strong management of fundamentals, and specifically by making taking on and excelling at that most difficult of defining just what innovation means to their organization.

Gandhi is quoted as saying "Be the change that you wish to be in the world." The innovative executive can exhibit leadership only by becoming an innovative person. This path relies on readily available tools and methods but is unique is some way for each person. Extended, it will be unique for each executive team and will certainly evolve as technology and challenges change over time.

# BB4

## Performance and Cultural Change Management Plans

*Billy Arcement*

### CONTENTS

The world hates change yet it is the only thing that has brought progress.

**(Charles Kettering)**

## INFLUENCES THAT IMPACT CHANGES IN OUR WORLD

Time stands still for no man. Nor does change. Like time, change *moves on*. Businesses and life are in a constant state of flux. For both to cope, they must learn how to effectively deal with the inevitable creep of change. It's ever present. It will impact. And this requires a vigilance to raise your change-coping mechanism. To illustrate this point, here are several items impacting change that demand the attention of everyone.

1. We are impacted by rapid technological changes.
2. Societal moral limits have shifted over the years. In some cases, the values of yesteryear have all but disappeared into the new atmosphere of 21st Century living.
3. Businesses face constant competition from the global community.
4. Workplace environments today are almost unrecognizable from years past. The *lean machine* has introduced the replacement of many workers. The result of such changes has diminished worker loyalty. It's no longer a "job for life" attitude with new employees. And such an attitude can be costly.
5. There is a shift in the level of accountability expected of employees.

This is a small portion of the many facets of change we find in today's world. If these ideas don't surface a desire to better cope with this changing world, your organization will be left behind. That is the message both business leaders and employees must embrace.

## CREATING BUSINESS SUCCESS IN A CLIMATE OF CHANGE

Decide what you want most in the world and then do it!
(Billy Arcement)

Change can cause chaos for the ill-prepared businesses. Survival demands we don't behave like the Dodo birds. Sometimes the obvious escapes our notice. Perhaps we've relied on past performance to maintain our future, an approach that can lead to your business joining the ranks of the extinct Dodo birds!

Business leaders understand growth depends on having a successful flow of cash. Yes, *cash is still king! (Or Queen if you prefer).* Whatever our business, we must sell our product or service at a profit. Success in business requires a greater sales income than it cost to run the business. Otherwise, we morph into a benevolent enterprise. It now becomes obvious that the number one reason a business fails is, *low sales.* Since it's our clients/customers that provide cash, to grow our business means we either grow our customer base or derive a higher income per client than previously collected. Growth is synonymous with the growth of the cash flow.

Now, the obvious becomes even more obvious. A business cannot ignore the importance of keeping their focus on the customer. A business has to create a growth strategy to some percentage above the previous year of income. To maintain a level above inflation, a suggested growth strategy would be a 10–30% annual increase in sales income. Without a growth plan, your business will stagnate. Growth is not an accidental activity. The more precise and well-thought-out your plan, the greater the odds of keeping the doors open. We will share strategies on how to best serve customers later in this chapter.

There are other factors that have an influence on the bottom line besides cash. Study the ideas and evaluate your work environment. Perhaps they can serve you as well.

A failure is but a temporary inconvenience in the path of life.
(Billy Arcement)

### Persistence Pays

Keep this phrase on top of your mind. Most business owner will tell you the unexpected will jump in and create a potential roadblock to growth.

Discouragement (The Big "D") can rear its ugly head at any moment once we sense an obstacle is in our path. Giving up is much easier than persisting. It's the business that learns how to persist against the odds that will clear hurdles like an Olympic athlete. If we let discouragement continually hover over our head, we risk losing the battle of persistence. The "Big D" will win the battle. And yes, there is a fine-line between persistence and stupidity! To distinguish, one must keep a sharp eye on reality. Falsehoods are not friends. It's reality that is the guidance tool for decisions. Illusions can lead one down the primrose path to failure. Gain sufficient accurate information to maintain a grasp on what you have the ability to do. And, that leads me to my next point.

## Create an Environment of Awareness

*Awareness* is the key trait every business owner must grow. It's hard to image a business having too much awareness. With the proper awareness, truth has the best opportunity to surface. Then, it becomes easier to determine the path to take and the adjustments that must be made. The truth sets you free to make the tough choices with the best opportunity to create positive results. Grasp the truth and follow the trail it produces. No need being stupid! That mindset can only lead one to a lack of awareness!

## A Passion for the Business

This is a critical component to combat the negative impact of change. It's passion that pushes you forward when quitting seems like an easier choice. Build a fire igniting your passion and providing energy to propel the business forward. Building knowledge is a method to build passion. The more we learn about the business, the easier it is to be passionate about it. Knowledge also creates enthusiasm. Knowledge can minimize obstacles and enhance the success potential of the business. Combine knowledge with passion and you've just created the dynamic duo for business success.

## Face the Fears

Possessing the right amount of courage can stop you from dropping anchor and prevent forward movement. We let our fears paralyze progress. It's those "imaginary ghosts" that frighten us into a warped window of fear. There is nothing wrong with being fearful. In fact, a little fear can be a motivator. We just can't let fear paralyze us into a position that will lead to failure. Look at fear as a challenge to be conquered, not an obstacle that stifles our progress. Again, it's reality that either validates a fear or dispels its existence. Make progress against the fears businesses owners face by utilizing the persistence and passion strategies. It's a synergy that works. But, it's important that you always keep reality in front of your decisions. The absence of reality is like attempting to play baseball without the ball and bat. It's not fun and it isn't baseball!!

> The significant problems we face cannot be solved at the same level of thinking we were where we created them.
>
> (Albert Einstein)

## It's the Vision Stupid!

Don't mistake this statement as an attempt to insult anyone. The intention is to bring light to your vision. It's obvious to the sound business thinker that one needs to have a clear view of many aspects of a business. For example:

1. What product(s) will you sell?
2. How will you structure the business?
3. How much cash will you need to start up and maintain business momentum?
4. What type of employees do we need and what skills must they possess?
5. Who are your best customers?
6. Who are your competitors?

These are just a few of the many questions business owners must answer to clarify the business vision. Don't let business cataracts cover your eyes to the true vision you need to articulate. The greater clarity you create, the greater the odds for your succeeding. No detail is unimportant as you begin to visualize the future of your business. The devil is in the details so get him out of your business by exposing those details. A clear vision is the beginning of your business success journey. See yourself as successful by using persistence, passion, conquering fears, and creating vision.

## Believe in the Business

This is the starting point for business development and continual success. After all, if you don't believe in the business, why should consumers believe in it? Belief can maintain momentum at a time when nonbelievers will quit. Once again, we caution that dealing with reality is the critical part of establishing an accurate belief system. Another caution is to understand that your lack of belief can sometimes be sensed by your employees. Words of discouragement or disillusionment are powerful deterrents for progress. Often, such words originate with our self-talk and thoughts. Deal with reality so that what you believe is accurate. Rumors and gossip are your enemies. Keep them out of your organization. Neither serve any useful purpose. Honest, truthful assessments are your friends and serve a most useful purpose. Use them to shore up your belief system and the confidence both consumers and employees support. It takes a team effort to build a successful enterprise. In this case, it's the belief of the business owner(s), the investors, customers, suppliers, financial institutions, and employees that count.

## Exhibit the Flexibility of a Gymnast

Picture your business like a piece of clay. It's malleable and can be shaped into many forms. Flexibility is a characteristic used to build skyscrapers. If they are very rigid and not able to "sway" a bit in the wind, they collapse. Like such buildings, rigidity in your business mindset is the perfect storm for failure. Business survival depends upon the malleable component of your business. In the world of business, failures happen often because flexibility isn't built into the organizational structure. A business must be able to bend and sway with the high winds affecting their activities. Being flexible allows for change. Rigidity produces ruins. A flexible mindset is open to a myriad of ideas and approaches to creating a successful approach to business practices. A rigid mindset that glues a business to one approach is assuring ruination is part of the future.

## Sometimes Rule-Breaking Is Your Only Choice

This statement begs for a bit of clarity. We are not referring to breaking the law! That's carrying rule-breaking a bit too far. Here we are referencing the ability to take a risk and venture into new territory or into what might be viewed as an unconventional choice. This approach to business success requires an adjustment to reality. (I know this has already been said a lot. Just want to be sure it sticks!).

Stop and think of the many new businesses that emerge each year. Many involve lots of risks. Many involve doing things differently. Did Orville and Wilber break the rules in order to record the first flight of the airplane? What rules did Thomas Edison, Benjamin Franklin, Bill Gates, and Steve Jobs break? The answer? *Lots!!* Their thinking challenged conventional thought about business building. They took the risk to persist until they succeeded. They followed a passion so strong that no obstacle was too great to smash their success. They bounced from idea to idea and were flexible enough to survive the tribulations of trial and error. No one can question their belief first in themselves and second in the vision created in their mind. All were grounded in a reality that allowed them to sense new directions needed to reach their conceptualized creations. Business success is not luck. It's the result of a well-thought-out strategy worked and refined until success is reached. And, in the process, every successful business removes the chaos surrounding their efforts. They create the proper changes needed. In this next section, we'll explore how to successfully lead change and turn the effort into a win.

## EFFECTIVELY LEADING CHANGE

Systematic innovation requires a willingness to look at change as an opportunity.

(Peter Drucker)

### Let's Talk Culture

For a business to succeed and effectively deal with change, there must be a clear understanding of organizational culture. It's becoming more and more prevalent that culture is the "make or break" component business leaders must address prior to attempting to implement any organizational change.

Lou Gerstner, former IBM chief executive said, *Culture is everything.* It is, by the observations of those seeking to incorporate change in an organization, the major and most critical element to the successful implementation of change. When executives plan to implement organizational changes, they cannot ignore the pro/con influence of culture in the workplace. Successful changes are much more likely to occur when leaders take advantage of the culture present rather than seeking to make a change in the culture. It may be easier to learn how to climb over a hill than to look for ways to bulldoze it out of the way. Culture is anchored deep within the organizational structure. (See Figure BB4.1.)

Most believe that it's the leader(s) that set the culture tone. Employees and leaders learn to live with the company culture or they go elsewhere. It's that critical an element of concern to employees and managers alike. Let's be more specific. It's the upper level of management that creates culture. Every manager at this level cannot forget it's their actions, not their words that influence culture creation. Managers that never follow-up on their orders may have them followed, or not.

What then are the major factors that create the culture? Here is a list for your consideration and, more importantly, examples of how to best approach each.

## Introducing Organizational Change

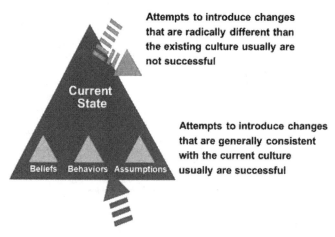

Attempts to introduce changes that are radically different than the existing culture usually are not successful

Current State

Attempts to introduce changes that are generally consistent with the current culture usually are successful

Beliefs  Behaviors  Assumptions

**FIGURE BB4.1**
Cultures Impact Upon Change.

1. *Values*: Values are often called principles. They serve as the organization's laws of government. All decisions that are made within an organization should be matched against these values to be sure they are in line. We all have them and leaders are not an exception. The values they display take root and can impact the attitude of employees and other lower level leaders. As an organization, there should be a clear position on corporate values. If you are a CEO, why not stroll through the workplace and ask employees their perception of corporate values. Might end up a scary moment! Contradiction is not the friend of executives. Consistency is key. The corporation either practices a value or it ignores it. It's the same with leaders. Don't tell employees "Safety is #1" and then don't provide equipment to prevent injuries. This inconsistency collapses culture. Values form the corporate foundation. And, never forget if the foundation crumbles, the house will fall.

   Values should be documented and well communicated. They never should set around unused to the point they get dusty. Values are not something that you change minute by minute throughout every day.

   We like to see the organization's value posted in every manager's office along with his set of personal principles. Personal principles should always be a reflection of the organization values.

2. *Beliefs*: What you believe directs your decisions and creates who you are. Companies follow the same idea. Leader beliefs direct employees to make their decisions in line with those beliefs. The major difference between value and beliefs is that values should never be compromised whereas beliefs are always considered when making a decision that may be compromised based upon a specific situation. Again, it's critical to avoid inconsistencies. Corporate beliefs form culture and should serve as a guidance on how to operate the business. The employees can be told that there is an important set of objectives, values, and beliefs, but if the employee does not see these pertinent factors driving the organization, they will lose belief in the organization.

3. *Attitudes*: In general, attitudes are impacted by beliefs. Several important attitudes are covered later in the chapter. It's attitude that creates behavior. It's behavior that creates actions. It's action that produces results. Don't like results? Why not go back to the attitudes that are part of the culture.

Other things like the accountability chain play an important role in the culture creation. Survival is impossible without proper accountability. Everyone in the culture has an accountability component they must follow and achieve. A no-accountability culture is a losing proposition.

## Ethics

Ethics is the other item of importance to creating strong, effective, and long-term survival practices. The ethics practiced by leaders will affect the practices undertaken by employees. Or, if the clash of values is too severe, people will leave the company. Can't say "honesty" is our policy when employees observe or engage in underhanded practices. It's that "inconsistent" factor again. Ethics can't be ignored if survival is the long-term goal.

----

## IMPORTANT CULTURE FACTS

Here are six important items about culture to keep in mind as you seek the best ways to use culture to enhance your business opportunities and employee engagement.

1. The success and/or failures experienced by employees is tied to the type of culture present. (Yes, it bears repeating.) A culture not supporting employee training is opening the door to increased mistakes and costly errors. Keep employees engaged to maximize their effectiveness. It's the right approach to using culture as a corporate benefit. Don't forget that culture is the fuel that drives the culture vehicle. So keep the tank full so you don't have to park it on the side of the road that leads to corporate success.
2. The role of values is directly related to the type of culture an organization creates. It represents the values shared by a majority of employees. If this is not the case, your organization will experience lots of turnover. People will not work very long in an environment that clashes with their values. So, don't let your "values vehicle" crash and wreck the organization.
3. When hiring, match prospective employee values with the organizational values. Misfits will quit and leave. Their motivation will

also be far less than the most energized employees. Misfits are costly. Choose carefully. Your culture survival depends upon it. Once hired, periodically emphasize important cultural values. It's essential every leader practice the values. An incongruent picture produces inconsistent performance. Neither is a welcomed event.

4. The ability to successfully lead and grow teams is lessoned when there is a misunderstanding of culture. Organizational culture has some blind spots that can cause difficulties. Eliminate these by an open discussion of your culture. It's not "I've got a secret" time. The more an organization is clear on its culture, the less the potential for blind spots to appear and confusion to exist.

5. Whenever you train, remain consistent to your cultural values. Any deviation from that focus point doesn't serve either the organization or employees well.

6. Lastly, culture can serve as a great problem solving entity. When issues arise, look for the inconsistency between the event and the culture. Study things a bit and the answer will surface. Rest assured that when culture and a problem are at odds, there is trouble.

Let's summarize important ideas. Experts say people join a company but leave managers. That is a significant point to remember. It's the leaders that create the culture. If managers create a culture that conflicts with employee values, they will leave the organization. Never forget the importance of having a culture all employees appreciate. Help them thrive in it. Help them look forward to working in the organization and considering it a good career move.

---

## PERFORMANCE

Definition of performance: the act or process of carrying out or accomplishing an activity, task, or function against preset known standards of accuracy, completeness, cost, and speed. Performance is deemed to be the fulfillment of an obligation.

As you can see, performance needs to be measured against a preset criteria. In well-developed organizations, the business plan should provide that standard. (See Figure BB4.2.)

| PURPOSE | 11 OUTPUTS | TIME FRAME |
|---|---|---|
| Direction | Visions | 10 - 20 years |
|  | Mission | Open-ended |
|  | Values | Open-ended |
|  | Strategic Focus | 5 years |
|  | Critical Success Factors | 3 years |
| Expectations | Business Objectives | 5-10 years |
| (measurements | Performance Goals | 1-5 years |
| Actions | Strategies | 1-5 years |
|  | Tactics | 1-3 years |
|  | Budgets | 1-3 years |
|  | Performance Plans | 3-12 months |

**FIGURE BB4.2**
Elements of a Complete Business Plan.

The five inputs that set the direction for the organization are developed by high-level management and approved by the Board of Directors. (See Figure BB4.2.) They provide the input necessary for the organization to develop a set of objectives and goals that along with other considerations will set the priorities for the change activities. The objectives and goals inputs are the primary performance measure for the organization. They are then subdivided down into activities that each employee is involved in completing. Failure to meet these objectives and goals is an indication of poor organizational performance. Meeting the goals and objectives indicates that the organization is doing its assignment. Exceeding these objectives and goals should result in extra rewards and recognition for the people involved.

## ORGANIZATIONAL CHANGE MANAGEMENT

> Research confirms that as much as 60% of change initiatives and other projects fail as a direct result of a fundamental inability to manage their social implications.
>
> Gartner Group

We all like to think of ourselves as change masters, but in truth, we are change bigots. Everyone in the management team is all for change. They want to see others change, but when it comes to the managers changing, they are reluctant to move away from their past experiences that have proven to be so successful for them. If the organization is going to change, top management has to be the first to change.

Change is inevitable and we must embrace it if we are going to be successful in this challenging world we live in. In *Change Management Excellence – The Art of Excelling in Change Management*, which is Book III in the series, *The Five Pillars of Organizational Excellence*, we discuss the change management system that is made up of three distinct elements.

- Defining what will be changed
- Defining how to change
- Making the change happen

> We must simply learn to love change as much as we hated it in the past.
> Tom Peters Thriving on Chaos

Most of the books written to date about change management have been theoretical in nature. They talked about black holes, cascading sponsorships, and burning platforms, but that is only the last phase of the change process. Most organizations do not understand or follow a comprehensive change management system. An effective change management system requires that the organization step back and define what will be changed. By that, we are not talking about reducing stock levels, increasing customer satisfaction, or training people; we are talking about the very fundamentals.

Which of the key business drivers need to be changed and how do they need to be changed? That means that you need to develop very crisp vision statements that define how the key business drivers will be changed over time. This requires that the organization have an excellent understanding of what its business drivers are and how they are operating today. Then the organization must define exactly how it wants to change these key business drivers over a set period of time.

Once the organization has defined what it wants to change, then it can define how to change. During this stage, the organization looks at the more than 1100 different improvement tools that are available today, determines which tools will bring about the required changes to these key business drivers, and schedules the implementation of these tools and methodologies. This schedule makes up a key part of the organization's strategic business plan.

The last phase in the change management process is making the change happen. This is the area where the behavioral scientists have developed a number of excellent approaches to break down resistance and build up resiliency throughout the organization. It is this phase that most change management books have concentrated on, but it is the last phase in the total change management system. This book focuses on all three phases of the change management system, discussing in detail how to define what will be changed, defining how to change it, and how to make the change happen.

> We (Japan) will win and you (USA) will lose. You cannot do anything about it because your failure is an internal disease. Your companies are based on Taylor's principles. Worse, your heads are Taylorized, too. We have passed the Taylor stage. We are aware that business has become terribly complex. Survival is very uncertain in an environment filled with risk, the unexpected, and competition.
>
> Konosuke Matsushita
> Founder
> Matsushita Electric Industrial Company

## Creating an Environment to Catapult Change

> Problem solving demands changes in our habits and way of thinking.
> (Billy Arcement)

To get a better understanding of how a corporation might deal with change, here are four approaches to consider. Each addresses critical components on an organization and how they work. The example that follows is the template USDA Rural began using a number of years ago to cope with the rapid rate of change within its walls.

1. *Staffing Levels*: Corporate leaders should examine their organizational structure for the level of efficiency present. Where deficiencies exist, implement changes to keep both internal and external customers aware of program deliveries. One wants staffing levels not only efficient but focused on the most important services and/or products important for corporate survival.
2. *Staff Performance*: Review the status quo and then create plans to enhance the performance of staff members. Review at mid-year

and end of the fiscal year. It's also important to maintain a constant vigil of results making the immediate necessary adjustments to maintain the results designed by the plans developed. Delaying can turn out to be detrimental.

3. *Training*: Everyone should be a participant at training aimed to develop greater performance and results. Help everyone understand and support the overall desired results. Keep everyone informed on any program changes and the impact on budget.

4. *Programs*: Again, it is the efficiency and streamlining activities to achieve program results. Know what must be achieved, have detailed plans to get that end results desired. It's important that everyone support program initiatives. It's a team sport to bring about the necessary changes that promote positive growth.

## Leader Conversations Are Critical

How does your management team speak to each other? How do they approach conversations with employees? In each case, business leaders need straightforward dialog. Again, it's the truth that sets everyone free to successfully navigate the seas of change management. Let's add these other important ingredients to the successful conversation recipe:

1. *A caring attitude*: This is so important yet often leaders want to give a command to make change occur. True change is easier to implement when recipients sense caring is part of the process. Empathy is an important entity. Have caring conversations.

2. *A confident attitude*: If a leader displays doubt that change is possible, it's contagious. Employees sense the doubt and become reluctant to be cooperative. It's the leader's confidence that produces momentum. Have a confident conversation.

3. *An honest attitude*: This is not the time to exhibit a devious mindset. Be truthful and honest when discussing what will happen as a result of change implementation. Have an honest conversation.

4. *A performance improvement attitude.* No deeply committed employee wants to take a step backwards when it comes to performance. A good worker wants to improve. And, when you can show how a change will produce that result, you have a winning conversation. Have a performance improvement conversation.

5. *A service attitude.* Servant leadership is the highest form of leadership. And, when you want to implement change, there had better be a sense of service present. Have a service-centered conversation.

## Leaders Must Lead the Way

Corporate leaders should be clear why they want changes instituted. Change just for change sake is wasted energy. Why are the suggested changes needed? What are the desired results needed for corporate and individual growth? How will all this be accomplished? When do we need these changes in place? What skills do the change agents need in order to accomplish the task? And finally, who are the specific individuals charged with making change occur? Important questions demanding answers before you begin the process. It's not the time to move blindly. Clear eyes and clear minds make the best judgments.

Changes don't take place in a vacuum. It's especially important for top management to "walk the talk." Remember, people are watching your actions, not just listening to your words. You will need the full cooperation, commitment, and participation by all levels of management. You will need a *passionate* commitment to bringing the change into reality.

Most importantly, without top management buy-in, completing change moves toward an impossibility level. If the CEO is not aligned with the change process, it will unlikely not succeed. It's also important to involve every level of leaders. When done properly, the path for change to occur is much smoother. These layers of managers are on the front line each day and have an accurate pulse assessing reality. Everyone understands change implantation can take more time than initially determined by involving these individuals. But, the delay is worth the effort to grow and support the change initiative. In the long term, this is the best approach. Involving early saves conflicts later. If lots of changes are required, corporate leaders should display patience, move slowly, and maintain focus. Taking the time to slow down a bit offers the opportunity to move at a faster pace later in the process. It's important the fog of rapid change not cloud vision and direction. Make the change expectations challenging but realistic. Better to move slowly and accomplish than move at such a rapid pace that vision is blurred and focus is lost. Consider implementing change as a journey, not a blueprint. There will be shifts and even complete movements in new directions. Be ready to adjust because adjustment produces less of a strain. Don't expect the thinking of everyone to cause a rapid change in behaviors. Change takes time and patience is a true virtue here.

## Leaders Must Provide Resources

Would a football coach not provide his team with helmets, pads, shoes, and footballs? No coach in his right mind would support such an absurd idea. Why then would a leader expect employees to achieve changes without providing the resources and training needed to accomplish the changes? At this point in the process, leaders must become boy scouts. In other words, they must "Be Prepared."

## Leaders Must Involve Everyone

Early in the process, leaders should make the effort to inform, involve, and include nonmanagement personnel in the process. A failure to move in this direction can result in a high level of resistance. To temper resistance, identify those employees that cannot or will not support the strategy and plans designed. They might also oppose the end result of change implementation. Leaders should welcome resistors. They are not necessarily the enemy. Their position might open eyes to a new view. If they are right, use their ideas. The most successful approach to deal with resistors is to keep everyone informed of the plans. Get their buy-in, support, and involvement. When you can successfully do this, resistance becomes like an ice cube in a heat wave. It melts away. Leadership should also remember that the change process should be treated as a team sport, not an exercise in isolation. Involvement creates support. Pushing change through without involvement is a ripe recipe for failure.

Important points to remember: Leaders must be transparent and bold in their desire to address questions and concerns. Neutralization of resistors is never a bad move. Involve everyone. It's the critical step toward the successful implementation of change. Support builds when one is involved in the action. Players in the game fight to achieve victory. It's hard to contribute when you sit on the bench. It's the contributions from those involved in the action that makes winning possible. If all your players are on the bench, there is no game and no victory.

## Leaders Monitor

As the process moves forward, monitor results and adjust as needed. Here, flexibility becomes an important part of the process. Rigidity can ruin the plan and stall the strategy. There may also be a need for making policy changes to get the buy-in. Leaders should arm themselves with options to increase the support in both a formal and informal manner. By leveraging both, the change transitions are more easily incorporated into the corporate culture. But obstacles identified by this monitoring process can be overcome by communication, communication, communication. It's not possible to overcommunicate and explain the plans and strategy. At the same time, listen, listen, listen. You've got to hear the conversations and observe the actions. Open your eyes and clean your ears and share the message. Let your passion for the new changes show to everyone you meet.

> United we stand, divided we fall ... a good thought to remember for successful change transition.
>
> (Billy Arcement)

## SOME SUGGESTIONS FOR CEOS TO AID CHANGE IMPLEMENTATION

Every CEO worth their salary and responsibilities understands the importance of *attitude* and the ability to turn lemons into lemonade. Here are several positive attitudes essential to making a smooth transition into a "change mode."

## Happiness

This attitude is not one to be pursued. It is self-manufactured as a by-product of the thought process. Let's ask a magic question at this point. *Will your folks experience greater happiness on the job because the change occurred?* Employees look at their job as a place that should bring happiness. By helping employees appreciate what they gain instead of crying over what they perceive they've lost. Misery doesn't produce happiness. So, make the move as free of misery as possible and as much about raising the reading on their happy meter. Doing this requires lots of pre-planning and a well-thought-out strategy. Never approach change in a haphazard manner and that includes a readiness to adjust. That's the approach winners take and we believe you are a winner.

## Growth

How will the change cause employees to grow in their skill set. Achievers want to grow a little each day. Satisfaction with the status quo is the first step toward stagnation. The recipe for perpetual ignorance is to be satisfied with your opinions and content with your knowledge. Go on a discovery trip to uncover talents that may be hidden from view. Make the change surface such talents whenever possible. Again, as planning for change is conducted, make this one of the goals to achieve at every opportunity. Remember, it's never too late to learn something new.

## Action

Nothing of any consequence ever occurs without action. It's the core element needed to make any progress. Just "wishing" for change won't make it happen. You must engage in a well-thought-out action process designed to achieve the desired change. It's worthy to add this thought from Francis Bacon.

> There's no comparison between that which is lost by not succeeding and that which is lost by not trying.
>
> (Francis Bacon)

## Belief

If people within the organization don't trust their leadership and believe in their vision, producing change is like trying to ask someone to throw a 100 pound weight 100 meters. It's impossible!

Leadership must address the beliefs that hold back momentum to change. Consider them the "box" in which people play. Most find it difficult to think or play outside the box. Such beliefs hold people back from adapting the new mindset of changing the status quo.

## Importance

We all have the urge to feel important. By helping those involved with making changes to feel worthy, their support is more likely to occur. We are not suggesting one use manipulation here. This position must be genuine. By establishing the "service first" mindset, this offers others the opportunity to feel important. Use this important human characteristic to smooth the transition required for incorporation of needed changes.

This list could be longer. But the intent is to stimulate your thinking; to incorporate, and be cognizant of the importance of maintaining a positive attitude. Negativity causes a deep dive into nothingness. Progress isn't made. People aren't happy. Cost may soar. Desired outcomes vanish. It's not a pretty picture. Be positive and change what ails you and perhaps you may even change the world.

## CONTROLLING THE COST FOR CHANGE IMPLEMENTATION

It's unlikely that one can put changes in place without some financial investment. The goal should be to make changes that lower cost. If that is the end product of your change process, give yourself a "gold star" for efficiency. If, on the other hand, to make positive changes, there is a cost, here are a few suggestions to help keep them under control.

1. *You must know what you're spending.* Look at every cent expended. It's the only way you can accurately state the cost. You may not like the picture but don't hid it from view. By watching everything, scrutiny is complete and maximum savings are achieved. This is a responsibility where management cannot stand on the sideline and observe. They must be a part of the cost-saving effort.
2. *Continuously strive to spend less.* Any business cost analysis includes ways to reduce expenditures. It's no different here. Keep turning the knob of cost down. You'll be proud of your effort when costs drop. Be willing to remove any item. Don't let pride of ownership sink the ship of sound fiscal practices.

3. *Use the proper tools and resources in the hands of employees.* Every decision within the corporate structure has a cost. Examine activities to determine where the dollars go. Reduce wherever processes are identified. Spend what you must. Just don't become a philanthropist! Also, grow the knowledge of employees as another tool to fight increasing and wasteful costs. In this case, knowledge is power!

4. *The more the merrier.* We're talking a numbers game here. The more employees involved in monitoring and reducing costs, the more funds can be saved. Remember that people matter. Ignoring any segment of the workforce is an opportunity for resistance to surface. Approach each group as an individual. Dialog in a fashion that is persuasive to them and enhance the buy-in. Be honest, thorough, and positive in your approach with each group. This trifecta is a winning combination.

5. *Simplify.* Don't complicate the monitoring process so everyone can become involved. The easier it is to spot excessive costs, the easier it becomes to save funds. It's that simple!

6. *Share the "why."* It's never a bad idea to keep employees informed as much as possible. When they understand which expenditures are able to be cut, this is a winning position. Create ownership whenever possible. We tend to watch more intently things we "own."

7. *Be clear on expectations.* When people understand their job responsibilities, they can more clearly see where costs can be reduced. Make excellence the goal. Winning organizations avoid "average" results. Your organization should also consider this position.

8. *Be prepared for the unexpected.* If things can go wrong, they often do. As leaders of the change management process, we must be ready and, as best we are able, anticipate the unexpected. You won't necessarily catch everything coming your way. But at least you will stop some when you are prepared to do so.

For more detail on Organizational Change Management, we recommend reading the book entitled, *Change Management – Manage the Change or it Will Manage You*, authored by Frank Voehl (published by CRC Press).

## ACHIEVING EXCEPTIONAL SERVICE

Any evaluation of performance and cultural change must also include a discussion of *service*. This is an appropriate topic to close out this chapter. Here is a list of eleven concepts corporate cultures can incorporate into everyday behaviors and possesses. Implementation of these strategies is a proactive approach to providing a high level of service.

(1) *Build customer loyalty and confidence.* A list of successful customer service strategies is at the end of this section. Essential to getting this right is to be proactive in meeting the needs of customers and building good will.

(2) *Empower your workers.* Provide your workers with the authority to take advantage of (problems, complaints, issues) improvement opportunities rapidly without consulting with a team or someone else first. Customers like individuals who can address their concerns personally without consulting with a higher authority. Empowerment builds stature in the individual and shows the organization's ability for him or her to make good decisions.

(3) *Emphasize with customers.* Be able to walk in their shoes. See things from their prospective and you've established a winning relationship.

(4) *Become effective communicators.* This includes a three-prong approach of speaking, writing, and listening. Serve other well by mastering these items and you will rise above the crowd and stand out in the workplace and among the vendors serving your customers.

(5) *Practice tolerance and patience under stressful situation.* Staying calm, cool, and collected is the right approach to successfully handling stress. Customers can be difficult. The stronger your ability to practice the three "C's," the greater your success odds.

(6) *Learn to process information well.* Go back to the previous points. Using the three "C's" works here as well. Educate yourself to a level that you understand issues your customers face. Use this to better understand their concerns.

(7) *Be self-motivated.* You are your motivator, not outside entities. For great service to others, become a caring, optimistic, and helpful individual and organization. Continuously learn to build

your self-confidence. Become a high energy-independent worker. Self-sufficiency can motivate.

(8) *Become a pro.* We equate professionalism as the upper level of performance. Present a good image and attitude.

(9) *Understand the organization, products, and/or services.* The more information you possess on these three fronts, the more value you bring to the organization. This is also a place where ignorance of these items is not bliss to your career.

(10) *Become a problem solver.* Few skills serve you better than the ability to address and solve problems. This is particularly important to grow your service reputation. Customers respect companies and individuals within its walls that can solve their problems. Learn this skill and you will advance to the front of the line.

(11) *Learn technical skills.* We live in a technological world. Invest in learning computer skills and state-of-the-art tools in your workplace. These all enhance your ability to serve.

We should not fall into the trap of thinking of change management in isolation. In truth, how a company serves its customers is a most important element of company success. After all, a company without customers has no reason to exist. On the other hand, changes within the corporate structure may be initiated by the relationship the organization establishes with its customers. This is the revenue stream that keeps the doors open. Perhaps, as you review this list, you will find information that prompts you to consider a change to shore up customer loyalty. If this isn't the case, it's still a good list!! Think through the steps following each of the twelve "rules" listed below and determine your position.

(1) ***Focus on problem identification. Turn them into opportunities to improve.***
   - You can't solve a concern that has not been properly identified.
   - Ask questions to discover information. Best handled with a prepared action plan.
   - Always be looking for ways to strengthen customer loyalty.
   - Take all complaints seriously but not personally.
   - Propose a solution and get the customer to agree with it.

- Focus on solving the complaint rapidly.
- Keep your word. Follow through on promises.

(2) *Keep accurate records, particularly for quality improvement opportunities.*
- Set up a system to document and classify complaints.
- Record all information given to you by the customer.
- Review records to prevent repetitive occurrences of a complaint.

(3) *Listen! Listen! Listen!*
- Listen to understand.
- Focus on problem identification.

(4) *Help customers understand who in your organization can address their concerns.*
- A customer must have easy contact with anyone who can help with their complaint.
- Use talents of people within the organization to build your service process.
- Channel problem to where it originates so service can be obtained immediately.

(5) *Practice empathy and sympathy.*
- This is not always easy but it is the right thing to do.
- Always try to see the complaint from the customers' perspective.
- Ask: "How would I like to do business with me?"
- Take a genuine interest in the customer as a person.
- Treat customer as a guest in your home.
- Gain confidence of customers by demonstrating sincere concern for their welfare.

(6) *Smile*
- A sincere smile is a pleasant thing to greet in person.
- Smile when you answer the phone so you will come across as friendly.

(7) *Use customers as the best source for new product or service ideas.*
- Learn as much as you can about the needs of your customers. This helps generate new ideas.

(8) *Be honest and level with customer when something goes wrong.*
- If you are wrong – admit it!
- Your customer is more interested in what you can do for him than he is in your goods or services.

- Right or wrong, the customer is always right.
- If you don't ever lie to a customer, you won't have to remember what you said.

(9) ***Never miss an opportunity to express appreciation for your customers' business.***
  - Be helpful, friendly on the phone, and in person.
  - Never forget to say "Thanks."
  - Be positive, polite, and patient. (3 P's)
  - Go the extra mile. Do something extra the customer doesn't expect.
  - Extend the concern throughout the organization.

(10) ***The customer isn't always right but she's always the customer.***
  - Customer perceptions are more important than facts.
  - Saying "I'm sorry" when a mistake is made goes a long way toward reducing confrontation.
  - Develop four characteristics: competence, honest, caring, and responsibility.

(11) ***Don't run down the competition – show the difference.***
  - Don't be a critic. No statue was ever dedicated to a critic.

(12) ***Periodically measure your customers' satisfaction.***
  - Everything in life needs periodic evaluation and customer satisfaction is no different.
  - Never forget a customer and never let the customer forget you.
  - Keep open lines of communication regarding needs, etc.

---

## SUMMARY

It's going to be the performance of everyone within the corporate structure that will impact the growth and success achieved. The importance of understanding the elements of culture has a great impact on performance. Cope with the barriers present in today's business environment by upgrading both individual and corporate performance. Create the culture that supports that end. It's the ultimate survival strategy and the best method to deal with the forces of change.

# BB5

## *Commitment to Stakeholders' Expectations*

*Bill Copeland*

## CONTENTS

## INTRODUCTION

Who is a stakeholder, why are they important, and how do you manage relationships with them? These very simple questions are the subject of this chapter.

Virtually every person in an organization from the CEO to the person working on an assembly line has a set of stakeholders they must be aware of and communicate with effectively.

From an organization or business standpoint, stakeholders are very important because they affect how an organization is managed and run, how significant financial decisions are taken, or how a project achieves its objective.

Stakeholders in most cases have a vested interest in a company. These interests can be quite different from one another and include financial, social, environmental, or social.

The issue of meeting expectations of stakeholders is an ongoing task. Every significant decision you make is geared to pleasing the most people in the most important ways most of the time. Success in meeting shareholders expectations assumes that you accomplish the following tasks:

- Define stakeholders
- Identify stakeholders
- Understand stakeholders' needs and wants
- Prioritize stakeholders' needs and expectations
- Develop a plan to communicate, implement, and manage stakeholder expectations

Meeting stakeholder wants and expectations may make the difference between success and failure of an organization, a project, or an individual within the organization.

## DEFINE STAKEHOLDERS

There are multiple definitions of stakeholders. The definition depends in many cases on the type of organization, industry, project, or role of a person within the organization.

Listed below are a number of common and widely used definitions that illustrate the broad range of definitions:

- collinsdictionary.com: "Stakeholders are people who have an interest in a company's or organization's affairs."
- businesdictionary.com: "A person, group or organization that has interest or concern in an organization. Stakeholders can affect or be affected by the organization's actions, objectives and policies."
- stakeholdermap.com: "A stakeholder is anybody who can affect or is affected by an organization, strategy or project. They can be internal or external and they can be at senior or junior levels."
- dictionary.cambridge.org: "A person or group of people who own a share in a business." "A person such as an employee, customer, or citizen who is involved with an organization, society, etc. and therefore has responsibilities towards it and an interest in its success."

- project-management.com: "Project stakeholders are individuals and organizations that are actively involved in the project, or whose interests may be affected as a result of project execution or project completion."
- psychologydictionary.org: "A person or company who has an interest in a research project that could be a sponsor, director, service recipient."
- Alan Li: "Stakeholders can be defined as all entities that are impacted through a business running its operations and conducting other activities related to its existence. The impact can be direct in the case of the business's customers and suppliers or indirect in the case of the communities in which the business chooses to place its locations."

The implication for this broad range of definitions is that the definition of stakeholders will vary depending on the organization, industry, project, or role of the leader.

Careful consideration should be given to developing a definition of stakeholders as the very first step to meeting their expectations.

## IDENTIFY STAKEHOLDERS

Failure is many times related to knowing who the stakeholders are. If you don't know who the stakeholders are, it's impossible to understand and meet their needs and wants and then satisfy those needs and wants.

Let's assume you decide on the definition of stakeholders for your project or organization. Using this definition of a stakeholder, you should be able to develop a comprehensive list of possible stakeholders.

Use brainstorming techniques to develop this list. Don't worry about assigning importance or priority or needs, as that will come later. At this stage "more is better."

Here are some typical questions to ask during a brainstorming session to help develop a list of stakeholders of your product, service, or project:

- Who has the most to gain or lose financially from the success or failure?
- Who can influence or decide on allocating resources?

- Who has the most influence?
- Who has the most direct influence on quality?
- Who is the ultimate customer or end user?
- Who actually delivers the product or service to the customer?
- Who interfaces with the customer on a regular basis?
- Who hears ideas from the salesforce or partners?
- Who needs to know the status on a regular basis?

Here are some traditional stakeholder groups. This list can be used to organize and bring structure to a potentially long list of stakeholders. Be sure to define specifically who is in each group. For example, in the customers group define customers of a specific product or service. In the employees group the stakeholders could be the product management team in the marketing department. The more specific you define the stakeholders, the more useful and relevant the following steps become.

- Customers: According to Peter Drucker, the purpose of a company is *to create customers*. Customers can be both external and internal.
- Employees: The employees are the ones who create and deliver the products or services that the customers consume.
- Management: This is a very broad term that can include the Board of Directors, CEO, functional VP's, direct supervisor, or project team manager.
- Investors, shareholders, and owners: The composition of this group will vary depending on the organization and the ownership structure. The common element is their focus on financial issues.
- Business partners, distributors, suppliers, distributors, and various other business partners: Partners are in many cases essential as they may have valuable skills or market access that the organization does not possess internally.
- The local community: Being a good citizen requires healthy links to the local community.
- Federal, state, local government, and regulatory authorities: These are important depending on the focus of the organization. For example, defense contractors will be highly focused on the federal government.
- Social media: The role of social media is expanding dramatically and must be considered.

- Creditors: Simply put, a creditor is a party to whom money is owed. As such, they have a vested interest in the organization.
- Trade unions: An organization of workers who have come together to achieve many common goals. Unions are important when work rules, compensation, and benefits are affected.

So now you have a comprehensive list of stakeholder groups. It is time to move to the next step.

## UNDERSTAND STAKEHOLDERS' NEEDS AND WANTS

Once you've identified your stakeholders, you need to understand their needs. Consider stakeholder needs and expectations in relation to your project goals, organization mission, or strategic direction. To what extent can you meet their needs and expectations within your objectives?

There are many ways to collect stakeholders' needs and wants. No one way is appropriate for use in all cases. The project or task at hand will determine the most valuable technique to use. It is suggested that several techniques or methods be included to gather all relevant information fully. It also may not be possible to reach all stakeholders with one technique. For example, it may not be feasible or appropriate to have board members fill out a questionnaire. However, it is highly recommended to start with interviews, if at all possible, as a first step. This will allow for a thorough discussion and understanding of the stakeholders' needs and wants. It also allows the stakeholder manager to develop rapport with stakeholders.

Here are just a few options to consider for identifying needs and wants:

- Interviews
- Questionnaires
- Focus groups and workshops
- Review documentation
- Observation
- Prototyping
- Feedback from process users
- Quality function deployment – can be used during the needs analysis and is a technique for deploying the "voice of the customer"

The purpose of using these various techniques is to capture the primary needs and wants of each identified stakeholder. This approach should develop a large number of needs and wants. The items must be well defined and differentiated from one another.

As an initial grouping, place the list of needs and wants into three categories: primary, secondary, and tertiary. Input from the stakeholder should determine which group is appropriate for each item. At this stage, it is important to focus only on the primary needs and wants. Primary needs are those defined as being first or highest in rank, quality, or importance. The primary category should include no more than two or three items.

This is a good time to review the list of stakeholders and their primary needs to ensure you have a comprehensive list. During this understanding stage, additional stakeholders may be uncovered who were not included in the identifying stage. If so, add them to the list and understand their needs and wants.

## PRIORITIZE STAKEHOLDERS' NEEDS AND WANTS

The importance of each stakeholder to the business determines the degree to which the organization or project manager attempts to accommodate the stakeholder in the course of planning its actions.

The Stakeholder Mapping Grid is a useful tool that helps provide structure to the analysis of needs and expectations. The tool uses a 2 × 2 grid that shows the stakeholder's relationship to the project or activity (see Figure BB5.1). This helps prioritize stakeholders and determine where stakeholder managers should direct their efforts. It is also a key input into the communications, risk, and scope plans.

In the grid, the horizontal axis identifies the stakeholder level of impact. This is the measure of how much a stakeholder will be directly affected by the outcome of the project from low to high. The vertical axis of the grid identifies the level of influence. This is the measure of how much clout a stakeholder has on the outcome of a project from low to high.

- *Top right is high influence, high impact:* Stakeholders in this square are the #1 priority and should be managed closely.
- *Bottom right is low influence, high impact:* Stakeholders in this square are the #2 priority and should be kept satisfied.

Stakeholder Mapping Grid

| Stakeholder Influence on Project | High | #3 Informed and Monitored | #1 Manage Closely |
|---|---|---|---|
| | Low | #4 Informed | #2 Keep Satisfied |
| | | Low | High |

Impact on Stakeholder from Project

**FIGURE BB5.1**
Stakeholder Mapping Grid.

- *Top left is high influence, low impact:* Stakeholders in this square are the #3 priority and should be informed and monitored.
- *Bottom left is low influence, low impact:* Stakeholders in this square are the #4 priority and should be informed.

Using the Stakeholder Mapping Grid is very straightforward. For each identified stakeholder, use the previously determined primary needs and wants to place the stakeholder in the appropriate grid.

Let's take, for example, two stakeholders for a company introducing new software. The Product Development Team stakeholder with primary needs of knowing the target customer and having the product specifications would be in the upper right grid as a #1 priority. They clearly have a high influence (vertical axis) on the product completion and are highly impacted (horizontal axis) by the success or failure of the product.

Conversely, a Local Community stakeholder with a primary need for general product awareness would be in the lower left grid as a #4 priority. They have very little influence on the product and are not impacted at all.

# TRADEOFFS

In reviewing stakeholder needs and wants, there are always some interesting and challenging tradeoffs between the needs and the wants of various stakeholders. During the understanding of stakeholder needs and wants activity, it will become quite clear that there are significant differences between stakeholders. The Stakeholder Mapping Grid analysis can put some structure into this discussion and decision-making process in order to help clarify the tradeoffs between stakeholders.

Here are two examples:

*Should we have a high price to maximize profit even if it means lower sales and market share?*

This is a historically difficult question. The VP of Finance will typically want higher prices and thus higher margins and profitability. Conversely, the VP of Sales would like lower prices to be more competitive and thus increase sales to achieve the sales target.

*Should we hire the best people we can afford in order to deliver better customer service or outsource offshore with a less expensive option?*

The Product Manager will typically want the best customer service possible to obtain high levels of satisfaction, which can lead to increased customer adoption. Conversely, the VP of Customer Support may have budget constraints, which will force less costly offshore alternatives.

Having an in-depth understanding of stakeholder needs as well as the priority of each one can provide the guidance to make these types of decisions and meet stakeholder expectations.

## DEVELOP A PLAN TO COMMUNICATE, IMPLEMENT, AND MANAGE STAKEHOLDER EXPECTATIONS

Managing stakeholders is an activity of communicating with stakeholders and meeting their information and involvement needs. The process is usually focused on establishing communications and gathering feedback in order to provide project or activity updates.

An effective stakeholder management approach is the key element to ensure timely and relevant feedback. The stakeholder manager assumes responsibility for managing stakeholder expectations, resolving conflicts, and uncovering and settling any issues that arise. In general, the process of managing stakeholders comprises the following key elements:

- *Stakeholder perception:* It is important to ensure that the stakeholders are engaged on a scheduled basis, and they are aware of the current status of the project or task at hand. High-level stakeholder

    perception increases the likelihood that the stakeholders provide the
    necessary support and the project can be successfully implemented.

- *Stakeholder feedback:* It is critical that stakeholders have the opportunity and are encouraged to provide feedback during the project. It must be made clear that communications are a two-way street and their feedback will be valued.

The stakeholder plan must be consistent with project objectives and resources available. First and foremost, it must be a practical, realistic, and achievable plan.

There are a number of ways to communicate, implement, and manage the stakeholder management plan. It is recommended that a project management software tool be used. These products help complete client requirements and manage time, budget, and scope constraints.

There are many options available, so choosing the right software tool can be a bit confusing. Software tools can be implemented in the traditional on premise manner where the software is installed on users' computers. However, the current trend is for software to be sold as a service and implemented as a cloud-based application. Cloud-based applications allow access anywhere, any time, on any device. There are free-to-use tools as well as pay-to-use tools.

Research and analysis will be required to pick the right tool to meet your needs and budget. There are a number of independent rating websites available to help in this selection process. Two of them are PM (https://project-management.com/) and Reviews (www.reviews.com/project-management-software/).

---

## SUMMARY

Here is a very simple scenario designed to summarize the key points of this chapter.

The stakeholder manager in this example is a Product Manager introducing a new software product targeted at the business user. The Product Manager has decided to include management of stakeholder expectations in the overall product introduction plan. Some stakeholders, the ones in grid #1 manage closely, for example, will have a major focus in the plan. Other stakeholders will have a secondary but yet important focus.

The Product Manager has settled on a definition of stakeholders as people who have an interest in the success of the product's introduction who can affect or be affected by the success of the new product.

Using this definition, the Product Manager has identified ten stakeholders.

(1) Software development organization developing the product
(2) Marketing department responsible for developing a website for online sales
(3) VP of Marketing
(4) VP of Sales
(5) Customers in small- to medium-sized companies across all industries
(6) VP of Finance
(7) Common stock shareholders
(8) VP of Human Resources
(9) Corporate creditors
(10) Local community

Using interviews and questionnaires the Product Manager identified the primary need(s) for each stakeholder.

- Software development organization developing the product
  ○ *Primary need*: Product specifications
- Marketing department responsible for developing a website for online sales
  ○ *Primary needs*: Product features and benefits, competitive analysis/competitive advantage, product pricing
- VP of Marketing
  ○ *Primary need*: Product introduction plan that increases market share
- VP of Sales
  ○ *Primary needs*: Sales forecast, competitive analysis/competitive advantage, product pricing
- Customers in small- to medium-sized companies across all industries
  ○ *Primary needs*: Product features and benefits, product pricing
- VP of Finance
  ○ *Primary needs*: Sales forecast, P&L, pricing
- Common stock shareholders
  ○ *Primary need*: Sales forecast

- VP of Human Resources
  - *Primary need*: Product features and benefits
- Corporate creditors
  - *Primary need*: Product features and benefits
- Local community
  - *Primary need*: General awareness of product and benefits

Now that the stakeholders and their primary needs have been established, the stakeholder manager uses the Stakeholder Mapping Grid to put each stakeholder in one of the four squares. In this case, there are five stakeholders in the #1 priority square and four of them are employee groups. This is not an uncommon mapping to have employees so highly represented as the #1 priority.

- #1 priority: Manage closely
  - Software development organization developing the product
  - Marketing department responsible for developing a website for online sales
  - VP of Marketing
  - VP of Sales
  - Customers in small to medium sized companies
- #2 priority: Keep satisfied
  - VP of Finance
  - Common stock shareholders
- #3 priority: Informed and monitored
  - VP of Human Resources
  - Corporate creditors
- #4 priority: Informed
  - Local community

The Product Manager decides to use a project management tool to manage stakeholder expectations effectively. His three selection criteria are a cloud-based application, easy to use, and no cost. These criteria led to the selection of Trello (https://trello.com). Trello allows the user to create boards to organize projects and is easy to use and easy to share with people you work. Trello works on any device and is completely free to use.

With the product introduction plan complete, the Product Manager has now put in place the tools to effectively meet stakeholder expectations!

# BB6

## Innovative Project Management Systems

*William S. Ruggles*

### CONTENTS

### INTRODUCTION

This chapter describes the fifth and final building block of "Tier II: Setting the Direction" for innovation and answers the fundamental questions: *Are there Project Management Systems applicable to TIME? If so, would you identify and describe them – both theoretical models and automated tools – and how can I learn more about them?*

The most important goal of an innovative project management system is to execute a plan to bring the idea to a productive and value-added position as quickly as possible. Whether this is a more profitable product (extrinsic value) or simply a better way of doing something (intrinsic value), it can create something completely new, or it can improve the quality of an existing service, process, or management model. In short, it is the addition of value to stakeholders, especially the customer. If no monetary reward is achieved with the addition of customer value, I would assume that the innovation at least offers an improvement to an individual, a group, or to society, in general. However, I would call that "creativity," not "innovation."

One can categorize innovation by product innovation, service innovation, process innovation, supply chain innovation, value stream innovation, marketing innovation, or the focus of this chapter (Innovative Project Management Systems).

## GLOSSARY OF TERMS AND ACRONYMS

Here, in alphabetical order, are the specialized terms and acronyms used in this chapter that aren't already defined for you:

- **PMS**: Project Management System
- **Portfolio**: A centralized collection of independent projects or programs that are grouped together to facilitate their prioritization, effective management, and resource optimization in order to meet strategic organizational objectives.
- **Project Portfolio Management**: Aligns organizational strategy by prioritizing projects and programs, prioritizing work, and allocating resources. It is the centralized management of one or more portfolios to achieve strategic objectives.
- **PPM**: Project Portfolio Management (see above)
- **Program**: A group of related projects, subsidiary programs, and program activities managed in a coordinated way to obtain benefits not available from managing them individually. May include work outside the scope of projects but will always have two or more projects within its scope.
- **Program Management**: The specialized application of management knowledge, know-how, tools, and techniques to a program to achieve its objectives and to obtain benefits and control not available from managing its components individually. It focuses on
  - ○ Creating cross-project interdependencies.
  - ○ Resolving resource constraints/conflicts among projects.
  - ○ Aligning strategic direction to impact PPP goals and objectives.
  - ○ Addressing issues and changes within the governance structure.
- **Project**: A temporary, change-oriented work endeavor undertaken to create or modify an innovative product, service, system, or result.

- **Project Life Cycle**: The series of phases through which a project passes from its initiation until its closure.
- **Project Management**: The specialized application of management knowledge, know-how, tools, and techniques to a project in a manner that is fundamentally proactive, integrated, and preventive.
- **WIP**: Used in a Lean context, it refers to "Work in *Process*," which is a company's partially finished goods waiting for completion; used in an Agile context, it refers to "Work in *Progress*," which is a Development Team's partially finished backlog of features waiting for completion at the end of a Sprint or Scrum.
- **WIP Limit**: Coined for use in an Agile context, it refers to a strategy for preventing bottlenecks that should be agreed upon by the Development Team BEFORE a project begins and which is enforced by the Team's Facilitator or Scrum Master.

## PROJECT MANAGEMENT SYSTEMS:

It is the central premise of this chapter that bridging organizational strategy by delivering a continual stream of successful, short-term outcomes must come through a pipeline or portfolio of projects and programs, each of which must be managed properly to drive incremental change and, in some cases, transformative innovation within the organization – one project at a time.

The increased presence of disruptive technology on 21st century projects has changed the "rules of the game" and created a demand for unique project life cycle choices and development approaches that will match their unique challenges and opportunities. This chapter focuses on the unique project life cycle and development approach choices available and used by Innovation Project and Program Management teams and the automated tools available to implement them.

### Project Life Cycle Options

Innovative projects and programs in the first quarter of the 21st century have been coming in varying shapes and sizes, and there are many ways to execute them, including the type of Project Life Cycle used to undertake each one. There are five types of Project Life Cycle from

| Option | Scope | Work | Deliverables | Priority |
|---|---|---|---|---|
| **Adaptive** | Flexible | Repetitive until accepted. | Smallest and most often | Frequent, customer value |
| **Incremental** | Flexible | Performed once per increment. | Smaller and more often | Speed |
| **Iterative** | Flexible | Repetitive until accepted. | Single | Acceptable solution |
| **Predictive** | Pre-Set | Performed once per project. | Single | Predictable cost & schedule |
| **Hybrid** | Fully customizable | Fully customizable | Fully customizable | Fully customizable |

**FIGURE BB6.1**
Project Life Cycle Options and Factors.

which to choose: *Adaptive, Incremental, Iterative, Predictive,* or *Hybrid.* See Figure BB6.1.

Another way to distinguish between the five main Project Life Cycle Options is displayed in the dual-axis matrix in Figure BB6.2:

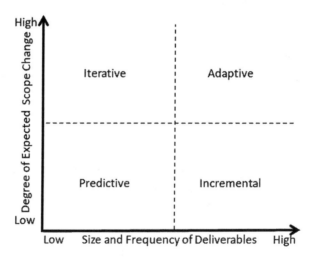

**FIGURE BB6.2**
Project Life Cycle Options Matrix.

Below you'll find brief narrative descriptions and illustrative examples for all five Project Life Cycle options:

*Adaptive (aka "Agile")*: When innovation Project Teams use this Life Cycle option, they iterate over the product to create smaller, finished, and more frequent deliverables. The team gains early feedback and provides customer visibility, confidence, and control of the product. Because the team can release things earlier, the project may provide an earlier ROI because the team delivers the highest value work first. It leverages both the aspects of incremental and iterative characteristics described below. It is also characterized by

- The requirements are elaborated frequently during deployment;
- Deployment occurs frequently with customer-valued subsets of the overall product;
- Change is incorporated in real-time during delivery;
- Key stakeholders are continuously involved; and
- Risk and Costs are controlled as requirements and constraints emerge.

There are two "sub-types" of Adaptive Project Life Cycles: "Iteration-based" and "Flow-based," which are illustrated separately in Figures BB6.3A and BB6.3B. (*Note*: The "S" Star at the left of the Life Cycle is the Project **Start** Milestone and the "F" Star at the right is the Project **Finish** Milestone for each one.)

*Incremental*: When innovation Project Teams use this option, the deliverable is produced through a series of product increments that gradually add functionality within a predetermined time frame. The

NOTE: Each "time-box" above is the same size and results in working features that have been tested.

**FIGURE BB6.3A**
Iteration-Based Adaptive Project Life Cycle.

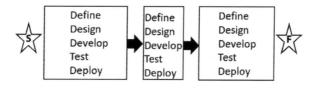

| Gather Define Design Develop Test | Gather Define Design Develop Test | Gather Define Design Develop Test | Iterate as needed ... | Gather Define Design Develop Test | Gather Define Design Develop Test |
|---|---|---|---|---|---|
| *# of Features in the WIP limit* | *# of Features in the WIP limit* | *# of Features in the WIP limit* | | *# of Features in the WIP limit* | *# of Features in the WIP limit* |

*NOTE: In a flow-based approach, the time it takes to complete a feature is __not__ the same for each one.*

**FIGURE BB6.3B**
Flow-Based Adaptive Project Life Cycle.

deliverable contains the necessary and sufficient capability to be considered complete only after the final increment. It provides finished deliverables that the customer may be able to use immediately. It is also characterized by

- The requirements can be elaborated at periodic intervals during deployment;
- Deployment can be divided into subsets of the overall product;
- Change is incorporated at periodic intervals;
- Key stakeholders are regularly involved; and
- Risk and Costs are controlled by progressively elaborating the plans with the new information.

You will find an example of an Incremental Project Life Cycle in Figure BB6.4:

**FIGURE BB6.4**
Incremental Project Life Cycle.

*Iterative*: When innovation Project Teams use this option, the Project Scope is generally determined early in the project life cycle, but time and cost estimates are routinely modified as the project team's familiarity with the product increases. Iterations develop the product through a series of repeated cycles, while increments successively add to the functionality of the product. It is also characterized by

- The requirements can be elaborated at periodic intervals during deployment;
- Deployment can be divided into subsets of the overall product;
- Change is incorporated at periodic intervals;
- Key stakeholders are regularly involved; and
- Risk and Costs are controlled by progressively elaborating the plans with the new information.

You will find an example of an Iterative Project Life Cycle in Figure BB6.5:

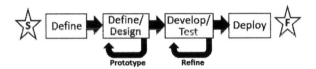

**FIGURE BB6.5**
Iterative Project Life Cycle.

*Predictive (aka "Waterfall" or "Traditional")*: When innovation Project Teams use this option, the Project Scope, Schedule, and Cost are determined in the early phases of the life cycle and any changes to the Scope are carefully managed after the Baseline has been set. It takes advantage of any variables that are known and proven. This reduced uncertainty and complexity allow teams to segment work into a sequence of predictable groupings. You can use the "Predictive" option when the requirements are very well known, clear, and fixed up-front; product definition is stable and the solution is known; no changes in the scope are expected; the technology is understood; resources with the required expertise are freely-available; and, project duration is expected to be relatively short. It is also characterized by

- The requirements are defined and the design is approved up-front before development begins;
- Define plans for the eventual deliverable; then, design, develop, test, and deploy only a single final product at the end of the project timeline ("Big Bang Delivery");
- Change is constrained or controlled as much as possible during the Project Life Cycle;
- Key stakeholders are involved at specific milestones; and
- Risk and Costs are controlled by detailed planning of mostly known or knowable considerations.

You will find an example of a Predictive Project Life Cycle in Figure BB6.6:

**FIGURE BB6.6**
Predictive Project Life Cycle.

*Hybrid*: It is a customizable combination or blend of both the Predictive and Adaptive Life Cycles in which those elements of the project that are well known or have fixed requirements follow a predictive approach, while those elements that are still evolving follow an adaptive one. You will find two examples of Hybrid Project Life Cycles in Figures BB6.7A and BB6.7B:

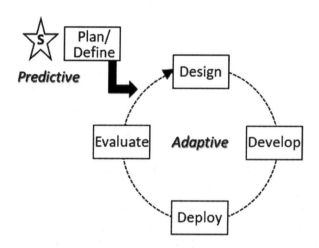

**FIGURE BB6.7A**
Hybrid Project Life Cycle Example "A".

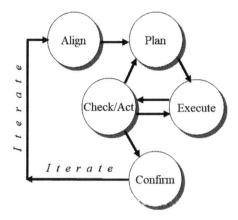

**FIGURE BB6.7B**
Hybrid Project Life Cycle Example "B".

## PROJECT MANAGEMENT SYSTEMS: THE 12 PERFORMANCE DOMAINS

Regardless of which Project Life Cycle approach you decide to use on innovative projects and programs in the current environment, you'll need to come up with answers to a set of questions for the following twelve Performance Domains throughout that Life Cycle:

(1) *Project Scope*: **What** are the REQUIREMENTS? **What** WORK needs to be done to complete them?

(2) *Project Schedule*: **When** does the project need to be done? **How Long** is the work expected to take?

(3) *Project Cost*: **How Much Money** do we expect to need to complete the work?

(4) *Project Resources*: **Who, What,** and **How Many** do we expect to need in order to perform and complete the work?

(5) *Project Quality*: **How Well** do we expect the REQUIREMENTS will need to be met?

(6) *Project Communications*: **What** INFORMATION do we expect to be needed? **From** WHOM? **To** WHOM? Via **which** MEDIA? **How Often**?

(7) *Project Risk*: **How Much** UNCERTAINTY is there on the project? **What** are the THREATS? **What** are the OPPORTUNITIES?

(8) *Project Procurement*: **Do** we expect to need CONTRACTORS or VENDORS? If so, **which** SKILL-AREA(S)?

(9) *Project Stakeholders*: **Who** is expected to IMPACT the project or be IMPACTED by it?

(10) *Project Change*: **How** DISRUPTIVE is the project? **What** IMPACT is it expected to have on the Requesting Organization? On the Performing Organization?

(11) *Project Management Technology*: Do we expect to **need help** using the PROJECT MANAGEMENT SYSTEM AUTOMATED TOOLS?

(12) *Project Integration*: **How comfortable** are we with the answers to #1–11 above? Is everything in a state of BALANCE?

## PROJECT MANAGEMENT SYSTEMS: AUTOMATED TOOL OPTIONS

Depending on which of the five Project Life Cycle approaches you decide to use and the twelve sets of Performance Domain Key questions, you'll need to answer for it, and you'll need to select an appropriate automated PMS or tool that is designed to work with them.

Table BB6.1, in alphabetical order, provides brief descriptions and pricing information for the thirteen most popular PMS and PPM automated tool vendors.

## PROJECT MANAGEMENT SYSTEMS INNOVATION: MORE INFORMATION

For more information and to increase the number of innovation project successes you'll have, I recommend that you read these two books (I co-authored with H. James Harrington) on Project Management and Project Portfolio Management Systems: *Project Management for Performance Improvement Teams* (CRC Press ©2018) and *Effective Portfolio Management Systems* (CRC Press ©2016).

**TABLE BB6.1**

Most Popular Automated PMS Tools

| Automated Tool Vendor | Brief Description | Pricing Options |
|---|---|---|
| 1. **Asana** (asana.com)<br>San Francisco, CA | A project and task management application (app) that facilitates team communication and collaboration. You can use it to create projects and tasks within the projects and follow the progress of those tasks from various browsers and devices. You can then add your team members to the projects and tasks, share files, and communicate with them. | • *Free* for Project Teams up to 15 users<br>• $9.99/user/month for 16+ users<br>• *Enterprise Plan* is also available for more control and support. (Contact the vendor for price.) |
| 2. **Basecamp** (basecamp.com)<br>Chicago, IL | A project management software that facilitates team communication and collaboration, primarily for entrepreneurs, freelancers, small businesses, and groups inside large organizations. It combines tools that teams need in a single package. | • 30-day *free trial*<br>• $99/month for unlimited users and projects. |
| 3. **Bitrix24** (bitrix24.com)<br>Alexandria, VA | A collaboration platform that provides a complete suite of social collaboration, communication, and management tools for your team, including CRM, file sharing, project management, calendars, and more. Available in both cloud and On-Premise editions. | • *Free Plan* for Project Teams of up to 12 users, 1 admin, and 5 GB of online storage<br>• *Plus Plan* for $39/month for Teams of up to 24 users, 2 admins, and 24 GB of online storage<br>• *Standard Plan* for $99/month for teams of up to 50 users, 5 admins, and 100 GB of online storage<br>• *Professional Plan* for $99/month for unlimited users, admins, and online storage. |

*(Continued)*

**TABLE BB6.1** (Cont.)

| Automated Tool Vendor | Brief Description | Pricing Options |
|---|---|---|
| 4. **CA Agile Central** (formerly **Rally Software**) (www.ca.com/us/products/ca-agile-central.html) Islandia, NY | An enterprise-class SaaS platform that's specially built for scaling agile development practices that transform businesses. You can connect your work to your company's most important business initiatives, empowering your teams to focus on the right work at the right time. Your teams can collaboratively plan, prioritize, track, and deliver value to your customers faster than the competition. Visibility into your real-time performance metrics demonstrates your levels of productivity, quality, and responsiveness. | • *Free 15-day trial*<br>• *Standard Plan* (contact the vendor for pricing).<br>• *Plus Plan* (contact the vendor for pricing).<br>• *Enterprise Plan* (contact the vendor for pricing). |
| 5. **Jira/Portfolio for Jira** (atlassian.com/software/jira) San Francisco, CA | A cloud-based project management tool for Agile (Adaptive) Project Teams that displays Scrum Boards, which help them stay focused on delivering iterative and incremental value as fast as possible. It can be scaled to meet an organization's needs by allowing it to choose a workflow or to make their own. | • *7-day free trial*<br>• $10/month flat fee for Teams of up to 10 users<br>• $7/user/month for teams of 11–100 users<br>• *Discounts* for 101+ users (contact the vendor for pricing). |
| 6. **KanbanFlow** (kanbanflow.com) Göteborg, Sweden | A cloud-based tool (portal) that performs simplified Lean Project Management and real-time collaboration via the virtual Kanban Board concept. | • *Free* (w/limited functionality but NO time or user limit)<br>• $5/user/month (w/Full functionality and 14-day free trial) |

**TABLE BB6.1** (Cont.)

| Automated Tool Vendor | Brief Description | Pricing Options |
|---|---|---|
| 7. **Monday** (Monday.com) Tel Aviv and NYC | A cloud-based tool (portal) that simplifies the way teams work together to manage workload, track projects, move work forward, and communicate with each other. | • *Free Trial* • Basic Plan $25/month (billed annually) • Standard Plan $39/month (billed annually) • Pro Plan $59/month (billed annually) • Enterprise Plan for $118/month (billed annually) |
| 8. **MS Project** (https://products. office.com/en-us/project/project-and-portfolio-management-software) Redmond, WA | A project, resource, and portfolio management tool to help you keep track of projects successfully. *Project Online* subscribers can work with their projects in a more agile way in the *Project Online Desktop Client*. If you are accustomed to using Kanban for Scrum methodologies to manage your projects, the *Project Online Desktop Client* allows you to create and manage your projects in a familiar way through the use of task board views of your projects and the ability to create Sprint-based projects. | • *Free Trial* (w/Partner) • *Project Online Essentials* ($7/user/month) • *Project Online Professional* ($30/user/month) • *Project Standard* (the standalone, on-premise version for $560 SRP) |
| 9. **Planview** (planview.com) Austin, TX | A multi-product menu of four options: • *Planview Enterprise One* (for enterprise-wide portfolio, resource capability, and technology management); • *Planview PPM Pro* (for project portfolio and resource management for Agile projects); • *Planview Projectplace* (for collaborative work management that empowers teams); and | • *Free Trials* (for all four options) • *Planview Projectplace* ($29/user/month when billed annually) • Contact the vendor for a free trial and pricing on the other three product options. |

(Continued)

**TABLE BB6.1** (Cont.)

| Automated Tool Vendor | Brief Description | Pricing Options |
|---|---|---|
| | • *Planview LeanKit®* (for enterprise Kanban for engineers). | |
| 10. **Slack** (slack.com) San Francisco, CA | A business communication platform that provides teams with a central place to instantly communicate with each other. Although it has customers in a variety of industries ranging from healthcare to ecommerce, this PMS is especially popular among tech companies and startups. Because many of its features help replace other tools, it has become a tool that helps companies streamline their communications. | • *Free Trial* • *Standard Plan* ($6.67/user/month billed annually or $8 billed monthly) • *Plus Plan* ($12.50/user/month billed annually or $15 billed monthly) • *Enterprise Plan* (contact the vendor for pricing). |
| 11. **Smartsheet** (smartsheet.com) Bellevue, WA | A project management system application emphasizing messaging with a spreadsheet-like interface to help teams collaborate, plan projects, and manage tasks. It offers a suite of project management applications, such as document management, reporting, resource management, and time tracking, with issue management offered through an add-on application. It standardizes key project elements, increases speed and improves collaboration with options that fit individual work preferences. It allows users to track all projects and improve visibility into team priorities such that important activities do not miss out on regular | • *Free Plan* • *Individual Plan* ($14/user/month billed annually) • *Team Plan* ($15/user/month billed annually) • *Business Plan* ($25/user/month billed annually) • *Enterprise Plan* (contact the vendor for pricing). |

**TABLE BB6.1** (Cont.)

| Automated Tool Vendor | Brief Description | Pricing Options |
|---|---|---|
| | work operations. It offers a cloud-based subscription model with native mobile apps for Android and iOS that includes accounts for multiple collaborators, so users can work or projects with a number of clients and colleagues. | |
| 12. **Trello** (trello.com) New York City | A project management app emphasizing task management. It utilizes the concept of boards (which correspond to projects) and within boards, there are cards (which represent tasks). The cards contain lists that can be used to track the progress of a project or to simply categorize things. (*Note:* In 2017, it was acquired by the same company that sells Jira – #4 above.) | • *Free Plan* <br>• *Business Class Plan* ($9.99/user/month if paid annually) <br>• *Enterprise Plan* ($20.83/user/month if paid annually) |
| 13. **Wrike** (wrike.com) San Jose, CA | An online project management software that was designed to improve the speed and efficiency of work in both co-located and distributed groups. You can use it to schedule, prioritize, discuss, and keep track of both work and progress in real time. | • *Free Plan* (up to 5 users) <br>• *Professional Plan* ($9.80/user/month for 5, 10, or 15 users billed annually) <br>• *Business Plan* ($24.80/user/month for 5–200 users if billed annually) <br>• *Marketing Plan* ($34.60/user/month for 5 unlimited users if billed annually) <br>• *Enterprise Plan* (for 5 unlimited users. Contact the vendor for pricing). |

*Note:* Inclusion in the table is NOT necessarily an endorsement of any one of these automated tools.

## SUMMARY

It doesn't make any difference if it is just a short continuous improvement activity for a major project like setting up a new production line or cultural transition: the same considerations apply, but they are implemented at different scales and degrees of complexity. For the complex or critical type projects/programs, a person who is trained and familiar with the project management processes and practices as defined in the PMBOK® Guide (*The Guide to the Project Management Body of Knowledge*) Agile Practice Guide, and Organizational Change Management should be assigned. For minor or noncritical short duration projects and corrective actions, it is usually not practical to assign a project or program manager. In these cases, the team leader should play the role of the project manager as adding a professional project manager could add additional cost and cycle delays that may not be justified. In the case of an innovation project that shows no continuous improvement, the nature of the project frequently requires a specialist and project manager to be assigned.

# BB7

## Innovative Management Participation

*Chuck Mignosa and H. James Harrington*

### CONTENTS

### INTRODUCTION

To start this chapter, it is extremely important that we have a common understanding of the difference between leadership and participation, as discussed in BB3 – Innovative Executive Leadership and in BB7 – Innovative Management Participation. First, let's define the two terms.
Definition:

- Participation – Notice that the first syllable in this noun is part-, as in, "take part." It is the act of taking part in an event or activity.
- Leadership – Leadership is both a research area and a practical skill, regarding the ability of an individual or organization to "lead" or guide other individuals, teams, or entire organizations. *Leadership* is the art of motivating a group of people to act toward achieving a common goal.

In BB3 – Innovative Executive Leadership, we emphasized the role that the executive team has in establishing an environment that is conducive to innovation. It included things like upgrading the business plan to reflect a transformed innovative culture, redistributing funds that could all increase creativity and innovation, job descriptions, changing key documents to reflect the need for improved creativity and innovation, and so on.

In BB7 – Innovative Management Participation, we focus on getting all of the management team from the top manager to the lowest level manager, supervisor, project leader, and foreman to transform the way that they are presently working so that they can become more creative and innovative, thereby setting an example for the people who report to him or her. In this Building Block we are discussing what the manager has to do to change the way he or she functions in order to increase their personal creativity and innovation as well as the people who report to them.

If we are putting on a play, the executive leadership would select the script, bring together the proper cast, obtain the funding, and approve the set and the wardrobes. He or she would direct the rehearsals and would be held accountable to the investors to get an above average return on their investment. A director to the best of his ability ensures that everything that can be done has been done in order to provide the participants (the actors) with an environment that allows the cast to bring to their character their own unique style and innovation.

On the other hand, management participation requires the management team to become actively and personally involved in the innovation initiative. There are two parts of management participation. The first part is the manager identifying improvement opportunities in the way the business is run and the way it operates. The second part is the identification of ways to help their employees become more creative and innovative related to the organization's goals and mission.

---

## THE RECORD

On the whole, government and business have performed very poorly over the last 40 years. That is at an all-time high. The middle class has all but disappeared. It is time that management steps up to its leadership responsibilities, thereby ensuring that all the stakeholders benefit from the organization's performance, not just management and investors. Management has stepped aside from its responsibility for the improvement efforts by saying, "The person closest to the job knows the job best, so they should be responsible for the improvement process." This is just a sophisticated dodge to get management off the hook. Eighty to ninety percent of all the problems were caused by management and can only be solved by them.

Why would any organization put the burden for management's mistakes on the workers? They are only pawns who have been misused by management over the years. Most of them are really trying to do their very best. Asking employees to take part in the improvement process too quickly only leads to frustration when they see that the really important issues have not been addressed by management. If you are a manager, ask yourself this question, "What have I done to change my work habits over the last 12 months that are innovative and how much value added did it generate?"

Management's role must change. They must remove the major roadblocks that they have put in the way of the employee before the employees' zest can be unleashed. A good rule of thumb is that the management team should solve 50% of its problems before the employees attack the 20% that they can control.

In order to manage, innovative team managers must have social skills as well as business skills. The question is, "What do we call the individuals that we used to call bosses?" Some options are associates, coaches, consultants, counselors, dictators, facilitators, leaders, managers, organizers, sponsors, supervisors, suppliers, and teachers.

I don't know what a psychiatrist would call a man who runs up and down the room yelling at the top of his lungs, and the next minute sits down to cry, but I call him a basketball coach. Surely a coach is not the type of person we need in organizations. The coach tells the team what they must do. A coach lays out the plays, makes up the playbook, and takes away the individual initiative. And if the players do not perform just as the coach directs them to, they will be pulled out of the game. Coaches play to win. A tie, or what I would call a win–win situation, is a loss for most coaches. "Coach" is certainly the wrong word to use for the individuals who will be working with our employees.

How about the word "leader"? Leaders are out in front. People follow them because they believe in them and are afraid of what would happen if they did not follow them. Few leaders have earned the respect of their followers by having the right answers in the past. Certainly, "leader" is a better description of what we need, but it still does not fill the total requirements, because it does not cover building the capacity of the followers. In fact, leadership that is under earned often gets very close to dictatorship. The military is a good example.

We have even heard of people wanting to call their managers "suppliers" because they supply direction, resources, and feedback to their employees. But to me, that is going from the ridiculous to the sublime. When I was first made a manager, I took a class on basic management skills. A 33-year-old book defined a manager as "a person who accomplishes tasks through others" (*The Improvement Process* by H. J. Harrington (1987)). This definition still holds true today, and with that as a definition, a manager utilizes all of the activities previously listed as part of their job.

After carefully considering all the options, I see no reason to call our managers anything other than managers. People who are trying to pull us away from using this term are usually consultants who are trying to establish their own personal niche.

## MANAGERS ARE ULTIMATELY HELD ACCOUNTABLE

When all is said and done, the management team is held responsible for the organization's performance. How will the organization's performance directly reflect to promotions, salaries, and longevity with the organization? In the United States, management's exposures are limited to reduced salary or loss of position. In China, poor performances are dealt with in a much more hostile manner.

China is not the only country that holds its managers accountable. Russia feels the same way about its managers. *Pravda* newspaper in 1985 reported that three female factory managers were sentenced to two years in a labor camp and fined $14,000 for producing poor-quality clothes at a government factory. In addition, they were fined 20% of all future salaries.

We are not recommending these types of stern actions on the U.S. government's part, but it is time that management steps up to the responsibility to improve the creativity, innovation, quality, and productivity of our organizations.

If our management team is going to be held accountable for the improvement, then they must be involved in the implementation of any improvement process. This involvement must extend far beyond knowledge of its existence. They must become the leaders of the movement. They must be the shakers, the movers, and the teachers. If our employees are to excel, then our management must excel. As Will Durant once said, "We are what we repeatedly do. Excellence, then, is not an act. It is a habit."

Sophisticated management methods rely on some basic beliefs that must be mastered before these methods can be applied. Managers who have not mastered these basic beliefs stand in major exposure to being the individuals who are left out in the cold during the next restructuring cycle. These basic beliefs are as follows:

- *Delegation.* Management must be able to accomplish assignments by delegating work to their direct reports. Management must be able to free themselves to do planning, break down barriers, teach, measure, and network.
- *Appraisal.* Management must be able to develop individual performance goals in cooperation with the employee and provide honest, continuous feedback on performance compared to these goals.
- *Disagreement.* Disagreements between management and employees can be healthy. Management needs to understand both sides of the situation and make the very best decision. "Yes" men or women are not helpful.
- *Be decisive.* Management cannot be reluctant to make a decision. Often, "gut feeling" is an extremely important part of managing the organization.
- *Positive attitude.* If the manager conveys a feeling of failure, the department is doomed to defeat.
- *Five-way communication system.* Management must establish excellence upward, downward, sideways, supplier and customer communication systems. They must be willing to share information with their employees. Information is power.
- *Investment.* Management should invest heavily in their employees, provide them with training, and help them grow and mature. This is one of the best investments an organization can make.

## TOMORROW'S MANAGERS

The term "management" should be treated as a set of concepts, not as a group of people. Traditional management, as we know it today, has evolved as follows:

- individual management
- professional management
- scientific management
- human relations management
- participative management

In the 19th century, the management style could have been called "individualistic management." The entrepreneur was responsible for creating most of the large organizations that we have today. Families such as the Ford's, Rockefeller's, Carnegie's, Durant's, Mellon's, Sloan's, and Watson's were all creative individualists who built and managed great organizations. This approach, driven by the economics of business, gave way to the Professional Management era, where management was measured by the short-term bottom line. The professional manager's goal was to produce the maximum output with the minimum expenditure.

This led naturally to Frederick Winslow Taylor's "scientific management" approach to running an organization. Scientific management was based upon four principles:

1. Scientifically designing the job.
2. Scientifically selecting workers to match job requirements.
3. Scientifically training workers to perform the job as designed.
4. Work must be done in a spirit of cooperation.

This worked well with workers who had a low skill level and low intelligence. This approach divided the work process into small assignments that required little training. As management's style became more and more autocratic and the employees became better educated, the system began to break down. The employees began to resent management who, from the employee's standpoint, was taking advantage of them. As a result, "human relations management" became the preferred management system. Human relations management is based upon the belief that if management treats the employee with respect and dignity, the employee's performance will be maximized. A simple idea for a simple situation. Unfortunately, today's working environment is anything but simple. As a result, the management style of the future must be a "participative management" style.

Tomorrow's managers will have to be much more effective than they are today. They will have a much bigger span of control or, as I like to think of it, a larger span of support and new, more demanding challenges. They will become more and more impacted with the soft side of management since most technical decisions will be made by intelligent computers. As employees become empowered to be responsive and accountable for their jobs, management's role must change. Table BB7.1 shows how the management environment at all levels is and will be changing.

## Management Job Description

You cannot manage today with a job description that was written for yesterday. Most of the manager's job descriptions could be best classified as prehistoric. In most organizations, literally all the job descriptions for management at all levels need to be changed so that it provides them with guidance and direction of how they should manage today and how they need to change to manage in the future. Basically, the manager's job description should be divided into three equal parts as follows:

**TABLE BB7.1**

The way management is changing

| Activity | Yesterday | Today | Tomorrow |
| --- | --- | --- | --- |
| Management style | Dictating | Coaching | Assisting |
| Providing direction | Orders | Consensus | The final results |
| Goal Setting | Management's Goals | Common Goals | Employee's goals |
| Evaluation | Criticize | Appraisal | Self-evaluations |
| Decision-making | Management decisions | Team decisions | Individual decisions |
| Compensation | Pay for years worked | Pay for performance | Pay for knowledge |
| Way to correct problems | Focus on the individual | Focus on the activity | Focus on the process |

(1) *Technical management* – Their knowledge and understanding of the department's mission that they are responsible for and their ability to come up with innovative ways to make the department's operation meet today's goals and recognize improvement opportunities that lead to innovation in the technical area.

(2) *Business management* – The ability to establish a culture that's in line with the organization's mission, goals, objectives, values, and objectives. The ability to understand and actively influence the department's contribution to the organization. This includes things such as effective, accurate bottoms-up budgeting, ability to understand and participate in setting aggressive business and departmental goals and objectives, effective staffing, use of resources, and correctly interpreting and living up to the organization's values.

(3) *Personnel management* – This includes understanding the emotional, as well as the technical, capabilities and requirements of each individual in the department. Recognizing the strengths and weaknesses of the individual. Then maximizing the effective use of their strengths with a plan to improve each individual's weaknesses that impact the organization's goals and objectives. It includes building up a career path for each individual and frequent job rotation that is in line with their growth objectives. The objective is to eliminate turnover of people and to maximize morale, job satisfaction, and organizational loyalty. Well I'm then having a lot of fun. Each person should feel that their job is their own company. They should treat the organization's resources like they were their own. If the manager is the most technically competent individual in the department, he or she is not doing the job because the job is to pass on the information and skills to his/her employees. After all, the employees are working 100% of their time on the technical aspects of the job and the manager should only be devoting 40% of his/her time to the technical management.

In this environment, management style must have many facets. Today, we expect managers to adjust their management style to meet the personality traits of the employee. In the future, we will have to adjust our management style to the individual's personality and to their job assignments. People's working personalities can be divided into four categories.

(1) *Planners* – People who excel in taking an idea and laying out the systematic approach to its implementation. Planners tend to be introverts.

(2) *Networkers* – People who establish excellent communications and working relationships between groups. They are excellent negotiators and politicians. Networkers tend to be extroverts.

(3) *Doers* – People who take a plan and implement it. They like to be assigned a problem and get it corrected. They make things happen. No matter how much work you give them, they always seem to want more responsibility, but they also need more praise for the work they do.

(4) *Leaders* – People who through their charisma, appearance, or example, attract others to follow them. People follow them because it is unpopular to do otherwise.

Each of these personality traits imposes very different needs on management. These needs can be classified into two types:

(1) *Social needs.* These needs are satisfied by management contact, public recognition, demonstrated interest in the individual and his or her career and personal life.

(2) *Technical needs.* The skills required to perform a given task.

The following two factors drive the degree and frequency to which both needs have to be fulfilled:

(1) How well the individual is performing the assigned task.

(2) The type of personality that composes the individuals make up.

There are five levels of employee performance and therefore five different interaction styles that a manager must be proficient in (see Figure BB7.1):

| | | | Coach | Teacher | Boss | Leader | Friend |
|---|---|---|---|---|---|---|---|
| M A N A G E M E N T | S U P P O R T | R E Q U I R E D | Much more than average | O | X | | | |
| | | | More than average | | O | X | | O |
| | | | Average | | | O | X | |
| | | | Less than average | | | | O | X |
| | | | | Does not meet req. | Meets min. req. | Meets req. | Exceeds req. at times | Always exceeds req. |

**FIGURE BB7.1**
Management support required versus job performance level.

(1) Employees who do not meet requirements need a "coach" – someone who will tell them what to do and show them the correct way when they cannot accomplish the task, minimizing their chance of making an error. They need someone who will help them feel good about themselves, even when they are not doing well. In these cases the manager needs to be a coach.

(2) Employees who meet minimum requirements need a "teacher" – someone who can help them understand the concepts and who will measure their performance and show them when they make an error. They need someone who recognizes their success and helps them to succeed.

(3) Employees who meet requirements need a "boss" – someone who gives them assignments and follows through to be sure they are accomplished. They need someone who helps them develop and improve the quality of their output and productivity.

(4) Employees who exceed requirements at times need a "leader" – someone who knows what needs to be done and has empowered the employees to take on responsibility and accountability for the jobs. The leader works with the employee to ensure that barriers to completing the job are eliminated. The leader focuses his or her

effort on coordinating the employee's interfaces and providing feedback. The leader sets the example for the employee – for his or her technical and personal style while at work.

(5) Employees who always exceed requirements need a "friend." At this level of performance management can delegate responsibilities for the assignment to the employees and hold them accountable for its outcome. Management should develop an open, two-way personal relationship with the employee, sharing experiences and family concerns. Technical interest and understanding are developed by providing a ready ear to discuss project operations and exchange ideas, but the technical decisions are made by the employee. The employee is empowered to make decisions and take actions on all tasks assigned to him or her, without management direction.

It is easy to see that a management style must change from coaching all the way to friendship, based upon varying degrees of performance. But performance is as much the responsibility of the manager as it is the employee (see Figure BB7.2). If a person has a networking personality and is assigned to do networking (coordinating between areas), his or her chances of meeting requirements are extremely high. But if a networker is

| Personality Traits | Type of Assignment | | | | Performance Level |
|---|---|---|---|---|---|
| | Planner | Networker | Doer | Leader | |
| Planner | Outstanding | Very poor | Good | Poor | |
| Networker | Very poor | Outstanding | Poor | Good | |
| Doer | Good | Poor | Outstanding | Very Poor | |
| Leader | Very poor | Good | Poor | Outstanding | |

**FIGURE BB7.2**
Expected performance level based upon personality traits and types of assignments.

assigned to a planning activity, it will be hard for him or her to meet requirements. Unfortunately, in today's and tomorrow's complex environment, employees will be moving back and forth through many types of assignments. As a result, management style for an individual employee will have to vary based upon the task that the individual is performing. Management cannot hold an employee responsible for poor performance if management miss assigns the individual and is not provided with the correct management style. This is a typical example of bad business management.

The three parts of the manager's job description should be weighted as follows when the performance is evaluated:

(1) 40% per technical management
(2) 30% for business management
(3) 30% for personnel management

You will note that if the individual manager does a poor job at business management and personnel management, even if they do a far-exceeds requirement on technical management, they will be rated as inadequate. And rightly so for these individuals should be removed from management and assigned where they can devote all their time to the technical aspects of the job.

## Work Ethics

Management's role is to get work done through others. We must realize that the work ethic is something that has to be learned. It is not an inborn trait. Many experiments with animals and people have proven beyond a doubt that the work ethic is a learned trait. In these experiments, individuals are provided with all their desires without doing anything to earn them, and to replace the work with less productive ways of occupying time. Unfortunately, work ethics are developed during the formative part of a person's life, between the ages of two and fifteen. By the time people enter into adulthood, their work ethics have already been formed.

As America has developed and prospered, work ethics have degraded. At the start of the 19th century, people lived to work. The harder you worked, the better person you were. Honest labor was a valued trait that would lead to success. As survival became a given, the government stepped in to provide a minimum living standard for everyone and work ethics began to slip.

As America became more and more successful, parents expected less and less of their children. Honest labor was replaced with time in front of the TV. Dishwashers eliminated the need for children to work with their parents when doing dishes. Product reliability improvements and increased financial wealth have reduced the need for the parents to work with the child in repairing the car, the washing machine, the plumbing, and so on. Store-bought frozen food, cakes, and bread have reduced the time that both the parent and the child spend in the kitchen working together. Fast food has for many families all but eliminated the need for a kitchen. This reduction in the time and effort required to run the home has freed up the wife to become a very important part of today's workforce, which has led to the emancipation of women. This added freedom didn't come too soon because as male earnings dropped off, women were forced to step in and shoulder part of the financial burden. As a result, families of both parents working are the rule rather than the exception, in order to maintain their desired standard of living.

Coupling this new financial security for women with the decrease in family work projects has had a very negative impact on family values, leading to a period where a one parent family is not unusual. The result is an ongoing decline in work values. As a result of these factors, there has been a drastic reduction in the honest work time that children are involved in. We estimate that an average 12-year-old today only works 25% of the time that a 12-year-old worked in 1940.

With the push for more and more people to get a college degree, and the loss of development of technical skills, the American society today is capable of creating new products but lacks the people with the necessary skills to produce them. This has led to offshoring manufacturing to Asia. Today, we are finding a shortage of electricians, carpenters, welders, and many other necessary skilled workers.

Innovation teams are an outgrowth of the former "research and development" departments. In the original R&D departments, research was focused on new technologies and the application of these technologies to possible future products. Innovation teams start with the end requirements and then search for the technologies that can be used to achieve the results.

In the 1970s Ned Herrmann studied the skills used in being creative and solving problems. He found that there are four sets of activities that, when brought together in a problem solving project, produce a better solution. He also found that individuals develop these skills as they grow into adulthood. He also found that an individual could learn to be more proficient in any of these skills but tended to fall into one of three areas of activities:

(1) Prefer to use
(2) Can use
(3) Avoids using

The four activities are identified as follows:

(1) Analytical
    (i) Deductive reasoning
    (ii) Factual
(2) Organizational
    (i) Financial
    (ii) Structured
(3) Communication
    (i) Empathetic
    (ii) Idealistic
(4) Holistic
    (i) Future thinking
    (ii) Possibility thinking

An understanding of the need to bring these four activities to bear on a given innovation project in order to attain the best result is a requirement. Because of this, the manager must be able to identify individuals' strengths and support them. The manager must also facilitate communication between individuals with different skill sets because each skill set looks at the situation differently and, therefore, complicates communication. For example,

• A holistic thinker will take an idea and project it into the future and visualize a finished product.
• An analytical thinker will see the idea and the finished product as a non-sequitur as they cannot see how to get from what we know to the end. They need to move toward the end product step by step.

- An organizational thinker looks at building a roadmap for getting from where the project is to where it needs to go. To do this, they need to take the analytical input and the holistic input and develop a step-by-step progression to attain the results in a given time.
- A communication thinker sees the discord created by the three other types of skills and thinkers and seeks to resolve conflict.

Management needs to bring a team together with individuals who are competent in all four of these skill sets and get them to work together.

The next thing to consider is a lesson demonstrated by Kelley Johnson of the Lockheed Skunk Works. Kelly developed a reputation for developing leading-edge airplanes on time and with better performance than asked for. To accomplish each innovative project, he handpicked a small team of people who represented every part of the business required. He then brought them together in a single location where they worked hand in hand through the development and implementation process. In this way if the development engineers found a problem, they could communicate directly with the manufacturing people to resolve it in a minimum amount of time.

A good example of this process and the complexity of any innovation project are found in the development of the SR-71 reconnaissance plane. The holistic goal for the plane was stated in three requirements:

(1) Fly 2,000 miles an hour
(2) Fly over 80,000 feet
(3) Have a small radar image

Starting with these three requirements, Kelley's team had to essentially reinvent the airplane. Some of the problems that they needed to overcome were as follows:

- Flying at 2,000 miles an hour the outside temperature will exceed 600 degrees
  - Fuels burn at 450 degrees
  - Aluminum will melt at these temperatures
  - The cockpit needs to be cooled
- They found a fuel that burns above 600 degrees
  - How do you ignite a fuel with that high an ignition point
- What material could be used to withstand the 600 degree temperature

  - ○ Titanium will work
  - ○ No one had worked with titanium, so they needed to develop manufacturing procedures
- The engines needed to be redesigned for the speed
- New engine configurations needed to be invented
- Pressurize and cooled pilot's suits needed to be designed

From this list, it is obvious that creating an airplane that would meet the three original requirements was not easy. The resultant airplane, delivered in 1959, is still listed at the fastest airplane ever built. It is also the first stealth plane that has less than 30% of the radar signature of an F-15 fighter, which is less than half the size.

It is obvious that managing such a team is a complicated endeavor. It is for this reason that managing any innovation team requires leadership and management with a wide variety of both management and people (soft) skills. Management must be able to

- Define the end product requirements
- If necessary, bring in a leading expert in the desired area being explored
- Identify the skill set required to reach the end result
- Identify the individuals who will provide the combination of skills required
- Bring the team members together, so they understand the significance of their contributions
- Set forth a project plan

After organizing the team, the manager needs to let them work on the problem, remembering that in any research and development project, failures are inevitable. The manager needs to be available to provide necessary support to the team so they can continue to move the project forward.

In today's industries innovation projects are given two years to achieve results. In many companies if the results have been achieved, or close, the company will continue funding for a short time. On the other hand, if the project is not deemed close enough to a product, funding will be ended and the project will be cancelled.

In some companies, the innovation teams are considered to be virtual and therefore members of the team are terminated from the company. In other companies, small teams of innovators are moved to new projects.

It is apparent that while all companies need to have innovation activities going on continuously, there is no consensus on how innovation teams should be treated within the company.

---

## SUMMARY

Talking about it won't do it. Telling someone else to do it won't really stimulate creativity and innovation. You cannot whip them into a frenzy and think that will turn on the creative juices. This may work for a while but sooner or later the employee will find a way to get even with you. We like to think that employees are all self-motivated, but that's not true.

The theory of participative management states that "people who are involved in the decisions that impact them have a tendency to implement these decisions much more effectively and efficiently." There are 5 levels of participation:

(1) *Dictator-type manager*: Makes the decisions. Employees participate by implementing.
(2) *Leader-type manager*: Listens and then makes the decision.
(3) *Politician-type manager*: One person, one vote. The majority rules.
(4) *Optimist-type manager*: Gets consensus.
(5) *Theoretical-type manager*: Gets full agreement.

Our professors and management consultants make all this sound easy. They talk about empowerment, employee involvement, participation, and motivation, all wrapped up in a simple three-step package.

Tomorrow's leaders will have to be much more creative in the way they manage their own work habits. Our workforce has become a digital workfare force. Computers and cell phones have replaced the office of yesterday with its mountains of paper. We have seen a steady and continuous worker evolution. They are as follows:

(1) *Land worker (farmer)* –Here the vast majority of the population needed to work the soil in order to produce enough food for the growing population.

(2) *Factory worker* – As the assembly line became popular, people grouped in small villages around the factories creating the factory worker.

(3) *Office worker* – As the production line became more sophisticated they required increased numbers of people working behind the scene to keep the production lines operating without interruption and with that the office worker was created.

(4) *Knowledge worker* – With the increased emphasis on improving the product and process, a higher and higher percentage of the workforce needed to be knowledgeable about a specific technology as it related to his or her assignment within the organization. As a result, the knowledge worker became an important part of the organization.

(5) *Information worker* – With large amounts of data being available, organizations that had established effective systems that transformed data into online information systems could achieve instantaneously a significant competitive advantage over their competition.

(6) *Innovation worker* – As technology became the driving force in making a buying decision, increasing the innovation and creativity of the employees became a necessity just to keep up with the competition.

(7) *Digital worker* – Analog data has given way to digital applications. The young people getting out of college are already digitized and feel comfortable in the digital world. Combining the advances that are being made in robotics, artificial intelligence, and digital applications, the business world is converting very fast with the digital world.

The way our people work has changed drastically over the past 50 years, but many managers are still trying to use the theories that didn't work back in the 1950s and blindly believe that they work even better in the digital environment. It is *time* for a major evolution in management theory. What creative approaches have you applied to the way you as a manager are operating? How can you build trust, confidence, and loyalty into your team?

# BB8

## Innovative Team Building

*H. James Harrington*[1]

## CONTENTS

---

[1] This chapter is based on the book by H. J. Harrington and Mitch Manning entitled *Making Teams Hum*.

Being part of a team or a group that provides security, acceptance,
and a sense of belonging is a basic need for most human beings.

**H. James Harrington**

## INTRODUCTION

Teams – what can I say new and interesting about teams? Every problem solving and management book you pick up talks about teams and how important they are to the organization. Thousands of teams have worked on improvement opportunities and/or problems that have generated massive return on investment. Many teams have existed that accomplished nothing and whose return on investment was negative.

"Teams" is not a new concept. Moses organized his followers in groups of 10. In reality, the caveman's group of people who shared a cave with him could easily be classified as a team. Jesus and his disciples met the team requirements. Every classroom in every school could be considered a team.

To start this chapter, let us explain that all positive innovations by definition are improvements and, in the broadest sense, all improvements are innovative. Keeping this in mind, the words improvement and innovation can be used interchangeably.

## Oh Hum OR HUM

This chapter is about making teams hum. Humming has long been used to describe the efficiency, timeliness, and effectiveness of the working process. Humming can be detected by the senses and evaluated by instinct. You can actually see, feel, smell, taste, and hear humming. By instinct, you can easily distinguish positive from negative humming. Positive and negative humming are comparable to what we think about when we contrast a bee hive with a wasp nest.

Another example is provided to us by the seven dwarfs in Snow White who taught many of us to whistle while we work. They also gave us a message that there is tremendous advantage to the positively humming team over a negatively humming team, and a ho-hum team. This is all humming.

> Definition: Team – Two or more entities (people, houses, oxen, dogs, etc.) bound together or dependent upon each other to achieve a specific goal.

So, what is a team in an organizational environment? A team is an organized group committed to work together to complete a well-defined piece of tedious work to achieve a shared goal. Many of our teams are committed more to play than to work. It helps to think that physically, there is little difference between work and play except in one's mind. To you and I, basketball is play. To Michael Jordan, it is work. Making teams is for achieving involvement in, and ownership of, appropriately delegated and assigned work.

There are 3 basic types of teams. They are:

- Type 1 – Golf Team – each team member does his or her own thing.
- Type 2 – Baseball Team – some interdependence.
- Type 3 – Football Team – everyone must work together.

There are 7 activities that we all perform naturally, which can be done better by a positively humming team. These activities are:

1. New product development – Determining new product opportunities, creation of a new and unique product or service.
2. Goal setting – Determining the desired end result.
3. Problem solving – Determining why actual doesn't equal expected and finding root cause.
4. Decision making – Determining the best balanced choice from all options.
5. Implementation – Transforming the concepts into value-added output.
6. Change – Determining what to stop, what to start, and what to do differently.
7. Action – Completing tasks that are too large for one person to do by themselves.

People and teams are naturals at problem solving and new product development. Let them solve a problem or develop a new product and they will want to move on to decision making. Change creates a whole new set of problems to be resolved and this restarts the natural cycle for continuous improvement that is driven by the human condition to be and do better. Individuals readily react by working together to accomplish tasks that they agree need to be done. This chapter is about how to build teams for new product development, opportunity development, problem solving, decision making, goal setting, making changes, and completing assignments because this is the work and the reward that people cherish. It is a natural predisposition of people and teams, which can be enhanced by providing appropriate resources such as capital, time, training, and tools.

In the 1980s and 90s, we learned how important teams were to the overall success of an organization. In the ensuing years, hundreds of organizations throughout the world have validated this. In the 90s, we realized that they have much more to offer than just their ability to solve problems. We gave them the authority to make decisions and manage their own actives. By doing this, we increased our return on assets (ROI) and increased the overall organization morale. It was a win–win for everyone.

Dr Kaoru Ishikawa, the "father" of the Japanese quality approach and quality circles, is no longer with us but the legacy he left is one of a more humanistic approach to management. We no longer need to answer the question, "Are teams right for our organization?" Of course, they are. "Should teams be expected to solve all problems that the organization has?" Of course not. A survey entitled "The International Quality Study" found that for organizations just starting their improvement efforts, building the human resource infrastructure and organizing teams into effective work unit is one of the best strategies. Very advanced organizations focus on empowering each individual to take advantage of the opportunity that they discovered. These advanced organizations focus on developing self-reliance in their people ahead of team problem solving. In these advanced organizations, teams are used primarily as a communication tool for individuals reporting their activities. Cooperation is a key ingredient in a team structure for these advanced organizations.

A team's reaction to a threat can be heard in a low, ominous drone. A team's reaction to an opportunity can be heard in an excited, higher pitched tone. This is how you know the state of the humming. This chapter is about how to achieve high-pitch humming. Humming is our way to describe getting the results that are desired for the minimum resources that are required within a planned timeframe and to the ultimate satisfaction of all the stakeholders in the process. When a team is really humming, the members get pleasure from the work that they do and the customers get added-value in the products and services that they receive.

Definitions:
Task Teams – Teams that are assigned to complete a specific work or problem assignment.

Organizational Teams – Teams that are defined by the way the organization is organized.

One premise of this chapter is that all teams have processes for work or play that convert resources from suppliers into products and services for customers and stakeholders. Another premise is that all teams can be categorized as either task teams or organizational teams. Task teams are teams chartered to complete a defined piece of work. Organizational teams are teams chartered to decide globally the nature of the organization's work, and how the work will be completed. Because decisions are products or services of a defined piece of work, organizational teams can be considered as the second category. From these premises, it is possible to make all teams hum using the same basic approaches, resources, processes, tools, and levels of team work. The objective of this chapter is to present in a systematic and logical way the information that is fundamental to planning and achieving the "humming" potential of all teams. To accomplish this objective, this chapter will address leadership, teams, team techniques, and team tools. The premises, theories, and concepts introduced in this chapter are very important to the operation of any organization.

## THE TEAM OPPORTUNITY/OPPORTUNITY CYCLE

Let's change the way we look at problems. Let's think about each problem we face each day as an opportunity to contribute to making the organization more successful. As these opportunities arise, we need to have a systematic way of addressing them so that they are not just put to bed, but buried. If you put a problem to bed, it can and will get up some time in the future to cause the organization more disruptions. It may be next week or next month or next year, or perhaps in five years, but it will come back unless the process that allowed the problem to occur initially is error-proofed. When you have error-proofed the process that allowed the problem to occur, then and only then have you buried the problem so that it will not come back. That's what the "Team Opportunity Cycle" is all about. (See Figure BB8.1.) Teams are designed to not only solve problems but also to identify and take advantage of other opportunities to make the organization successful. For the rest of this chapter, we will refer to opportunities rather than problems.

Phase 1. Opportunity Selection Phase

- Activity 1: Listing for the opportunity
- Activity 2: Collecting data
- Activity 3: Verifying the opportunity
- Activity 4: Prioritizing the opportunity
- Activity 5: Selecting the opportunity
- Activity 6: Defining the opportunity

Phase 2. Protection Phase
- Activity 7: Taking action to protect the customer
- Activity 8: Verifying the effectiveness of the action taken

Phase 3. Analysis Phase
- Activity 9: Collecting opportunity symptoms
- Activity 10. Validating the opportunity
- Activity 11: Separating cause and effect
- Activity 12: Defining the root cause

Phase 4. Correction Phase
- Activity 13: Developing alternative solutions
- Activity 14: Selecting the best possible solution
- Activity 15: Developing an implementation plan
- Activity 16: Conducting a pilot run
- Activity 17: Presenting the solution for approval

Phase 5. Measurement Phase
- Activity 18: Implementing the approved plan
- Activity 19: Measuring cost and impact
- Activity 20: Removing the protective action (installed in Phase 2)

Phase 6. Prevention Phase
- Activity 21: Applying action taken to similar activities
- Activity 22: Defining and correcting the basic process
- Activity 23: Changing the process documentation to prevent recurrence
- Activity 24: Providing proper training
- Activity 25: Returning to Phase 1, Activity 1

**FIGURE BB8.1**
The Opportunity Cycle.

When you investigate each opportunity, go through the six distinct phases of the Opportunity Cycle as indicated in Figure BB8.1. Each phase contains a number of individual activities. The total cycle consists of 25 different activities.

Begin the opportunity cycle by selecting the opportunity that is a bottleneck, represents wasted effort, is not meeting customer expectations, or provides a means to add value to the organization's product and process. Team activity is most appropriate when applied to solving a long-standing, nontrivial problem or when developing a new product and/or service.

When teams follow these six phases (or a similar process), their life becomes much easier. Unfortunately, the more experienced the team becomes, the more likely they are to take shortcuts. Process shortcuts have probably led to the demise of more teams than can be counted.

When a team elects to circumvent the correct problem-solving process, they automatically reduce their ability to function in an innovative (continuous improvement) environment. The team may ultimately be successful, but it will be by accident, not by design. I would estimate that more than seventy five percent of the team meetings I have attended are not managed in keeping with good team practices.

There are four stages of team development.

- Getting Together,
- Staying Together,
- Working Together,
- Growing Together.

Effective team leadership and management of these four stages of team development are key to making teams hum.

There are personal and professional benefits for enhancing your knowledge, skills, and abilities in the areas of helping teams get together, stay together, work together, and grow together. Committing yourself to making teams hum will help you to accomplish spiritual, physical, family, work, financial, and learning goals in your life. You may not even be aware of some of your goals until after you have accomplished them. Accomplishing something, even before you know that you want it, is a very rewarding experience.

## THE PURPOSE OF STEPPING UP TO LEADERSHIP

Making teams hum is focused on teams that are involved in value-added activity. This requires that the experts be in charge at all times to provide focus and to inspire innovation, efficiency, and teamwork. The members of the team expect position leadership to provide initial direction and support for the team, and need shared leadership by the experts on the team to achieve the goal.

## Focus

The team leader position enhances the team's direction by providing focus through a shared vision, mission, goals, and objectives. Focus requires more than a one-time communication. It requires constant emphasis so that all team members know the direction for the team and see the path that lies in front of the team. Focus is a shared responsibility within the team. Focus can be attained by providing the employees with a clear vision, mission, goals, and objectives that they understand and believe are important and relevant to their assignment. Focus can be maintained and sustained by posting critical team measurements and current status against the team plan. Sharing one-by-one, the team members can help to focus on how they can help the team reach goals on an individual basis.

> Leaders and take everyone from Roosevelt to Churchill to Reagan, inspire people with clear visions of how things can be done better. Some managers, on the other hand, muddle things with pointless complexity and detail. They acquaint it with sophistication, with sounding smarter than anyone else. They inspire no one.
>
> Jack Welch, CEO of General Electric

## Creativity and Innovation

Shared team leadership encourages creativity and innovation in teams by recognizing and improving methods, the efficient use of materials, mastery of machines and technology, achieving key measures, and the development of the members and the team. Shared team leadership fosters an appreciation for diversity within the group by encouraging challenging of the status quo and helping all members to think out of the box.

## Efficiency

Shared team leadership promotes the enhancement of team functions and tasks in order to exceed customer and other stakeholder needs by setting high expectations for the efficient use of resources and processes. Team members need to encourage simplicity of the team processes and passion for cycle-time reduction without compromising the quality of the output.

### Teamwork

Shared team leadership promotes teamwork and totally involves people in their work. The position leader must be a part of the team and be perceived as a steward of the team's efforts. Without teamwork, a talented group cannot achieve synergy, a phenomenon where the whole is greater than the sum of the parts, which leads to achieving the full team potential.

## THE FOUR FUNCTIONS OF LEADERSHIP

There are four functions that are absolutely essential to making teams hum. The greatest leaders are revered for their unique ability, usually in only one or two of the functional areas. The functions are: communicate, motivate, educate, and administrate.

Definitions:

- Communicate – To transfer understanding.
- Motivate – To draw out the potential of another person.
- Educate – To transfer knowledge and skill.
- Administrate – To direct and manage resources.

President Ronald Reagan is known as the "great communicator." One example of his communication ability helped the nation to see the growing national debt. He described the debt in terms of 27 stacks of 1,000 dollar bills each equally as tall as the Empire State Building. Only a few questioned the math. Everyone acknowledged that the debt was huge.

President John F. Kennedy is known as a powerful motivational speaker. He told a nation to "ask not what your country can do for you; ask what you can do for your country." Only a few questioned the origin of the words or the fact that he trembled from fear of public speaking. Everyone was motivated and the nation became a nation of volunteers.

President Bill Clinton is known as a great educator. He told the nation that "we can do better." Only a few questioned if we really could do better. As a nation, we have done better in education, government, and business.

President Harry Truman is known as a great administrator. He told the nation "I have a job to do" and "the buck stops here." Only a few questioned his record and his credentials. He did the job and the buck did stop there.

In an ideal world, an ideal leader would allocate personal time to each function with approximately thirty percent to communicate, thirty percent to motivate, thirty percent to educate, and ten percent to administrate. Studies by Dr. Warren Bennis of the world's greatest leaders document that they average spending sixty percent of their scheduled time communicating. In reality, at lower levels of leadership, administration usually consumes far more than ten percent of the leader's time. The challenge then is to focus on creative and innovative ways to reduce the demands of administration in order to have more time to spend on communicating, motivating, and educating.

Why not pause here and reflect on your knowledge and experience with the leadership functions? Record your answers on a sheet of paper.

- Think of ways that shared leadership can contribute to enhancing the leadership functions.
- Identify ways that the leadership functions can be assigned within the team.
- Identify ways that the leadership functions can be delegated within the team.
- Decide your priorities for the leadership functions by percentage of your schedule for each.
- Set targets for allocating your time to the leadership functions to match your priorities.

Now let's reflect on your knowledge and experience with leadership behavior. Record your answers on a sheet of paper.

- Identify examples of other leaders for each function.
- Think about their effectiveness as behavior for you to model.

- Where are you most effective? Least effective?
- How can you enhance your strengths and eliminate your weaknesses?

Now that we know the four things that we must do to lead, we need to know our preferred leadership style for doing the work.

---

## ESTABLISHING THE TEAM MISSION

The Executive Improvement Team (EIT) should either pick or approve the task the team wants to focus on. Once this is decided, the EIT should determine a preliminary mission of the team. The team mission should simply give the team a clear perspective of why it (the team) exists. Very early in the team meetings the team should prepare their mission statement and have it reviewed by the appropriate individual on the executive team.

One of the most frustrating experiences a team can have is to be assigned an unclear task or opportunity by the EIT. An example of this is forming a team to look at the "communication" issue. This is referred to as a divergent opportunity or a opportunity that tends to grow in size and complexity as the team moves forward in their efforts to solve, develop, and control it. In other words, it keeps getting bigger and bigger. It's up to the EIT to ensure the team is working on opportunities that are convergent or those that tend to become more clearly defined as a team moves toward solution and implementation. In the case of "communication," a more convergent problem would be, "We have a problem communicating between management and the employees." The EIT would then give the team a mission that might say:

> The mission of the communication task team is to identify ways to enhance communication and understanding between management and employees.

The mission sets the stage for how you want the opportunity or issue to change. It should be very brief, no more than two or three sentences.

Once the mission is set, the team can establish the rest of its own Team Charter. The charter consists of three key elements:

- The mission – why the team exists
- Team goals – what the team hopes to accomplish
- Team guidelines (or Code of Conduct) – how the team will manage and measure itself

As you can see, the clearer the team mission the easier it will be for the team to complete a team charter. Once the team charter is established, it is typically signed off by each team member and the team's EIT sponsor. This sign-off shows "ownership" by both the team and their sponsor and helps the team in identifying team process issues that may inhibit their performance.

Another element that supports the team charter is the project plan. This plan gives the team specific direction in the following areas:

- Team meeting schedule
- Resources required
- Schedule of activities
- Completion time frame
- Measures of success

Both the completed Team Charter and the Team Project Plan should be reviewed and approved by the EIT. This review and approval authorizes the use of the organization's resources for a specific period of time to complete a specific task.

> Team participation should never occur until the management team is participating in the cultural change activities, if you don't want the employee to believe that they are being manipulated. Management must provide visible evidence of the organization's total commitment to a policy of encouraging change, rather than reacting to change.
>
> H. James Harrington

Does every opportunity require a formal team structure? The answer is a resounding no. It should be the objective of the management team to develop the individuals to the point that they can be empowered to make decisions on their own and take advantage of the opportunities they observe. In other cases, the team meets for one meeting. At this meeting, the opportunity is defined and assignments are made. Each individual has a commitment and honesty to live up to his or her commitment without team follow-up to be sure it gets done. The single team meeting is becoming a larger and larger percentage of the team activities in the more advanced and proficient organizations.

Teams operate on the basic assumption that 1+1=3. This assumption indicates that two people working together will accomplish the work of three individuals working separately. This is often true but we have seen occasions where 1+1=0.5. This occurs when two individuals have had different approaches to taking advantage of an opportunity. In order to get a consensus, a third idea is developed that is not as effective as either one of the other two by themselves. A good example of that is when a group of people trying to make up their mind about if and where there go for supper. James is tired and just wants to go to bed. Bob likes Chinese food and he suggested going to his favorite Chinese restaurant. Tom suggests going to a smorgasbord because he's very hungry. Mary suggests going to San Francisco that is 60 miles away. After hours of discussion, the team agrees that the compromised position is to go to Sunnyvale only 30 miles away for corned beef hash. No one is really excited about the compromise but no one feels that their suggestion was turned down in favor of someone else's suggestion.

## KEY ELEMENTS OF A TEAM

We find there are four key elements in the team environment. The elements that must be in place prior to teams being formed is the Executive Improvement Team's (EIT) commitment to the process. The second is the team member's themselves. The third is the team leader, and last, but certainly not least, is the facilitator. Let's look at one of them – the Executive Improvement Team.

### The Executive Improvement Team (EIT)

The Executive Team has overall responsibility for the entire improvement effort. If the effort succeeds, much of the credit should go to them, and, if it fails, all of the blame should be directed at them. Why?

When the team environment is first being established in an organization, its early success will depend on the amount of support and encouragement given teams and team members by management. Early team planning by the EIT will eliminate many of the problems that plague organizations with a poorly organized team structure. However, there is one ingredient that comes before establishing the team, and that's training.

## Basic Team Effectiveness Training

The smart executive team will train as many employees as possible in the basics. By basics, we mean:

- Understanding the organization's goals and objectives
- Understand the improvement process
- Team dynamics
- Team effectiveness
- Effective meeting skills

## BASIC OPPORTUNITY DEVELOPMENT TRAINING

In every organization where we have conducted opportunity development assessments, the tactic that always made the employees' "top 5" list is "training" or the lack thereof. However, it most often isn't their number one issue. At Xerox, effective Improvement Teams participation grows, in part, from the affected opportunity development training. At a minimum, every Xerox employee had received 28 hours of training. Xerox initial training investment is estimated at more than 4 million employee hours and $125 million. The training of teams is just as important as training individuals to do their job. There are two primary ways of providing training. The most popular is formal classroom training and the other is on the job training.

## Formal Classroom Training

Teams can be trained as a group, where all members of the team go through training together; or as individual participants, where several (normally 10 to 20) employees are trained together and assigned a team at a later date. Either way works well; however, in both cases, the training should not be conducted until the participants are within 30 days of using what they have learned. Don't waste valuable organizational resources by training and waiting three to six months to put the training to use.

An additional word of caution: Timid or less aggressive team members may never become completely competent through this approach. We recommend team and opportunity development training be a part of the New Employee Orientation process, thereby providing everyone in the organization with a common language and approach.

For more than 40 years, teams have been effectively used to solve problems. The approach used varies based upon the product, process, complexity, and skills of the team. Teams should evolve through the following 6 levels:

1) Seven Basic Tools
2) Plan-Do-Check-Act – the basic problem-solving cycle defined by Shewhart
3) Same as #1 and#2 plus the Seven Management Tools
4) Add Statistical Analysis and Design of Experiments
5) Add Simulation Modeling, Structured Analysis, and Causal Modeling
6) TRIZ (Russian acronym for "Theory of Solving Problems Inventively")

Of course, not all teams need to or should progress through all six opportunity development levels. In fact, many teams can stop at level 2.

All employees should be trained in the seven basic tools. They are:

• Brainstorming
• Checksheets
• Graphs
• Nominal Group Technique (NGT)
• Force Field Analysis
• Cause-and-Effect Diagram
• Pareto Diagram
• Flow-Charting

There are a number of other tools that every member of a formal team should be trained to use. They are:

- 5W's and 2H's
- Delphi Narrowing Technique
- Failure Mode and Effect Analysis
- Five S's
- Histogram
- Milestone Graph
- Mind Map
- Shewhart Cycle
- Root Cause Analysis
- Run Charts
- Business Process Improvement (BPI)

The more advanced teams need to be trained in the seven new management tools. They are:

- Affinity Diagram
- Interrelationship Diagram
- Tree Diagram
- Matrix Diagram
- Prioritization Matrix
- Process Decision Program Chart (PDPC)
- Arrow Diagrams

Process Improvement Teams, which are involved in Reengineering, Redesign, or Benchmarking, need to be trained in the following 12 basic Business Process Improvement Tools:

- BPI concepts
- Flowcharts
- Interviewing Techniques
- Value-Added Analysis (VA)
- Bureaucracy Elimination Method
- Process and Paperwork Simplification Techniques
- Simple Language Analysis and Improvement Methods
- Process Walkthrough Methods
- Cost and Cycle-Time Analysis
- Statistical Process Control (SPC)
- Organizational Change Management (OCM)
- Knowledge Management (KM)

In addition, the process owners, who chair Process Improvement Teams, should be trained in the 12 sophisticated tools. They are:

- Quality Function Deployment (QFD)
- Program Evaluation and Review Technique (PERT) Charting
- Business Systems Planning
- Process Analysis Technique
- Structured Analysis/Design
- Value Analysis/Control
- Information Engineering
- Process Benchmarking
- Poor-Quality Cost (PQC)
- Design of Experiments
- Simulation Modeling
- Project Management

In Appendix B, we provide a list of 77 innovation tools that have been divided up into 3 categories. They are:

1. Creative Tools, Methods, and Techniques That Every Innovator Must Know
2. Evolutionary Tools, Methods, and Techniques That Every Innovator Must Know
3. Organizational and Operational Tools, Methods, and Techniques That Every Innovator Must Know

## Establishing the Team Process

Establishing the team process should take place prior to forming the first team. The EIT should know what type of team is being established. (See Figure BB8.2.) The EIT should also decide how the team process will be managed. For example, will EIT itself be responsible for team training and day-to-day management? Probably not, but it is important to decide who is! Listed below are several areas an EIT should consider in establishing the team process.

1. Who is responsible for overall management of the teams?
2. Who is responsible for setting the team mission?

3. How empowered is the team?
4. What type of team reporting will be required?

Each team, however, should be required to submit for approval their Team Charter and Project Plan. In addition, minutes of all team meetings should be prepared and distributed to members as soon as possible.

For organizations just starting their improvement efforts, we recommend the EIT set up and/or approve each individual opportunity team mission statement.

## EIT'S SUPPORT OF TEAMS

The EIT should be willing to run interference for the team and guide them on policy issues and potential barriers. As the team progresses, the EIT should hold periodic reviews on progress to eliminate any surprises during the Innovation Systems Cycle. Team recommendations should be reviewed and approved by the EIT prior to implementation. This should not make the team feel less empowered. Remember, the EIT still has final responsibility for utilizing the organization's resources wisely.

Last, but certainly not least, the EIT helps drive the implementation effort. This becomes much easier, even for a team totally empowered, when management has been a part of the process from start to finish.

### Team Leader

The individual selected to lead the team may be elected by the team, or more often, appointed by the EIT. In the case of natural work group teams, it may be the supervisor or manager of that organization or department. It is usually someone with a deeper knowledge of the opportunity area, someone having more experience in the Innovation Systems Cycle or someone that has an excellent understanding of the team process.

For those of you with a more autocratic management style, learning to be an effective team leader can be a challenge. While it is one of the harder jobs in the team process, we feel it is one of the most rewarding. Two of the most important traits that an effective team leader should have are being able to guide the team without dominating it and acting as an effective role model to the team.

Some of the duties of the team leader are to:

- Coordinate team meetings and activities
- Teach members
- Promote and sustain the team synergy
- Encourage individual member participation without coercion
- Follow up on meeting action items
- Assist the team in monitoring and measuring its progress
- Ensure the team process is being followed

Frequently, the team leader does not take a position related to a debate or disagreement between two or more of the team members. This neutral position encourages both sides of the discussion to be creative and not feel overpowered by the team leader. In most cases, the only time the team leader will vote on an issue is when there is an equal vote for both proposed action. The team leader is responsible for being the tie breaker when there is a time between two proposals.

## Team Members

The team member is certainly the "heart" of the team. The idea of "Participative Management" is based on allowing employees to help management make better decisions. The whole concept of "synergy" is based on two heads being better than one. If the team leader is there to guide, the team members should assume responsibility for successfully completing the tasks. Some specific team member responsibilities are:

- Willingness to express opinions or feelings
- Active participation
- Listen attentively
- Think creatively
- Avoid disruptive communication
- Be willing to call a time-out when necessary
- Be protective of the rights of other members
- Be responsible for meeting the goals and objectives of the team

**Team Facilitator**

Probably the most difficult role in the team environment is that of the facilitator. There are several different thoughts as to what the role of the facilitator should be. Some organizations use the facilitator as a full member of the team. Other organizations believe the facilitator should be an expert or have a lot of knowledge in the team issue.

There are essentially three types of facilitators. They are:

1. Integrator/coordinator
2. Group process specialist
3. Session leader

The Integrator/Coordinator can, and in many cases, does fill the role of assistant team leader. Duties for this individual are typically in the administration of the team processes and in communicating with others outside the team process. It has been said that this role is that of the Team Secretary or Team Assistant.

The Group Process Specialist is the more traditional facilitator role and is primarily that of facilitating the team meeting with a focus on process. This is the facilitator role that was developed as part of the Quality Circle and group problem-solving process developing in Japan. This facilitator is not a full-time member of the team. His or her role can be described as that of teaching, coaching, and supporting the team.

The Session Leader Facilitator is simply one who leads a session, often in the form of a training session or workshop where a more traditional facilitator is not required. He or she is usually a subject matter expert on the opportunity or activity being presented.

We believe the more traditional view of the team facilitator, the Group Process Specialist, is best when an organization is developing a team culture. First of all, the team facilitator should not be part of the team. The key responsibility of the team facilitator is to assist the team in focusing on process, not content. The most effective facilitators are those with the ability to tune out most of the team's content discussion and focus on the overall effectiveness of the team. In other words, is the team reaching its goals and objectives? Do they stay on track? Do they start and end on time? Are they using the proper tools and techniques at the proper time?

We have included a chart that shows the team roles and responsibilities. (See Figure BB8.2.) The key is to remember that the team leader's

|  | Team Facilitator | Team Leader | Team Member |
|---|---|---|---|
| Purpose | To promote effective group dynamics | To guide teams to achieve successful outcomes | To share knowledge and expertise. |
| Major Concern | *How* decisions are made | *What* decisions are made | *What* decisions are made |
| Principle Responsibilities | • Ensure equal participation by team members<br>• Mediate and resolve conflicts<br>• Provide feedback and support team leaders<br>• Suggest problem solving tools and techniques<br>• Provide TQM training | • Conduct team meetings<br>• Provide direction and focus to team activities<br>• Ensure productive use of team members' time<br>• Represent team to management and EIT<br>• Assist team in developing and maintaining measures | • Offer perspective and ideas<br>• Participate actively in team meetings<br>• Adhere to meeting ground rules<br>• Perform assignments on time<br>• Support implementation of recommendations<br>• Maintain measurements |
| Position Type | Organization-wide | Team-specific | Team-specific |
| Selection Criteria | Personal characteristics | Job title and/or description | Ownership of/in the process |

**FIGURE BB8.2**

Team Roles and Responsibilities.

and members' major concern is what decisions are made (content) and the facilitator's concern is how decisions are made (process).

# THE OPPORTUNITY DEVELOPMENT PROCESS

The first step in the Innovation Systems Cycle is Opportunity Identification. Most of us come in contact with many potential improvement opportunities every day. However, we don't take the time and effort to evaluate them to determine if we reacted to them, would they create significant value-added or not. I'm sure that a high percentage of the improvement opportunities that you will identify will be outside your realm of responsibility/capabilities. The question is, "In the cases where the improvement opportunity is outside your responsibility/capabilities, is it your responsibility to make the appropriate individuals aware of the opportunity?" The answer is sometimes it is and sometimes it isn't. It all depends upon the culture that has developed within your organization. The truly innovative organization wants to know and understand all the potential improvement opportunities that anyone has so they can select the ones to attack that will create the greatest value-added content.

The team environment really exists for one reason only – to improve the organization's performance. Let's face it; we probably wouldn't have a participative management process like teams if it only gave the organization a "warm and fuzzy good feeling" and didn't produce tangible results that translate into dollars and/or customers satisfaction. In other words, "If it doesn't make the organization money, don't do it!"

There are as many approaches to opportunity development as there are to structuring teams. The one we've chosen is probably the most detailed approach.

## USING THE TEAM APPROACH TO ORGANIZE AND RUN MEETINGS

One of the quickest paybacks to the team process is better meeting management. A study conducted a few years ago identifies ineffective meetings as the number-one time waster of management in American businesses. (This includes conference call also.) Most of us can quickly relate to this since we all spend an inordinate amount of time in meetings.

If you are a senior-level manager, you probably spend anywhere from sixty to eighty five percent of your time in meetings. Mid-management spends from fifty to seventy percent of their time in meetings. When asked, most managers will tell you that maybe ten percent of the meetings they attend are beneficial and those would be more valuable if they were conducted with some structure.

We feel there are three pieces to the meeting "pie." They are:

1. Logistics. This includes the where; that is, things such as getting the meeting notice out on time, preparing the meeting room, etc., look out for conferences that are scheduled for one or two hours; they often are poorly planned and poorly managed. Meeting schedule should be based upon covering the agenda, which, in most cases, is not an exact hour or two hours. A typical well-planned and manage meeting with the scheduled to start at 1:10 PM and end at 1:40 PM.
2. Process. This is the how. Here we're looking at how the meeting is conducted, what type of meeting style is in use. What tools and techniques will be required and how do we use them?
3. Content. Here is the heart of the meeting, or the what. What do we hope to accomplish, what action do we need to take, etc.?

## Five Elements of a Successful Meeting

Equally important are what we call the Five Elements of a Successful Meeting.

1. Before the meeting:
   a. Plan the meeting.
   b. Develop a complete agenda.
   c. Prepare for the meeting.
2. At the beginning of the meeting
   a. Start the meeting on time.
   b. Utilize a scribe or recorder.
   c. Reach agreement on the agenda and the key objective of the meeting.
   d. Define each participant's role.
   e. Define the meeting process style. There are basically four types of meeting styles. They are; informational, discussion, problem-solving, and decision-making.
3. During the meeting
   a. Be as positive as possible.
   b. Stick to the agenda and meeting time limits.
   c. Keep the discussions on track.
   d. When necessary, conduct a process check or "time-out."
   e. If new items come up, post them on an "Issues List" (parking lot) for discussion at a later date.

4. At the end of the meeting
   a. Beach agreement on the results.
   b. Establish action items.
   c. Review the process. Take time to evaluate the meeting.
   d. If required, set a time and place for the next meeting.
   e. Prepare the agenda for the next meeting.
   f. End the meeting on time.
5. After the meeting
   a. Follow up on any items.
   b. Prepare and distribute the minutes of the meeting.

## Team Benefits for the Organization

There are many benefits of teams from the organization's standpoint. Some of them are:

- Makes the team more effective and efficient.
- Aligns the team's activities with the organization's objectives.
- Improves the problem-solving cycle by providing better solutions.
- Improves morale.
- Improves trust in management.
- Improves communications.
- Develops new leaders.

## THE SIX LEADERSHIP STYLES

There is more than one way to lead. There are at least six styles of leadership that are effective for making teams hum.

They are force, seduction, persuasion, integrity, empowerment, and wisdom. Style can be, and often is, selected to fit the immediate situation. However, force, seduction, and persuasion do not have the staying power of integrity, empowerment, and wisdom.

Integrity, empowerment, and wisdom are the only true leadership styles for making teams hum and for helping other people.

- Force – Force inspires fear. The forceful leader compels others by physical, moral, or intellectual means. People will flee from forceful leaders at the first opportunity.
- Seduction – Seduction inspires expectations. The seductive leader entices others by attracting or charming. People turn away from seductive leaders when reality falls short of expectations.
- Persuasion – Persuasion inspires demands. The persuasive leader moves others with promises or arguments. People become hostile when promises are broken and arguments are defeated.
- Integrity – Integrity inspires trust. The leader with integrity moves others by consistency of words and deeds. People admire honest leaders and support often continues to grow after the situation.
- Empowerment – Empowerment inspires development. The empowering leader moves by giving authority and power. People need to feel responsible and accountable to self-actualize. They always remain loyal to the leader who makes a positive difference in their lives.
- Wisdom – Wisdom inspires confidence. The wise leader moves others by applying great understanding of people and situations.

Saddam Hussein is perceived by many to be a forceful leader. The power of force is that it moves the team in the leader's desired direction. The problem with force is team resentment.

President Lyndon Johnson is perceived by many to have been a great persuader. The power of persuasion is that people are moved by expectations. The problem with persuasion is that the expectations continue to grow and the team is angered when they are not fulfilled.

Madonna, the pop star, is perceived by many to be a seducer. The power of seduction is the hypnotic control over people. The problem with seduction is the brevity of the control.

General Colin Powell is perceived by many to have great integrity. The power of integrity is the trust that it instills in people. The problem with integrity is that it must be sustained.

President George Bush is perceived by many to be an individual who was effective at empowering people. The power of empowerment is that it fosters creativity and innovation and attracts self-managing people. With empowerment people can rightfully say "we did it." The problem with empowerment is that the leader is still held accountable for the outcome even if he or she did not make the decision.

Albert Einstein is perceived by many to have possessed great wisdom. The power of wisdom is that it is respected. The problem with wisdom is that it is expected in all areas.

Leaders are by nature the type of people that make things happen.

It has been said that there are three kinds of people: those who make it happen, those who do the work, and those who sit by and say, what happened? A good leader makes it happen but does it in a way that others think it was their idea and that they made it happen. People work hardest when they are implementing their own ideas. A good leader helps people mold their ideas so that both parties win.

Why not pause here and reflect on your knowledge and experience with the leadership styles? Record your answers on a sheet of paper.

- Identify other models for each leadership style.
- Describe situations where each style could be most effective.
- Describe situations where each style could be ineffective.
- Decide your preferred style.

## BECOMING A LEADER

A single finger and a piece of string to teach you all you need to know about leadership. (See Figure BB8.3.) The pleasures finger at the end of the string and move your finger forward the string follows were ever you want to take it. If you push back on a string, all it does is wad up and you make no progress.

We now know the key functions of a leader and six leadership styles. The next task is becoming a leader. A cartoon character, Pogo, once said that the quickest way to become a leader is to find a parade and step in front of it. There is more to leadership than Pogo is telling us. Today, great parades are being created by people who have compelling visions for how things and the world can be and the rest of us are stepping in behind them as they parade into the future.

There are definite paths and accountability to leadership. Although the paths can vary from leader to leader, and situation to situation, the accountability for leadership behavior is always predictable.

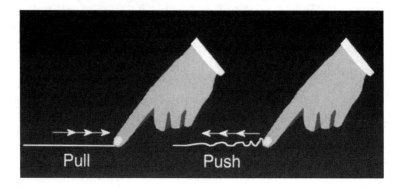

**FIGURE BB8.3**
Impact of Pushing/Pulling.

- Inherited – If you are an inherited leader, the family is forever accountable.
- Appointed – If you are an appointed leader, the appointer is always accountable.
- Promoted – If you are a promoted leader, the promoter is held accountable.
- Elected – If you are an elected leader, the voters are reluctantly accountable.
- Earned – If you have earned leadership, you are expected to be accountable.

Stepping up to shared leadership brings with it the responsibility and accountability for making teams hum. All leaders, regardless of position, role, team level, and path to leadership, can enhance personal knowledge, skills, and abilities by mastering the basic concepts, strategies, tools, and techniques for making teams hum. This in effect can put all paths to leadership on the earned leadership path. (See Figure BB8.4.)

A team leader evolves through four steps. They are:

Step 1 – Controller
Step 2 – Facilitator
Step 3 – Advisor
Step 4 – Leader

**FIGURE BB8.4**
Unlocking Your Leadership Potential.

What step are you at? If you are not at step 4, what are you going to do to move up to the next step? (See Figure BB8.5.)

Now let's pause to reflect on your knowledge and experience with earned leadership. Record your answers on a sheet of paper.

- List positives and negatives of earned leadership accountability.
- List how you can "accentuate the positives and eliminate the negatives."
- Decide your level of commitment to earned leadership.

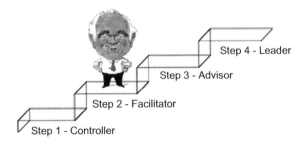

**FIGURE BB8.5**
The Stairway to Leadership.

## LEADERSHIP RESPONSIBILITIES AND ACCOUNTABILITIES

Shared leadership can make teams hum by meeting the needs of the member, team, and organization. This is how to do it.

- Member – Use skills that increase the sense of dignity and self-esteem.
- Team – Use skills that increase team cohesiveness and team spirit.
- Organization – Use skills that motivate productivity and the achievement of organizational and team goals. Use skills that help members and teams reach goals.

## MEETING THE MEMBERS' NEEDS

Member needs must be met on five levels, one person at a time. Each level builds on the level just below it. A person is severely challenged when expected to perform at a higher level when the lower level does not provide a solid foundation. If there is a secret to motivating people, it is in helping them to identify and then to meet their own needs. Motivation is the art of balancing the emotions of desire and fear to bring out the best that is within another person. (See Figure BB8.6.)

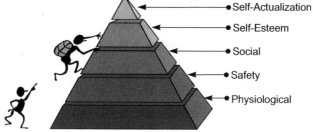

**FIGURE BB8.6**
Hierarchy of Needs.

There are five categories of needs that Abraham Maslow describes as the "hierarchy of needs." (See Figure BB8.6.)

1. Physiological – Physiological needs are met by the team member on an individual level. Physiological needs are things like hunger, shelter, and thirst.
2. Safety – Safety needs are met through greater control of work and environment.
3. Social – Social needs are met through team acceptance. People need a sense of belonging and pursue it through family, friends, work group, sports teams, and religious affiliations.
4. Self-Esteem – Self-esteem is enhanced by rewarding work, responsibility, achievement, recognition, and advancement. A well-developed sense of self-esteem is fundamental to development.
5. Self-Actualization – Self-actualization is achieved by self-direction, self-learning, self-management, and self-rewarding. Providing opportunities for self-actualization is a great motivational tool because it provides the greatest sense of accomplishment.

## MEETING THE TEAM'S NEEDS

There are four needs that must be addressed if the team is going to hum.

### Teams Need #1 – Culture

All cultures have four components in common.

- Institutions – Places and procedures to assemble, interact, and govern.
- Language – How to talk to each other.
- Technology – The tools, hardware and software, to do the work.
- Arts – The means for artistic expression. High achievement in work is artistic.

Institutions provide structure, direction, and support for the team. Other names for institutions are meetings, procedures, routines, charters, regulations, and contracts. The chapter entitled "The Team Process" provides more information on institutions.

## Teams Need #2 – Resources

Teams need ample time, timely and relevant training, and the best in technology (tools) to do the team's work. Knowledge, information, power, and rewards are key enablers for making teams hum.

## Teams Need #3 – Processes

The fundamental processes are procure, protect, promote, and propel. Methodologies like Business Process Improvement, TIME and Six Sigma define the approaches to streamlining and reducing costs for the organization processes. We suggest reading the book entitled *Business Process Improvement* produced by McGraw-Hill to provide more information on processes improvement.

## Teams Need #4 – Routines

Time, training, and technology are used most effectively by teams that have team spirit and group cohesiveness. Group cohesiveness and team spirit can be achieved and enhanced with icebreakers, warm-ups, activities and exercises, and closures that direct and support the work of the team.

---

## MEETING THE ORGANIZATIONAL NEEDS

We tend to forget that teams and organizations are man's creations to serve man. Meeting organizational needs enhances the service to the people who are the stakeholders in the organization. The people can be customers, employees, suppliers, management, investors, regulators, and neighbors (communities). These people are all caretakers and care providers of the environment where the team works.

The leader, the team, and the other stakeholders meet organizational needs by continuously improving the inputs, processes, and products and services. There are five inputs and four processes that are common to all teams, organizations, and cultures. (See Figure BB8.7.) By focusing on these inputs and processes, the leader and team can accomplish approximately eighty percent of the planning and work required to meet the organizational needs.

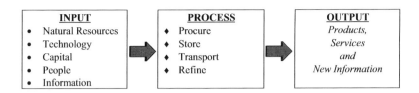

**FIGURE BB8.7**
Input, Process, and Output Model.

The organization's process takes inputs, adds value to them, and provides output to its customer. The objective of all organizations is to increase the value of the output while consuming less and less resources. This allows the organization to make more profits while providing their customers with products and services that are more valuable to the individuals and organizations that receive them.

Innovative products and services are achieved with innovative inputs through innovative processes. A systems view, to look at the whole, is essential to success. Improving one input could be a detriment to the whole. Improving only one process can do the same. A balanced approach is best for achieving products and services to exceed customer expectations and to meet the organizational needs. Other chapters will provide more information.

Now, why not pause to apply your current knowledge and experience to meeting organizational needs by using the process model?

- Select an output (product or service) that your team provides.
- Describe the inputs and processes with team words (e.g., procure becomes recruit, store becomes protect, transport becomes propel, refine becomes promote, or, develop).
- Compare your completed model with your actual experiences.
- Identify the gaps between the model you just developed and your experiences.
- Ask yourself "how do I feel about the gaps?" and "what would I do differently?"
- List three to five leadership things to do to close the gaps, with target start and completion dates.

All the teams that have ever been, and all the teams that will ever be, will hum from desire and from fear. Creating fear and desire are leadership approaches for making teams hum. The leader decides which approach is appropriate. They both work. Fear is difficult to sustain and desire is challenging to maintain. Fear can be effective short term for goals that do not require individual commitment to achieve full potential. Desire takes longer to nurture but is more effective in achieving maximum potential through individual discretionary effort over longer periods of time. The challenge is finding new things to desire. The team's purpose and situation should always govern the decision when selecting fear or desire.

The essential tools and techniques for making teams hum have always been, and always will be available to all teams. This has been documented in, and validated by, the ruins of prehistoric society around the globe. These tools and techniques have been in use for thousands and thousands of years. Cultural anthropologists tell us that the tools are common to all cultures in all ages. The leading question might then be "why have there been winners and losers in the human race for improvement?" Part of the answer, of course, is the misuse and abuse by leaders of fear and desire as motivators for change. Another answer is the imposed limitation by leaders on information, knowledge, power, and rewards, which are the cornerstones of successful teams. Yet another answer is that each individual and each team must learn to use the tools effectively for the team to achieve its full potential. An answer for the information age is expressed in comic wisdom by an insightful, successful business executive. He likes to say, "I now know so much stuff that I can't remember a lot of it, and I can't use a third of what I do remember." Many of us do feel almost overwhelmed by information overload. This provides another reason for Making Teams Hum. It can be a resource and reference book for the tools and techniques that have transcended time and culture translated into current business terms. The team that is most successful with the tools is usually the winner.

The essential tools and techniques are used for identifying, collecting, analyzing, evaluating, and applying relevant information. The tools are interaction, creativity, innovation, diagnosis, prognosis, and measurement. They are fundamental to communication, motivation, education, and administration for making teams hum. There are many, many ways to design and apply the tools and techniques. More ways are being developed and promoted daily as the "latest and greatest." This can lead to analysis paralysis and prolific paranoia. The bottom line is that when the approach is appropriate and the tools and techniques are clear, concise, and correct, teams can hum at five different levels, which we call the Team Alphabet Soup. Every team has the right to decide its desired "humming" level as one of its driving goals.

## Team Alphabet Soup

The Alphabet Soup of teams, or measures of humming, can be described in an easy-to-remember alphabetic order. The levels are:

- A – Aware
- B – Believe
- C – Comprehend
- D – Do
- E – Excel

These levels apply to all teams and to all work. Identifying, planning for, and ensuring the achievement of the desired level of humming is the most important work of the team. In the simplest organizational form, it is almost totally the leader's responsibility. As the organizational form and the technology becomes more complex, the responsibility must be increasingly shared by the leader with the team members. For a team to be aware requires the team leader to be an informed and effective communicator. **Awareness** is the lowest level of humming and obviously requires less energy from the team and the leader. To get a team to believe that something is happening, could happen, or should happen requires a higher energy level from the team and the leader. The knowledge, skill, and ability requirements of the team and the leader have to expand exponentially to achieve the **believe** level. The leader must be able to motivate others toward the desired decision making and goal setting. The team members must be ready to enhance their capability for informed decision making and goal setting.

To reach the **comprehend** level, the team needs to gain understanding of the work the team does and purpose of the team. To fully comprehend requires awareness and belief. The knowledge, skill, and ability requirements of the team members and the team leader must take another exponential leap forward. The leader needs to become an educator. This requires knowing how to gain and transfer understanding of the technical and behavioral information needed by the team in an effective and timely manner. The team needs the capability to process and apply the transferred knowledge.

After comprehension comes the **do** level. To do something well requires passage through the levels of to be aware, to believe, and to comprehend. The leader now needs to have the knowledge, skill, and abilities to effectively administrate the process. This requires understanding the technical and behavioral information requirements well enough to identify, track, analyze, and apply the key drivers of continuous improvement to your process. The team members need the knowledge, skills, and abilities to take informed risks, recover from failure, and to find new reasons to continuously improve. Doing well requires goal-setting capabilities of the leader and the team members to continuously "raise the bar," "look beyond the horizon," and to "commit to a compelling vision."

> The very essence of leadership is that you have to have a vision. It's got to be a vision you articulate clearly and forcefully on every occasion. You cannot blow an uncertain trumpet.
> Father Theodore Hesburg Former President of Notre Dame University

The fifth level of making teams hum is the **excel** level. This requires the team members and the team leader to acquire and develop the knowledge, skills, and abilities to self-learn, self-direct, self-manage, and self-reward. To make teams hum at the excel level requires awareness, belief, comprehension, and doing. This is further complicated by the natural laws of teaming.

Law No. 1 is that most team members never report to the team leader that they would prefer to follow and most team leaders never have exactly the team members that they would select. Birds of a feather like to flock together. This tendency discourages diversity that can limit creativity and innovation. Law No. 2 is that none of us can be as great as all of us.

It is true that two heads are better than one, especially when they're humming by thinking differently and complementarily. However, you have to get to excel from where you are. So, this chapter is really about determining where you are on your journey to make teams hum, deciding where you need to be, and determining how to get there. To excel requires the team leader and the team members have the capability to change.

## Team Benefits for the Individual

There are many benefits of being a member or a leader of a team to the individual. Some of them are:

- Learn better ways to solve problems.
- Develop better interpersonal skills.
- Get more satisfaction from finding better answers to problems.
- Get a better understanding of the organization.
- Develop friendships.
- Develop leadership skills.
- Become more satisfied with their job.

## HOW TO IMPLEMENT A TEAM INITIATIVE

We talked about implementation of the team concept. We like to do it in the following four target areas in the order presented below:

1. Focusing on changing executive behavior patterns.
2. Focusing on increasing external customer satisfaction levels.
3. Focusing on Improving Internal Organization Interfaces.
4. Focusing on lowering operating costs.

### Focusing on Changing Executive Behavior Patterns

All major initiatives within an organization need to start with the executive team leading the way, setting the example, and living up to the initiatives concepts. For this reason, the team initiative starts with the executive team and, better still, both the executive team and the board of directors implementing an error measurement for themselves.

1. Executive Team Error Measurement

   The executive team assignment is to lead the organization and make major decisions related to how the organization functions. This results in them having the possibility of making two types of error. These are:

   - Decision Making Errors.
   - Behavioral Errors.

   Decision-making errors are extremely expensive to the organization and the executive team needs to be expert in risk analysis and the functions they are assigned to. It is unfortunate that most decision-making errors are not immediately recognizable. In an attempt to quantify decision making, we have looked at the decisions that were made by the executive team 6 months after they were made. We classify each decision as a poor decision, an acceptable decision, and the best-possible decision. In this case, only 8.5 percent of the decisions were the best-possible decision. The difference between an acceptable decision and best-possible decision can be hundreds of million dollars a year for a major company.

2. Increasing External Customer Satisfaction Levels.

The second priority is forming a dedicated task team to improve customer satisfaction level to the point it meets its goal. The goal we like to set is ninety percent of the customers rate the organization as "exceeds requirements." Organizations that meet requirements or exceeds requirements at times are not going to have loyal customers, unless the customer has no better opportunity and often will try other brands in hopes that they will find one that consistently exceeds the requirements. Of course, anything below meeting requirements is a reflection of customers that are actively looking for other organizations to fill their needs and requirements. This usually is accomplished with assigning a task team to each major product to study what the customer wants but is not getting. They asked the question of external customers, "What would it take to make the organization as outstanding?"

3. Focusing on improving internal organization interfaces

The four most important tools in building an innovative culture in order are:

1. Measuring executive behavior errors
2. Brainstorming
3. Area Activity Analysis
4. Business Process Improvement

Developing a cohesive internal supplier–customer relationship is the basis that all team activities should be directed at. Many books on team building stress the importance of establishing both the external and internal customer–supplier interface. A great deal of emphasis has been placed on building the external partnership but few tools have been affected for developing the internal supplier–customer relationship between the natural work teams that make up the organization. The only tool that we have found effective at developing the customer–supplier internal relationships is the Area Activity Analysis (AAA) methodology. The following are the four major improvements that AAA usually brings about in an organization when it is implemented.

a. Establishes agreed-to efficiency measurements throughout the organization.
b. Establishes four-way communication links.
c. Establishes performance standards.
d. Establishes internal supplier–customer relationships.

4. Focusing on lowering operating costs

## AREA ACTIVITY ANALYSIS (AAA)

I cannot overemphasize the importance and effectiveness of this tool in improving innovation and internal organizational support. The only effective way we have found in establishing an organization-wide customer supplier relationship is through the use of Area Activity Analysis (AAA). I strongly suggest that AAA is the best starting point to change the culture and habits within the organization. It quickly defines all of the overlaps and establishes efficiency and effectiveness measures for frequently used processes. It affects everything from payroll, to snow removal, customer retention, and all the activities in between.

### Abstract

Area Activity Analysis (AAA), sometimes called "Department Activity Analysis," is the most effective approach developed today to establish the internal and external supplier/customer relationships. It also establishes Individual Performance Indicators (IPI) related to major activities that go on in all of the organization's natural work teams (NWTs). These individual performance indicators define and measure what each level of management and all employees do and what they are responsible for. This allows improvement efforts to be focused upon real problems and to take advantage of real opportunities that impact the total organization's performance.

## Introduction

Definition: Area Activity Analysis is a methodology to establish agreed-to, understandable efficiency and effectiveness measurement systems and communication links throughout the organization. It is designed to define and set up all of the internal and external supplier/customer relationships and measurements. (See Figure BB8.8.)

The methodology consists of seven phases. The first six phases of AAA process usually have fixed start- and end-points; only the last phase, Continuous Improvement, is a continuous process. The first six phases are normally treated as an innovation project and they are included in the organization's strategic business plan. This by no means indicates that the measurements and associated requirements are developed and not updated on a regular basis. It provides a set of IIPs that are relative to the activities going on within each natural work team and presents

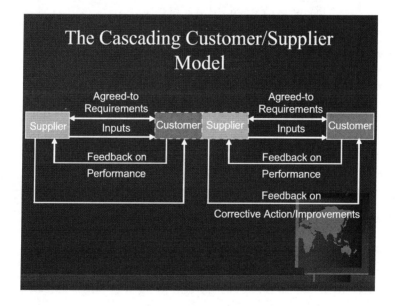

**FIGURE BB8.8**
The Cascading Customer/Supplier Model.

the results in a way that is easily understood by the employees. At least one of the IPIs should be an innovation measurement related to the natural work team's activities. (See Figure BB8.8.)

By monitoring the IPIs, the people that can realize they have a problem at least 30 days before the problem can be recognized in the Key Performance Indicators (KPIs).

## Benefits of AAA

AAA has many benefits to an organization. Some of them are:

- It aligns the mission statement throughout the organization from the president's office all the way down to first-line-foremen's group (Natural Work Team).
- It ensures that the individual Natural Work Teams (NWT) are conducting activities that are in line with their mission statements.
- It provides a good understanding by all of the NWT members of what is going on within the NWT and how its innovation is measured and reported.
- It provides agreed to, understandable output requirements as viewed by the internal and external customers.
- It establishes a performance-feedback system from the internal and external customers.
- It establishes agreed-to and documented work standards for all major processes within the NWT scope of work.
- It documents the major processes that go on within each NWT.
- It sets up a visual, innovation opportunity and performance tracking system for each NWT.

Definition: Natural Work Team (NWT) or Natural Work Group (NWG) is a group of people who are assigned to work together and who report to the same manager or supervisor. AAA projects are implemented by NWTs.

## Features of AAA

The features of a typical AAA methodology include:

- It develops aligned, interdependent mission statements for NWTs at all levels within the organization from the CEOs NWT to the janitorial NWT.
- It defines the major processes that are going on in each NWT.
- It documents customer agreed-to, signed-off output requirements for the major processes that each NWT is involved in.
- It defines and documents the performance feedback loop for the internal and external customers for each output from the major NWT processes.
- It defines and documents signed-off work standards for the major processes for each NWT.
- It documents the processes that create the output for each NWT.
- It documents a set of supplier agreed-to input requirements for each major process for each NWT.

Few incentives are more powerful than membership in a small group engaged in a common task, sharing the risks of defeat and the potential rewards of victory.

Robert B. Reich, *The Work of Nations: Preparing Ourselves for the 21st Century Capitalism* (Vintage Books 1992)

## The AAA Methodology

The AAA methodology has been divided into seven different phases to make it simple for the NWT to implement the concept. Each of these phases contains a set of steps that will progressively lead the NWT through the methodology. (See Figure BB8.9.) These seven phases are:

We will briefly describe each of the seven phases AAA. Implementing these 7 phases will bring about a major improvement in the organization's measurement systems, increase understanding and cooperation, and lead to reduced cost and improved quality throughout the organization.

### Phase I – Preparation for AAA

This phase is normally conducted in BB2 – Innovation Organizational Assessment, BB3 – Executive Leadership, and BB6 – Project Management Systems.

AAA is most effective when it precedes other innovation improvement. It is also best to implement the AAA methodology throughout the organization. This does not mean that it will not work if other

| Phase | Number of Steps |
|---|---|
| Phase I—Preparation for AAA | 5 |
| Phase II—Develop Area Mission Statement | 5 |
| Phase III—Define Area Activities | 15 |
| Phase IV—Develop Customer Relationships | 7 |
| Phase V—Analyze the Activity's Efficiency | 4 |
| Phase VI—Develop Supplier Partnerships | 6 |
| Phase VII—Performance Improvement | 8 |
| Total: | 43 |

**FIGURE BB8.9**

AAA Phases.

improvement activities are underway or if it is only used by one area within the total organization. In the preparation phase, the good and bad considerations related to implementing AAA within an organization should be evaluated. A decision is made whether or not to use AAA within the organization. If the decision is made to use AAA, an implementation strategy is developed and approved by management. Phase 1 – Preparation for AAA is divided into 5 steps.

### Phase II – Develop Area Mission Statement

This is normally conducted during BB15 – Innovative Organizational Structure.

> Definition: Mission Statement – A mission statement is used to document the reasons for the organization's or area's existence. It is usually prepared prior to the organization or area being formed, and is seldom changed. Normally, it is changed only when the organization or area decides to pursue new or different set of activities.

For the AAA methodology, a mission statement is a short paragraph, no more than two or three sentences, that defines the area's role and its relationship with the rest of the organization and/or the external customer. An area's mission statement must reflect a part of the mission statement that the area reports to. A manager can't delegate responsibilities to a group that reports to him/her that the delegating manager is not responsible for. (See Figure BB 8.10.)

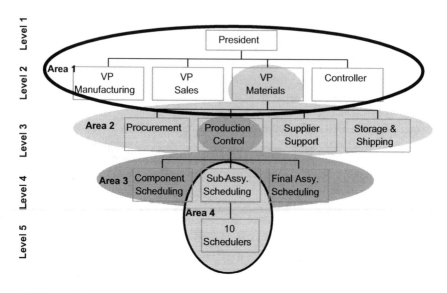

**FIGURE BB8.10**
How AAA Worked in a Five-Level Organization.

Every area should have a mission statement that defines why it was created. It is used to provide the area manager and the area employees with guidance related to the activities on which the area should expend its resources. Standard good business practice calls for the area's mission statement to be prepared before an area is formed. The mission statement should be reviewed each time there is a change to the organization's structure or a change to the area's responsibilities. It should also be reviewed about every four years, even if the organization's structure has remained unchanged, to be sure that the mission statement reflects the current activities that are performed within the area.

During Phase II, the NWT will review and update the area's mission statement. If a mission statement does not exist, the NWT will prepare a mission statement. In all cases, any change to the mission statement must be approved by upper management before it is finalized. Phase II – Develop Area Mission Statement, is divided into 6 steps.

### Phase III – Define Area Activities

This phase is normally conducted during BB15 – Innovative Organizational Structure.

During this phase, the NWT will define the activities that are performed within the area. For each major activity, the NWT will define the activity's output(s) and the customers that receive that output. Phase III – Define Area Activities is divided into 8 steps.

### Phase IV – Develop Customer Relationships

This is normally done during the time BB14 – Comprehensive Measurement System.

During this phase, the NWT will meet with the internal and external customers who are receiving the outputs from the major activities conducted by the area to:

- Define the customer's requirements.
- Develop how compliance to the requirements will be measured.
- Define acceptable performance levels (performance standards).
- Define the customer feedback process.

Phase IV – Develop Customer Relationships, is divided into 7 steps.

### Phase V – Analyze the Activity's Efficiency

This is normally conducted during BB14 – Comprehensive Measurement Systems.

For each major activity, the NWT will define and understand the tasks that make up the activity. This is accomplished by analyzing each major activity for its value-added content. This can be accomplished by flowcharting or value-stream mapping the process and collecting efficiency information related to each task and the total process. Typical information that would be collected is:

- Innovation-related information cycle time
- Processing time
- Cost
- Rework rates
- Items processed per time period

Using this information, the NWT will establish efficiency measurements and performance targets for each efficiency measurement, these targets/

measurement are signed off by the person that the area reports to and the work standards group, if there is one. These work standards are often used to calculate the area's work load and budget,

Phase V – Analyze the Activity's Efficiency is divided into 6 steps

### Phase VI – Develop Supplier Partnerships

This is normally conducted during BB10 – Supplier Partnerships and BB14 – Comprehensive Measurement Systems.

Using the flowcharts generated in Phase V, the NWT identifies the supplier that provides input into the major activities. This phase uses the same approach discussed in Phase IV, but turns the customer/supplier relationship around. In this phase, the area is told to view itself in the role of the customer. The organizations that are providing the inputs to the NWT are called internal or external suppliers. The area (the customer) then meets with its suppliers to develop agreed-to input requirements. As a result of these negotiations, a supplier specification is prepared that includes a measurement system, performance standard, and feedback system for each input. This completes the customer/supplier chain for the area.

> Definition: Supplier – An organization which provides a product (input) to the customer (source ISO 8402).

> Definition: Internal Supplier – Areas within an organizational structure that provide input into other areas within the same organizational structure.

> Definition: External Supplier – Suppliers that are not part of the customer's organizational structure.

Phase VI – Develop Supplier Partnerships is divided into 5 steps.

### Phase VII – Performance Improvement

This is normally conducted during BB8 – Team Building and BB9 – Individual Innovation, Creativity and Excellence.

This is the continuous opportunity development phase that should always come after a process has been defined and the related measurements are put in place. It may be a full innovation effort or just a redesign activity. It could be a minimum program of error correction and cost reduction or a full-blown TIME project.

During Phase VII, the NWT will enter into the Opportunity Development and error prevention mode of operation. The measurement system should now be used to set challenge improvement targets. The NWT should now be trained to solve problems and take advantage of improvement opportunities. The individual efficiency and effectiveness measurements will be combined into a single performance index for the area. Typically, the area's key measurement graphs will be posted and updated regularly.

During Phase VII, management should show its appreciation to the NWTs and individuals who expended exceptional effort during the AAA project or who implemented major improvements.

Phase VII – Performance Improvement is divided into 8 steps.

## Benefits of AAA

The AAA methodology provides you with five major benefits. They are:

1. *Understanding*

   Often the authority and responsibilities of an area are not defined and understood by the area and the other parts of the organization that interfaces with them. This often leads to activity voids and overlaps that are very costly. With AAA each NWT has a defined and documented mission statement that defines what activities it is responsible for. A NWT should not perform activities that are not directly in line with their mission statement.

   The AAA methodology is needed because most individuals and groups do not really understand just why they do the things they do. They don't know who their suppliers are, nor who their customers are. Even if they do know, it is unlikely that they and their customers, suppliers, and management have a common, agreed-to understanding of how their output should be measured and what is acceptable performance related to each of these measures. Improvements cannot be made without understanding these items. AAA can provide this understanding because it is a systematic and disciplined method of looking at the inputs from the suppliers, the value-added content of the area, and the outputs the customers receive.

2. *Involvement*

   AAA is a methodology that involves managers and nonmanagers (administrative personnel, accountants, salespeople, operators, technicians, engineers, etc.) in analyzing what goes on within an area and defining what acceptable performance is.

3. *Opportunity*

   AAA's structure makes it an ideal tool for opportunity discovery, and opportunity development. Defining improvement opportunities is one of the first steps in the improvement journey. Too often, organizations train people to identify opportunities and then tell them to go out and find an opportunity that will add value to the stakeholders. With AAA, the employees are provided with information that defines if they have business-related opportunities, as well as defining the magnitude of the opportunity. If they do have business-related opportunity and/or improvement opportunities, the employees are then trained to take advantage of these opportunities. Using this approach, problem solving is truly a value-added business activity.

4. *Communication*

   AAA is designed to capture vital information and keep management and the employees aware of how the area is integrated with the overall goals and strategies of the organization.

5. *Measurement*

   AAA is a methodology that will help an area develop and use meaningful measurements and performance standards. Typically, each area will have its innovation standard, 3–6 effectiveness measurements and 3–6 efficiency measurements with their associated performance standards. Often, these measurements are combined mathematically to develop a single improvement measurement for the many activities that go on within the area. This measurement system will help to integrate what is done within the area with the overall strategies and goals of the organization. Each area should have its own performance board. (See Figure BB8.11.)

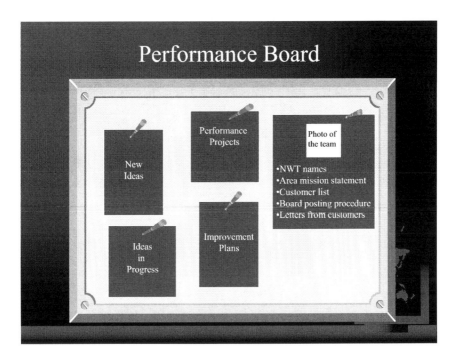

**FIGURE BB0.11**
Performance Board.

## Advantages

Using AAA has many advantages over some of the other improvement techniques. Some of these include:

- All individuals in the organization can be actively involved in the innovative AAA process.
- Those employees that contribute to the success of the organization can be identified and rewarded appropriately.
- The organization's operating skills are improved, especially leadership skills.
- Burning issues and problems are addressed.
- A team environment is established within the area.
- Teamwork between areas is greatly improved.
- The area manager maintains the role of leader of the area.
- Employees become more responsible for their own actions.
- Employee self-esteem improves.

- The system provides realistic and meaningful specifications that have been agreed to by the customers, suppliers, management, and the employees.
- Critical, meaningful measures of effectiveness and efficiency are identified at the area level for each major activity.
- Employees have a better understanding of how they fit into the area and total organization.
- External customer service is improved.
- An appropriate escalation process is established for those issues that cannot be resolved by the NWT.
- Interpersonal relationships are improved.
- The organization maximizes its knowledge base.
- A firm foundation is developed that leads to major quality improvement and cost reduction.

## AAA Summary

Too many of the improvement programs that I see being implemented today remind me of Don Quixote's quest. They are full of good intentions, but they are misdirected. They are limited to a few peoples' view of what is important and have little long lasting substance. People are trained to use tools, but they are not given the time or the opportunity to use them. We are relying more and more on technology to interface with ourselves and our external customers and less and less on our people. For example, people send text messages to the person sitting at the desk right beside them instead of talking to them. AAA provides a systematic way of helping each employee understand what is going on within the natural work team and how the natural work team and he/she fits into the bigger picture. It also establishes a direct connection to the people that get the output from each employee's activities thereby building a sense of ownership within the individual.

In addition to having a very positive impact on all the employees, AAA also provides the organization with an effective way to measure and control the organization down to the individual level. The individual performance indicators become the key drivers in the continuous improvement process activities. Progress or the lack of progress at the activity level is continuously visible so action can be taken immediately to keep it on track. Truly, AAA is a technique that all organizations should be using as the basis for building their team activities and their continuous improvement programs.

---

## TEAMS NOT THE BEST ANSWER

Teams are the in-thing today when trying to make an improvement or create a new product. They are usually recommended for significant new product development and for major problem solving activities. For example:

- Example 1 – As an organization progresses and becomes more mature in its improvement approaches a higher percentage of the initiatives are handled by an individual rather than a team. The more advanced organizations are empowering individuals to make decisions on their own without relying on a groups inputs. Picture someone calling into Apple with the problem that the computer will not start and gets the help desk. After the customer describes his problem, the help desk operator states, "That's a very interesting problem. I'll bring it up at our next team meeting and see what the team thinks about it. I'll be back to you in a week or more." Of course, that is ridiculous. Properly trained people need to be empowered to make decisions on their own without added input of team members or the management. As employees gain more trust and commitment to an organization, they should become more empowered.
- Example 2 – Teams have often been described as "one plus one equals 3 not 2." This higher value is based upon bringing together a group of people with different backgrounds and experiences to look at an individual opportunity. All too often the team will go along with a suggestion made by its leader even though there are better alternatives. This is the safe way to plan it as they cannot be blamed if it does not work. In other cases two options will be developed with each one supported very strongly by 1 or 2 of the team members. In these cases in order to reach a consensus, both options have to be compromised often creating a third option that is not as good as either one of the individual options. In this case, we have $1+1+1+1+1+1=0.7$

In these two examples, example 1 is a favorable condition and one that should be encouraged. Great care should be taken that you don't empower an individual who has not developed to a point that he or she can properly handle the things that empowered to do. Example 2 is a very unfavorable condition and usually requires a strong, well-trained leader or a facilitator to find not a win–win answer but a best answer. Teams are usually run by a majority vote to agree on a course of action rather than full consensus.

## THE MAJOR PROBLEM WITH TEAMS

The general structure of any organization is built on subdividing work into small groups or teams. Once an organization expands past 10 to 15 employees, it is time to subdivide work by classification of jobs. This automatically creates organizational-based teams. The problem occurs because the organizational teams in most cases have not been trained in the tools required to improve the efficiency, effectiveness, and adaptability of the processes they are involved in.

Every large organization is made up of a large number of teams. In most cases, these are not assigned the responsibility for improving the way they operate. They are used primarily as communication teams where pertinent business information is provided to the team members and the team members report back on the status of the work they are doing. The problem is not that we don't have enough teams. The problem is that the teams are either untrained or not assigned the responsibility to bring about improvement within the organization.

## SUMMARY

Do teams have a place in the future of an organization's improvement efforts? The Ernst & Young "Best Practices Report" makes a point work considering. It states "Building the human resource infrastructure is essential ...." According to the report, lower performing organizations show less than five percent of the work force is participating on teams while higher performing organizations show over twenty five percent.

The United States was introduced to participative management and the team concept almost four decades ago. It's changed the way we do business.

Ford Motor Company almost cut the Mustang automobile from the line-up. A team known as the "Gang of Eight" researched innovative ideas and changes, presented the changes to top management and, after very tough questions from CEO Harold Poling, they got the go-ahead. The team promised a 37 -turn-around. This was several months quicker than any previous turn-around on new car design. Working together, the team slashed bureaucracy and delivered the new Mustang in just 35 months. Will Boddie, Ford's Mustang boss, said, "We made decisions in minutes around the coffee pot that would normally take months."

Richard De Vogelaere and the folks at GM took a team approach to taking on water leaks in the Camaro and Firebird model automobiles. They called themselves the F-car SWAT team. Not only did they fix the water leaks but also that "scree" noise made when window glass rubs against the rubber. They also took care of some shakes and squeaks in T-top models by using under-body braces. De Vogelaere's comment:

> You say to yourself, "if we'd done this five years ago, how many more could we have sold? How many more thousands of owners would be out there saying what a great, exciting car this is." We thought we were meeting the customer's expectations, but we weren't really listening, I guess.
>
> Why be a hermit when teams are so much more rewarding.
>
> H. James Harrington

# BB9

## Individual Creativity, Innovation, and Excellence

*Frank Voehl*

## CONTENTS

> Above all, we know that an entrepreneurial strategy has more chance of success the more it starts out with the users – their utilities, their values, their realities. An innovation is a change in market or society. It produces a greater yield for the user, greater wealth-producing capacity for society, higher value, or greater satisfaction. The test of an innovation is always what it does for the user. Hence, entrepreneurship always needs to be market-focused, indeed, market-driven.
>
> **Peter F. Drucker, Innovation and Entrepreneurship**

## INTRODUCTION

The purpose of this chapter is to present some ideas for individual creativity and innovation, and how it contributes to both personal and organizational excellence. It describes some descriptive models and the associated factors influencing individual innovation and creativity in an organization that is focused on achieving excellence in all that it does. Additionally, the model for individual creativity is presented and shown how it integrates into the model for organizational excellence.[1] Our premise is that this model contains four criteria for both individual and organizational innovation as follows: (1) The entire process of individual creativity is considered as a critical element in the process of organizational innovation; (2) There needs to be an attempt at incorporating all aspects of organizations that influence innovation; (3) The model needs to show all the major phases in the innovation process; and (4) The model will describe the influence of the organizational factors on individual creativity and innovation.

## PROLOGUE

As outlined in this chapter, the initial problem faced by all practitioners and researchers is to be able to accurately define the terms "creativity" and "innovation" as they pertain to both individual and organizational practices. In fact, precise definitions of creativity and innovation have long been a source of dispute and debate among academic researchers (West 2002). Fortunately, ISOs Technical Committee 276 on innovation has acquired a consensus agreement on the definition of innovation. They define innovation as the introduction of something new. It often includes the development and implementation of a new idea, design, method, product, or service. Creative is defined as using the ability to make or think of new things involving the process by which new ideas, stories, products, etc., are created. Create is defined as making something: to bring something into existence.

Facing rapid technological changes and being challenged by emerging markets, the modern organization has to adapt quickly in order to maintain

---

1 JSTOR. According to the Amsterdam University Press, Chapter Title: Innovation and creativity in organisations: individual and work team research findings and implications for government policy Chapter Author(s): Neil R. Anderson and Rosina M. Gasteiger Book Title: *Micro-foundations for Innovation Policy* Book Editor(s): B. Nooteboom, E. Stam Published by: Amsterdam University Press. (2008) Stable URL: www.jstor.org/stable/j.ctt46mwvr.14.

or increase their effectiveness – they need to innovate or evaporate.[2] *Innovate or Evaporate* by Jim Higgins explains The Innovation Quotient (IQ) concept is truly innovative in its own right and is worth the price of the book. For more details, see BB2 – Innovative Organizational Assessment.

The tools and techniques in Higgins book are organized around a four-step innovation methodology – define, discover, develop, and demonstrate. Within this scope, the development and adoption of innovations have become a critical determinant of organizational productivity, competitiveness, and longevity. Hence, it is not surprising that a major research effort has focused on variables that facilitate or hinder the development and implementation of innovations. One of our main reasons for focusing upon these variables and levels of analysis was the summary description of this whole project area itself. To quote from the homepage related to the project on "Innovation: The Need for Renewal": "The fundamental unit of analysis is people in interaction with other people, within and between businesses, with businesses, macro-conditions and institutions as 'enabling constraints'. The analysis at micro-level provides a basis for recommendations, which are largely situated at the institutional level" (www.wrr.nl/english/content.jsp?objectid=3949&pid=3947).[3]

> I sat down and made a quick list of some of the things I think about when I talk about improving the individual's ability to be creative, and to transform that creative spark into a finished product. Probably the most important thing is their personal commitment to implementing their ideas … The belief in what they're doing and their desire to contribute … No innovator can wait for someone else to turn ideas into value added.
> H. James Harrington, On Individual Innovation Excellence

The NSF (National Science Foundation) reports starting in 2005 and moving forward consistently communicate the findings of individual

---

2 *Innovate or Evaporate: Test and Improve Your Organization's I.Q., Its Innovation Quotient* by James M. Higgins. Used as the criteria for selection for the Global Innovation Award, this book features questionnaires that allow firms to test their current levels of innovation in the areas of product, process, marketing, and management. It includes lengthy and numerous descriptions of the 49 characteristics of innovative organizations.

3 One essential point needs to be made at this introductory stage. Most of the research efforts by work psychologists referred to in the present chapter have focused upon larger organizations, usually on the basis of attempting to maximize sample size once access has been negotiated. Many of the studies cited in our chapter concern individual and team-level innovation in larger, often multinational organizations. The generalization of these findings to smaller organizations, family businesses, and the like can be open to question.

versus team innovation.[4] Specifically, in particular, five umbrella research areas are identified as critical how-to pathways in helping the United States regain the lead in the process of individual innovation:

1. studies that expand *understanding of the cognitive mechanisms of innovation/creativity* and the ways in which strategies and external tools influence these cognitive mechanisms;

2. *computational modeling and agents simulations of innovation/creativity* that allow for theoretical development across levels of individual, group, and organizational analysis;

3. empirical studies and computational models that explore the *temporal dynamics of individual and group factors* on creativity/innovation;

4. interdisciplinary programs of *research that coordinate psychology laboratory and design engineering experiments*;

5. empirical studies that *explain and unfold cognitive and social/ motivational factors of group cognition in more realistic group settings*: including horizontally integrated across disciplines, vertically integrated (with leaders), and evolving group structure over long time periods.

While many books discuss the various aspects of corporate creativity, the fact is that corporations cannot imagine and think, nor can they come up with new ideas without the individuals that they employ. The common fallacy of innovation diminishing as individuals' age is a fallacy and simply is not true. What may be the case is as one becomes older, we are the one that has more to lose. What this can directly translate to is the need for organizations to make it safer for individuals to be creative.

One company we researched and documented a few years ago referred to the innovation program as *"prairie dog innovation."*[5] When

---

4 Final Report from the NSF Innovation and Discovery Workshop: The Scientific Basis of Individual and Team Innovation and Discovery, Christian D. Schunn (University of Pittsburgh), Paul B. Paulus (University of Texas, Arlington), Jonathan Cagan (Carnegie Mellon University), Kristin Wood (University of Texas, Austin) August 2006.

5 On the hardscrabble lands of the American West, blood is spilled by the most innocent-looking of outlaws – the white-tailed prairie dog. These social rodents, native to Colorado, Wyoming, Utah, and Montana, ruthlessly bite and thrash Wyoming ground squirrels to death, leaving their bloody bodies to rot, a new study says. The killers' offspring then live longer, healthier lives – probably because their parents bumped off their competition for food. It's the first time that a herbivorous mammal has been seen killing competitors without eating them, suggesting that a plant-based diet doesn't preclude mammals from having a taste for bloodsport.

I contacted them and asked them to explain this, they outlined the concept as follows.

> The company had a very public program to solicit innovative ways to deliver healthcare to patients. They wanted new products, better ways to do things and ways to connect with customers and fellow employees in new and novel ways. The problem was that employees' felt like they were prairie dogs, and management was a guy with a shotgun. If they stuck their heads (ideas) out of the hole, they better be sure that it was a good one. If not, it was likely that they would get their heads shot off (fired, censured, reassigned, etc.).

In other words, management made it clear by their actions that innovation was only good when the idea was good. So, no one brought forth ideas for fear that it wouldn't be the ideas that management was looking for. Additionally, in this particular organization, the individual responsible for starting and building a world-class innovation department was not promoted when it was decided that they needed a Chief Innovation Officer, as the position was filled with an acquaintance of the CEO, but it was a person who had no innovation-related qualifications.

## SOME THOUGHTS ON INDIVIDUAL INNOVATION EXCELLENCE[6]

The following is an extract from a recent documentary interview by Frank Voehl, Chair of the US TAG for Innovation and Dr. Jim Harrington, who is a Working Group Leader of Innovation Frameworks. We will use these

---

6 *Knowledge Management Excellence*. Firms contend with increasingly knowledge-driven competition. Many attempt to meet the challenge by investing in expensive knowledge management systems. However, these are useless for making strategic decisions because they don't distinguish between what's strategically relevant and what isn't. This book focuses on identifying and managing the specific, critical knowledge assets that your firm needs to disrupt your competitors, including tacit experience of key employees deep understanding of customers' needs, valuable patents and copyrights, shared industry practices, and customer- and supplier-generated innovations. *Knowledge Management Excellence* (by Harrington & Voehl, 2005), contains world-renowned experts, cutting-edge research, and practical tools to help you identify and manage the many kinds of knowledge you and your firm can use to innovate. Other outcomes can be accelerated-organic growth, reconfigure your competitive approach to new and existing markets, target power-producing acquisitions, and forge powerful alliances. And, because an estimated 80 percent of competitive knowledge is not numeric, you will explore new strategies for identifying, developing, and managing talent.

25 How-to Individual Innovation Action Items as a guidepost for the TIME Pyramid for the remainder this Chapter.

JIM HARRINGTON: Frank, *you wanted some of my thoughts on the chapter you're writing on individual excellence. In this case we are talking about what we can do to help the individual be more creative and come up with more ideas that are innovative. The chapter before this we talked about how you do it with teams. Most of the real big breakthroughs occur by individuals coming up with ideas. 70% of our gross national product comes from small to midsize organizations. How do you get your wife, your son, yourself, be more innovative? How much more value-added are you and your spouse doing today than you both were doing 5 years ago. How do we get the individual to issue more patents? Shark tank is a good example of something that was effective at motivating individuals. It has been said that every individual sometime in their life will have an idea worth $1 million if they just implemented it. How do you get the individual to recognize an opportunity and motivated to the point that they mortgage their home to finance the development of her/his innovation? The following are some 30 ideas that I have; I'm sure you can add a lot more (in this Chapter). I hope this helps in getting started.*

– H James Harrington, Innovation Author

## TOP 20 HOW-TO INSIGHTS

The following are the Top 20 How-to Insights

1. Providing the environment for personal development – opening the door to individual excellence
2. Improvement-related training and experience.
3. Job- and career-related training and experiences.
4. Career growth training to boost personal Creativity.
5. Rewrite all job descriptions including management – and understand the psychological foundations for make personal innovation a requirement in every job. No more hanging up your mind at the timeclock.
6. Developing individual performance plans and performance evaluation (appraisal). Provide a way so that his or her progress. We know

of organizations that expect approved suggestions a month from every employee including the CEO.

7. Use helpful Suggestion systems. Good tracking system and even better response.
8. New employee training and Career-Building. If you Promote, rotate.
9. Building a bond with your manager and your neighbor.
10. Reinforcing desired individual behaviors.
11. Cross discipline training.
12. Turning employee complaints into profit.
13. Getting ideas flowing.
14. Empowering the individual closest to the customer.
15. Self-managed employees.
16. How to recognize improvement opportunities.
17. How to evaluate the value of your ideas.
18. How to perform Area Activity Analysis (AAA).
19. How to excel in selling your ideas.
20. Dealing with Empowerment: Setting personal excellence goals and award programs for individual excellence (quality, productivity).

**How-to Innovation Insights #1, 2 and 3: In order to boost organizational creativity, it is critical that the organization provide an environment that includes Training, including Improvement and Job-Related skillsets.**

*Learning and technology go side by side, hand in hand.* As high-tech innovations accelerate, so does the opportunity to create better corporate training programs and delivery methods. (Who is he/she?) As the president and CEO of one of the oldest learning and development providers in South Florida, I have learned that organizations need personalized training that incorporates cutting-edge technology, supports professional development, and encourages employee engagement. More than ever, training is effectively providing skills that match the way we learn in a high-tech world. The knowledge and skills acquired and applied by employees is shared freely in a learning culture, creating a sustainable and adaptable organization.

Management can help develop future leaders and managers as soon as new employees enter the door by providing mentors and helping them build professional networks. Improving your leadership development program helps you build teams that are agile and capable of evolving with the times. Think of using training clips on a YouTube channel, a classroom training session, a MOOC (massive online open course), or a post shared on Facebook Workplace as elements that can be turned into learning content.

However, there is widespread concern among recruiters that the soft skills gap is widening with the technologically savvy but soft-skill-poor Gen Z employees entering the workforce. Learning and development personnel can overcome this challenge by offering soft skills training to employees and encouraging them to refine their social skills, with gamification simply a process of building a progressive reward system into training that imitates modern video games. In many innovation-building environs, delivering training on multiple platforms, such as classroom, mobile, and on-demand, can help eliminate the time crunch for busy individuals involved with innovation. Oftentimes it's about a high level of personalization, coupled with ongoing support and making the most of today's cutting-edge technologies, which gives your innovators-in-the-making the incentives and social interactions they need to actively engage.

In addition universities need to change their curriculum providing the students with better insight related to the skills of opportunity they need to survive in a competitive environment. The need for great increase in the study work programs that prepare the student for the shock of real business. University curriculum and offerings need to reduce the emphasis on upper income jobs and start preparing curriculum that will provide individuals that will fall into the midrange salary bracket. More that there are immediate short- and long-term needs for employees with math and science degrees and is not being met by the University. University curriculum and offerings need to be restructured, preparing the students for entry-level assignments.

In addition to training and development, the package needs to include:

- *Trust*. Employees must trust management before they will share ideas with management. Employees must not feel their jobs or their future prospects will be threatened should they propose a bad idea. Employees must feel they will be rewarded for sharing ideas with the company rather than have their ideas stolen by the company.

- *Sharing.* An environment that actively encourages the sharing of new ideas. Stop promoting people based only on what they know give equal consideration to what they share.
- *Good communications.* Those that ensure everyone's voice is heard, everyone can find out what is happening throughout the company and everyone can share ideas across the company. Everyone should be using the organization's knowledge management system.
- *Evaluation of ideas.* Individuals must be capable of grossly analyzing a specific idea and making a decision if the idea will be value-added.
- *An idea management structure.* One that ensures good ideas are shared with the organization, recognized, and implemented for the organization.
- *Recognition.* Likewise, it is important for companies to recognize who their creative thinkers are and to take advantage of them.

Creative thinkers can lead – or at least participate in – creative teams that review problematic issues within the organization and propose solutions. (I will look at creative teams in organizations in the future.)

### How-to Insight #4: Use Career Growth Training to Boost Your Individual Creativity Ability

In the book *Problem Solving for Results*,[7] authors Bill Roth and myself discussed the need for shaping the right attitude and perspectives for creativity to flourish in light of the need for improving creativity in problem-solving in any business operation. Ten years later, on his seminal work on the subject, "Creativity," Mihaly Csikszentmihalyi said that an

---

7 *Problem Solving for Results*, by Bill Roth, Frank Voehl and Jim Ryder, St Lucie Press, Delray Florida, 1996. Turbulence is not new to the entrepreneur in business world. In fact, the turbulence is increasing and managers are seeing teams spinning their wheels. But now there is a book that addresses these realities *Problem Solving for Results*. Management systems are in a state of crisis and operations are more complex. The old top-down operations mode no longer suffices. Today's businesses demand speed and increased accuracy, forcing everyone to re-evaluate chains of command and tear down the walls between functions. Amid the responsibilities of traditional management lies problem solving. The push is toward moving decision-making authority down the ladder to all levels. Entrepreneurs are no longer equipped to or capable of making the number and variety of necessary decisions in a vacuum.

The five steps "How-to" Steps for improving both individual and group creativity in any organization are:

1. **Presentation & Preparation** – understanding the problem or issue that peaks your curiosity and has a good chance of being improved.
2. **Incubation** – letting the initial thoughts and ideas percolate inside your mind subconsciously.
3. **Insight Idea Generation** – finally knowing that you understand the true essence of the problem and it all starts to make sense. You now have a fundamental understanding of this issue.
4. **Evaluation/Idea Validation** – consideration of the value that the idea brings compared to the cost and resources necessary to implement the solution.
5. **Elaboration of Outcome Assessment** – development of an action plan with steps, **INNOVATION SYSTEMS CYCLE.**

**FIGURE BB9.1**
The 5 "How To" stages for problem solving.

effective career-growth training process in almost any type of problem-solving or opportunity-finding situation usually consists of five steps or stages. See Figure BB9.1.

## INNOVATION SYSTEMS CYCLE

The Innovation Systems Cycle (ISC) consists of three phases with 12-process groupings as shown in Figure BB9.2.

We've focused on these five steps and their associated tools, which are covered in our *Innovation Tools Handbooks and the Global Innovation Science Handbook (GISH),* to provide a clear and practical way for you to think about individual innovation and creativity, and to use these methods every day in your life. Over the years, we have seen as many as 20-steps involving a process for creativity often used with lesser impact and success than the five steps outlined above. We like the idea of five steps because – in the areas of creativity and directed problem-solving rules and steps – less is more.[8]

---

8 Drucker says:

> Effective innovations start small, not grandiose. They try to do one specific thing. It may be to enable a moving vehicle to draw electric power while it runs along rails – the innovation

The Innovation Systems Cycle

Phase I. Creation

- Process Grouping 1. Opportunity Identification
- Process Grouping 2. Opportunity Development
- Process Grouping 3. Value Proposition
- Process Grouping 4. Concept Validation

Phase II. Preparation and Production

- Process Grouping 5. Business Case Analysis
- Process Grouping 6. Resource Management
- Process Grouping 7. Documentation
- Process Grouping 8. Production

Phase III. Delivery

- Process Grouping 9. Marketing, Sales, and Delivery
- Process Grouping 10. After-Sales Services
- Process Grouping 11. Performance Analysis
- Process Grouping 12. Transformation

**FIGURE BB9.2**
Three phases of ISC.

**How-to Insight #5: Rewrite All Job Descriptions Including Management – And Incorporate the Psychological Foundations For Making Personal Innovation a Requirement**

Every job description should have a portion of it set aside that defines the assignment expectations related to innovation and what percentage of the total grading that it influences.

Understanding the psychological foundations for making personal innovation real can be divided into four meta-categories:

---

that made possible the electric streetcar. Or it may be as elementary as putting the same number of matches into a matchbox (it used to be fifty), which made possible the automatic filling of matchboxes and gave the Swedish originators of the idea a world monopoly on matches for almost half a century..

**Peter F. Drucker, Innovation and Entrepreneurship**

- Those used to improve the creativity and enhance the problem identification skills of the individual
- General techniques used to improve the creativity of groups
- Systems-oriented techniques used to work with problem networks or "messes" as systems scientists call them
- Tools used to specifically measure an organization's productivity and innovation creativity IQ

Understanding *the psychological foundations of individual and team innovative engineering design* has taken on new urgency. A National Science Foundation-commissioned report from the National Academy of Engineering warned:

> Leadership in innovation is essential to U.S. prosperity and security. In a global, knowledge-driven economy, technological innovation, the transformation of new knowledge into products, processes, and services, is critical to competitiveness, long-term productivity growth, and the generation of wealth. U.S. leadership in technological innovation seems certain to be seriously eroded unless current trends are reversed.[9]

Many individuals feel that patents is a good indicator of a country's innovation capabilities. In 2014, China applied for over 929,000 patents. United States in 2014 applied for less than 579,000 patents. (See Figure BB9.3.) In other words, China filed for more than 60 percent more patents than the United States and, since 2014, all indications are that this significant negative difference has continued to get worse. What the data does not show is how many of the patent are the result of basic research versus applied research. China has set an objective to be the

| | | |
|---|---|---|
| China | 928,177 |
| United States | 578,802 |
| Japan | 325,989 |
| South Korea | 210,292 |

**FIGURE BB9.3**
Patents filed by country in 2014.

9 Assessing the Capacity of the U.S. Engineering Research Enterprise. [www.nae.edu/nae/engeco com.nsf/weblinks/MKEZ-68HQMA?OpenDocument].

leading country in artificial intelligence taking the lead away from Silicon Valley.

A second NSF-commissioned study by the American Society of Engineering Education concurs, "U.S. engineers lead the world in innovation," but "this great national resource is at serious risk because America has an engineering deficit."[10] It is difficult to overemphasize the economic importance of innovative design.[11]

Furthermore, individuals high on openness to experience as well as lacking conscientiousness and agreeableness have been found to have a higher propensity to innovate in their job role, as shown in Figure BB9.4.

**How-to Innovation Insight #6: Developing Individual Performance Plans and Performance Evaluation (Appraisal)**

Sixty-five percent of total revenues for technology-based companies have come from "performance-planning products" that are less than five years old.[12] Cross-national studies show a high correlation between patents per million and a nation's standard of living.[13] The Design Council (U.K.) found that companies known for innovative design outperformed the average Financial Times Stock Exchange Index by 200 percent from 1994 to 2003.[14]

According to a 10-year research study, the results clearly showed that the top 25 companies with performance-based product development most often cited by papers as well as other patents far outperformed the Standard & Poor's 500 from 1999 to 2013.[15] These findings are compounded by the

---

10  Engineering in the K-12 Classroom. An Analysis of Current Practices & Guidelines for the Future [www.engineeringk12.org/educators/taking_a_closer_look/documents/Engineering_in_the_K-12_Classroom.pdf].

11  Within that scope, the so-called "big five" or the "Five-Factor Model" (see Figure BB9.1) of human personality plays an important role. In terms of individual personality types found in the applied research to be likely to be more innovative, the profile is not particularly surprising. Individuals with distinct self-confidence, tolerance of ambiguity, unconventionality, and independence were shown to be more likely to be innovative than individuals showing these attributes to a moderate extent.

12  Fagerberg, J., Mowery, D., & Nelson, R. (2004). *The Oxford Handbook of Innovation.* Oxford: Oxford University Press.

13  Shavinina, L. V. ed. (2003). *The International Handbook of Innovation.* Elsevier Science.

14  Ozgur, E. (2004). *Effective Inquiry for Innovative Engineering.* Academic Press.

15  Ulrich, K. T., & Eppinger, S. D. (2004–2014). *Product Design and Development* (3rd ed.). New York: McGraw-Hill.

1. Fact #1: In 1963, the United States filed more than 81 percent of the world's patents. Since that time, other countries – particularly Japan, China, South Korea, and India – have made substantial gains, filing more than 52 percent of world patents in 2001. Also, Asia is forecast to have nearly 80–90 percent of all practicing engineers by 2020.[16]
2. Fact #2: The United States will graduate 60,000 engineers in 2019, while China is forecast to graduate nearly 500,000 engineers.[17] (China's own estimates are 800,000.)
3. Fact #3: U.S. college graduation rates increased by 26 percent from 1985 to 2015, while graduation rates for engineers decreased by 23 percent during the same period.
4. Fact #4: In some countries, 10–20 percent of the engineering curriculum is devoted to design. By contrast, in most U.S. engineering schools, design makes up only 5–10 percent of the curriculum and innovative design even less than 5 percent.

**FIGURE BB9.4**
Personal traits' impact on innovation.

fact that an increased global competition is clearly threatening the U.S. 0economy and undercutting its competitive advantage, as indicated by the following facts:

In keeping with the job description, each person should have innovation and a portion of their total performance assessment. We recommend that this be a agreed-to target that both the manager and employee can agree to. Managers should have targets related to their total department innovation often measured related to inputs into the organizations knowledge management system.

> **How-to Insight #7: Use Helpful Suggestion Systems to Highlight Individual-level Antecedent Factors: Individual and Job Characteristics[18]**

---

16 National Research Council. (1991–2011). *Improving Engineering Design: Competitive Advantage.* Washington, DC: National Academy Press.
17 Bilén, S. G., Devon, R., & Okudan, G. E. (2002). Forecast of core methods in teaching global product development. ICEE 2002, Manchester, 22 August.
18 JSTOR. According to the Amsterdam University Press, Chapter Title: *Innovation and creativity in organisations: individual and work team research findings and implications for government policy,* Chapter Author(s): Neil R. Anderson and Rosina M. Gasteiger Book Title: *Micro-foundations for Innovation Policy* Book Editor(s): B. Nooteboom, E. Stam Published by: Amsterdam University Press. (2008) Stable URL: www.jstor.org/stable/j.ctt46mwvr.14. We are indebted to JSTOR, a not-for-profit service that helps scholars, researchers, and students discover, use, and build upon a wide range of content in a trusted digital archive. JSTOR uses information technology and tools to increase productivity and facilitate new forms of scholarship. For more information about JSTOR, please contact support@jstor.org. Our use of the JSTOR archive indicates our acceptance of the Terms & Conditions of Use, available at https://about.jstor.org/terms

The term "employee suggestion systems" refers to a variety of efforts businesses make to solicit and utilize input from their employees in hopes of achieving cost savings or improving product quality, workplace efficiency, customer service, or working conditions. These efforts range from simply placing suggestion boxes in common areas to implementing formal programs with committees to review ideas and rewards for those that are adopted. The ideas generated can range from simple quality of work life improvements, like putting a refrigerator in the coffee room, to larger streamlining issues that can save the company thousands of dollars per year, like switching all salespeople's cellular phones from individual contracts to a group contract with a discount vendor.[19]

According to the Amsterdam University Press, four key factors have been found to be predictive of work role innovation at the individual suggestion-system level-of-analysis: – Personality; – Motivation; – Cognitive ability; – Mood states.

In addition, job characteristics, for example the autonomy in ones work role, have been shown to be important predictors for individual innovation at the workplace. In early studies on creativity and innovation, scholars thought that certain personality characteristics constitute an individual's potential to be creative and to innovate (Barron and Harrington 1981). Correspondingly, it was attempted to find measures to identify a "creative personality." Contemporary studies analyze the relationship between personality and innovation in more detail.

As part of the bronze Metal Innovation Certification activities, a self-evaluation using a Herman Brain Dominance Instrument is used to measure the degree and potential of an individual that is studying to complete the Bronze metal certification level. The following is a typical output from 1 of these self-assessments. (See Figure BB9.5.) A one on one session is then held with a trained specialists to discuss long-term goals and activities that can help to improve creativity.

---

19 "Suggestion programs create a win-win situation," Kate Walter wrote in *HR Magazine*. "More involvement and input for employees and improved efficiency and cost-savings for employers."

"Companies that set up effective suggestion systems are finding that employees have great ideas that can lower costs, increase revenues, improve efficiency, or innovate for greater quality," said Charles Martin, author of *Employee Suggestion Systems: Boosting Productivity and Profits*. "Employees work both individually and together as a team, and often submit ideas both individually and as a team. And they begin to think more like managers, looking beyond the scope of their own jobs."

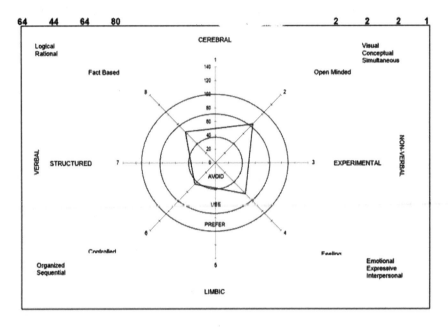

**FIGURE BB9.5**
One on one session.

## How-to Insight #8: Integrate New Employee Training and Career-Building = Link Resources to Personal Motivation

Learning and technology walk hand in hand. As high-tech innovations accelerate, so does the opportunity to create better corporate training programs and delivery methods. As the president and CEO of one of the largest learning and development providers in the United States, innovators have learned that organizations need personalized on-boarding and training that incorporates cutting-edge technology, supports professional development, and encourages employee engagement. In many books about innovation, you'll find a number of interesting observations covering how to increase personal productivity in organizations, such as building new offices, adding a coffee bar, rearranging the furniture, moving the water cooler, or holding creative retreats.

While many of these ideas will perhaps help to improve personal creativity, the fact is that many companies that are doing the most innovative things have not changed a thing in their operating environments, such as furniture, color schemes, or cubicles. In fact, much of the innovation actually happening in the world isn't happening in Silicon Valley. This innovation is happening in the consumer-packaged goods (CPG), oil and gas, and automobile manufacturing, just to name a few.

So how these companies get innovation of new employees? The answer is actually surprisingly simple. They allow employees to be unique. Organizations that force strict compliance with rules, change of command, and rigidity in everything they do, find that employees act the same way.

> Entrepreneurs, by definition, shift resources from areas of low productivity and yield to areas of higher productivity and yield. Of course, there is a risk they may not succeed. But if they are even moderately successful, the returns should be more than adequate to offset whatever risk there might be.
>
> **Peter F. Drucker**, *Innovation and Entrepreneurship*

If you've ever coached children sports, you know what this means. Simply telling your kids to play better does not make the site better. Instead, you practice and keep them to play better and when the time comes for games, you encourage them and get excited about what it is that they're doing. Creativity and employees are similar in that you need to give them the tools, teach the most tools, and allow them to be creative. In a recent survey done by the IAOIP, of executives from around the world, we found that one of the most underserved areas of innovation is creativity.

But face it, all humans are becoming creative. This creativity is what makes us humans different than other animals in the world. This is how we are different when compared to the remainder of the animal kingdom. This ability to creatively solve problems is a natural tendency and part of human nature.

Unfortunately, however, creativity and innovation are often used as interchangeable terms or are meshed together as one concept; the difference between the two is an important one that actually helps us to understand each more fully. One way to understand the subtle difference is to think about creativity as a precursor to innovation. Creativity can happen without innovation but innovation seldom happens without creativity. Think about all the wonderful and creative ideas you have in your lifetime but have never turned into a product.

Now consider all of the innovations that you have come up with in your lifetime, and you would probably be hard-pressed to take creativity out of that equation. You might imagine creativity as a relatively random event. Innovation is the ability to organize these creative thoughts into new ideas, products, processes, and services for the real world. So, if you have a creative workforce that lacks the processes and systems to translate that creativity into innovation, all you have is a creative workforce.

## How-to Insight #9: Build a Bond with Your Manager[20]

Building a bond with your manager works both ways: Managers must also show enthusiasm and commitment toward the program if it is to generate the desired results. A small business owner might begin by sharing his or her vision for the company with employees to start the bonding process. Employees who understand the company's overall mission are more likely to submit valuable ideas that will help build a better bond and help the company achieve its goals. The next step might be to make sure line managers support the suggestion system and do not feel threatened by it. It is also important for managers to raise the topic frequently in meetings and incorporate the positive results of employee suggestions into periodic progress reports. Managers should also be encouraged to submit suggestions themselves, although they should not generally be rewarded for ideas that fall under their normal strategic planning responsibilities.

Some researchers have proposed that practices facilitating learning and knowledge transfer are particularly important to innovation. Some of the practices that researchers have studied include how organizations collaborate with other organizations, how organizations promote learning, and how an organization's culture facilitates knowledge transfer and learning. And while some have proposed the importance of combining practices,

---

20 Individual innovation programs tend to be more successful when employees are encouraged to make reasonable suggestions within the parameters of their own work experience. "The real goal is to generate as many ideas as possible, and, over time, to improve the quality of the suggestions through feedback and encouragement," Bell noted. It is important to develop a clear policy statement that covers all aspects of the suggestion program and make sure that both managers and employees understand it. If employees view the process as open and above-board, it will help eliminate any suspicion about how ideas are reviewed and rewarded.

there has been a distinct lack of empirical studies that have explored how these practices work together to facilitate learning and knowledge transfer that leads to the simultaneous achievement of incremental and radical innovation, what we refer to as innovation ambidexterity (IA). Yet, a firm's ability to combine these practices into a learning capability is an important means of enabling them to foster innovation ambidexterity.[21]

## How-to Insight #10: Reinforcing Desired Individual Behaviors

The results of this study make four important contributions. First, they demonstrate that the combination of these practices has a greater impact on innovation ambidexterity than any one practice individually or when only two practices are combined. Second, the results demonstrate a relationship between innovation ambidexterity and business performance in the form of revenues, profits, and productivity growth relative to competitors. Third, the results suggest that innovation ambidexterity plays a mediating role between learning capability and business performance. That is, learning capability has an indirect impact on business performance by facilitating innovation ambidexterity that in turn fosters business performance.

Therefore, creativity requires an unrestrained openness of originality that is not always in sync with the organization. When the organization can recognize creativity and see the connections between creative people, ideas, in the problems of the organization, then it becomes inspirational, useful, and enjoyable.[22]

---

21  Managing the Exploitation/Exploration Paradox: The Role of a Learning Capability and Innovation Ambidexterity, Hsing-Er Lin, Edward F. McDonough III, Shu-Jou Lin, Carol Yeh-Yun Lin. First published: 25 October 2012, **https://doi.org/10.1111/j.1540-5885.2012.00998.x**. In this study, learning capability is defined as the combination of practices that promote bonding via intraorganizational learning among employees, partnerships with other organizations that enable the spread of learning, and an open culture within the organization that promotes and maintains sharing of knowledge among all levels with bosses.

22  If you believe the premise that creativity is separate from innovation, and you take personal creativity as a stand-alone topic, then you can begin to sort out creativity from the process of innovating. Creativity is another of those topics where there is much agreement but subtle differences in that agreement. The fact is that there is no universal way to define creativity that makes sense for all of us trying to understand it in the context of our own lives. A standard definition the creativity might look something like this, "creativity is the ability to create original ideas, connections, alternatives, or possibilities for effective in solving problems, communicating with others, and inspiring new and useful ideas and others."

## How-to Insight #11: Use Cross Discipline Training to Achieve High Levels of Personal Productivity

Understanding personal productivity requires us to recognize that creativity as a process requires that the organization recognize and harness it in a way that changes business. In the work of Arin Reeves, she describes research that she has done with dozens of individuals in a multitude of industries and professions. Specifically, she asked the questions of how to generate original effective ideas. She states that this requires:

1. Diverse inputs/inclusive thinking
2. Context articulation
3. Divergent thinking
4. Convert and thinking

## How-to Insight #12: Turning Employee Complaints into Profit

The complaint is a signal that should not be ignored. When customers complain, they are giving your company a golden chance to fix what is wrong and improve your business. Why? Employees as well as customers act in their own self-interest, and they are in a unique position to tell your company the unvarnished truth – something your employees historically were unlikely to do because it might have reflected negatively on their performance or they may fear that you might "kill the messenger" rather than listen to the message. Just about every comprehensive study done on this subject points to greater success for companies that turn the negatives represented by complaints into positives.[23]

---

23 *John Goodman* did pioneering research on complaints through *TARP*, the company he founded in 1971. He showed that, while customer service is typically a cost center in most companies, it could be turned into a powerful marketing machine to drive sales, repeat business, and greater profits. His research showed that roughly 4 percent of customers (1 out of 26) that were "wronged" by a company complain. The other 96 percent (25 out of 26, or the silent majority) stop buying and tell 9 to 10 others within a week about their poor treatment. This means that a negative word of mouth pyramid averaging 250 is created. If the company is able to satisfactorily solve the problems of the 4 percent that complain (turn the negative into a positive), they will tell 6 to 7 others within a week that the company solved their problem and this will result in a positive word of mouth pyramid of 250 customers that say good things about the company.

**Insight #13: Getting Ideas Flowing**
**Insight #14: Empowering the Individual Closest to the Customer**

Great innovation brands start with great service cultures. And while great service cultures may start at the top management level, they focus on the front: they explicitly give customer-facing employees the power to go out of their way to delight customers. A huge part of this is giving them the right training without overkill, as previously described. Make sure that they know how to properly respond to customer issues without reading off a script. Instead of massive rule books showing what agents can't do, have a few principles that focus on the goal: happy customers who tell others about their service experience. Then let your agents do what they need to do to make that happen.

This means letting your rmployees know what's possible, and proving it. Many of those *exceptional customer service stories* we've heard about started with an employee who pushed the limits of the norm. Encourage your service agents to think and go above and beyond, and support them along the way. This is a major change from the "idiot-proof," productivity-at-all-costs service approaches that many times we've all been victimized and turned off by. And the impact on innovation can be enormous.

While conventional thinking on innovation is far from settled, there are certain stereotypes that typify a creative thinker. Examples include your behavioral differences, cultural differences, differences in education and intelligence, and natural ability to be creative. While we may imagine an artist as a naturally creative person drawn to a certain field, there are many artists such as those they create animation for movies, which may be doing it for the money. As an example, we know of several individuals working in film who are more attracted to the computer programming in the visual arts. If one were to view their work, they would think the opposite, that they were creative types who are forced to program. And while tempting to stereotype different groups of people such as Asians and Indians in the math and sciences, there are no shortages of "creative" in this space.

**How-to Insight #15: Self-managed Employees via Self-organization**

The model suggests that individuals with strong self-leadership will consider themselves to have more innovation and creativity potential than individuals who have weak self-leadership, and that individuals who have innovation and creativity potential will be more likely to practice innovation and creativity when they perceive strong support from the workplace than individuals who perceive weak support from the workplace.[24]

As Langdon Morris points out in his seminal work Agile Innovation:[25]

A new movement is emerging.

Product and technology development teams all over the world are now quietly engaged in a highly effective revolution that is changing business forever.

They are self-organizing to adapt to the accelerating rate of change and the complexities of the global digital age. Industry after industry, from Internet software, to aviation, to digital health care, to mobile telephony, is using a process called Agile to turn out better results in less time.

Agile is fundamentally changing the way that business works.

Soon Agile will move beyond the technology world because the insights it reveals are applicable across the entire organization.

When this happens, argues Morris, a new *revolution* will occur, one that will affect every industry, not just the software industry. It involves a paradigm shift that was envisioned by Thomas Kuhn 60 years ago in his work *The Structure of Scientific Revolutions.*[26]

24 *Maximizing organizational leadership capacity for the future: Toward a model of self-leadership, innovation and creativity,* Trudy C. DiLiello (Defense Acquisition University, Port Hueneme, California, USA), Jeffery D. Houghton (Department of Management, Abilene Christian University, Abilene, Texas, USA). The purpose of this paper is to develop and present a model of self-leadership, innovation and creativity. Drawing upon existing theoretical and empirical evidence, the paper develops and presents a conceptual model of the relationships between self-leadership, innovation, creativity, and organizational support. The paper also presents research propositions based upon the relationships suggested by the model.

25 See Agile Innovation references and book profile at end of this chapter.

26 Kuhn challenged the then prevailing view of progress in "normal science." Normal scientific progress was viewed as "development-by-accumulation" of accepted facts and theories. Kuhn argued for an episodic model in which periods of such conceptual continuity in normal science were interrupted by periods of revolutionary science. The discovery of "anomalies" during revolutions in science leads to new paradigms. These new paradigms then ask new questions of

**How-to Insight #16: Learn How to Recognize Improvement Opportunities**

Using the Innovation Lens Mindset, improvement opportunities abound, with the world being one big hammer, and innovation improvements being the stick of dynamite. The first edition of *The Structure of Scientific Revolutions* ended with a chapter titled "Progress through Revolutions," in which Thomas Kuhn spelled out his views on the nature of scientific progress and how to recognize improvement opportunities. Since he considered problem-solving to be a central element of science, Kuhn foresaw that for a new improvement paradigm to be accepted by a scientific community, "First, the new (improvement) candidate must seem to resolve some outstanding and generally recognized problem that can be met in no other way. Second, the new improvement paradigm must promise to preserve a relatively large part of the concrete problem solving activity that has accrued to science through its predecessors."[27]

**How-to Insight #17: Learn How to Evaluate the Value of Your Ideas**

Learning how to evaluate the "value" of your ideas is the secret-sauce of innovation, and often challenges can build individual character and with organizations, it can bond teams, which enhances innovation and builds operational efficiencies. Many organizations have lots of ideas but

---

old data, move beyond the mere "puzzle-solving" of the previous paradigm, change the rules of the game, and the map directing new research leading to self-managing teams, among other breakthroughs.

27 In the second edition, Kuhn added a postscript in which he elaborated his ideas on the nature of scientific progress. He described a thought experiment involving an observer who has the opportunity to inspect an assortment of theories, each corresponding to a single stage in a succession of theories. What if the observer is presented with these theories without any explicit indication of their chronological order? Kuhn anticipates that it will be possible to reconstruct their chronology on the basis of the theories' scope and content, because the more recent a theory is, the better it will be as an instrument for solving the kinds of puzzle that scientists aim to solve. Kuhn, T. S. (1970). *The Structure of Scientific Revolutions* (2nd ed.). Chicago, IL: Chicago University Press. p. 206. Discussed further in Weinberger, D. (2012). Shift Happens. *Chronicle of Higher Education* April 22, 3023

there is a lot of innovation wastage due to poor management of innovation at the corporate level, especially in the selection, implementation, and deployment phases. Achieving the innovation goals of high value creation (i.e., both in terms of returns on investments and competitive differentiations) in the face of uncertainty and associated risks requires using adequate innovation management system with appropriate measurement practices to guide the company along its innovation journey. These issues are so important that the International Standards Organization decided to develop a complete set of innovation management standards.

You cannot manage something unless you measure it is a summary of what Lord Kelvin said in 1883

> I often say that when you can measure what you are speaking about, and express it in numbers, you know something about it; but when you cannot measure it, when you cannot express it in numbers, your knowledge is of a meagre and unsatisfactory kind ...

For individual innovation, as for most activities, success is predicated on proper management and progress measurements to enable better decisions to be made on progress achieved, what to change, and how to do better.

### How-to Insight #18: Perform Area Activity Analysis

As Innovation Expert H. James Harrington wrote about in his 1998 book *Area Activity Analysis*,[28] you need to align your workforce – to get maximum value from each employee! Are your organization's management and employees in complete harmony, not only about how each activity's quality and productivity are measured, but also about what is considered acceptable performance? Area Activity Analysis provides a methodology to align your organization's mission, activities, and measurements systems so that each work team understands the critical nature of their output, along with each individual customer's (and management's) expectations. This comprehensive approach communications package shows you how to develop signed, documented partnership agreements with your Natural Work Teams' customers, suppliers, and upper management that: define

---

28 See Area Activity Analysis Profile at end of this chapter.

each area's purpose and activities; develop quality and productivity measurements for each activity; develop a performance standard for each measurement; gain commitment to the performance standard by employees and management; identify where improvement opportunities exist; and gain supplier commitment. Uncover and correct your organizational chain's weakest links! Area Activity Analysis is the essential approach for ensuring that each employee understands his or her area's overall mission, and which strategies will best measure and improve the employee's performance in every activity. For details, see www.amazon.com/Area-Activity-Analysis-H-Harrington/dp/0071347038.

## How-to #19: How-to Excel in Selling Your Ideas

Chances are you are required, on a regular basis, to sell ideas. Time and again in my work as an innovation coach, I see that the ability to build the buy-in for our ideas is a key determinant of success, both internally and externally. How can you improve your skills in this vital arena? Here are six suggestions:[29]

1. **Individual innovators need to realize that selling ideas is job #1.** Far from being an after-thought, once the idea is ready for launch (or thrown over the wall to the marketing and sales team to handle) successful innovators know that selling is a constant need and never-ending requirement.
2. **Focus on benefits, not features.** Will the new product or service that you have come up with save the customer time, improve his or her social standing, and solve a problem better than existing solutions? Every effective sales professional knows the importance of how to concentrate on such benefits. Prospective buyers don't care how your product works, how many switches it has, etc., or anything else about its features, until they buy the benefits.
3. **Emphasize the role of persuasion.** Innovators need to constantly emphasize the need to "win friends and influence people" internally and externally to the organization and its units. You need to work on communication skills and develop energizing, creative,

---

29 Source: www.innovationexcellence.com/blog/2011/09/27/selling-your-innovation-ideas/

briefings, descriptions, boardroom reports, etc. Also, focus on crafting messages so that people pay attention, and learn to make everyone on the team an idea evangelist.

4. **Test out ideas on skeptical individual first.** Your friends are likely to give you the positive feedback you want to hear. But before you really decide to commit all out to an idea, try it out on your toughest critic. Humbly invite them to tear it apart, find the weaknesses. Then, see how you feel. If you're still convinced you've got something, go for it. If not, you probably don't have the fire in the belly to see it through to fruition.

5. **Speak the language of the people you are selling to.** Effective idea evangelists find out as much as they can about the thinking styles of those they are pitching. Are they analytical, quantitative? Then provide numbers. Emotionally-driven? Come with anecdotes that convey your message. If "big picture" oriented, don't bore them with details.

6. **Help others to really visualize your idea**. Embrace the old adage: a picture is worth a thousand words. And the more others can feel, taste, touch, and, most of all, see your idea represented, the greater your chances of getting a green light. People don't like to admit that they don't understand, or that you've confused them. But as every champion knows, people don't buy what they don't understand.[30]

The experts claim that we are now a country of skeptics because many people had lost their life savings. Several trillion dollars languished in money market accounts for the last 20 years, and now many people are naturally afraid of the stock market. Emotions about losing are much stronger than feeling good about investments increasing in value. Regretfully, they missed out in billions of positive stock market returns from 2009 to 2019. Like it or not, it might appear people feel the financial profession failed them twice, while Wall Street walks away with

---

30 There is an outstanding book on the subject of selling your ideas: *The Language of Trust: Selling Ideas in a World of Skeptics*. It provides valuable insight into winning over the minds of those in America's "Post-Trust Era." Using relevant and modern case studies and experiences from his own life, author Michael Maslansky debunks many myths associated with how to properly advertise, and subsequently sell, ideas, products, and even yourself. By contrasting practices that have worked in the past with those that are more effective in today's skeptical society, you can sell your ideas to the clients you serve and innovate with.

billions in government bailouts and the bonuses still awarded. People are not stupid, they are angry.

The solution: financial information must use language that people understand in the form of a story. From our research with many focus groups, the participants made it clear there are words that build trust and words that no longer work.

- Positive not risk. Risk is negative.
- Maximizing gains not minimizing losses. Loss is an offensive word, for good reason – 2008!
- Voluntary not default or auto-enrollment. People want to feel like they are in control.
- Costs and charges are preferred over fees. People do not like the word fees. They feel that they pay more fees everywhere they go, national parks, toll roads, etc.
- Financial security not financial freedom. Freedom is too vague.
- A portion of is superior to all or nothing. People want choices and control.
- Straightforward not transparent or clear. Transparent and clear might be too vague.

One of the most important messages of the innovation movement: The process of creating and selling products, services, and ideas has moved in a totally different direction, from the one-sided approach of the salesperson to one of being the customer's advocate and educational resource of the trusted communicator.

## How-to #20: Creating an Individual Empowerment for Innovation

The challenge with innovation is finding products and services that are easier to use, easier to maintain, and more appealing to customers. Where can you draw the creativity and drive to make this happen? Often the best source for innovation is the team within your business. A great leader can turn them into entrepreneurs who are hungrily looking for new opportunities. The key is empowerment. By empowering people you enable them to achieve goals through their own ideas and efforts. The leader sets the destination, but the team chooses the route. People need clear objectives so that they know what is expected of them.

They need to develop the skills for the task. They need to work in cross-departmental teams so that they can create and implement solutions that will work. They need freedom to succeed. And when you give someone freedom to succeed you also give them freedom to fail. Above all, empowerment means trusting people. It is by giving them trust, support, and believing in them to make relevant decisions related to their work.

In fact, it may be that certain people are trained to restrain their creative tendencies because of their job title, training, or background. For example, you may prefer to have your barista or bartender be creative than your CPA. Does this mean that people who are accountants are not creative? Before you answer that question, consider the fact that one of the authors of this book was a CPA in his first career. As an aside, the reason he left accounting was that of the rules and structures which did not easily allow for creativity. On the other hand, a tax accountant, especially for a large corporation, is probably encouraged to explore creativity within the law.

## A VIEW TO THE FUTURE

To summarize, it is of course possible that the nature of research may change, both in the directions of studying the process and the way innovation takes place. In the next five years, there will be an increase in studying the way innovative design takes place. However, first and foremost, we may have to learn how to work together in an effective interdisciplinary manner.

- Creation of interdisciplinary centers to study innovation/creativity; open solicitations in the science of innovation/creativity, graduate training grants (e.g., in engineering design), interdisciplinary conferences.
- Separate interdisciplinary panels should be created, rather than attempting to review or co-review this kind of interdisciplinary work within the traditional disciplinary panels.
- An increase in our ability to collaborate effectively and investigate the key issues. Funding and publication opportunities will be very important for growth, so within the next five years, the rewards for this type of interdisciplinary approach must continue to grow.

- In 10 years, there perhaps will be some significant impact on education, the economy, and the actual design processes.
- There may be some national centers for innovation research.
- In 20 years by 2035 or so, there will be new perspectives on how we can more effectively study creativity and innovation using a solid scientific and multidisciplinary approach.
- At that point, there will be a sophisticated community of scholars and practitioners communicating with one another regularly about this research.

Today is the starting point for this journey and the pathways are sure to be filled with excitement, along with some dead ends, and perhaps many unpredictable breakthroughs.

Overall, the approach for collaboration is to focus on design thinking as the common context to more clearly highlight the actual phases of the creative process. It is clear that at this time a multidisciplinary approach is expected to make significant progress because design thinking involves issues of motivation, problem formulation, evaluation, and phenomenology. Moreover, psychologists tend to focus on the process of working toward a given end state or goal while engineers tend to focus more on the outcome – the creation of end states.

There are rich areas of collaboration among the three disciplines as pairs or as a whole. Between engineering and cognition research areas include: effective strategies for goal-directed search, the importance of representations and how they change over time, cognitive mechanisms of creativity (including impasses and fixation), understanding analogy, understanding and development of methods and tools to enhance creativity, and ontologies (e.g., for functional reasoning) to enable better communication and simulation. (See Figure BB9.6.)

Shah and Smith propose a basic model,[31] shown in Figure BB9.7.

In the above model, the goal is to combine the strength of the disciplines in laboratory experiments versus design engineering experiments. Fundamental innovation components and interactions are hypothesized, or observed, and tested within the separate disciplinary approaches, and are then correlated to form working models.

31 Shah, J., Smith, S., Vargas, N., Gerkens, D., & Muqi, W. (2003). Empricial studies of design ideation: Alignment of design experiments with lab experiments. ASME Design Theory & Methods Conference.

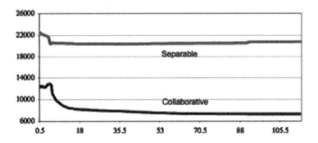

**FIGURE BB9.6**

Collaboration between engineering and social science research. Some areas include studies of engineering teams, ways to build design teams that work more effectively, the creation of new ethnographic techniques, and the impact of disciplinary cultures on creative design.

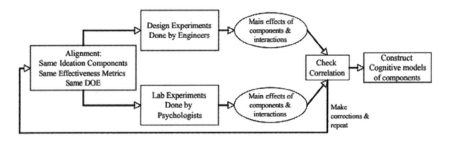

**FIGURE BB9.7**

Design experiments vs. lab experiments.

Initial results of this model are promising yet challenging. Great potential exists to identify the fundamental components and interactions, where the alignment and collaborative spirit of the disciplines are the catalysts. Historically, the study of groups has been the domain of social rather than cognitive psychologists. Recently, progress has been made to show that many of the basic theoretical pieces of individual cognition can be applied to complex group setting.[32] But there remains emergent processes by which the group is more than just the sum of the parts, and these emergent processes involve a rich interplay of cognitive and social/motivational factors.

---

32 Hutchins, E. (1995). *Cognition in the Wild*. Cambridge, MA: MIT Press.

## SUMMARY

*"The entrepreneur always searches for change, responds to it, and exploits it as an opportunity,"* Drucker wrote. *"Efficiency is doing things right, and effectiveness is doing the right things."* What's true for individual managers is also true for organizations, which often squander time and resources trying to improve processes for products not worth producing. The solution? It was Drucker who first suggested that choosing what not to do was a decision as strategic as its opposite. Drucker's theory of *"purposeful abandonment"* exhorted business leaders to quickly sever projects, policies, and processes that had outlived their usefulness.

> The first step in a growth policy is not to decide where and how to grow, *it is to decide what to abandon. In order to grow, a business must* have a systematic policy to get rid of the outgrown, the obsolete, the unproductive.[33]

---

33 The Wisdom of Peter Drucker from A to Z. Known widely as the father of management, Peter Drucker formulated many concepts about business that we now take for granted. In honor of the 100th anniversary of his birth, we take a look at Drucker's contributions, from A to Z. By Leigh Buchanan, Editor-at-large, Inc. magazine. Source: www.inc.com/articles/2009/11/drucker.html.

# BB10

## Innovative Supply Chain Management

*Doug Nelson*

## CONTENTS

## INTRODUCTION

The primary goal of Innovative Supply Chain Management is value creation by providing products and services to customers through optimally managed processes, resources, and capabilities. Innovative Supply Chain Management is a cradle-to-grave process that is involved from the earliest recognition of customer need through end-of-life and final disposal or retirement of products and services.

APICS, formerly founded as American Production and Inventory Control Society (APICS) defines Supply Chain Management as "the design, planning, execution, control, and monitoring of supply-chain activities with the objective of creating net value, building a competitive infrastructure, leveraging worldwide logistics, synchronizing supply with demand and measuring performance globally."

There are five basic steps that provide an analytical and objective structure to formulate a strategic linkage between the supply chain and marketing. These are:

1. Define organizational objectives.
2. Determine marketing strategies to meet these objectives.
3. Assess how different products qualify in their respective markets and win orders against competitors.

4. Establish the appropriate process to manufacture or outsource production of these products.
5. Provide the infrastructure to support the manufacturing or sourcing of these products and related supply chain infrastructure.

Collaboration is at the heart of Supply Chain Management. The Supply Chain Management process should look at the needs of the entire enterprise and processes should be designed accordingly. While the Supply Chain Manager may not own the individual process, it is important to understand and participate in decision making at all levels from the inception of the product to its final discontinuance, retirement, disposal, and recycling. This will mean establishing a close working relationship with other departments. An important example is Sales and Marketing, which controls customer facing processes such as Customer Relationship Management and Demand Forecasting.

## CUSTOMER RELATIONSHIP MANAGEMENT PROCESS

Customer-relationship management (CRM) is used to manage a company's interactions with current and potential customers. It uses data analysis of the customers' history with an organization to improve business relationships with customers, focusing on customer retention and driving sales growth.

Also, important is the Engineering department, which innovates and provides new product designs.

Determination of stakeholder needs, and requirements is accomplished through an engineering process. Several areas of engineering are very much involved with collaboration and directly involve the supply chain management process. Ensuring that proper feedback from throughout the organization is available to engineering can help to ensure a successful innovative product development program.

## SYSTEMS ENGINEERING

Systems engineering is an interdisciplinary approach and a means to enable the realization of successful systems. It focuses on defining customer needs and required functionality early in the development cycle, documenting requirements, and then proceeding with design synthesis and system validation while considering the complete problem: operations, cost and schedule, performance, training and support, test, manufacturing, and disposal. Systems Engineering considers both the business and the technical needs of all customers with the goal of providing a quality product that meets the user needs (INCOSE).

## COLLABORATIVE ENGINEERING

Collaborative engineering is defined by the International Journal of Collaborative Engineering as a discipline that "studies the interactive process of engineering collaboration, whereby multiple interested stakeholders resolve conflicts, bargain for individual or collective advantages, agree upon courses of action, and/or attempt to craft joint outcomes which serve their mutual interests."

## CONCURRENT ENGINEERING

Concurrent engineering (CE) is a work methodology emphasizing the parallelization of tasks (i.e., performing tasks concurrently), which is sometimes called simultaneous engineering or integrated product development (IPD) using an integrated product team approach. It refers to an approach used in product development in which functions of design engineering, manufacturing engineering, and other functions are integrated to reduce the time required to bring a new product to market.

In many organizations, functional managers are measured by their departmental efficiency rather than overall effectiveness. Consequently, Managers often make trade-offs that are suboptimal for the business as a whole. The Supply Chain Manager should collaborate with other departments to ensure that decisions are made that will optimally benefit the organization.

## SCOR MODEL

The supply chain operations reference model (SCOR) is a management tool used to address, improve, and communicate supply chain management decisions within a company and with suppliers and customers of a company. The model describes the business processes required to satisfy a customer's demands. It also helps to explain the processes along the entire supply chain and provides a basis for how to improve those processes. (See Figure BB10.1)

The SCOR model was developed by the supply chain council (www. supply-chain.org) with the assistance of 70 of the world's leading manufacturing companies. The model integrates business concepts of process re-engineering, benchmarking, and measurement into its framework. The supply chain council refers to this process as spanning from "the supplier's supplier to the customer's customer."

This framework focuses on five areas of the supply chain – plan, source, make, deliver, and return:

- **Plan** – Demand and supply planning and management are included in this first step. Elements include balancing resources with requirements and determining communication along the entire chain. The plan also includes determining business rules to improve and measure supply chain efficiency. These business rules span inventory, transportation, assets, and regulatory compliance, among others. The plan also aligns the supply chain plan with the financial plan of the company.
- **Source** – This step describes sourcing infrastructure and material acquisition. It describes how to manage inventory, the supplier

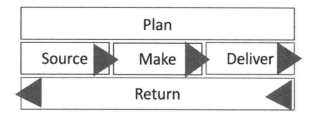

**FIGURE BB10.1**
SCOR Model

network, supplier agreements, and supplier performance. It discusses how to handle supplier payments and when to receive, verify, and transfer product.

- **Make** – Manufacturing and production are the emphasis of this step. Is the manufacturing process make-to-order, make-to-stock, or engineer-to-order? The make step includes, production activities, packaging, staging product, and releasing. It also includes managing the production network, equipment and facilities, and transportation.

- **Deliver** – Delivery includes order management, warehousing, and transportation. It also includes receiving orders from customers and invoicing them once product has been received. This step involves management of finished inventories, assets, transportation, product life cycles, and importing and exporting requirements.

- **Return** – Companies must be prepared to handle the return of containers, packaging, or defective product. The return involves the management of business rules, return inventory, assets, transportation, and regulatory requirements.

The SCOR process can go into many levels of process detail to help a company analyze its supply chain. It gives companies an idea of how advanced its supply chain is. The process helps companies understand how the five steps repeat over and over again between suppliers, the company, and customers.

## DEVELOPING AN INNOVATIVE SUPPLY CHAIN STRATEGY (OPERATIONS STRATEGY)

### Porter's Five Forces

Porter's Five Forces Framework is a tool for analyzing the competitive environment of an organization. It draws from industrial organization (IO) economics to derive five forces that determine the competitive intensity and, therefore, the attractiveness (or lack of it) of an industry in terms of its profitability. An "unattractive" industry is one in which the effect of these five forces reduces overall profitability. The most unattractive industry would be one approaching "pure competition," in which available profits for all firms are driven to normal profit levels. The five-forces perspective is associated with its originator, Michael E. Porter of Harvard University. This framework was first published in Harvard Business Review in 1979. (See Figure BB10.2)

## THREAT OF NEW ENTRANTS

Profitable industries that yield high returns will attract new firms. New entrants eventually will decrease profitability for other firms in the industry. Unless the entry of new firms can be made more difficult by incumbents, abnormal profitability will fall toward zero (perfect competition), which is the minimum level of profitability required to keep an industry in business.

## THREAT OF SUBSTITUTES

A substitute product uses a different technology to try to solve the same economic need.

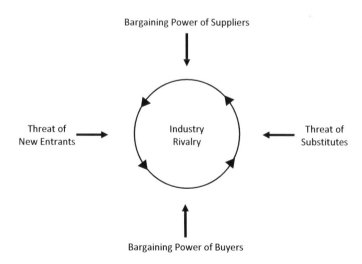

**FIGURE BB10.2**
Porter's Five Forces

## BARGAINING POWER OF CUSTOMERS

The bargaining power of customers is also described as the market of outputs: the ability of customers to put the firm under pressure, which also affects the customer's sensitivity to price changes. Firms can take measures to reduce buyer power, such as implementing a loyalty program. Buyers' power is high if buyers have many alternatives. It is low if they have few choices.

## BARGAINING POWER OF SUPPLIERS

The bargaining power of suppliers is also described as the market of inputs. Suppliers of raw materials, components, labor, and services (such as expertise) to the firm can be a source of power over the firm when there are few substitutes. If you are making biscuits and there is only one person who sells flour, you have no alternative but to buy it from them. Suppliers may refuse to work with the firm or charge excessively high prices for unique resources.

## COMPETITIVE RIVALRY

For most industries the intensity of competitive rivalry is the major determinant of the competitiveness of the industry. An understanding of industry rivals is vital to successfully market a product. Positioning pertains to how the public perceives a product and distinguishes it from competitors. A business must be aware of its competitors' marketing strategies and pricing and be reactive to any changes made.

### SIPOC Diagram – Describes Suppliers, Inputs, Processes, Outputs, and Customers Diagram

A SIPOC diagram is a tool that summarizes the inputs and outputs processes in flow chart form. The acronym SIPOC stands for suppliers, inputs, process, outputs, and customers. The SIPOC diagram is used by a

**FIGURE BB10.3**
SIPOC Diagram

team to identify all relevant elements of a supply chain process before work begins. It helps define a complex project that may not be properly scoped. A SIPOC diagram defines the inputs the process receives and the suppliers providing those inputs and the outputs that a process delivers to the customers receiving the outputs. In traditional manufacturing processes, these represent the physical flow of all inputs to the product and, finally, the completed product to the customer. (See Figure BB10.3)

# VALUE STREAM

The Value Stream encompasses all actual value-added and nonvalue-added activities and associated processes used to transform information and/or raw material into a final product/service for delivery to the customer.

# VALUE STREAM MAPPING

Value Stream Mapping is a method used to define, measure, analyze, improve, and control the flow of the product or element being transformed, which could be inventory, a medical patient, paperwork, or anything in any segment of any value chain. The Value Stream Map provides a graphical representation of the information and physical flows of the value chain for a defined set of customers, suppliers, or product family from a systematic view. The informational flows are communicated across the top of the map and flow from left to right from customer to seller and provide the signal that sets the supply chain in motion resulting in communication of demand to suppliers and production facilities. The physical flows of product are communicated along the lower portion of the map and are represented as flowing from right to left from the Supplier through manufacturing and delivery processes to the customer. Metrics such as cycle time or Overall Equipment Effectiveness may be represented. Finally, a time line that compares Value-added time and Nonvalue-added time, the combination of which represents Total Lead time is displayed across the bottom of the graphic. The maps are normally drawn as Current State reflecting "as-is" conditions and Future State with the desired improvements being shown. (See Figure BB10.4) Performance improvement programs are used to bridge the gap between the Current State and Future State.

## CURRENT STATE VALUE MAP

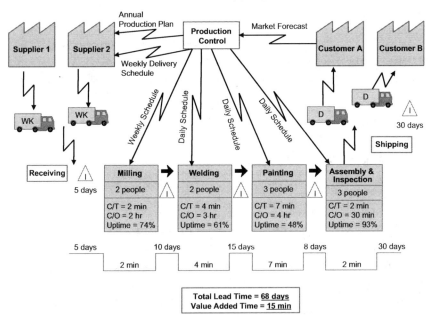

**FIGURE BB10.4**
Value Stream Map

## SUPPLIER MANAGEMENT (PURCHASING)

Procurement process – Procurement is the process of finding and agreeing to terms, and acquiring goods, services, or works from an external source, often through a tendering or competitive bidding process. Procurement is used to ensure the buyer receives goods, services, or works at the best possible price when aspects such as quality, quantity, time, and location are compared. Organizations often define processes intended to promote fair and open competition for their business while minimizing risks such as exposure to fraud and collusion.

Supplier Management and the relationship with suppliers have never been more important than it is today. This reflects the increasing importance of innovation, and the supply chain. Organizations are increasingly called upon to justify the quality of products based on how they are designed and produced, including the materials procured from suppliers to create them. The importance of a safe, cost-effective, high-quality, integral, traceable, and agile supply chain cannot be overstated.

## SUPPLIERS AND QUALITY

The quality organization provides one of the two key interfaces with suppliers. The other key interface is procurement whose primary focus is on cost and delivery date. The quality organization has the responsibility for ensuring that a supplier has added controls in place to prevent them from shipping detective parts and/or materials. As a starting point, ISO 9000 defines the basic quality system that needs to be in place in order to meet these requirements. This is only the start of a long-term relationship for items like correlation of measurement and test equipment, lot acceptance of product, changes in production activity, and supplier performance reporting.

## DR. W. EDWARD DEMING

Deming's book, "!4 Points, Out of the Crisis," includes "end the practice of awarding business on the basis of price tag alone. Instead, minimize total cost." Deming went on to discuss the differences between procurement strategies of Western and Japanese organizations. Deming thought of sourcing strategy as a strategic advantage and advantageous to any firm. Deming's arguments include:

- We can no longer leave quality, service and price to the forces of competition and price to the forces of competition and price – not in today's requirements for uniformity and reliability.
- What one company buys from another is not just material: it buys something far more important, namely engineering and capability.

Deming suggested moving toward a single supplier for any one item and not doing business and negotiating with suppliers based on the lowest price. It is worthwhile in the long term to build a good and long-standing relationship with suppliers, which enables trust and increases loyalty. An organization should be able to rely on their suppliers; they supply the parts for the production line and are the first link to a high-quality product.

While it has been more than three decades since Deming stated his 14 points, many companies are still learning the lessons of failure to incorporate these points into their strategies and culture.

## SPECIFICATIONS AND DESIGN RESPONSIBILITY

Suppliers may have valuable input to offer for design consideration. They often can provide input that would improve the design, reduce the cost of manufacture, or improve quality, such as

- The manufacturability of a design
- Establishment of nominal specification and tolerances on dimensions, features, and various performance related specification
- Use of alternate materials or manufacturing processes

A supplier might have specialized equipment, processes, and capabilities that influence the optimum design approach or requirements.

Some innovative supply chain improvement techniques include methods for reduction of number of new parts in the supply chain.

# THE EIGHT RUNAWAY BY-PRODUCTS OF ONE NEW PART

(Gwendolyn D. Galsworth), Visual Thinking, Inc.

They fall into eight broad categories:

1. **Exploding Active Parts Count**. When new products are developed, new parts get added; the question is: Is each of these new parts required and unavoidable? Even if a new part is required, it may bring an escalation in the number of service parts the company must stock.

2. **Pressurized Sourcing and Procurement Activities.** As a part number is added, sourcing and purchasing teams respond; the continuous need for new purchased or made parts exert pressure on the parts procurement function as well as on other related functions.

3. **Unwarranted Processes, Dies, Tooling, Fixtures, Equipment, and Changeover Times**. New parts often require new production processes, and new equipment, dies, fixtures, or tooling, and associated extra changeovers; these burden already-loaded shop-floor activity.

4. **Congested Floor Space, Shelving, and Storage Racks**. As with parts in general, new parts need homes, however temporary, and add clutter to floors, racks, shelving, and stores; over time, multiplying service parts, and dead stock (obsolete but not yet retired parts) further cramp already congested storage areas.

5. **Overburdened Material Handling.** If the company accepts material handling as a given, added parts tax an already burdened transportation system, as each part requires its share of handling in the form of receiving, counting, inspecting, storing, retrieving, and otherwise moving it.

6. **Ballooning IT Input and Maintenance.** Each part that enters or leaves the system must be individually logged in and maintained; pressure to keep data systems up to date can be staggering.

7. **Mushrooming Control Points.** Literally hundreds of paper, computer, and other transactions across all departments (known as control points) support each new product and its new parts – drawings, catalogs, cost estimates, supplier searches, purchase orders, faxes, invoices, receipts, tracking checklists, inspection sheets, etc.

8. **Loss of Opportunity.** The resources needed to support runaway parts proliferation are astounding. They rob the company of assets it could otherwise use to develop and grow.

## COTS

It may also be possible to make innovative improvements through the use of readily available commercially available of the shelf products.

**Commercially available off-the-shelf (COTS)** products are packaged solutions, which are adapted to satisfy the needs of the purchasing organization, rather than the development of custom fabricated materials or coded software solutions. Use of COTS solutions can reduce costs and time in product development and overall supply chain costs.

## INVENTORY MANAGEMENT FOUNDATIONS

### Sales Forecasting

Forecasting is a prelude to planning. Before making plans, an estimate must be made of what conditions will exist over some future period. The Sales Forecast is an input to Demand Planning.

- Point 1: Forecasting is being done in virtually every company. The issues are who does it and at what level it's done.
- Point 2: Sales and Marketing people "own" the Sales Forecast.
- Point 3: Better processes yield better results and forecasting is no exception; better forecasting processes will yield better forecasts. (T. Wallace)

### Sales and Operations Planning

The purpose of Sales and Operations Planning is to achieve a balance in Supply and Demand It is a business process that focuses on aggregate volumes byproduct families and groups so that mix issues may be resolved later to fill individual customer orders. (See Figure BB10.5)

**FIGURE BB10.5**
The Monthly S&OP Process

**Step 1** – Gather the data and run month end reports.
**Step 2** – Plan the Demand.
**Step 3** – Review capacity constraints and plan the supply.
**Step 4** – The Pre-SOP Meeting is where representatives from the demand and supply departments meet and look to combine their work to determine the Sales and Operation Plan recommendations and alternative.
**Step 5** – The Sales and Operations meeting is held monthly under the auspices of the Business Owner and final decisions are made as to volume and mix and the Sales and Operation Plan is agreed to.

The Sales and Operations Plan is updated monthly and provides a rolling plan of demand and planned production for the future 12 to 18 months by dollar volumes attributable to individual product families.

## MASTER PRODUCTION SCHEDULING

After developing the production plan, within the Sales and Operations planning process, the next step is to prepare a master production schedule. The MPS is a statement of which end items are to be produced, the quantity of each and the dates they are to be completed. The MPS is a vital link in the production planning system. It constitutes the link between production planning and what operations will produce. It forms the basis for calculating the capacity and resources needed. The MPS drives the materials requirements plan based on finished goods. The MPS sets the priority plan for manufacturing.

## MATERIALS REQUIREMENTS PLANNING

The MPS serves as an input to Materials Requirements Planning. Materials Requirements Planning is used to break down the MPS and determine which materials you need to purchase and components you need to make, the quantity of these materials and components, and when they are needed. It uses time phasing, but the time phases are shorter time periods than those used in the MPS. Time phases in an MRP may be in weeks, days, or even hours, depending on organizational needs.

## SUPPLY CHAIN RISK MANAGEMENT

Supply-chain risk management (SCRM) is "the implementation of strategies to manage both every day and exceptional risks along the supply chain based on continuous risk assessment with the objective of reducing vulnerability and ensuring continuity" (Wieland).

## DISTRIBUTION RESOURCE PLANNING (DRP)

Distribution resource planning (DRP) is a method used for planning orders within a supply chain. DRP enables the user to set certain inventory control parameters (such as safety stock) and calculate the time-phased inventory requirements. It is able to both respond to customer demand and coordinate planning and control. This process is also commonly referred to as distribution requirements planning.

## BUSINESS-PROCESS INTEGRATION

Business Process Integration (BPI) is essential for organizations looking to connect systems and information efficiently. BPI allows for automation of business processes, integration of systems and services, and the secure sharing of data across numerous applications. Overcoming integration challenges allows organizations to connect systems internally and externally. BPI allows for the automation of management, operational, and supporting processes. This gives businesses an advantage over competitors as they can spend more time developing new and innovative processes.

## ENTERPRISE RESOURCE PLANNING (ERP)

Enterprise Resource Planning, or ERP is a business software system that supports business or enterprise throughout ongoing operations and projects in organizing, planning, maintaining, tracking, and utilization of resources effectively.

ERP allows organizations to integrate all the operational units such as financing, human resources, production, sales, marketing, finance and accounting, procurement, and inventory management, etc.

ERP helps the organization to achieve real time business information processing, increase productivity, improve delivery, reduce cost, increase profits, improve product quality, enhance reporting, and improved performance management.

Successful SCM requires a change from managing individual functions to integrating activities into key supply-chain or operational processes. An ERP system integrates the core functional processes within an organization. The ERP system is used to collect, store, manage, interpret, and report data from these many business processes.

Understand the processes, innovate, implement, and standardize, automating where possible. The ERP integrates and provides for automation of many of the organizational processes.

## SUPPLY CHAIN PERFORMANCE METRICS

Supply Chain Metrics may include measurements for procurement, production, transportation, inventory, warehousing, material handling, packaging, and customer service. Some of the more useful include:

1. Perfect Order Measurement – The percentage of orders that are error-free.
2. Cash to Cash Cycle Time – The number of days between paying for materials and getting paid for product.
3. Customer Order Cycle Time – Measures how long it takes to deliver a customer order after the purchase order (PO) is received.
4. Fill Rate – The percentage of a customer's order that is filled on the first shipment. This can be represented as the percentage of items, SKUs or order value that is included with the first shipment.
5. Supply Chain Cycle Time – The time it would take to fill a customer order if inventory levels were zero.
6. Inventory Days of Supply – The number of days it would take to run out of supply if it was not replenished.
7. Freight bill accuracy – The percentage of freight bills that are error-free.
8. Freight cost per unit – This is usually measured as the cost of freight per item or SKU.
9. Inventory Turnover – The number of times that a company's inventory cycles per year.
10. Days Sales Outstanding – A measure of how quickly revenue can be collected from customers.
11. Average Payment Period for Production Materials – The average time from receipt of materials and payment for those materials.
12. On Time Shipping Rate – The percentage of items, SKUs or order value that arrives on or before the requested ship date.

---

## BUSINESS PROCESS MANAGEMENT (BPM)

Business Process Management is a management discipline that integrates the strategy and goals of an organization with the expectations and needs of customers by focusing on end-to-end processes. It brings together strategies, goals, culture, organizational structures, roles, policies, methodologies, and IT tools to:

- Analyze, design, implement, control, and continuously improve end-to-end processes, and
- Establish process governance.

It is focused on delivering operational improvement, or, in a large-scale change, transformation. This process-centric approach to business management is supported by automated tools to deliver an operational environment that supports rapid change and continuous improvement. BPM provides a view of the business activity through the use of process models with clearly visible associated business and technical operational rules (ABPMP).

A business process is the complete, and dynamically coordinated set of collaborative activities that deliver value to customers (Fingar).

Upper management provides the vision and direction, teams correct the problems, and individuals provide the creativity, but it is the processes within any organization that get things done (Harrington).

## WORKFLOW

This is a generic term for the sequential movement of information or materials from one activity in a process or subprocess to another in the same overall process. This is the aggregation of activity within a single Business Unit. Activity will be a combination of work from one or more processes. Organization of this work will be around efficiency. The activities within the workflow will be shown as a flow that describes each activity's relationship with all the others performed in the Business Unit. Modeling will show this work as a flow that describes each activity's relationship with all the others performed in the Business Unit.

Workflows can be manual, automated, or more likely a combination of both. Workflow models often include both the diagram and the specific rules that define the flow of information from one activity to the next. When used in conjunction with the workflow system or engine, it usually refers to a software-based workflow system that will move information from a database to one computer or organization after the other (ABPMP).

## SUPPLY CHAIN PROCESS IMPROVEMENT AND AUTOMATION

While the discussion of best Supply Chain Management practices and appropriate customization thereof to individual organizations is beyond the scope of this text, there are several process improvement methodologies that may be useful in this regard. These may include tools for definition and management of existing processes, or improvement of these processes through Area Activity Analysis, Business Process Improvement, Streamlined Process Improvement, or Lean Six Sigma methodologies. Finally, once these processes are fully understood and streamlined, they may be candidates for automation.

Automation may make use of artificial intelligence or machine learning. Artificial intelligence has the potential to make supply chains run faster, better, and cheaper. In an extreme case, a fully automated supply chain could use artificial intelligence to make decisions and take actions autonomously. (See Figure BB10.6)

- **Understand** – A thorough understanding of the current state of practice and the actual processes of the industry and organization is an important first step.
- **Streamline** – This is the improvement methodology.
- **Automate** – This covers a range of activities from eliminating the human element from the production process to increasing the productivity of humans throughout the supply chain by automating processes.

## ELEMENTS OF INNOVATIVE SUPPLY CHAIN MANAGEMENT LEADERSHIP

The core elements of Innovative Supply Chain Management include customer satisfaction, design, and operational efficiency (Figure BB10.7).

**FIGURE BB10.6**
USA Process

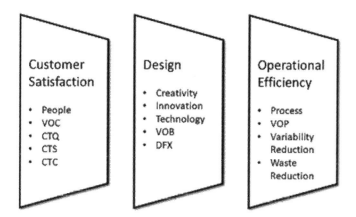

**FIGURE BB10.7**
Elements of Innovative Supply Chain Management Leadership

## PLOSSL'S SEVEN SUPPLY CHAIN POINTS

George Plossl, one of the key innovators credited with the popularization of Material Requirements Planning, the forerunner of what we now know as a component of Supply Chain Management, developed a simple set of Seven Supply Chain Points that are as relevant advice today as they were when written and provide a good starting point for the development of an effective supply chain management system.

1. Satisfy the customer's real needs, not wants.
2. Understand how the real world works.
3. Have a complete integrated system.
4. Use accurate data.
5. Manage cycle time.
6. Eliminate nonvalue-added activity.
7. Use fully qualified people.

## SUMMARY

The development of innovative supply chains remains a great opportunity for many organizations. Innovations in supply chain have fundamentally changed the way business is done globally. Amazon has disrupted traditional retail through creating flexible supply chains that serve to meet customer needs efficiently with minimal variability. Wal-Mart and other retail organizations have worked to significantly improve their supply chain performance. Uber has shown a pathway for automating the balancing of supply and demand in service organizations through their software platform. Opportunities abound for innovation that will automate many repetitive processes and augment others to enhance human performance in supply chains of the future.

# BB11

## Innovative Design

*Doug Nelson*

## CONTENTS

## INTRODUCTION

An innovative design is not one that gradually changes even though the change is in a positive direction. An innovative design is one that jumps forward in the march of progress, rather than a step forward. After a short time period an innovative design is no longer innovative because it is no longer significantly better than what is available from other sources. The product life cycle has grown shorter as we have moved forward in time. Nothing lasts forever. The design may later be reviewed with improvements made in future iterations or versions based on recognized continuous improvement methodologies – or may become a candidate for another innovative design. It should be noted that ISO document 50501 recognizes continuous improvement as part of the innovation system.

Back in 1991, Robert Hayes, a professor at the Harvard Business School, said, "Fifteen years ago companies competed on price. Today it's quality. Tomorrow it's design." Tomorrow has arrived. The world continues to move toward a more knowledge-based society, where organizations compete on the strengths of their intellectual property and their ability to create new and innovative products and services.

The creation of an innovative design is one of the most important projects that an organization can embark upon to ensure future growth and profitability. An Innovative Design project, to be successful must, of course, be effectively driven and carefully managed.

For the organization to be successful in producing new products, it is important to utilize and build core competencies of the organization and develop or purchase intellectual property that can add to the organization's core competency capabilities. Ideally, the organization should be the purveyor of that technology, methodology, or service to customers and should market and support the needs of the customer, with no outsiders coming between the organization and its customers.

## THE SMILING CURVE

The smiling curve is a graphical representation of the concept that shows how value added varies across the different stages of bringing an innovative product to market. (See Figure BB11.1.) It was proposed by Stan Shih, the founder of Acc Computer, in Taiwan, in 1992. Shih observed that, within the personal computer industry, the two ends of the value chain – conception and marketing – as compared with the actual manufacturing command the highest returns for the organization. When presented graphically, with the Y axis representing the value

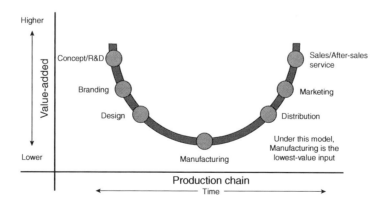

**FIGURE BB11.1**
Smiling Curve.

added and the $X$ axis representing the stages of production of the value chain, the resulting curve appears as a smile. And indeed, the adopters of strategies (within multiple industries) as recognized within the smiling curve have had a lot to smile about.

Control of concept/R&D, branding, and design (the intellectual property side of the curve) and the distribution, marketing, sales/after market service (customer facing side of the curve) can be recognized in multiple techno-logical designs, supply chain and marketing strategies. The manufacturing or assembly of the product is often seen as least contributory to the overall value of the product and is, therefore, often a candidate for outsourcing.

## TRIZ

TRIZ (pronounced treesz) is a Russian acronym for *teoriya resheniya izobretatelskikh zadatch*, the theory of inventive problem solving, origi-nated by Genrich Altshuller in 1946. It is a broad title representing methodologies, tool sets, knowledge bases, and model-based technolo-gies for generating innovative ideas and solutions. It aims to create an algorithm to the innovation of new systems and the refinement of existing systems, and is based on the study of patents of systems, scientific theory, organizations, and works of art.

TRIZ is one of the most effective tools we have found for innovation. TRIZ may be used within the creation phase to help design new products or to improve existing products or services. It also may be used in the phase to solve manufacturing problems and to improve manufacturing procedures.

## LEAN TRIZ

Lean TRIZ is a new workshop-based process that brings together teams to focus on specific processes, evolutionary product designs, and improvement opportunities. (see *Lean TRIZ: How to Dramatically Reduce Product-Development Costs with This Innovative Problem-Solving Tool (Management Handbooks for Results)*, Productivity Press; (2017).

## 20 Questions to Encourage Ideas

 (1)  What if ...?
 (2)  How can we improve ...?
 (3)  How will the customer benefit?
 (4)  Are we forgetting anything?
 (5)  What's the next step?
 (6)  What can we do better?
 (7)  What do you think about ...?
 (8)  How can we improve quality?
 (9)  How can we streamline ...?
(10)  What should we modify?
(11)  What should we replace?
(12)  What should we add?
(13)  What should we eliminate?
(14)  Can we make any new assumptions?
(15)  What will make it work ...?
(16)  What other ideas do you have ...?
(17)  What issues should we explore ...?
(18)  What patterns can you see?
(19)  How can we simplify ...?
(20)  Why?

## Engineering Management of Innovative Design Projects

### *The Waterfall Approach*

The waterfall approach is a traditional project management approach where the project is completed in distinct stages, moving linearly and sequentially from inception toward ultimate completion (see Figure BB11.2).

The waterfall approach is effective when project work is clearly definable. Definable projects are those that involve clear procedures, are well understood, and involve low levels of execution uncertainty and risk, for example, building of a new home and manufacturing of automobile. This approach works well when predictive approaches can be used to determine the bulk of the requirements up front and changes may be controlled through the change request process. This is often not the case, during certain phases of the Innovative Design project.

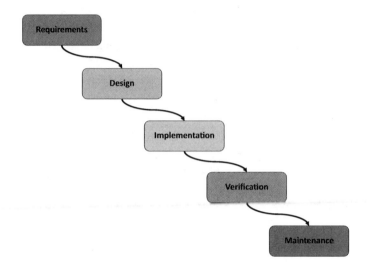

**FIGURE BB11.2**
Waterfall Approach.

## The Agile Approach

The agile approach originated in the software industry in the early 2000s. The agile movement has been adopted within a broad range of industries. The goal of the agile approach is to achieve competitive advantage in today's fast-paced, complex marketplace through becoming quicker, more responsive, and more flexible.

Innovative design, research, and development – any work done for the first time is exploratory in nature. It requires subject matter experts to collaborate and develop opportunities to create solutions. It is highly uncertain and is characterized by high rates of change, complexity, and risk, including failure.

## The Hybrid Approach

Projects to create innovative design often require multiple approaches, tailored to the organizational culture and operating environment, to drive successful outcomes. A hybrid approach may be instituted including the methodologies of innovation design, lifecycle management, and multiple project management approaches.

As we discussed in BB6 – Innovative Project Management Systems, the Project Management Institute (PMI) has recognized this need with the issue of the 6th edition of the *Guide to the Project Management Body of Knowledge*. For the first time, PMI includes specific and detailed information about agile approaches to project management. The *Agile Practice Guide* is provided as a companion, serving as a bridge that connects waterfall and agile approaches.

The goal within the Innovative Design Hybrid Approach is to move from an environment of high uncertainty to one of certainty as rapidly and flexibly as warranted. The Innovative Design project often requires progressive elaboration. This is the iterative process of increasing the level of detail in a project management plan as greater amounts of information and more accurate estimates become available. The Innovative Design process should begin with an agile approach that provides flexibility and responsiveness in the early stages of development and transitions to a more structured approach with timelines, defined scope, and accountabilities that can be more effectively observed, acted upon, and managed, as the level of certainty and information increases.

## Requirements

Requirements planning is the process of turning our concepts into actual product features by way of developing and documenting requirements for those features as early as we can in order to minimize surprises and high costs later in the delivery process. Failure to create requirements early in the development process is one of the greatest risks to project success.

Product requirements are how we communicate our understanding of what a product will be. They ensure that all stakeholders have the same understanding of a product's important features. When creating product requirements, it is important that we capture everything that is important to our customers, our organization, and other relevant stakeholders (e.g., government and regulatory requirements). Otherwise, the results are likely to be different from our expectations, and significant costs and delays may be incurred.

For each Innovative Design project, a Requirements Management Plan is developed that describes how requirements will be analyzed, documented, and managed. A requirement is a condition or capability that is necessary to be present in a product, service, or result to satisfy a business need. Requirements documentation is a description of how individual requirements meet the business needs of the project. Ideally, the requirements part of this document should be developed by marketing based upon their close contact with the customer. Unfortunately, marketing doesn't always have the skills or understand the customer well enough to crisply quantify the requirements. The Requirements Traceability Matrix is a grid that links product requirements from their origins to the deliverables that satisfy them. When this is the case, the matrix is often prepared jointly by research and development and marketing.

Requirements articulate what the product must do for it to be successful and to be accepted by the customer. Here we focus on what the product must do, as opposed to how we will meet the requirements. This can be challenging since there is a tendency to focus on solutions and propose implementations too early in the process. The requirement specifications are a part of the documentation that guides the entire project, and if properly developed, provide flexibility for creativity and innovative solutions.

One of the most important components of requirements management is traceability. Tracing allows us to understand why the requirement exists, the impact of change, if the set of requirements is complete, and helps prioritize requirements.

The Requirements Traceability Diagram shows how traceability starts off with the business requirements' outcomes/benefits and traces through the stakeholder requirements, solution requirements, supplementary requirements/nonfunctional, and drops down into testing scenarios and test cases.

**Requirements Traceability Diagram**

See Figure BB11.3.

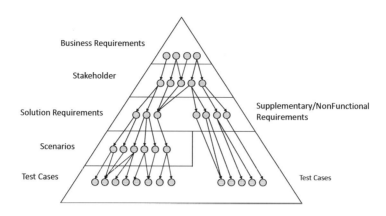

**FIGURE BB11.3**
Requirements Traceability Diagram.

## Introduction to Innovation Systems Cycle

See Figure BB11.4.

The Innovation Systems Cycle

Phase I. Creation

- Process Grouping 1. Opportunity identification
- Process Grouping 2. Opportunity development/action
- Process Grouping 3. Value proposition
- Process Grouping 4. Concept validation

Phase II. Setup and Producing

- Process Grouping 5. Business case analysis
- Process Grouping 6. Resource management
- Process Grouping 7. Documentation
- Process Grouping 8. Production

Phase III. Delivery

- Process Grouping 9. Marketing, sales, and delivery
- Process Grouping 10. After-sales services
- Process Grouping 11. Performance analysis
- Process Grouping 12. Transformation

**FIGURE BB11.4.**
Innovation Systems Cycle.

## DMADV FRAMEWORK

DMADV is a framework that focuses on creation of a design for new products, services, or processes. Proper use of the DMADV methodology serves to define the needs of the customer as they relate to a product, service, or process and to ensure that designed architectures optimally meet these needs. As such, the DMADV framework is utilized primarily within the Concept and Development Stages, but the Production, Utilization, Support, and Retirement Stages need to be fully considered. Early, proactive consideration of these stages will allow necessary changes to be made at the most cost-effective point in the product's life cycle. See Figure BB11.5.

- *Define* – Define the design goal to meet the needs of the customer, business objectives, and other relevant stakeholders.
- *Measure* – Measure risk, process, and product capabilities.
- *Analyze* – Analyze and test early concepts and ideas.
- *Design* – Design the final architecture of the product, service, or process.
- *Verify* – Verify that design specifications are being met and release.

### Defining Customer Needs

Standard methodologies for determining customer needs include defining and identifying the customer, visiting customers, interviewing customers, and surveying customers. This can be incredibly useful in determining the current state of the marketplace but may be insufficient in realizing the unmet, yet unrealized, needs of the customer – those that require innovative design.

There is a popular quote, often attributed to Albert Einstein that says, "If I had an hour to solve a problem, I'd spend 55 minutes thinking about the problem and 5 minutes thinking about solutions." While, it is unclear

**FIGURE BB11.5**
DMADV Framework.

whether Einstein ever made such an utterance, there is clearly supporting data to be found in spending adequate time in the full definition and understanding of the issue at hand before proceeding. Further, the author, may have somewhat underestimated the time required to implement an effective solution. However, it should be noted that often there is an interest on the part of team members in moving too rapidly through the Define Phase. If the opportunity is clearly understood from multiple perspectives, the solution will more quickly and correctly be initiated and resolved. This will proactively set in place the iterative cycles that occur within the Measure, Analyze, and Design phases. Thereafter, the project should move rapidly and expediently through the verification process (see Figure BB11.6).

## Measure – Analyze – Design Phases

### Measure Phase

Within the measure phase, customer specifications and needs are measured. When Innovative Design teams have accurate, timely data to evaluate, they can make better decisions that lead to more profitable products.

### Analyze Phase (Define, Breakdown, Assess, and Decide)

Within the analyze phase, early concepts and ideas are analyzed and tested. Alternative combinations of methodologies, features, and technologies are tailored to meet the best possible solution within any constraints. While Innovative Development teams must access and analyze vast amounts of product data, they must also leverage their

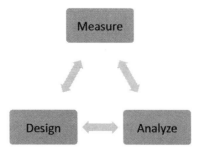

**FIGURE BB11.6**
Iterative Cycle.

product, domain, and organizational knowledge to create viable marketing and product development strategies. Knowledge and data are important assets to the Innovative Design team because they help identify important market patterns and trends that lead to vital insights.

### Design Phase

Within the design phase, the final architecture of the product, service, or process is determined. An initial low-fidelity prototype, a prototype that is sketchy and incomplete, that has some characteristics of the target product but is otherwise simple, to quickly produce the prototype and test broad concepts may be produced within the progressive iterations of the measure, analyze, and design phases. These models may be changed or upgraded as the team discovers and learns more about the design under study.

## DESIGN FOR X

See Figure BB11.7.

Design for Excellence (DFX) is the systematic thoughtfulness of all applicable life cycle factors, such as testability, reliability, manufacturability, maintainability, and affordability, and it includes human rights, labor rights, and internal corporate governance.

DFX is both a philosophy and a methodology that can help organizations change the way they manage product development and become more competitive. DFX is defined as a knowledge-based approach for designing products to have as many desirable characteristics as possible.

This approach goes beyond the traditional quality aspects of function, features, and appearance of the item.

AT&T Bell Laboratories coined the term DFX to describe the process of designing a product to meet the abovementioned characteristics. In doing so, the life cycle cost of a product and the lowering of downstream manufacturing costs would be addressed.

Any number of factors might be relevant to the definition of quality during a systems' design initiative. DFX involves being able to incorporate a variety of factors "X" into a design, working toward a solution set that optimizes their interaction against customer needs and requirements. Common "X" factor examples include Assembly, Reliability, and Testing.

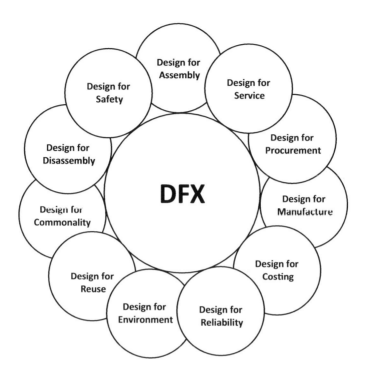

**FIGURE BB11.7**
Design for X.

The DFX toolbox has continued to grow in number from its inception to include hundreds of tools. The usual practice is to apply one DFX tool at a time. DFX tools may be incorporated as part of the Innovation Design process. Design for X is frequently used within concurrent engineering. Concurrent engineering objectives include improving quality, reducing costs, compressing cycle times, raising productivity, and improving image. This requires achieving these objectives through cooperative teamwork between multiple departments and functions to consider all interacting issues in designing products, processes, and systems from creation through production and use to retirement.

The use of DFX tools is likely to increase the number of design changes in early stages but reduce the number of late design changes significantly. Because it is easier to change early than late, substantial savings can be achieved, better products can be produced, while products and processes may be realigned more easily and at lower cost. As we pointed out earlier in this book, in today's environment, with a reduced sales life frequently problems identified and corrected during the manufacturing process have little or no effect on the customer's perspective and cost of our product. An organization's reputation is based upon the first three months of production more than the last two months of production. The objective is to detect all potential errors and correct them before the design is released.

Design guidelines: DFX methods are usually presented as design guidelines. These guidelines provide design rules and strategies. The design rule to increase assembly efficiency requires a reduction in parts count and part types. The strategy is to verify that each part is needed or that common part types could be used.

A number of general Design for X guidelines have been established to achieve higher quality, lower cost, improved application of automation, and better maintainability. Examples of these for Design for Manufacturing include

- Reducing the number of parts to minimize the opportunity for a defective part or an assembly error, to decrease the total cost of fabricating and assembling the product, and to improve the chance to automate the process.
- Mistake-proof the assembly design so that the assembly process is unambiguous.
- Design verifiability into the product and its components to provide a natural test or inspection of the item.
- Avoiding tight tolerances beyond the natural capability of the manufacturing processes and make sure to design in the middle of a part's tolerance range.
- Design "robustness" into products to compensate for uncertainty in the product's manufacturing, testing, and use.
- Design for parts orientation and handling to minimize non-value-added manual effort, to avoid ambiguity in orienting and merging parts, and to facilitate automation.
- Design for ease of assembly by utilizing simple patterns of movement and minimizing fastening steps.
- Utilize common parts and materials to facilitate design activities, to minimize the amount of inventory in the system and to standardize handling and assembly operations.
- Design modular products to facilitate assembly with building block components and sub-assemblies.

- Design for storage and handling during the manufacturing process.
- Design considerations for serviceability into the product.

Every organization should set up a community of practice that makes up a set of guidelines and DFX parameters that are in line with the product that the organization is handling.

*Design analysis tools*: Each DFX tool involves some analytical procedure that measures the effectiveness of the selected tool. A typical design for assembly procedure should be provided for analysis of such elements as handling time, insertion time, total assembly time, number of parts, and assembly efficiency. Each tool should have some method of verifying its efficiency.

While each design tool is typically considered individually, exploration of synergies and trade-offs can be useful in optimal positioning of products along the product life cycle curve.

## Design for X Procedure

- Step 1: Product Analysis – Information related to the product is collected. Bills of Material (BOMs) are used to display product structure. Other types of product data can be easily correlated with the product BOM. It is useful to obtain the product hardware to examine and understand its features.
  - ◦ This is typically done during the design review activity where manufacturing, manufacturing engineering, test engineering, production control, and quality all review the proposed prints and requirements.
- Step 2: Process Analysis – Process Analysis is primarily concerned with the collection, processing, and reporting of process-specific and resource-specific data. Operation process and flow process charts are established.
- Step 3: Measuring Performance – The process and product interactions can be measured in terms of the relevant performance indicators as relevant within the specified DFX tool. Additional data collection and processing may be required.
- Step 4: Benchmarking – The objective is to determine whether or not the subject processes are good and what areas contribute to it. Benchmarking primarily involves setting up standards and comparing the

performance measurements against the established standard. Individual and aggregate benchmarks may be established. Once the performance standards and measurements are available, the areas where performance measurements are below the standard can be identified.

- Step 5: Diagnosis – Based on performance measurement and benchmarking, a determination is made as to what is good and what is not. In order to solve problems, it is necessary to know their causes. A cause-effect diagram may be useful in determining major causes of a problem. Root cause analysis techniques may be used further to identify specific conditions related to the problem.

- Step 6: Advise on Change – Explore as many improvement areas as possible for each problem area. Brainstorming is a useful technique. Redesigning of the product and processes is dependent upon specific circumstances. Changes may take place to composition, configuration, and characteristics at different levels of detail. Product changes may be made across the entire product ranges, working principles, concepts, structures, subassemblies, components, parts, features, and/or parameters. Process changes may be made across product lines, business processes, procedures, steps, tasks, activities, and/or parameters. Product and processes are closely interrelated. It is important to consider the interrelationships between the two when making a change to either product or processes. A "what if" analysis may be helpful.

- Step 7: Prioritize – The analysis may reveal a large number of problem areas within the product and processes. There may be many causes and solution alternates for each problem. Prioritization is often required due to limited resources. Prioritization should be based on some form of measurement. A Pareto chart may be constructed and can be used to show relative frequency of events such as products, processes, failures, defects, causes and effects. Analysis of the Pareto chart should aid in prioritization of the problem areas.

## DESIGN FOR PRODUCT LIFE CYCLE

Design for Product Life cycle is a "cradle to grave" approach. Design for X methodologies can be used in Design, Production, Useful-life, and finally, End of Product Life.

There are currently hundreds of DFX tools that have been developed. A few of the more popular design tools are discussed herein.

## Design for Safety

Design for safety requires the elimination of potential failure-prone elements that could occur in the operation and use of the product. The design should make the product safe for: manufacture, sale, use by the consumer, and disposal or reuse. Failure Modes and Effects Analysis (FMEA) and Fault-tree Analysis are often incorporated within Design for Safety. FMEA is a fundamental hazard identification and frequency analysis technique that analyses all the fault modes of a given equipment item for their effects both on other components and the system. A Fault-tree analysis is a hazard identification and frequency analysis technique that starts with the undesired event and determines all the ways in which it could occur. These are displayed graphically.

## Design for Reliability

Design for Reliability describes the entire set of tools that support product and process design (typically from early in the concept stage all the way through to product obsolescence) to ensure that customer expectations for reliability are fully met throughout the life of the product with low overall life cycle costs. FMEA is a good tool to assess risk. It is used to identify potential failure modes for a product or process, assess the risk associated with those failure modes, prioritize issues for corrective action and identify and carry out corrective actions to address the most serious concerns. Always identify where the risk is and design parallel circuits to provide for all the groups where failure occurs. Usually reliability analysis is supported by test data either at normal conditions or under stress conditions.

## Design for Testability

Design for Testability aims to make the product test procedures as easy and economical as possible during manufacturing, use, and servicing. Design for Testability includes techniques that add certain testability features to a hardware product design. The idea behind Design for Testability is that features are added to make it easier to develop and apply manufacturing tests for the designed hardware. The purpose of manufacturing tests is to validate that the product hardware is free of manufacturing defects that may affect the product's correct functioning. Tests are applied at several steps in the hardware manufacturing flow and may also be used for hardware maintenance in the field. The tests generally are driven by test programs that execute within Automatic Test Equipment processes. These tests may also be conducted within the assembled equipment during maintenance procedures. In addition to finding and indicating the presence of defects, tests may log diagnostic information about the nature of the subject test fails. The diagnostic information can be used to locate the source of the failure.

Always be sure that there is a correlation between the development measurements that are recorded and specifications and the test equipment results. Test equipment should be 10 times more accurate than the measurement equipment. In extreme cases due to measurement limitations that requirement is reduced to 4 times

## Design for Assembly/Manufacturing

Design for Assembly means simplifying the product so that fewer parts are required, making the product easier to assemble and the manufacturing process easier to manage. Design for Assembly is often the most effective DFX tool providing increases in quality while reducing costs and time to market. Design for Assembly is accomplished using fewer parts, using the same parts in different parts of the product, reduction of engineering documents, lowering of inventory levels, reduced inspection, minimization of setups, and materials handling. If a product contains fewer parts it will take less time to assemble, reducing its assembly costs. If the parts are provided with features, which make them easier to grasp, move, orient, and insert, assembly time and assembly costs will be reduced. The reduction of the number of parts in an assembly has the additional benefit of generally reducing the total cost of parts in the assembly. Major cost benefits of the application of Design for Assembly are achieved through this reduction of number of parts and using the same part in other applications within the product. This results in lower cost and higher quality.

## Design for Environment

Design for Environment aims to create minimal levels of pollution over the product life cycle. Manufacture, use, and disposal are considered. The idea is to increase growth without increasing the amount of consumable resources. Some considerations include recovery and reuse, disassembly, waste minimization, energy use, material use, and environmental accident prevention. Design for Environment techniques may include life cycle assessment, technology assessment, sustainable engineering, reusable parts, and sustainable design.

The Design for the Environment program of the US Environmental Protection Agency helps consumers, businesses, and institutional buyers identify cleaning and other products that perform well and are safer for human health and the environment. Lists are available that identify safer chemical products for use in manufacturing processes and aid in determining safer reuse/recovery techniques or appropriate disposal.

## Design for Serviceability

Design for Serviceability aims to return operation and use easily and quickly in order to repair the item after failure. This is often associated with Maintainability. Design for Serviceability/Maintainability objectives include reduction of service requirements and frequency, facilitation of diagnosis, minimization of the time and costs to disassemble, repair/replace, and reassemble the product within the service process, and reduction of the cost of service components. The primary benefit is reducing the impact of a failure on the customer.

## Design for Ergonomics

Human factors engineering must ensure that the product is designed for the human user. Some of the attributes that may be considered are fitting the product to the user's attributes, simplifying the user's tasks (user-friendliness), making controls and functions obvious and easy to use, and anticipation of human error.

Design specification best practices include (1) use of global anthropometry considerations (North America, Europe, Asia, and Latin America), (2) use of dimensions and ranges that support adjustability and reconfiguration, (3) designs to accommodate neutral postures and task variation, (4) minimization of manual material handling requirements, and (5) environmental considerations such as lighting, temperature, noise, vibration, and ability for colorblind people to read the product controls and reporting system.

## Design for Aesthetics

Aesthetics is the human perception of beauty, including sight, sound, smell, touch, taste, and movement. Aesthetics is the aspect of design and technology which most closely relates to art and design, and issues of color, shape, texture, contrast, form, balance, cultural references, and emotional response are common to both areas. Products are becoming smaller and lighter. Customers desire that products be appealing in appearance. While considering customer image requirements, it is important to consider how the product will be manufactured to meet these aesthetic characteristics during the design process. Incorporation of a good industrial design leads to products that are genuinely appealing and represent a synthesis of form and function.

## Design for Packaging

The most effective packaging for the product must be determined. The size and physical characteristics of the product are important. Design for automatic packaging methods may be considered. Packaging may be designed for maximum benefit in shipping or for product protection in distribution, storage, sale, and use. Design for Packaging incorporates package design and development as an integral part of the new product development process. Products that are designed with packaging in mind can help ensure cost savings and product protection as it moves through the supply chain. We have seen products where the packaging design changes create more sales and loyal customers than changes to the product has. Do not underestimate the importance of the packaging. Look at the number of packaging options that were evaluated and why each option that is presented was selected.

## Design for Features

Design for Features considers the accessories, options, and attachments that may be used in conjunction with the product. Adding or deleting options is often used in creating products with similar manufacturing characteristics while meeting customer requirements within targeted marketing segments. It allows for expansion of product line offerings without the cost and time involved in complete redesign.

## Design for Time to Market

Design for Time to Market helps to ensure that timeliness of product launches may be maintained even as product life cycles continue to shorten. The ability to make the product either earlier or faster than the competition can provide a market leadership advantage. Reducing time to market has a significant positive impact on revenue realization. With optimized processes, prelaunch development costs can be lower, time to launch can be faster, and market share gains can be faster and larger creating a first mover advantage. First mover advantage is the advantage gained by the initial significant occupant of a market segment. Part of this advantage may be attributable to the fact that the first entrant can develop or gain control of resources (such as patents or other intellectual property) that followers may not be able to match.

### Testing

Higher level testing, or product validation, should be conducted as early as possible within the Design process. This is looking at how usable the product is for our customers, and how the hardware, software, and mechanical subsystems work together, known as integration test or system test. Early testing of circuits, software, and mechanicals decreases costs and decreases the time required for product development.

### Verify Phase

An innovative design must undergo tests to verify efficacy. This requires a system of tests and models to check that customer specifications are being addressed within any constraints that may be present. This may include simulations, pilots, and prototypes to verify the innovative design solution. Product verification can be extremely time-consuming and costly. Frequently an emphasis is placed upon comprehensive simulation models and 3D printing.

### Validation

Validation is the assurance that a product, service, or result meets the needs of the customer and other identified stakeholders (PMI).

Simply put, Validation answers the question, "Did we build the right product?"

### Verification

Verification is the evaluation of whether a product, service, or result complies with a regulation, requirement, specification, or imposed condition (PMI).

Verification answers the question, "Did we build the product right?" See Figure BB11.8.

### V-Model

The V-Model means Verification and Validation model. Just like the water-fall model, the V-shaped model provides for a sequential path of execution of processes. Each phase is completed before the next phase begins.

## SPIRAL MODEL FOR SOFTWARE DEVELOPMENT

The spiral model is a risk-driven software development process model. (See Figure BB11.9.) Based on the unique risk patterns of a given project, the spiral model guides a team to adopt elements of one or more process

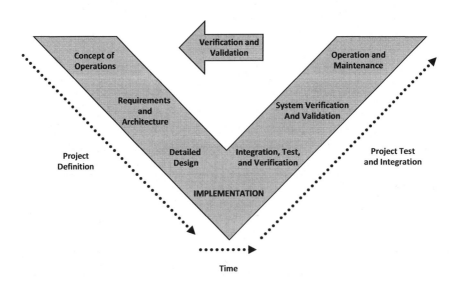

**FIGURE BB11.8**
V-Model.

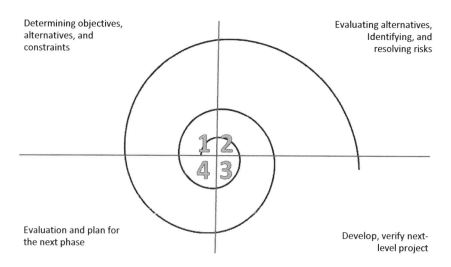

Determining objectives, alternatives, and constraints

Evaluating alternatives, Identifying, and resolving risks

Evaluation and plan for the next phase

Develop, verify next-level project

**FIGURE BB11.9**
Spiral Model.

models, such as incremental, waterfall, or evolutionary prototyping. The spiral development model is a combination of a waterfall and iterative model. Each phase in the spiral model begins with a design goal and ends with the client reviewing progress.

The spiral model builds on the strengths of other process models, such as early V and V concepts within the V-Model, concurrency concepts within the concurrent engineering model, agile and lean models, and risk-driven concepts.

The development team using the spiral model starts with a small set of requirements and goes through each development phase for those set of requirements. The engineering team adds functionality for the additional requirement in ever-increasing spirals until the application is ready for the production phase.

## RISK IDENTIFICATION AND ANALYSIS

When assessing the importance of a project risk, consider the two key dimensions of risk: uncertainty and the effect of the project's objectives. The uncertainty dimension may be described using the term "probability," and the effect dimension may be called "impact" (though, other descriptions are possible, such as "likelihood" and "consequence").

Risk includes both distinct events, which are uncertain but can be clearly described, and general conditions, which are less specific but may give rise to uncertainty. The two types of project risk, those with negative and those with positive effects, are called, respectively, "threats" and "opportunities" [*Practice Standard for Project Risk Management* (PMI, 2009)].

Qualitative risk analysis is the entry step for risk analysis. It must be performed before quantitative risk analysis is used. Qualitative risk analysis is the process of prioritizing individual project risks for further analysis or action by assessing their probability of occurrence and impact as well as other characteristics.

Quantitative risk analysis is the process of numerically analyzing the combined effect of identified individual project risks and other sources of uncertainty on overall project objectives. The key benefit of this process is that it quantifies overall project risk exposure and can provide additional quantitative risk information to support risk response planning. (See Figure BB11.10)

## FMEA

Product recalls, in-service warranty problems, and safety issues can destroy the reputation of an organization, cause financial ruin, and result in potential harm or loss to consumers.

FMEA is a design technique used to define, identify, and manage known or potential failures or errors from a system during all phases of the product life cycle. A successful FMEA activity helps identify potential failure modes based on experience with similar products and processes – or based on common physics of failure logic.

Global competition, high liability risks, and shorter product life cycles increase the need for prevention of problems in the design process – the point at which they are least costly to correct. FMEA can reduce costs by making products more reliable, lowering warranty and other costs incurred through product failure. FMEA can shorten product development time by addressing problems early in the design process, thus

| RISK RATING KEY | LOW<br>0 – ACCEPTABLE<br>OK TO PROCEED | MEDIUM<br>1 – ALARP (AS LOW AS RESONABLY PRACTIABLE)<br>TAKE MITIGATION EFFORTS | HIGH<br>2 – GENERALLY UNACCEPTABLE<br>SEEK SUPPORT | EXTREME<br>3 – INTOLERABLE<br>PLACE EVENT ON HOLD |
|---|---|---|---|---|
| | SEVERITY | | | |
| | ACCEPTABLE<br>LITTLE TO NO EFFECT ON EVENT | TOLERABLE<br>EFFECTS ARE FELT, BUT NOT CRTICAL TO OUTCOME | UNDESIRABLE<br>SERIOUS IMPACT TO THE COURSE OF ACTION AND OUTCOME | INTOLERABLE<br>COULD RESULT IN DISASTER |
| LIKELIHOOD | | | | |
| IMPROBABLE<br>RISK IS UNLIKELY TO OCCUR | LOW<br>- 1 - | MEDIUM<br>- 4 - | MEDIUM<br>- 6 - | HIGH<br>- 10 - |
| POSSIBLE<br>RISK IS LIKELY TO OCCUR | LOW<br>- 2 - | MEDIUM<br>- 5 - | HIGH<br>- 8 - | EXTREME<br>- 11 - |
| PROBABLE<br>RISK WILL OCCUR | MEDIUM<br>- 3 - | HIGH<br>- 7 - | HIGH<br>- 9 - | EXTREME<br>- 12 - |

**FIGURE BB11.10**
Risk Assessment Matrix Template.

reducing the costly and time-consuming need to rework on designs. FMEA can help organizations meet ever-increasing customer expectations for reliability by eliminating or mitigating failures before they are encountered by customers or users (see Figure BB11.11).

Engineers and managers throughout the organization make decisions concerning risks every day. Providing a set of clear strategies along with guidance allows the organization to appropriately mitigate risks on a regular basis.

Mitigation approaches include avoid, accept, reduce/control, or transfer.

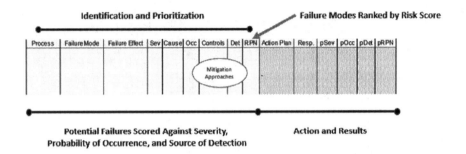

**FIGURE BB11.11**
FMEA.

## STREAMLINED PROCESS IMPROVEMENT

Although what we have discussed so far provides an excellent approach to product-related innovation, it is not quite as effective at process innovation in a nonmanufacturing environment (finance, after-sales services, quality assurance, procurement, HR, and so on) This methodology was originally introduced in Business Process Improvement and updated in Streamlined Process Improvement (SPI). Figure BB11.12 shows the five phases of SPI.

SPI also takes advantage of the continuous improvement and relevant systems methodology to improve performance. Typical examples are ISO 14000, ISO 9000, Quality Circles, Lean, Six Sigma, and TQM. The

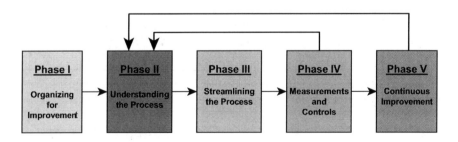

**FIGURE BB11.12**
Five Phases of SPI Methodology.

continuous improvement methodology should result in a continuous performance improvement of 5 to 10 percent per year in a step function improvement when the breakthrough methodologies are used in IT business processes.

## BUSINESS PROCESS IMPROVEMENT

Just as we have to have innovative creative output for the external customer, the same thought pattern has to relate to public service ourselves. This means that we have to continuously modify, upgrade, and reinvent the processes that control our internal operation and/or service and social interface with their external customers. To accomplish this, we recommend a methodology called Business Process Improvement (BPI). It is a methodology designed to help the organization maximize the efficiency and effectiveness of their processes.

To get economy of scale, most companies organize themselves into vertically functioning groups, with experts of similar background grouped together to provide a pool of knowledge and skills capable of completing any task in that discipline. This creates an effective, strong, and confident organization that functions well as a team, eager to support its own mission. Unfortunately, however, most processes do not flow vertically; they flow horizontally (see Figure BB11.13).

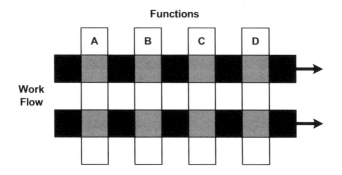

**FIGURE BB11.13**
Horizontal Workflow versus Vertical Organization.

A horizontal work flow combined with a vertical organization results in many voids and overlaps, and encourages sub-optimization, negatively impacting the efficiency and effectiveness of the process. Consider an order entry department that decided to stop comparing the item order number to the written description, even though they had been finding 3.3 percent errors. They reasoned that it was the salesperson's responsibility to ensure that the order was filled out correctly, and they could use the extra 40 hours per week currently devoted to confirming the order to process the growing backlog of orders. This had a very positive effect on the order entry department's primary measurement. The number of hours required to process an average order dropped from 38 to 12 hours. Other benefits include

- Saving the time involved in making the comparison.
- Saving the time and telephone cost required to contact the sales person to determine whether the number or the narrative was correct.
- Reduction of overtime from 10 to 0 percent by applying the time spent to check the orders to inputting orders into the computer.

Upper management was so impressed with the improvement that it gave the whole department a "night on the town" at the company's expense.

Sounds great, doesn't it? Unfortunately, while the intention was good, the end results were disastrous. In this case, 2 percent of the customers began to receive the wrong product. The day before a major trade show, one customer, who had ordered 10,000 balloons with Ajax Tools printed on them, received 10,000 coats with Ajax Tools embroidered across them. The result was a spoiled promotional campaign for the customer – and it proved very difficult for the supplier to sell 10,000 coats with Ajax Tools embroidered on them.

When you don't look at the total process, it creates a group of individual small companies being measured on goals that are not in tune with the total needs of the business. This leads to sub-optimization.

Despite cases like these, a functional organization has many benefits, and a strategy is available to take maximum advantage of its effectiveness, as well as ensure that the processes provide maximum benefits to the company. That strategy is BPI.

What we must do is stop thinking about the functional organization, and start looking at the process we are trying to improve. I am always surprised when I sit down with a group of managers who are involved in a critical business process, such as accounts payable, and ask them, "Who owns the process?" Usually, I encounter eight different managers all sitting on their hands. In most cases, no one owns these critical parts of a business. Everyone is doing a good job, but no one makes sure that the activities interrelate. A critical part of business process improvement is to assign someone to own each critical business process. Thomas J. Watson, Jr., former chairman of the board of IBM, explained the problem, saying,

> I believe the real difference between success and failure in a corporation can often be traced to how well the organization brings out the great energies and talents of its people. How does it help these people find common causes with each other? How does it keep them pointed in the right direction, despite the many rivalries and differences which may exist among them?[1]

BPI ensures the effective and efficient use of resources – facilities, people, equipment, time, capital, and inventory.

## Five Phases of BPI

The following identifies the five phases of BPI and how to implement them within your organization. Figure BB11.14 shows these five phases. With this methodology, you will be able to manage your business processes.

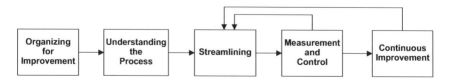

**FIGURE BB11.14**
The Five Phases of BPI.

---

1 https://www.azquotes.com/quote/578476

- Phase I – Organizing for Improvement (Ernst & Young Technical Reports TR 90.002 HJH And TR 90.003 HJH).
  Objective: To ensure success by building leadership, understanding, and commitment.
  Activities:
  (1) Establish an Executive Improvement Team.
  (2) Appoint a BPI champion.
  (3) Provide executive training.
  (4) Develop an improvement model.
  (5) Communicate goals to employees.
  (6) Review business strategy and customer requirements.
  (7) Select the critical processes.
  (8) Appoint process owners.
  (9) Select the Process Improvement Team members.

- Phase II – Understanding the Process (Ernst & Young Technical Reports, TR 90.004 HJH And TR 90.005 HJH).
  Objective: To understand all the dimensions of the current business processes.
  Activities:
  (1) Define the process scope and mission.
  (2) Define process boundaries.
  (3) Provide team training.
  (4) Develop a process overview.
  (5) Define customer and business measurements and expectations for the process.
  (6) Draw a flow diagram of the process.
  (7) Collect cost, time, and value data.
  (8) Perform process walk-throughs.
  (9) Resolve differences.
  (10) Update process documentation.

- Phase III – Streamlining (Ernst & Young Technical Report TR 90.006 HJH).
  Objective: To improve the efficiency, effectiveness, and adaptability of the business processes.
  Activities:
  (1) Provide team training.
  (2) Identify improvement opportunities:

(i) Errors/rework

(ii) Poor quality

(iii) Backlog

(iv) High cost

(v) Long time delays

(3) Eliminate bureaucracy.

(4) Eliminate no-value-added activities.

(5) Simplify the process.

(6) Reduce process time.

(7) Error proof the process.

(8) Upgrade the equipment.

(9) Standardize.

(10) Automate.

(11) Define the improvement approach.

(12) Document the process.

(13) Select the employees.

(14) Train the employees.

(15) Measure results.

- Phase IV – Measurement and Control (Ernst & Young Technical Report TR 90.007 HJH).
  Objective: To implement a system to control the process for ongoing improvement.
  Activities:

  (1) Develop in-process measurements and targets.

  (2) Establish a feedback system.

  (3) Audit the process periodically.

  (4) Establish a poor-quality cost system.

- Phase V – Continuous Improvement (Ernst & Young Technical Reports TR 90.008 HJH, TR 90.009 HJH, and TR 90.010 HJH).
  Objective: To implement a continuous improvement process.
  Activities:

  (1) Qualify the process.

  (2) Perform periodic qualification reviews.

  (3) Define and eliminate process problems.

  (4) Evaluate the change impact on the business and on customers.

  (5) Benchmark the process.

  (6) Provide advanced team training.

## SUMMARY

Complexity pervades the world today. Our products continue to become increasingly complex. Mistakes in design can be catastrophic to the organization. Sometimes, the best solutions, the best designs are those that refrain from unnecessary complexity. In closing this chapter, the "Good design" principles of Dieter Rams are a refreshing reminder of the basics of good design.

Dieter Rams is a German industrial designer closely associated with the consumer products company Braun and the Functionalist school of industrial design. By designing electronic devices that were remarkable in their austere aesthetic and user friendliness, Rams helped make Braun a household name in the 1950s. He introduced the idea of sustainable development and of obsolescence being a crime in design in the 1970s. Accordingly, he asked himself the question: "Is my design good design?" The answer he found became the basis for his acclaimed ten principles. According to Rams, "Good design"

(1) *is innovative* – The possibilities for progression are not, by any means, exhausted. Technological development is always offering new opportunities for original designs. But imaginative design always develops in tandem with improving technology and can never be an end in itself.

(2) *makes a product useful* – A product is bought to be used. It has to satisfy not only functional, but also psychological and aesthetic criteria. Good design emphasizes the usefulness of a product whilst disregarding anything that could detract from it.

(3) *is aesthetic* – The aesthetic quality of a product is integral to its usefulness because products are used every day and have an effect on people and their well-being. Only well-executed objects can be beautiful.

(4) *makes a product understandable* – It clarifies the product's structure. Better still, it can make the product clearly express its function by making use of the user's intuition. At best, it is self-explanatory.

(5) *is unobtrusive* – Products fulfilling a purpose are like tools. They are neither decorative objects nor works of art. Their design

should therefore be both neutral and restrained, to leave room for the user's self-expression.

(6)  *is honest* – It does not make a product appear more innovative, powerful, or valuable than it really is. It does not attempt to manipulate the consumer with promises that cannot be kept.

(7)  *is long-lasting* – It avoids being fashionable and therefore never appears antiquated. Unlike fashionable design, it lasts many years – even in today's throwaway society.

(8)  *is thorough down to the last detail* – Nothing must be arbitrary or left to chance. Care and accuracy in the design process show respect toward the consumer.

(9)  *is environmentally friendly* – Design makes an important contribution to the preservation of the environment. It conserves resources and minimizes physical and visual pollution throughout the life cycle of the product.

(10)  *is as little design as possible* – Less, but better – because it concentrates on the essential aspects, and the products are not burdened with nonessentials. Back to purity, back to simplicity.

# BB12

## Innovative Robotics/Artificial Intelligence: The Future of Innovation

*Sid Ahmed Benraouane*

## CONTENTS

## INTRODUCTION

Just a few years ago, the topic of artificial intelligence (AI) was a specialization of academic research institutions and tech labs, and speculation of scientific movies such as the Matrix and Her. Today, AI seems to have moved to mainstream society and became the center of the discussion of CEOs, business leaders, policy makers, strategists, and entrepreneurs willing to capitalize on this historical shift that will change the way we conducted business during the last one hundred years. More than half of CEOs surveyed in 2019 think that AI will have a larger impact than internet, while 80 percent of CEOs think AI will significantly change the way we conduct business in the next five years.

Andrew Ng, a leading scientist in machine learning, argues that the impact of AI on our society will be similar to the impact of electricity on the world civilization. When electricity was discovered and became cheap and accessible to everyone, it became the engine that fueled innovation in every single segment of the economy, and the spark that lit up progress and scientific development in the twentieth century.

James Harrington, an American thought leader in quality and innovation and the editor of this book, argues that, because of its power to transform the way we do business today, AI will be the most important source of innovation in the near future; it will shape the global economy in a profound way. Successful companies will be those who move first on introducing this new technology into different segments of the economy to take advantage of its disruptive nature. Economic sectors, such as transportation, logistics, manufacturing, defense, and national security, will be deeply affected by AI, while traditional management functions such as operations, logistics, HR, finance, marketing, and customer service will experience a fundamental shift.

So what is AI and how it is different from human intelligence? How will AI affect business and the global economy and what should managers do to take advantage of this technological breakthrough? What will be the impact of this new technology on social norms and how will society react to it? These are some of the questions that we will address in this chapter.

## DEFINITION OF AI

Before we get into all these questions, let's start with some conceptual frameworks that will help us understand the nature of this nascent technology and how it will impact our lives.

AI is a branch of computer sciences that has been evolving since 1950. The term was first coined by the American cognitive scientist and inventor John McCarthy in a conference paper presented in 1956 to Dartmouth College Conference. The ambition, at that time, was to create a machine that mimics the activities a human brain performs during the learning process. In McCarthy's mind, by automating different learning tasks a human brain goes through, we may be able to program a machine to learn and behave in similar ways to humans.

Haugeland (1985), an American professor of philosophy and cognitive science, provides another definition. For Haugeland, AI refers to "the exciting new effort to make computers think … machines with minds, in the full and literal sense." In this definition, Haugeland believes that AI in the future could acquire capabilities that are similar to the ones humans have. These capabilities are abstract thinking, emotions, feeling, and consciousness.

Kurzweil (1990), an American inventor and futurist, provides yet another definition of AI. He argues that "AI is concerned with building machines that can act and react appropriately, adapting their response to the demands of the situation." In this definition, Kurzweil adopts a behaviorist approach to AI in order to point out the ability of machines to act intelligently.

For this book we will define AI as:

(1) a branch of computer science dealing with the simulation of intelligent behavior in computers.
(2) the capability of a machine to imitate intelligent human behavior.

## DIFFERENT TYPES OF AI

To understand better the definition of AI, we need to address the different types of AI. They are:

(1) Artificial Narrow Intelligence (ANI) or narrow AI,
(2) Artificial General Intelligence (AGI) or general AI,
(3) Artificial Super Intelligence (ASI) or super AI.

Because not all of the types of AI we talk about today have the same power and impact, it is important to remind the reader about the distinction that needs to be made between three types of AI. In the field of AI, we make the distinction between Artificial Narrow Intelligence (ANI) or narrow AI, Artificial General Intelligence (AGI) or general AI, and Artificial Super Intelligence (ASI) or super AI. Important to mention that at this junction of history, we have been able to discover only narrow AI. We are not able yet to use the general AI or super AI.

### Artificial Narrow Intelligence (ANI)

This type of AI, also called weak AI, is designed to perform a very precise and well-defined task. It is narrow because it does not go beyond what it has been programmed for. It operates according to the rules and the pre-defined parameters. A good example of a narrow AI is the language processing programs we are all familiar with, such as Apple's Siri and Amazon's Alexa. Another example of narrow AI is the AI algorithm behind search engine, such as the RankBrain program Google uses, to map queries, organize searches, and rank pages according to a specific parameter that is provided by the programmer.

These applications, while they appear to be very intelligent in interacting with us, they perform in a very narrow fashion. They perform only actions for which they were programmed. Apple Siri, for instance, while it may seem that it knows everything, it interacts only from within what has been provided to it by the data sets. In other words, it cannot go beyond the parameters from which it reads. That is why Siri, or any other language processing application, is unable to understand language subtleties such as humor, jokes, sadness, or emotion in general.

It has been said that a computer can be no more intelligent than the individual that is supplying it with information. This is true. But when 100 people are provided with information soon becomes more intelligent and advanced to any 1 of the 100 people.

H James Harrington

## Artificial General Intelligence (AGI)

The second type of AI is general AI. This type of AI, also known as full AI or strong AI, has the potential of mimicking human cognition, and the decision-making process that a human brain goes through. This is the type of AI that we see in Sci-Fi movies and makes us scary about the prospect of AI. While we are still too far from this kind of AI, the exponential nature of technology will one day lead us to strong AI where computers will be sovereign to make decisions outside of human control. These decisions will not be narrow. They will involve abstract thinking, strategic thinking, and judgment calls about situations that are surrounded by ambiguity and uncertainty. There already has been one case per hour in which computers generated their own language to talk to each other that humans could not understand.

## Artificial Super Intelligence (ASI)

The third category of AI is called super AI. In this type of AI, we reach the Singularity moment where the machine intelligence surpasses human intelligence. In this type of AI, the machine acquires qualities that are so far exclusively part of the human experience: consciousness, a term that characterizes humans and refers to our ability to know, feel, perceive, and be aware of our surrounding, including the meaning of time and space.

## AI: THE FUTURE GROWTH STRATEGY

Today the interest in AI is largely because of the advances in computing, big data, and the availability of large data sets with affordable access to cloud computing. Peter Diamandis, an entrepreneur and a co-founder of Singularity University, argues that the sudden emergence and interest in AI today is the result of a deep disruption that started to shape up two decades ago. The explosion of many different exponential technologies at the same time, as he argues, created a disruption that has led to the AI revolution.

The computing power of today's processors, the advances in sensors and network, the relatively easy access to cloud computing, and advances in material science have accelerated the AI revolution and made it more accessible to a large spectrum of economic agents. He calls this moment the "Unexpected Convergent Consequences."

Most of the studies that looked at the impact of AI on the global economy agree on the fact that AI is a game changer. The automation of tasks that used to be performed by humans, such as the maintenance of transportation fleet, the management of loan and the detection of fraud, and customers experience, will be the new opportunity that companies have to seize on to capitalize on the power of AI. In a study conducted by Accenture in 2018, it was predicted that AI will increase productivity in the USA by 40 percent, resulting thus in a net improvement in GDP growth from 2.6 percent to 4 percent.

Furthermore, AI will not only impact productivity but also will be an important source for the development of new products and services that will have a direct impact on the performance of national economies. In the USA, AI is poised to deliver more than $15.7 trillion in economic growth by 2030 according to a PWC study. Other countries that make the top 50 percent of the global economy will also see similar improvements. Sweden will see an increase of 37 percent, Finland 35 percent, and Japan 34 percent in their GDP, according to the same study.

The following are three products that would bring fundamental changes in the way we live and think when they are developed to the point they are ready for the general public.

- *Teleportation*: Ping Koy Lam, Australian National University, transported a beam of light.
- *Altering gravity*: Dr. Ning Li, Researcher, University of Alabama, constructed a super-conducting disc.
- *Synthetic humans*: In Sandia National Laboratories, a chip that will synthesize the eye's retina.

## ECONOMIC SECTORS THAT WILL BE IMPACTED BY AI

As we transition from the current economy to an AI-powered economy, most economists agree that the first sectors that will reap the benefits of AI are manufacturing, health care, banking, transportation, cybersecurity, and national defense.

## The Manufacturing Sector

In manufacturing, for instance, optimization will be the most important outcome of AI. Cohen (2018), from the Economic Strategy Institute, argues that AI will impact three areas: assets optimization, fleet optimization, and network optimization. With AI, manufacturing facilities can become better at managing their performance and optimizing their outputs.

## The Finance Sector

In the finance sector, AI is poised to have a major disruption. According to Forbes (2018), the banking industry is expected to save more than $1 trillion by 2030. Areas such as risk assessment, fraud detection and management, financial advising service, customer experience, and trading will take more advantage of AI technical advances. Automated algorithmic trading can process a huge amount of data and learn from the pattern of trading to make suggestions for stock trading while watching for triggers to identify anomalies. Similar applications are also used in loan processing and loan management. AI and automation of loans can result in many advantages. It can reduce credit loss, lower due diligence costs, and increase orientation revenue.

## The Transportation Industry

In the transportation industry, the AI revolution is already happening. From driverless trains to self-driving cars, AI breakthrough is expected to change the way consumers perceive transportation. Currently, AI applications are being tested on traffic control systems in order to eliminate jams, reduce waiting time at traffic lights, and synchronize the flow of vehicles in intersections.

## National Security and Law Enforcement Sector

Another economic sector that is considered critical to the USA national strategy is the national security and law enforcement sector.

Facial recognition applications have improved tremendously and now they can be used to monitor traffic, detect suspicious behavior in major events, and predict when a crisis will hit in the future. Predictive policing, an AI application that runs in some of USA police departments, can now analyze crime areas and map out crime hotspots to predict where crime is more likely to happen. Predictive policing is based on algorithms that learn from the historical data to make forecasts about the spike in crime in a specific region.

## The Health Care Sector

In health care, AI will be a true game changer. The ability of AI to read images and identify the discrepancy on the image with a higher level of accuracy than a human being will have a deep impact on the economics of this industry. Patients will benefit greatly by getting an accurate reading of their medical images. In a study conducted by Siemens, deep networks were able to detect tuberculosis with an accuracy rate of 97 percent, and a specificity of 100 percent, thus surpassing the human rate set at an average of 60 percent. The speed of reading and the accuracy level will be of great help to hospitals producing large amount of data. Estimates put the data produced by hospitals, in the forms of X-rays, CT scans, MRI, and medical imagining, at around 50 petabytes of data per year. Only machine learning algorithms can process this amount of data and provide meaningful reading of this huge amount of data to doctors in order to make an accurate diagnosis to patients.

## The Cybersecurity Sector

Finally, cybersecurity is another sector of interest to companies where AI can be critical. AI is more effective with a large amount of data that run in large networks. AI applications can now spot better and more efficiently malicious activities and can identify intruders that cannot be caught by conventional signature-based detection software. The ability of AI to study and detect patterns that are suspicious and learn from their behavior is what makes AI a powerful tool in protecting national assets and critical infrastructure.

## STRATEGY IMPLICATIONS: THE CURRENT STATE OF AI ADOPTION

A quick survey of AI users shows that worldwide AI adoption is getting some attraction. In a survey conducted by McKenzie in 2018, nearly half of the respondents said that they have integrated at least one aspect of AI and machine learning into their standard business operations, while 30 percent said that they are testing new AI solutions. Most companies tend to start with robotic process automation (RPA), language processing, computer vision, and conversational interfaces.

A study conducted by Davenport and Ronanki in 2018 reveals that out of 152 companies using AI, 71 use the technology for process automation, 57 use it for cognitive insights, and 24 use it for cognitive engagement. While process automation seems to be the obvious and easy application of AI, cognitive insights and cognitive engagement are the future of AI and hold more promising opportunities. Companies willing to understand market behaviors and connect better with customers to enhance and improve the overall customer experience will find a great strategy in AI.

### AI in Automation: RPA

RPA represents the most basic form of AI. In general, any process that is rule-based, has a digital input, and is routine can be automated. Companies that use RPA, use it for back-end office operations such as reading and transferring emails and file, transferring data, toggling systems, applying business rules, orchestrating business processes, execute ERPs instructions, and record keystrokes. This type of AI is programmed to execute simple instructions and cannot "think" by itself. It is a good example of a narrow AI.

The impact of this kind of AI on the business bottom line is tremendous given the cost-saving benefits it provides to companies. According to a study conducted by Deloitte in 2018, RPA has an average return of 20 percent of full-time equivalent capacity provided by a robot, with 92 percent of improved compliance, 86 percent improved productivity, and 59 percent cost saving. Companies engaged in RPA will continue to do so primarily to focus on continuous improvement, increase the level of automation, and develop analytics capabilities.

## AI in Prediction: Gaining Cognitive Insight

The second type of AI implementation is cognitive insight. According to the study conducted by Davenport and Ronanki, many companies use AI as a tool to understand better their customers and their markets. In this type of applications, companies use AI as a predictive tool to understand users' behavior, detect patterns of clicks, and be able to predict how customers react to different campaigns. According to Davenport and Ronanki, companies using AI use it to achieve the following goals:

- Predict future customers' choices in terms of what product or service they will acquire.
- Understand how to personalize ads to target specific customers.
- Use data on warranty or fraud to decide about trends and what type of customers are likely to benefits from a specific service.

## AI in Cognitive Engagement: Building Customers Relationship

The third category of AI users is companies using AI to engage with their customers in order to enhance personalization and impact the customer experience. Bots can identify clues during the conversation with a customer to make suggestions or custom products to the specific needs of the customer. Spotify, a music start up, uses AI to customize music offering to customers based on their preference, tastes, and habits. This musical site is one of the most powerful sites in customers' engagement as it gets better by the day at predicting customers' mood and tastes with high accuracy. Another example of companies using cognitive engagement is China Merchant Bank, one of the largest credit card companies in China. The bank uses a bot called WeChat Messenger to handle more than 1.5 million customer conversations a day. These conversations are about banking products, balance inquiry, and payments.

Another example of AI application to engage with customers is the partnership KFC China has established with the Chinese search engine Baidu. This application uses a facial recognition in order to customize menus based on the facial expression, the gender, and the mood of the customer walking into the store.

## AI AND ROBOTICS

Definition:

**Robotics** is an interdisciplinary branch of engineering and science that includes mechanical engineering, electronic engineering, information engineering, computer science, and others. Robotics deals with the design, construction, operation, and use of robots, as well as computer systems for their control, sensory feedback, and information processing. These technologies are used to develop machines that can substitute for humans and replicate human actions.

A robot is a mechanical or virtual artificial agent, usually an electro-mechanical machine that is guided by a computer program or electronic circuitry. Robots may be constructed to take on human form but most robots are machines designed to perform a task with no regard to how they look.

Of all the applications of AI, robotics seems to be the one that presents more promises and excitement for the business world. Because of the expected value that programmed robots will deliver, especially in manufacturing, the excitement about robotics has grown exponentially. While we have lived with robots for a long time, the ability now to program robots to be autonomous, presents a historical moment that gets everyone excited from business leaders to average people.

From an engineering point of view, a robot has two parts: the mechanic infrastructure, which refers to the electronics, the sensors, and the navigation system that robot needs in order to move around and gain agility, and the cognitive dimension, which is the dimension that helps robots think, reason, and make a decision. This dimension is performed primarily by neural networks, a subfield of AI that has seen a revival during the last two decades. This dimension is also important because it helps us connect robotics to AI. Many believe that AI and robotics are two different fields and should not be mixed. While this was true for the old generation of robots, which operated under the "rule-based" theory (If/Then), it is not true for current generation of robots using neural network. Neural network-based robots do not follow strict rules, but make decision on their own based on the data, the examples, and the training models they are fed.

## INDUSTRIAL ROBOTICS AND AI

In manufacturing, robots perform an outstanding job in helping companies produce more with less. In assembly lines, robots execute pre-programmed tasks, such as material handling, welding and painting, and help companies reduce human errors, produce better quality products, and reduce time delivery. Three factors are driving the interest in robotics: the falling prices of robots, the ability of companies to seamlessly integrate robots into manufacturing, and the ability of robots to perform complex task while still collaborating with people. According to 2018 survey conducted by the International Federation of Robotics, robotics sales grew by 15 percent per year in 2018. The main markets for this growth were USA, China, South Korea, Japan, and Germany. In China alone, robotics sales grew by 56 percent reflecting the nature of the economic transformation China is undergoing. In the USA, the field of robotics has gained momentum as companies deploy more robotics capabilities at a higher speed. According to the International Federation of Robotics, this trend, if it continues, will increase robotic density in the USA which is set at 164 industrial robots per 10,000 employees, well above the global average of 74 industrial robots by 10,000 employees. This trend will also reverse the outsourcing movement as it becomes cheaper to use robots on American soil.

## MEDICAL ROBOTS

The introduction of robotics into medicine and health care is one of the most important AI breakthroughs. While robots have been used in the medical field for the last twenty-five years, mainly as a tool for guided precision and repeatability, new developments of this technology are revolutionizing the health care industry. Robots now in hospitals can perform many functions to support doctors and nurses. Robots can take blood samples, transport analyses, and store them. They can detect easily the right vein when drawing blood thus reducing stress and anxiety for vulnerable patients. They can also carry carts and beds in large facilities and can even help physical therapists in administering their physical therapy.

## MILITARY ROBOTS AND AI

Military robotics aims at helping soldiers on the battle ground to overcome natural obstacles, difficult tasks, and dangerous missions such as walking around minefield or deactivating explosives. Military robots are programmed to operate in an unstructured area and aim at replacing humans in dangerous situations. Most of the military applications of robotics tend to be a programmed robot controlled by an operator and equipped with image recognition software to help robots identify and adapt to what they see. A rover, for instance, can map out the terrain and check the type of obstacles against its database to choose the right path in case of an obstacle. In the United States, the most known military robot is the Big Dog robot developed by Boston Dynamic and Crusher developed by DARPA and designed by Carnegie Mellon's National Robotics Engineering Center (NREC).

Another military application of robotics and AI is in the field of autonomous weapon and weapon targeting, an application that combines AI and robotics to train robots at using weapon autonomously. According to Daniel Faggella, who leads the Emerj Artificial Intelligence Research group, autonomous weapon today can identify targets in the specific area they have been assigned to and autonomously track it. This AI application is one of the most important breakthroughs in the defense sector. And while today there is no autonomous weapon that can fire on its own and without clear and explicit instructions from a human agent approving the fire, this type of autonomous weapon will one day be developed. This is why it is important to develop a strong code of ethics that guides and regulates this type of weapon.

## IMPACT OF AUTOMATION ON SOCIETY: HOW WILL SOCIETY REACT TO AI AND AUTOMATION?

When a new technology emerges there are a lot of unknowns. In the case of AI, the discussion so far is centered on fear, excitement, and hypes. While there are a lot of studies that show the positive impact of the new technology on society, there are also calls for the need to be careful in the way we adopt and use AI. So far the research conducted on the subject of AI falls into two categories. Those who believe that automation will have a positive impact on the economy, the wider society, and will create more opportunities for people, and therefore we need to embrace it. And those who take a cautious perspective on AI and think that AI will increase job loss and will displace entire segments of the economy, in addition to the risks that it will produce like in the autonomous driving, autonomous weapon, and AI-powered cyberattacks.

So how does society react to AI? And what will be the impact of AI on society? How do people react to automation and would they accept it or reject it?

In addressing these questions, the World Economic Forum (WEF 2019) presents a framework for policy makers with three possible scenarios.

1. Scenario One: Society will accept AI because there is a balance between automation and technological breakthrough.

   In this scenario, and according to the WEF, people will accept automation because automation may not develop to its fullest. Automation may simply stumble against some technical obstacles such as the quality of data and the lack of computing power. In this scenario, we face limited progress of automation that will put a break on the momentum and the power of AI. In the labor market, for instance, it will not be possible to automate every single aspect of a job family because jobs tend to have a high level of task diversity, according to WEF. It will be difficult for companies to automate an entire spectrum of tasks. For instance, it will not be possible to automate the job of a financial analyst because, in addition to the repetitive task a financial analyst conducts, he or she also performs other tasks that are based on judgment, creativity, and communication. The complexity that is inherently built into the nature of the job makes it simply difficult to fully automate.

2. Scenario Two: Society will reject AI because of our own irrational behavior.

   In this scenario, society may reject automation because of the irrational behavior that tends to characterize humans. In this scenario, the WEF argues that humanity may not be interested in the full automation, not because automation is not good, but because, as a human species, we are not always rational in our choices. Even though automation may be the right path for us, as human beings, and because we do not always follow rational paths, we may simply choose not to fully automate our lives. The irrational aspect of our behavior may simply make it difficult for automation to take place thus forcing us to make a selective choice between what we want to automate and what we don't want to automate. As well argued by WEF, much of the support of this scenario comes from the newly produced research in the field of behavioral economics. Behavior economist Dan Ariely, a researcher at MIT, argues that human beings are fundamentally irrational in their decisions and they can be predictably irrational in their choices, their behavior, and their policy-making decisions.

3. Scenario Three: Society will accept automation but at a slow pace and with a planned process.

The third scenario described by the WEF on the spectrum of acceptance/rejection of full automation is called "planned automation." In this scenario, humanity may reach full automation by developing a rational process for data collection and machine behavior with a clear definition of what is exactly needed. Policymakers can define the ethical and moral framework that will govern this process of full automation. In this scenario, the decision of whether to automate or not, and to what extent we should automate our lives, has to take place through discussion, iteration, and consultation about what society needs and expects from full automation. As well explained by WEF, the government may provide more help to those who may be adversely impacted by the full implementation of automation by providing incentives, such as training programs for displaced workers, ethical guidelines on when AI can be used for, and tax breaks to help local governments and disadvantaged communities take advantage of full automation.

## THE JOBS AI WILL CREATE

As with any digital transformation, AI impact on the job market will also be positive. While researchers agree that AI and robotics will eliminate a lot of jobs, they also agree that AI will create other types of jobs. Those who are poised to benefit from this disruption will be companies that are moving simultaneously on three fronts: changing and reinventing the business process, rebuilding human capital of the organization, and utilizing data by intelligently capturing its power.

According to a study conducted by Accenture 2018, AI will create new jobs that we have not seen in the past. These jobs are the jobs of trainers, explainers, and sustainers.

### Trainer

According to the research conducted by Accenture, the first category of jobs needed is the people who will need to train AI on how to respond adequately to input from customers. There are two types of training needed. Those who will help natural language processors and translators understand the meaning of input on one hand, and those who will train algorithm on how to imitate human behavior on the other hand. Examples of this category of jobs include training AI on language subtleties, recognizing sarcasm, and identifying the true meaning of a statement.

### Explainer

When companies deploy new algorithms, the result sometime may not be what the company has predicted. In many cases, AI behaves in a way that was not programmed. What we refer to as the "block-box problem" could be solved by training people on how to explain the decision made by AI and make sense of it. Take the example of a bank's algorithm that was built to depict the creditworthiness of customers so the lender can make the judgment about the loan approval process. If the algorithm starts to reject a specific segment of customers, then the lender is expected to explain the why of this situation. Explainers are an important category of the AI value chain because they provide AI with the credibility it needs when it is deployed for the first time. Explainers help business leaders make sense of AI behavior and provide an answer to the public. In Europe, the need for "explanation" has become a legal requirement. The General Data Protection Regulation (GDPR) recently implemented requires companies to provide an explanation about their decision.

### Sustainer

The third category of new jobs that AI is expected to create, according to Accenture, is the type of jobs that will help companies keep AI on a check.

In their research of more than 1,000 companies, Accenture found that less than one-third of companies trust with high degree their AI system. This is a challenge if companies still don't have full confidence of this new technology. Sustainers will need to understand the purpose of the AI system implemented and the mission of the organization as well as the type of stakeholders. Their role is to watch for behavior that could go wrong, much more like a compliance officer or ethical committee tracking algorithm's behavior.

## THE USA ARTIFICIAL INTELLIGENCE NATIONAL STRATEGY

Because of its transformative nature, AI has become a powerful economic tool that will provide countries with a global leadership position. In the last five years, many countries have launched different documents that outline their AI strategy. Some of these countries are Canada, France, China, the UAE, and the USA. The underline thread for these documents is a political will to organize the countries' resources and capabilities into a coherent framework that will spur innovation around AI and other exponential technologies. While these strategies are different from one another, their common objective is to create an AI ecosystem that targets funding, R&D, education, and private–public partnership. Some of these countries, like China, have also set large budgets to encourage investments in infrastructure and digital transformation, *a sine qua none* condition to AI growth.

In the USA, most observers agree that the US government has not done what it needs to do in order to organize resources and rally the nation behind this new technology. What the USA has done, in terms of policy, was the publication of a collection of documents that were produced in 2016 and 2019 to lay out the national AI agenda. The first set of documents was released by the White House Office of Science and Technology Policy in 2016, and set the following objectives as a framework for AI national policy:

1. The development of a long-term investment plan in AI research and the prioritization of the investment choices the federal government makes to push for sectors and appreciation in which the USA wants to have a leadership position.

2. The development of strategies that focuses on human–machine collaboration to make sure that machines are always subject to a human decision and not the other way around.
3. The design of AI systems that are easily integrated and can easily comply with current laws, regulations, and ethics.
4. The development of safety and security standards in order to create AI that can be controlled and subject to the safety and security needs of the community.
5. The importance of developing a high-quality data set in order to guarantee a much better training opportunity for AI.
6. The need to develop a framework to measure and benchmark AI in order to be able to evaluate its impact on common performance and social development.
7. The need to develop more research to understand the impact of AI on the labor market and how the United States can better develop educational opportunities that will allow an increase in the talent pool that is needed for AI jobs.

The second step in the development of the US national AI strategy was in 2019 when the White House launched the American AI Initiative. In this document, the White House identified the following objectives to boost AI:

(1) Investing in AI and R&D.
(2) Unleashing AI resources.
(3) Setting governance standards.
(4) Building the AI workforce.
(5) International engagement and protecting the AI advantage.

## SUMMARY

While these two steps set a good framework for national AI strategy, most of critics agree that the USA needs to do more to catch the AI global race. The current initiative seems to lack details, funding, and is short on the ethical framework that will serve as a model for AI governance. China for example has set an objective of becoming the world leader in AI technology. (Watch out Silicon Valley.)

# BB13

## Knowledge Assets Management

*Mitchell W. Manning, Jr. and Mitchell W. Manning, Sr.*

## CONTENTS

## OVERVIEW

Today, more than ever before, knowledge is the key to individual and organizational success. To fulfill this need, the Internet and other information technologies provide access to more information than we can ever manage. Instead of having a source of information, the Internet provides us with hundreds, if not thousands of inputs, all of which must be researched for the critical nuggets of knowledge. We become so overwhelmed with information we don't take time to think about how to use it.

The term "knowledge assets" was first introduced in the Baldrige Glossary in 2003. It refers to the accumulated intellectual resources of an organization. It is the knowledge possessed by the organization and its workforce in the form of ideas, learning, understanding, memory, insights, cognitive and technical skills, and capabilities. The organization's databases, documents, guides, policies and procedures, software, and patents are repositories of organizational knowledge assets. Knowledge assets are held not only by the organization but also reside within its customers, suppliers, and partners. They are the "know how" that the organization has available to use, to invest, and to grow. Building and managing knowledge assets are strategic priorities to creating value for stakeholders and to helping sustain overall organizational performance success.

Baldrige21.com as edited by Mitchell W. Manning, Sr.

Most individual and therefore organizational knowledge is undocumented. Knowledge rests in the minds and experiences of the individuals/ employees. Left unharvested, knowledge disappears from the organization's knowledge base every time an employee leaves an assignment. In many organizations today, the knowledge assets are more valuable than the combined facility, equipment, and unsold inventory. An organization's first knowledge priority is to collect and document the undocumented knowledge of its employees. The second knowledge priority is, preventing inside and outside sources from hacking the knowledge base. The knowledge asset database can be hacked not only by competitors and disinterested third parties, but also by the people you hire, the tools you buy and use, your suppliers, your vendors, the language you allow to be used, the behavior you overlook, and the things you celebrate and reward. If you have ever questioned your changing individual or corporate culture, look to uncontrolled innovation, and changing knowledge assets for root cause.

Total Innovation Management Excellence provides a descriptive approach to tasks, functions, processes, and systems for adding value. The biggest problem with the information age is too much information. Now, I know so much I can't remember it all.

The number of definitions for innovation has passed 40 and continues to increase. This proves someone somewhere has been innovative. Knowledge Assets Management (KAM) is the process leading innovation excellence.

KAM is found in the fourth tier of the TIME Pyramid, which is the Delivery Processes Level. This tier of the pyramid focuses on the organization's processes and the outputs the customer/consumer receives. There are three building blocks:

(1) Building Block 11 – Innovative Product, Services, Processes Designed
(2) Building Block 12 – Innovative Robotics/Artificial Intelligence
(3) Building Block 13 – Knowledge Assets Management

## TIME FOR CAUTION

Excellence in KAM will change your culture and your attitude. It will change the language you use; your tools and how you use them; your institutions and how you meet; and your arts (how you express yourself with recognition, rewards, and celebration). All cultures build and decline on four components: language, tools, institutions, and art. Tools are the most impactful component on culture change. Tools change the language, the institutions, and the art. You don't have to drive innovation. Innovation drives you and your culture. You need to manage innovation, and you need to begin with identifying your knowledge assets and the sources of the culture influencers.

### Culture Development Exercise

Brainstorm the knowledge asset sources using Figure BB13.1 for an individual, a family, and an organization. Describe/discuss/draw the connections. Develop and share ideas on how to manage these influencers.

### Knowledge Assets Flow Exercise

Three examples of Total Innovation Management Excellence (TIME) have been provided. Identify the knowledge assets procured and where and when; describe how they might have been protected (how, why, and who); describe how they might have been promoted, developed, improved, and innovated; finally think about how the knowledge assets and their sources might have been propelled if useful and if not useful.

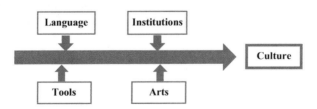

**FIGURE BB13.1**
Culture Development Exercise.

**FIGURE BB13.2**
Knowledge Assets Flow Exercise.

Describe/discuss/draw the connections and discuss the value of managing knowledge assets to achieve TIME.

## Example One

The young man in this picture was 18 years old in 1952. He is at the train station in Mobile, Alabama, with $1.50 in his pocket; two changes of clothes in the bag by his right foot; along with his mama's fried chicken and ham biscuits. He was on his way to Indiana to take a job.

He was going to play baseball for the Indy Clowns of the Negro Leagues. Apparently, he was pretty good at it. He played for the Milwaukee Brewers for two seasons, and for the Milwaukee Braves, before later following them to Atlanta.

On his 85th birthday he was still working, but as the senior vice president of the Atlanta Braves. His retired number, 44, still hangs on the outfield wall of the old Atlanta-Fulton County Stadium near where he belted a home run to break Babe Ruth's all-time record. "Hammerin' Hank" Aaron, born on February 5, 1934, learned how to manage his knowledge assets and mastered innovation.

## Example Two

He was born on July 30, 1863, on a farm in Michigan to an Irish immigrant father and an orphaned first-generation Belgian mother. His father gave him a pocket watch in his early teens. At 15, he learned to dismantle and reassemble the pocket watch. He quickly gained the reputation of a watch repairman by doing the same with timepieces of friends and neighbors. He left the farm to work as an apprentice machinist in Detroit, first with James F. Flower & Bros., and later with the Detroit

Dry Dock Co. In 1882, he returned to work on the family farm, where he became adept at operating the Westinghouse portable steam engine. He was later hired by Westinghouse to service their steam engines. During this time, he also studied bookkeeping. He went on to convert an expensive curiosity into a practical tool that profoundly changed the landscape of the 20th century. He became one of the richest and best-known people in the world. He is credited with promoting mass production of inexpensive goods coupled with high wages for workers. He had a global vision, with consumerism as the key to peace. His intense commitment to systematically lowering costs resulted in many technical and business innovations, including a franchise system that put dealerships throughout most of North America and in major cities on six continents. Ford left most of his vast wealth to the Ford Foundation and, arranged for his family to control his company permanently. Henry Ford knew how to manage his knowledge assets to drive innovation (as edited by Mitchell W. Manning from Henry Ford/Wikipedia, 02/22/2019).

## Example Three

He was born on an Oklahoma farm that didn't provide enough income to raise a family. Despite moving frequently from town to town and state to state, he became the youngest Eagle Scout ever in Missouri. He helped his family make financial ends meet by hiring out to do chores, carrying a paper route, selling magazines, and milking the family cow and selling the surplus to neighbors. His high school class voted him "Most Versatile Boy." He worked odd jobs and waited tables in exchange for meals while attending the University of Missouri as an ROTC cadet. He earned a bachelor's degree in economics and his graduating class elected him "permanent class president." He went to work for J. C. Penney three days after graduation as a management trainee for $75 a month. He left that job to begin working in a DuPont munitions plant anticipating joining the military for World War II. He attained the rank of Captain in the Army Intelligence Corps while supervising security at aircraft plants and prisoner of war camps. At age 26, Sam Walton purchased his first retail variety store where he began to pioneer innovations in purchasing, merchandizing, transportation, and assets management (as edited by Mitchell W. Manning, Sr. from Sam Walton/Wikipedia, 02/22/2019).

## LEARNING OBJECTIVES OF THE CULTURE AND ASSETS EXERCISES

1. You are the product.
2. You innovate or deteriorate.
3. KAM is the critical building block for excellence/success.

### Recognizing Knowledge Assets

The cause and effect diagram in Figure BB13.3 is provided to stimulate thinking about your knowledge assets and where to place the responsibility and accountability for managing them. The practice of managing knowledge assets is key to excellence for the individual, the family, and the organization.

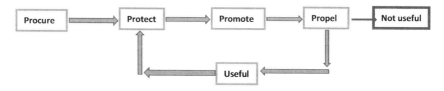

**FIGURE BB13.3**
Cause and Effect Diagram.

My mind went to – of all things – the plow. The plow is an excellent embodiment of the history of innovation.

Humans have been using them since 4000 BCE when Mesopotamian farmers used sharpened sticks to aerate soil.

We've been slowly tinkering with and improving them ever since, and today's plows are technological marvels.

Bill Gates – www.gatesnotes.com, February 27, 2019.

## UNDERSTANDING INNOVATION AND KAM

Table BB13.1 is provided to stimulate your thinking about innovation in KAM.

About the same time the farmers were tilling the ground with their sticks, leaders there and around the world were developing ideas about ethical behavior, relationships, core values, and societal norms. By 1000 BCE, more than one group of people had created documents with rules, laws, literature, poetry, history, and science. This is an early example of KAM. The effectiveness of their KAM is evident in the world today as much of what was written is still being practiced, debated, and innovated.

The U.S. Constitution is an example of an innovation of their early work. "The Genius of the People revealed itself in the strange mix of bankers, farmers, politicians, merchants, scholars and generals who struggled throughout the long summer of 1787 to construct a constitution unique in the history of nations. By the end of the convention, none of the delegates, not one, was entirely happy with the constitution they had written. Some refused entirely to sign the completed work; and those who did sign signed in varying degrees of reluctance, dismay, anguish, and disgust" (The Genius of the People, Charles L. Meeks, Jr., Harper and Row, New York, 1987; as edited by Mitchell W. Manning, Sr. 02/27/2019).

KAM for TIME is challenging, rewarding, and has long-term impact. Give it your best, and then some.

**TABLE BB13.1**

Dominant Technology Innovation versus Time

| Phases | Introduction | Elaboration | Conclusion |
|---|---|---|---|
| Demographics | Trendsetter | Follower | Resister |
| Processes | Design/Develop | Implement/ Enhance | Assimilate |
| Life Cycle | 25% | 50% | 25% |

**Dominant Technology Innovation**

| 1840 | 1880 | 1920 | 1960 | 2000 | 2040 |
|---|---|---|---|---|---|
| Steel Plow | Interchangeable Parts | Petrochemical Fertilizers | Computer | Artificial Intelligence | The Next Big Thing. |

## RESPONSIBILITY AND ACCOUNTABILITY FOR MANAGING KNOWLEDGE ASSETS

The responsibility and accountability for managing knowledge assets belongs at the top of the food chain. The individual is responsible and accountable for procuring, protecting, promoting, and propelling value added knowledge assets at the personal level. The head of the family is responsible and accountable at the family level. The chairperson is responsible and accountable at the organizational level. Hank Aaron, Henry Ford, and Sam Walton are excellent examples of "the buck stops here."

### What Can Possibly Go Wrong? The Theranos Case Study

#### "She Never Looks Back": Inside Elizabeth Holmes's Chilling Final Months at Theranos

At the end, Theranos was overrun by a dog defecating in the board-room, nearly a dozen law firms on retainer, and a CEO grinning through her teeth about an implausible turnaround (Vanity Fair, February 20, 2019, at 7:03 PM by Nick Bilton; as edited by Mitchell W. Manning, Sr. on 03/04/2019).

**Elizabeth Holmes** appeared to know exactly what she needed to do. It was September 2017, and the situation was dire. Theranos, the blood-testing company she had dreamed up more than a decade ago, during her freshman, and only, year at Stanford, was imploding before her very eyes. **John Carreyrou**, an investigative reporter at *The Wall Street Journal*, had spent nearly two years detailing the start-up's various misdeeds – questioning the veracity of its lab results and the legitimacy of its core product, the Edison, a small, consumer blood-testing device that supposedly used a drop of blood to perform hundreds of medical tests. Carreyrou had even revealed that Theranos relied on third-party devices to administer its own tests. Theranos, which had raised nearly $1 billion in funding for a valuation estimated at around $9 billion, now appeared less a medical-sciences company than a house of cards …

In Silicon Valley, founders and CEOs often embrace a signature idiosyncrasy as a personal branding device. Steve Jobs wore the same black turtleneck every day and tended to only park in handicap spots.

**Mark Zuckerberg** went through a phase during which he would only eat the meat of animals he had personally killed. **Shigeru Miyamoto**, the Nintendo video-game legend, is so obsessed with estimating the size of things that he carries around a tape measure. It can get even weirder. **Peter Thiel** has expressed an interest in the restorative properties of blood transfusions from young people. **Jack Dorsey** drinks a strange lemon-water concoction every morning and goes on 10-day silent retreats while wearing designer clothing and an Apple Watch. Holmes, too, had seemingly cherry-picked from her elders. She wore a black turtleneck, drank strange green juices, traveled with armed guards, and spoke in a near baritone. In an industry full of oddballs, Holmes – a blonde WASP from the D.C. area – seemed hell-bent on cultivating a reputation as an iconoclastic weirdo …

Silicon Valley can often feel like a lawless place, and for good reason. Many of the people who run the largest technology companies on earth don't often suffer the consequences of their actions. Despite their unequivocal role in upending our democracy, Zuckerberg and Sheryl Sandberg still run Facebook. Dorsey is still the CEO of Twitter, even though he has not been forthright about the number of bots on the service and has done almost nothing to stop the spread of hate speech on his platform. The CEO of Tesla, Elon Musk, was charged with securities fraud. He agreed with the S.E.C. to step down as chairman and pay a $20 million fine …

The fascination with Holmes often fixates on her extraordinary rise – her ability to convince Stanford scientists to believe her idea despite a lack of formal training; her aptitude for getting wisemen (**Henry Kissinger, James Mattis, and George Schultz**) to sit on her board; and her skill for obtaining early funding from eminences such as **Rupert Murdoch**, the Walton family, and others. But the final days of Theranos were equally chilling. After all, Holmes wasn't just an inexperienced scientist; she was also a wild-spending fiduciary …

Holmes faces consequences, but it may take a while. Justice Department officials, according to a filing from January 2019, are combing through between 16 and 17 million pages of documents. And there could be more charges filed against Holmes and Balwani (her former boyfriend and Theranos COO), and even other people close to them.

Assistant U.S. Attorney John C. Bostic said in court recently that the "story is bigger than what's captured in the [original] indictment." And that it "doesn't capture all the criminal conduct" that the investigation has uncovered so far. Holmes faces up to 20 years in prison.

### Learning Objective for the Theranos Case Study

1. List the KAM stakeholders.
2. List the knowledge assets obvious to each stakeholder.
3. Discuss and decide where the buck stops.
4. Review managing knowledge assets: with technology systems (see the following paragraph and Figure BB13.4).
5. Identify, discuss, and decide the critical knowledge asset system (see Table BB13.2).

### Managing Knowledge Assets: With Technology Systems

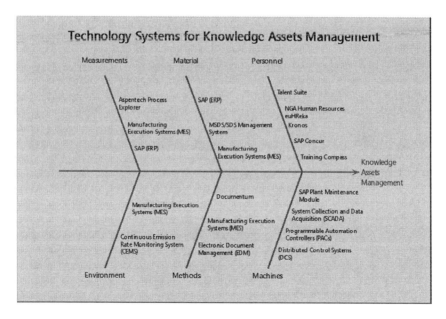

**FIGURE BB13.4**
Technology Systems for Knowledge Management.

**TABLE BB13.2**

Knowledge Asset Management System Definitions

| Knowledge Asset Management System | Definition |
|---|---|
| Aspentech Process Explorer | Aspen ONE Process Explorer is the easiest, fastest, and most convenient way yet of accessing and analyzing tag data, characteristics and unstructured data using the most innovative operations data visualization platform on the market – in a web application with desktop power and performance. |
| SAP Concur | SAP Concur simplifies travel, expense, and invoice management for total visibility and greater control. |
| Continuous Emission Rate Monitoring System (CEMS) | A CEMS is the total equipment necessary for the determination of a gas or particulate matter concentration or emission rate using pollutant analyzer measurements and a conversion equation, graph, or computer program to produce results in units of the applicable emission limitation or standard. |
| Distributed Control System (DCS) | A DCS is a computerized control system for a process or plant usually with many control loops, in which autonomous controllers are distributed throughout the system, but there is central operator supervisory control. This contrasts with systems that use centralized controllers – either discrete controllers located at a central control room or within a central computer. The DCS concept increases reliability and reduces installation costs by localizing control functions near the process plant, with remote monitoring and supervision. |
| Documentum | Documentum is an enterprise content management platform, now owned by OpenText, as well as the name of the software company that originally developed the technology. |
| Electronic Document Management System (EDMS) | An EDMS is a software system for organizing and storing different kinds of documents. This type of system is a more particular kind of document management system, and a more general type of storage system that helps users to organize and store paper or digital documents. |
| NGA Human Resources euHReka | NGA Human Resources euHReka supports 921 individual Core HR features and functions to include Talent acquisition, Personnel Management, Payroll, Benefits, Workforce Management, Training Management, Employee Self-Service, and Product Technology. |

(Continued)

**TABLE BB13.2**  (Cont.)

| Knowledge Asset Management System | Definition |
| --- | --- |
| Kronos | Kronos online system is the time reporting system used for submitting employee hours to payroll. |
| Manufacturing Execution Systems (MES) | MESs are computerized systems used in manufacturing, to track and document the transformation of raw materials to finished goods. |
| Programmable Automation Controllers (PACs) | A PAC is an industrial controller that combines the functionality of a programmable logic controller with the processing capability of a PC. |
| SAP (ERP) | SAP stands for Systems Applications and Products in Data Processing. SAP is also named of the ERP (Enterprise Resource Planning) software as well the name of the company. SAP Software was Founded in 1972 by Wellenreuther, Hopp, Hector, Plattner, and Tschira. |
| SAP Plant Maintenance Module | SAP Plant Maintenance (SAP PM) is a software product that manages all maintenance activities in an organization. The Plant Maintenance module consists of key activities to include inspection, notifications, corrective and preventive maintenance, repairs, and other measures to maintain an ideal technical system. |
| System Collection and Data Acquisition (SCADA) | SCADA is a control system architecture that uses computers, networked data communications, and graphical user interfaces for high-level process supervisory management but uses other peripheral devices such as programmable logic controller and discrete proportional integral derivative controllers to interface with the process plant or machinery. |
| Talent Suite | Talent Suite is a talent management system. It is an integrated software suite that addresses the "four pillars" of talent management: recruitment, performance management, learning and development, and compensation management. |
| Training Compass | Learning and Development system for employee training and tracking. |
| MSDS/SDS Management System | A document management system for material safety data sheets and safe data sheets. |

## NEXT STEPS

You can be the Hank Aaron, Henry Ford, or Sam Walton in your category or even Elizabeth Holmes, if you will. Google, Facebook, and Amazon with a little help from Cambridge Analytica can take you there, if they already haven't done so. Artificial Intelligence (AI) is here if you want it and are willing to pay for it. Airlines and the military have been training and assessing pilots with AI for decades. We once took turns landing a simulator in San Francisco over 30 years ago. The green faces and the rush to the rest rooms after the landings confirmed for us anyway, the reality of the training. Both of us have validated logistics, manufacturing, and laboratory technology with technological capacity that far exceeded the actual use for more than 25 years. And, the last three cars I've owned have had technology I paid for but never used, or at least didn't know I was using. And you guessed it, I'm not comfortable with that. We've taken the low-tech approach favored for machinists training in this chapter. We feel you need to know the feel of the metal of your knowledge assets as you shape them for use to achieve TIME.

We recommend starting with what you have. Look at your individual knowledge assets first to build experience, and then your organization(s). If you don't already know your KAM systems, you can do a brown paper exercise to identify where they are and look at what they are doing. The second step is to do a SWOT analysis. Knowing your strengths, weaknesses, opportunities, and threats relative to your individual and organizational knowledge assets will be useful for you. The third step is to apply the quality principles of elimination, simplification, and acceleration to your KAM. The fourth step is to establish 3 to 5 needs and set 1 to 10 priorities for no more than 10 wants. If you are divided into functional groups, you can do this by group (Human Resources, Operations, Finance, Engineering, Marketing, Sales, and Quality). Validate the alignment and integration of your knowledge assets. The final step is to monitor, control, and close. The close needs to be documented in a KAM file. Repeat once annually minimum, and more often if needed. Use Figure BB13.5 to develop a KAM plan using the six faithful servants.

The faithful servants are numbered in priority order. If we've learned anything important about project management through education and experience, the most important is to put the first thing first and the last

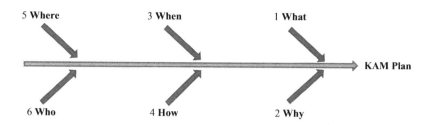

**FIGURE BB13.5**
KAM Plan Using Six Faithful Servants.

thing last. What then why lead the way to TIME. If you are serious about on or ahead of schedule, on or under budget, and meet and exceed expectations, this is the path to take.

We have been using and teaching the SOPPADA presentation technique since 1984. How we found it is a mystery. You can find a SOPPADA template in Google documents. How we used SOPPADA is nothing short of a miracle. All levels and all disciplines of people can use the process to present issues, requests, ideas, project plans, recommendations, and subjects. In one ten-year period in one company, 73 Quality Circles presented, gained approval, and implemented over 1,000 projects which returned over $100,000,000 to the company in EBITDA (earnings before interest, taxes, depreciation, and amortization). We wanted to leave you with a gift for reading this chapter. Now, let's go exploring KAM to achieve TIME.

> When a person dies, a library is lost.
>
> H. J Harrington

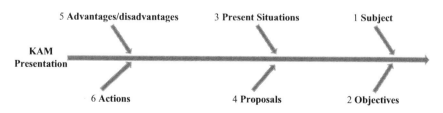

**FIGURE BB13.6**
KAM Presentation: Using SOPPADA.

# INTRODUCTION TO KNOWLEDGE MANAGEMENT

Dr. Donald S. Feigenbaum, Executive Vice President and COO, General Systems Company, Inc. stated,

> Dr. Jim Harrington's lifetime career of highly successful, hands-on, knowledge-based organization leadership is in itself an example of the role of knowledge in both personal and enterprise success. And it is why he is so highly qualified to write and to teach us about the enormous transition that is taking place today in the powerful new character of emphasis upon knowledge in the work of all of us.

"Knowledge is Power" was the traditional – and, today inaccurate – term that an earlier business generation inscribed in granite blocks over major buildings from educational and research edifices to corporate headquarters. Today, the very different and correct term is, instead, "Knowledge is Power – When Managed with Excellence."

A basic principle of corporate strength has become recognition that effective knowledge management is a basic requirement in today's constantly changing global marketplace. It is a major key for business growth and profitability strength in the 21st century. And for effectiveness it requires systematic and rigorous implementation and attention as the key business asset it has become. An increasing number of today's corporate leaders recognize this. They understand that knowledge is an integral business leadership component of management and has to be organized and systematically structured as an integral component of business operations. In Knowledge Management Excellence, the authors clearly explain to us how to accomplish this successfully. In specific, clear terms the book discusses the fundamental factors in implementing the ongoing knowledge management excellence results.

> If only HP knew what HP knows, we would be three times more productive.
>
> Lew Platt, Former CEO of HP

Good is no longer good enough. Doing the right thing "right" is not good enough. Having the highest quality and being the most productive will not do it today. To survive in today's competitive environment, you need to excel. To excel, an organization needs to focus on all parts of the organization, optimizing the use and effectiveness of all of its resources. To excel, you need to provide "knock their socks off" products and services. You need to be so innovative and creative that your customers say, "I didn't know they could do that!"

Today, more than ever before, knowledge is the key to organizational success. In order to fulfill this need, the Internet and other information technologies have provided all of us with more information than we can ever consume. Instead of having one or two sources of information, the Internet provides us with hundreds, if not thousands, of inputs, all of which need to be researched to be sure you have not missed a key nugget of information. We are overwhelmed with so much information that we don't have time to absorb it.

> One of the biggest problems facing organizations around the world is the lack of a knowledge sharing and learning culture.

To make matters worse, most of the organization's knowledge is still not documented; it rests in the minds and experiences of the people doing the job. This knowledge disappears from the organization's knowledge base whenever an individual leaves an assignment. Most organizations need a Knowledge Management System (KMS) that is designed to sort out unneeded and/or false information and capture the "soft" knowledge needed to run the organization.

> At the individual level, it (capabilities) includes personal knowledge and individual skills and talents; while at the organizations level, competence includes infrastructure, networking relationships, technologies, routines, trade secrets, procedures, and organizational culture. Knowledge is today's driver of company life.
> N. Bontis, N.C. Dragonetty, K. Jacobsen & G. Roos "The Knowledge Toolbox" *European Management Journal*, 17(3), 343–356

With the almost endless amount of information that clouds up our computers, desks, and minds, the KMS needs to be designed around the organization's key capabilities and competencies.

As professionals, we try to express everything in a formula. The original formula for Organizational Excellence was:

*Best Practices + Best Technology = Excellent Performance*

Today's formula is:

*Best Practices + Best Technology + Energized*
*Knowledgeable People = Excellent Performance*

## WHAT IS KNOWLEDGE?

Definition: Knowledge is defined as a mixture of experiences, practices, traditions, values, contextual information, expert insight, and a sound intuition that provides an environment and framework for evaluation and incorporating new experiences and information.

Definition: Knowledge management is defined as a proactive, systematic process by which value is generated from intellectual or knowledge-based assets and disseminated to the stakeholders.

Knowledge takes us from chance to choice.

The true standard of success for knowledge management is the number of people who access and implement ideas from the knowledge networks. These networks bring state-of-the-art ideas and/or best practices into the workplace. This allows the organization to develop areas of critical mass that implement standards that work, and also provides access to everyone so they can make comments to improve those standards. Even the newest novice to the organization can look at the materials and make recommendations based upon personal insight, creativity, and experience.

Benjamin Franklin once said, "If a man empties his purse into his head, no one can take it away from him. An investment in knowledge always pays the best interest."

Knowledge management is an evolving broad umbrella of topics and viewpoints, and in this book you will find major thoughts and trends. A successful knowledge management program begins with a foundational strategy that integrates the organization's strategy.

However, strategy is not enough for we must also consider the question of how knowledge is shared. To do so, we must consider what techniques or approaches are useful for managing knowledge, and what techniques have produced less than satisfactory results.

Knowledge is the only instrument of production that is not subject to diminishing returns.

-J. M. Clark

We are living in a knowledge economy. The value of most organizations is defined by its intellectual capital, rather than by its physical assets, often by over 600%. The Mecca for knowledge in organizations today is located in Northern California (Silicon Valley). Yes, today knowledge is king. In the late 1800s Andrew Carnegie was the wealthiest man in the world. His wealth was made up of assembly plants, steel mills, raw materials, equipment, and the finished goods of Carnegie Steel. Today Bill Gates' wealth comes from the "heads of his programmers." The Financial Accounting Standards Board is working on establishing standards for measuring intangibles.

The organization of the future is held together by information.

-Peter Drucker

Not too long ago, back in the "dark ages" of the 1970s, a coffee machine or water cooler was the only technology needed to facilitate in-house knowledge sharing. But as the information needs of the modern business organization grew ever more demanding, formal systems and practices were needed to encourage the transfer of knowledge between the workers, other departments, and other organizations. With the advent of the knowledge revolution, and once digital networks emerged as the central resource for communication and information retrieval, many companies are discovering that making individual knowledge common property has the potential to significantly improved operational efficiency and decision quality.

People perish from the lack of knowledge.

-Proverbs from The Old Testament

There has been more information produced in the last 30 years than during the previous 5000 years. We cannot go back to what we used to do for this "old world" has changed. The amount of information available to each of us doubles every five years. According to Richard Worman in "Information Anxiety," the weekday edition of the *New York Times* contains more information than the average person was likely to come across in a lifetime in 17th Century England. There is 1,000 times more information in that little 15″ computer screen on your desk than there is anyone's personal home library.

Today horsepower has given way to brainpower. Knowledge has become more precious than equipment in our fast changing world. In the 1950s organizations were searching for information. Today organizations and their employees are drowning in information. No one has the time to sponge up the information relevant to their interests, let alone sort through the mountains of information that is available to find the relevant information. And as many of us have experienced, you can get lost for days "surfing" the Internet just looking at interesting things.

## THE BASICS OF KNOWLEDGE MANAGEMENT

Knowledge Management (sometimes called Intellectual Capital[1]) is defined as (a) the practice of adding actionable value to information by capturing, filtering, synthesizing, summarizing, storing, retrieving and disseminating tangible and intangible knowledge; (b) developing customized profiles of knowledge for individuals so they can access the kind of information they need when they need it; (c) creating an interactive learning environment where people share what they know and apply it to create new knowledge.

According to the "father" of knowledge management, Karl-Erik Sveiby,[2] companies usually take one or more of the following approaches to knowledge management to achieve their objectives:

- Capturing, storing, retrieving, and distributing tangible knowledge assets, such as copyrights, patents, and licenses.
- Gathering, organizing, and disseminating intangible knowledge, such as professional experience, creative solutions, and the like.
- Creating an interactive learning environment where people readily transfer and share what they know, internalize it, and apply it to create new knowledge.

---

1 *Intellectual Capital: The New Wealth of Organizations*, Thomas Stewart, Doubleday, 1997.
2 *The New Organizational Wealth: Measuring and Managing Knowledge-Based Assets*, Erik Svilby, Berrett-Koehler, 1997. One of the few authors with hands-on experience of running a business, Sveiby was one of the first to emphasize the importance of the physical office environment and the impact of information overload.

Organizations today are challenged to progress through the wisdom filter. (See Figure BB13.7)

- Filter One – Collect data
  - Data is bits and pieces that are not put into organized patterns and analyzed.
- Filter Two – Information
  - Used to draw a conclusion (reports, white papers, budgets, bills, etc.)
- Filter Three – Knowledge
  - At this level information is screened to identify trends and best practices. Duplications and obsolete material is discarded.
- Filter Four – Wisdom
  - At this level knowledge has been applied based upon experience, impact studies, and results analysis. Enough knowledge has been collected to validate the worth of the knowledge. At this level it can be applied to future projects and you will get very predictable results. It is validated knowledge.

Knowledge is not like a tangible product. If you have five apples and you sell one, you have four left. However, knowledge is intangible; it can be sold, given away, or traded, and you still have the knowledge. In fact, the more you use knowledge, the more valuable it becomes. But knowledge is also perishable. If it is not renewed and replenished, it

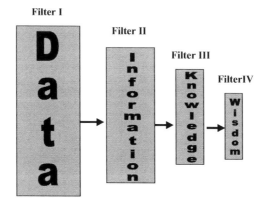

**FIGURE BB13.7**
Wisdom Filter.

becomes worthless. Yes, knowledge has a shelf life. An MBA who does nothing to renew his/her knowledge becomes obsolete within four years. Knowledge is always changing, and this requires every organization to become a learning organization or become an obsolete organization.

## Two Categories of Knowledge

There are two categories of knowledge: explicit and tacit.

> *Definition*: Explicit knowledge is defined as knowledge that is stored in a semi-structured content, such as documents, e-mail, voicemail, and video media. It can be articulated in formal language and readily transmitted to other people. We like to call this *hard or tangible knowledge*. It is conveyed from one person to another in a systematic way.

> *Definition*: Tacit knowledge is knowledge that is formed around intangible factors embedded in an individual's experience. It is personal, content-specific knowledge that resides in an individual. It is knowledge that an individual gains from experience or skills that he or she develops. It often takes the form of beliefs, values, principles, and morals. It guides the individual's actions. We like to call this *soft knowledge*. It is embedded in the individual's ideas, insights, values, and judgment. It is only accessible through the direct corroboration and communication with the individual that has the knowledge.

> Humans, left to their own devices, will build isolated fiefdoms, and pretty soon it is hard to pull the information together that you really need on an ongoing basis to manager the organization.
> —Robert J. Herbold, Retired COO (Microsoft)

Unfortunately, up to 80% of an organization's knowledge assets are the soft knowledge that is retained by the individual. Just ask yourself, "Of everything you know, how much of it would be classified as 'hard' knowledge?" The big challenge that organizations face today is how to convert as much of the soft knowledge as possible into hard knowledge. Here is a recent example of how one major corporation, IBM, handled this problem. IBM held an electronic "WorldJam," which ran for three days, for the purpose of converting soft knowledge into hard knowledge. Over 52,000 IBM employees participated by logging in from offices, hotel rooms, homes, and airports. They discussed 10 key subjects, ranging from building customer relationships to how to keep the employees on the road feeling like they are part of IBM. This proved to be a very successful means of converting soft knowledge into hard knowledge for more than 6,000 ideas and comments were posted.

Table BB13.3 was prepared to show you the differences between explicit and tacit data.

Organizations tend to focus on one of the two types of knowledge strategies – a hard knowledge or a soft knowledge strategy. The knowledge strategy you select will define how you select your employees, train them, and reward them.

If your organization selects a soft knowledge strategy, you will want to hire people that can live in turmoil and like to solve problems, that is, independent thinkers. They will require lots of personal one-on-one training. They like to learn by experience, not reading. You reward these people based upon how effectively they share their knowledge with others. Organizations should not select one strategy for today, but they need both the soft and hard knowledge strategies or they will be left behind the parade. Using either the soft or the hard strategy only will get you 30% of the way to your knowledge goal. However, when you effectively combine them, you will hit a home run, positioning yourself as the band leader in front of the parade.

**TABLE BB13.3**

Differences between Explicit Data and Tacit Data

| Explicit (Hard) Knowledge | Tacit (Soft) Knowledge |
| --- | --- |
| Based on documented skills, competencies, experiences and expertise, policies, procedures, instructions, standards, and results | Based on undocumented experience and expertise. Reflects ways of doing things |
| Exists as part of an organization | It is personal to the owner |
| Often well documented | Rarely documented |
| Held within an organization | Held within individuals |
| Accessible and easy to share | Not easily accessible and difficult to share |
| Accessed and enabled through collection and codification | Accessible only through personal exchanges, learning, and practice |

See Maja Van der Velden, *Journal of International Development*, (14), pp.27, 2002.

## KNOWLEDGE CAPITAL

Knowledge capital can be divided into three categories:

(1) Customer Capital – customer base, trademarks, brands, and so on
(2) Human Capital – know-how, creativity and innovation, knowledge, competencies, education and training, experiences, and so on
(3) Structure Capital – Information Systems, processes, databases, operating procedures

The five points of the Knowledge Capital Star represent the five-key knowledge-asset areas (see Figure BB13.8).

*Definition*: Knowledge Capital (same as Intellectual Capital) is the intellectual material, knowledge, information, intellectual property, and experience that can be put to use in order to create wealth. It is collective brainpower.

*Definition*: Knowledge artifact is a specific instance of a knowledge asset.

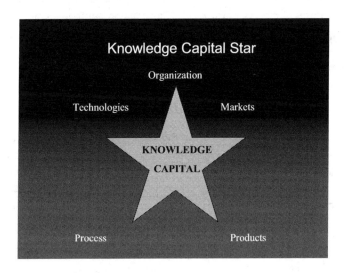

**FIGURE BB13.8**
The Knowledge Capital Star.

Knowledge is part of the social process. In Ikujiro Nonaka and Hirotaka Takeuchi's book, *The Knowledge Creating Company,* the authors point out that knowledge is passed on through four different modes of knowledge conversion.

## Four Modes of Knowledge Conversion

| Conversion Process | Knowledge Change |
|---|---|
| 1. Socialization | From tacit knowledge to tacit knowledge |
| 2. Externalization | From tacit knowledge to explicit knowledge |
| 3. Combination | From explicit knowledge to explicit knowledge |
| 4. Internalization | From explicit knowledge to tacit knowledge |

The knowledge management methodology was developed so that intellectual capital can be managed as an organizational asset. Knowledge management is designed to capture the flow of the organization's data, information and knowledge, and deliver it to the knowledge worker that uses it on a day-to-day basis. Dow Chemical developed a six-step approach to managing intellectual assets (Knowledge Capital) as follows:

- Step 1. Strategy – In this step they defined the role that knowledge would play in Dow Chemical.
- Step 2. Competitive assessment – Next, they set about to study their competition to define their knowledge strategy and assets.
- Step 3. Classified portfolio – They then set about to understand what their core competency knowledge base was, how they used it, and where it should be used.
- Step 4. Evaluation – In this step they studied their knowledge assets to define their worth and to maximize their total value.
- Step 5. Investment – They invested additional effort to fill any identified weaknesses or voids.
- Step 6. Assemble their knowledge portfolio – This was their continuous improvement phase where they continuously refined and identified their knowledge assets.

Information acts like a force of gravity that pulls the decision-making power lower into the organization.
–Richard Danzig, Former U.S. Secretary of the Navy

## KNOWLEDGE CAPITAL PARADIGMS

What happens when research team members grounded in the two paradigms described in Table BB13.4 I try to collaborate? They may seem
uncooperative or unproductive to each other, and thus be unable to work
together. Likewise, competitors who fail to understand each other's modus
operandi may cry "foul play." Nonetheless, working together across paradigms can be fruitful. Some behaviors and practices on both sides help this
process, while others are a hindrance. It takes a concerted effort to appreciate – and take advantage of – team members brought up in different
cultures. Good communication and a positive learning attitude are required.

## THE KNOWLEDGE CULTURE

> The climate we create as leaders has a major impact on our ability to share
> knowledge across time and space.
> – Robert Buckman, Buckman Laboratories

Knowledge sharing is first and foremost a cultural issue. When
employees start to share knowledge, the organization's culture will
change, becoming much more open. And so it is understandable that
installing a KMS is more a cultural challenge than it is a technological
challenge. In fact, cultural resistance is the most significant barrier to

**TABLE BB13.4**

Two R&D Paradigms

| Cartesian paradigms | Holistic paradigms |
|---|---|
| Causal | Acausal and causal |
| Divisible into small parts | Entire system is the unit |
| Single-valued | Multi-valued |
| Mainly goal-oriented | Mainly process-oriented |
| Often short term | Often long term |
| Uses thought experiments | Prefers physical experiments |
| Alphabetic expression | Ideogrammatic expression |
| Individual creativity | Group creativity |

knowledge management implementation as shown in this Microsoft study (see Table BB13.5).

To reiterate, the major problem we face in implementing a KMS is the culture of the organization. This stems from the fact that knowledge is power and as you make more and more knowledge available throughout the organization, there is a decided shift in power away from management to the staff. There is also a major problem at the staff level with sharing the individual's tacit knowledge. For years we have paid and promoted people based upon their knowledge and the way they use it. Individuals look upon their tacit knowledge as their competitive advantage. To share it with others is viewed as taking away this advantage. This means as you go about implementing a KMS, the culture and rewards structure has to undergo major changes. We need to reward people based upon the way they share their knowledge, as well as how they create and use the knowledge that is available.

To establish a knowledge culture, we need to understand the type of people we have in the organization and their approach to obtaining knowledge. Karen Stephenson, a professor at Harvard's School of Design, performed a study to define the informal pathways by which knowledge is communicated. She points out that there are three types of people:

(1) Hubs – People who collect and share data
(2) Pulse takers – People who build relationships that keeps them informed about what is going on in the organization
(3) Gatekeepers – People who control the flow of information that is communicated to a specific part of the organization

These three types of people transmit tacit (soft) knowledge throughout the organization and, in most cases, they do this more effectively that the

**TABLE BB13.5**

KMS as a Cultural Challenge

| | |
|---|---|
| • Cultural resistance | 48% |
| • Immaturity of technology | 19% |
| • Immaturity of industry | 16% |
| • Cost | 12% |
| • Lack of need | 5% |

formal organization structure does it. Different people will take the same information and reshape it to their own thinking pattern. Each person has a different background that has shaped his/her beliefs, prejudices, hopes, needs, wants, reactions, and interpretations. It is just normal for a person to selectively select the parts of the information that is presented to them, embracing parts of it and ignoring the other parts. A good KMS will help to offset these misconceptions and help them draw the correct conclusions from the information that is available to them.

## THE KNOWLEDGE MANAGEMENT LIFE CYCLE

Installing a KMS is not easy; it requires that the total organization undergo a transformation that includes its culture, structure, and management style, but the results are well worth the effort. However, before we talk about the KMS, let's look at the Knowledge Management Life Cycle. In its very simplest term, it is made up of six phases. (See Figure BB13.9)

### Phase I – Creating Knowledge

Information and knowledge creation can and does occur at any place, which includes all parts of the organization and the outside world. It is the result of an individual's creative thoughts and actions. All individuals must be encouraged to become involved in contributing and increasing the availability of information and knowledge.

### Phase II – Capturing Knowledge

This is the act of preserving knowledge by identifying its value. This includes both hard (explicit) and soft (tacit) knowledge. This is so crucial that IBM hired outside journalists to interview their own people to capture how they made the decisions that led to successful outcomes.

### Phase III – Transferring Knowledge

This is the act of transforming knowledge inputs into a standard format, which can be addressed by the stakeholders. It includes organizing the

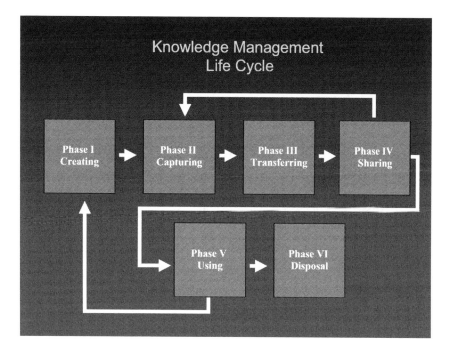

**FIGURE BB13.9**
Knowledge Management Life Cycle.

data into subject-matter groups to meet the needs of the users. Furthermore, enabling processes must be put in place that will prompt the system to update the most current knowledge.

## Phase IV – Sharing Knowledge

The knowledge-sharing phase is the most important phase of the life cycle. People throughout the organization must be willing to share their knowledge and experiences if the KMS is going to succeed. However, there are many reasons why people do not want to share their knowledge. Here are some of them:

- "I am valuable because I know something that no one else knows."
- "I am not rewarded for sharing."
- "Sharing is a waste of time."
- "People should be able to think it out themselves."

- "I am too busy to share information."
- "It is not worth the time."
- "The timing is not right."

The truth of the matter is that people are afraid of losing their personal competitive advantage if they share their knowledge.

Share your knowledge. It's one way to achieve immortality.

## Phase V – Using Knowledge

This is where the KMS pays off. Its big advantage is that the sharing of past experiences and knowledge helps to prevent errors from occurring and to create new and better answers to the organization's opportunities. It is also during this phase that new knowledge is created and fed back to Phase I.

## Phase VI – Disposal of Knowledge

As new ideas are created, better ways are developed, and best practices change, it is important to keep the knowledge warehouse purged of any obsolete information and past best practices. This must be done with care for sometimes historical data is very helpful as new approaches prove to be unsound.

## THE KNOWLEDGE SYSTEM

We are drowning in information but starved for knowledge.
–John Naisbitt, Author (Mega trends)

The KMS (Figure BB13.10) is a filtering and analysis system. The raw materials that go into this system are data from the many measurement points within and outside the organization. The data is accumulated and stored in a data warehouse. The data in the data warehouse is then analyzed and distilled into information that takes the form of reports, statements, bills, etc. This information is typically stored in an information warehouse. The information warehouse also receives information from many other sources, such as minutes of meetings, external reports,

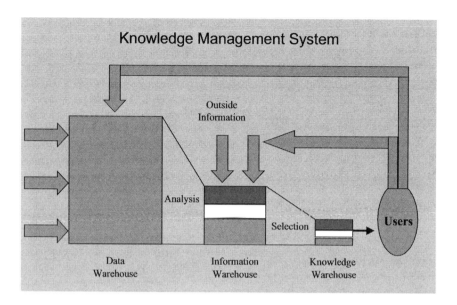

**FIGURE BB13.10**
KMS.

books, literature reviews, conferences, and papers, and from tacit knowledge that is converted into explicit information. Don't underestimate the amount of excellent information that can be collected from external sources (outside information).

> Books are not lumps of lifeless paper but minds alive on the shelves. From each of them goes out its own voice ... and just as the touch of a button on your stereo set will fill the room with music, so by taking down one of these volumes and opening it, one can call into range the voice of a man far distant in time and space, and hear him speaking to us, mind to mind, heart to heart.
>
> –Gilbert Highet, Literary Critic

> The need to acquire knowledge from outside – which you may call benchmarking – and the need to acquire knowledge from inside – the sharing of best practices – and then make it portable is a universal concept that will remain long after modern metaphor has changed.
>
> –Steve Kerr, CEO, GE

The 5 "Cs" that differentiate data from information are condensation, calculation, contextualization, correction, and categorization.

(1) Condensation – Data is summarized in a more concise form
(2) Calculation – Analyzed data similar to condensation of data
(3) Contextualization – You know why the data was collected
(4) Correction – Errors have been removed
(5) Categorization – The unit of analysis is known

The information within each silo is then reviewed to determine if it represents new or added-value information that should be added to the knowledge warehouse. This is often accomplished by subject matter experts. They will maintain the knowledge warehouse, updating it as new information becomes available and removing obsolete records. For example, the best practices for an individual knowledge subject are continuously changing so that the old best practices need to be removed and replaced by the current best practices. The knowledge warehouse never has raw data stored in it.

The output from the knowledge warehouse (repository) usually takes the form of a restricted portal that is set up for the users of the knowledge category. The knowledge warehouse can be considered the "bank" of our intellectual capital (see Figure BB13.11). The knowledge warehouse usually contains structured electronic repositories of knowledge; either

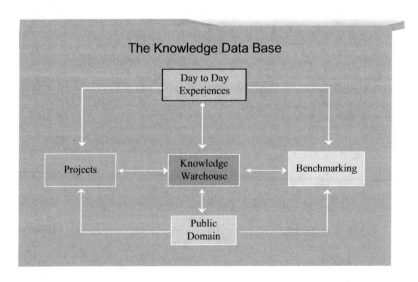

**FIGURE BB13.11**
The Knowledge Database.

structured document-based knowledge, information discussion-type knowledge, or repositories of "who knows what."

When organizations were asked by the Conference Board, "What were the obstacles to successful Knowledge Management?" they replied (see Table BB13.6):

**TABLE BB13.6**

Obstacles to Successful Knowledge Management

- 78% – Perceived need for KM
- 69% – Culture of hoarding knowledge
- 68% – Functional silos
- 67% – Incentives for sharing
- 46% – Proper technology for sharing
- 46% – Cost, financial support
- 30% – Top leadership
- 29% – Globalization
- 30% – Internal politics

## THE SIX PHASES TO INSTALL A KMS

Although in a learning organization everyone needs access to knowledge, most KMSs are designed around the core competencies of the organization. We recommend a six-phase approach to implement a KMS (see Table BB13.7). The six-phases are made up of 63 activities.

1. Phase I – Requirements Definition (8 activities)
2. Phase II – Infrastructure Evaluation (16 activities)
3. Phase III – KMS Design and Development (13 activities)
4. Phase IV – Pilot (15 activities)
5. Phase V – Deployment (10 activities)
6. Phase VI – Continuous Improvement (1 activity)

It would take a great deal of space to go into the details of each activity in each phase so we recommend reading "Knowledge Management Excellence" published by Paton Press.

**TABLE BB13.7**

The Six-Phase Approach to Implementing a KMS

| | | Knowledge Management Road Map | | | |
|---|---|---|---|---|---|
| Phase I *Requirements Definitions* | Phase II *Infrastructure Evaluation* | Phase III *KM System Design & Development* | Phase IV *Pilot Activities* | Phase V *Deployment* | Phase VI *Continuous Improvement* |
| Activities | Activities | Activities | Activities | Activities | Activities |
| 1. Develop a KM Vision Statement | 1. Survey existing sources | 1. Conduct a Benchmark Study | 1. Define layer capacity | 1. Define roll out stages | 1. Evaluate performance, measure ROI, continuously improve |
| 2. Define KM categories (K-spots) | 2. Identify KM Communication Systems | 2. Identify integrated functional requirements | 2. Install Internet | 2. Define incentives | |
| 3. Define KMS users | 3. Identify analysis tools | 3. Select platform | 3. Define platform interdependencies | 3. Deploy measurements | |
| 4. Identify input sources | 4. Identify tacit data & exchange | 4. Define intelligence layers | 4. Establish security controls | 4. Appoint subject matter experts | |
| 5. Identify measurements | 5. Change risk analysis | 5. Define search components | 5. Install filtering layers | 5. Set up portals | |
| 6. Prepare the change management plan | 6. Define K clusters | 6. Define silos | 6. Integrate middleware | 6. Conduct promotional campaign | |
| 7. Prepare project plan | 7. Define IT gaps | 7. Develop the KMS | 7. Connect legacy layers | | |
| 8. Organize the KM team | 8. Conduct SWOT | 8. Audit K assets | 8. Integrate and test total system | | |
| | 9. Prepare knowledge maps | | 9. Develop training package | | |
| | 10. Update the OCM plan | | | | |

11. Set priorities
12. Define ground rules
13. Conduct user survey
14. Perform a preliminary business needs analysis
15. Align KM and business strategy
16. Update project plan

9. Define KMS interfaces
10. Define tacit to explicit transfer
11. Develop KM organization
12. Create the KMS blueprint
13. Develop the KMS Rewards and Recognition System

7. Organize Communities of Practice
8. Train the effected personnel
9. Balance change management and technical factors
10. Implement communication plan

10. Implement the change management plan
11. Train the effected personnel
12. Establish the data, information, and knowledge warehouses
13. Start the pilot
14. Monitor the pilot
15. Make required improvements

## BENCHMARKING

To write about knowledge management and not include a discussion related to benchmarking would be a major error. Benchmarking provides an excellent means, if not the best, obtaining information related to best practices. It is one tool that any organization striving to have a comprehensive KMS will be using. Let me start by giving you a definition of benchmarking.

- Benchmark (BMK) – standard by which an item can be measured or judged
- Benchmarking (BMKG) – a systematic way to identify, understand and creatively evolve superior products, services, designs, equipment, processes, and practices to improve your organization's real performance.

There are four types of benchmarking:

(1) Product and Services
(2) Manufacturing Processes
(3) Business Processes
(4) Equipment

Darel Hall, manager of Transportation and Planning at AT&T's MMS division, stated "AT&T went into benchmarking for the right reason: to improve our business and culture."

A key to be successful at this is having meaningful measurements and challenging targets. You need to understand how and why other organizations perform as they do. In addition, you need to close negative gaps between best practices and the performance of its organization's processes. All too often the management team does not know the level of performance that is possible for the organization to reach. They don't believe that major improvements are possible. They don't know how to bring about major breakthrough improvements in their key KPIs (key performance indicators); the answer to this limitation is benchmarking.

There are five types of benchmarking processes:

(1) Internal Benchmarking
(2) External Competitive Benchmarking

(3) External Industrial (Comparable) Benchmarking
(4) External Generic (Trans Industry) Benchmarking
(5) Combined Internal and External Benchmarking

The benchmarking process today is very well defined. It is typically implemented in a five-phase process, consisting of 20 activities and 144 tasks. (See Figure BB13.12)

> The objective of benchmarking is to define places where you can improve, not to show how good you are.
>
> H. James Harrington

Table BB13.8 provides a more detailed breakdown of the five phases and 20 activities of the benchmarking process.

It is common practice for large organizations to establish a benchmarking office. This office is a point of contact for all external organizations that wants to benchmark an item within the organization.

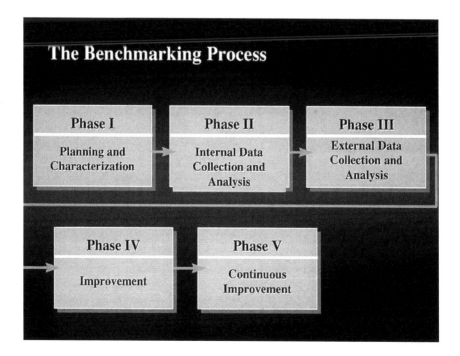

**FIGURE BB13.12**
The Five Phases of the BMKG Process.

**TABLE BB13.8**

Benchmarking's Five Process Phases

| BENCHMARKING PHASE | RELATED ACTIVITIES |
|---|---|
| **Phase 1**<br>Planning the Benchmarking Process and Characterization of the Item (s) | 1. Identify what to benchmark<br>2. Obtain top management support<br>3. Develop the measurement support<br>4. Develop the data collection plan<br>5. Review the plans with location experts<br>6. Characterize the benchmark item |
| **Phase II**<br>Internal Data Collection and Analysis | 7. Collect and analyze internal published information<br>8. Select potential internal benchmarking sites<br>9. Collect internal original research information<br>10. Conduct interviews and surveys<br>11. Form an internal benchmarking committee<br>12. Conduct internal site visits |
| **Phase III**<br>External Data Collection and Analysis | 13. Collect external published information<br>14. Collect external original research information |
| **Phase IV**<br>Improvement of the Item's Performance | 15. Identify corrective actions<br>16. Develop an implementation plan<br>17. Gain top management approval of the future-state solution<br>18. Implement the future-state solution and measure its impact |
| **Phase V**<br>Continuous Improvement | 19. Maintain the benchmarking database<br>20. Implement continuous performance improvement |

## Benchmarking Summary

Management's problems are as follows:

- They don't know what level of performance is possible.
- They don't believe that major improvements are possible.
- They don't know how to bring about major breakthrough improvements within the organization.

Benchmark is the answer to all three of these problems

## PATENTS AND TRADEMARKS

*Note*: This section of the book is written by Christopher Voehl in a book we co-authored – *Making the Case for Change* (published by CRC Press).

Business case recommendations involving potential candidates for patents and/or trademarks is a data-driven approach that involves proactive action related to community speaking the opportunities being pursued; yet, it cannot be treated as a stand-alone item. This is the point at which organizations need to investigate the use of patents and trademarks/copyrights in order to link the business plan recommendations with the organizational policies and management systems.

### Starting the Patent/Copyright Process

If the proposed idea/concept proves that it is an original idea/concept, which has not been registered by any other organization, the Business Case Analysis (BCA) team will contact the originator of the idea/concept and recommend that he/she register it. If the decision is made by the originator not to register the idea/concept, the BCA team should escalate the decision to the sponsor of the proposed project and record the results in their final report.

Learning how to avoid patent and trademark infringement is crucial to an inventor, entrepreneur, or any type of business case involving these items. It is best to spend a little time and money during the business case planning stage in order to avoiding patent infringement rather than defending a costly, time-consuming patent infringement lawsuit later. Considering that the concept of patent infringement can be complex and confusing to many, it is easy to understand why many business case developers choose to hide their heads in the sand rather than investigate the potential infringement issues up-front. This can be a path that can sometimes derail the best-developed business plan and even bankrupt the healthiest business. It is never too late to take the necessary steps to avoid patent infringement whether you are developing a product or have been manufacturing a product for many years and are attempting an upgrade.

## Issues to Consider

Some possible issues to consider during your BCA to determine whether or not you have any patent infringement issues prior to producing a product (or continuing to produce a product) are as follows:

- Possible costly lawsuit. A patent infringement lawsuit is extremely expensive compared to other types of lawsuits. A patent infringement lawsuit typically will cost $1 million or more in legal fees alone. It is not uncommon for even simple patent infringement lawsuits to end up costing a company many millions of dollars. If you lose the lawsuit, you will then be responsible for paying damages to the patent owner along with the potential for the associated damages and attorney's fees. The attorneys' fees alone can put many small businesses out of business when the lawsuit could have been avoided by spending as little as $10,000 – $15,000 hiring a patent attorney to review a patent for patent infringement issues. It is also important to note that many insurance policies do not cover patent infringement requiring you to pay the legal fees and damages yourself.
- Possible preliminary injunction. A patent owner may be able to get a preliminary injunction early in a lawsuit that stops the manufacture and sale of the alleged infringing product. An injunction can be costly to defend against and the "unknown" of whether the injunction will be granted can be negative to your business planning (and your customers).
- May be time consuming. A patent infringement lawsuit requires the officers and technical people of the company to participate heavily in litigation decisions. While one may believe that the lawyers will do most of the work, it is fair to say that the client's business developers will end up doing as much as 20% of the total work involved in a lawsuit.
- Your customers may be sued. Some patent owners may sue your clients, which can be very destructive for your continued business relationships. It can also be expensive for you since you may have an indemnification clause with your customer where you agree to pay their legal fees and any damages.
- May be able to identify non-infringing alternatives. By identifying potential infringement issues up-front, you can then determine

how to best design your product to avoid infringing upon one or more patents. The longer you wait in the product development process, the harder it will be to redesign your product when a patent infringement issue is identified.

## The Common Patent Mistakes Made

"We know about all the patents in our industry." One of the most common mistakes a BCA team makes is taking the attitude that they know all of the products that exist and their related patents. This fails to consider the technology that may be developed by a competitor that hasn't been commercialized yet. It also fails to consider that a small company with limited geographic reach may have a patented product.

Another mistake made by some BCA teams is in believing a smaller company will not sue them. This view fails to consider that a small company may be very tenacious in defending its intellectual property. This view also fails to consider that the patent owner may later sell the patent rights to a larger company that can afford a patent infringement lawsuit. Finally, there has been an increase in the number of infringement attorneys willing to take patent infringement lawsuits on a contingency arrangement.

## Steps to Avoid Patent Infringement

(1) Start early and keep your diligence: Do not delay your business case development efforts even for a day to avoid patent infringement. The best place to begin your infringement review is during the product concept stage (i.e., prior to developing a prototype) when you are busy characterizing the current state. This is the stage when usually more than one alternative exists. By identifying potential infringement issues at this stage, you can weed out product designs which carry a high risk of liability.
(2) Keep your business development heads above the sand: Some people will intentionally avoid becoming aware of a competitor's patent believing this will help them later. The fact is, ignoring a patent will not help you later in litigation, and it can potentially result in a judgment finding that you have intentionally infringed upon a patent. It is best to respect the intellectual property rights of others by becoming aware of and understanding their rights.

(3) Find out about the patent(s) you may be infringing upon: Before a proposed project reaches the business case level, the possibility of patent infringement should be thoroughly analyzed by the individual who created the idea/concept and the results validated by the sponsor. The BCA team cannot take for granted that all the possibilities have been thoroughly evaluated. As a result, the BCA team should identify what patent(s) exist that their project/initiative could possibly be infringing upon by doing the following activities or verify that someone else has already completed the following activities:

(i) Online patent search. You can search for patents via the U.S. Patent Office or by using any type of software product such as Patent Hunter, which has a 60 day free trial. When doing your patent search, you will want to search for patents related to your technology using keywords describing your product and by also searching the assignee records for patents owned by specific competitors. Keep in mind that some smaller companies may not assign a patent to their company, so you will have to search by any known inventor names (e.g., oftentimes the owner of a small company will be an inventor on the patent). In addition, some larger companies use separate intellectual property holding companies that own their patents so searching by company name may not result in the patent being found.

(ii) Review the competitor's product. In addition to performing a patent search for patents related to your new product, you should also review all known competitor products for any patent notices. Most companies that have a patent on a product will conspicuously mark the product with the patent number (e.g., U.S. Patent No. 14,8253,547). If the competitor's product does not have a patent number directly on it, you can also check the packaging, marketing materials, and website for any patent notices. After you have identified a patent number of interests, you can perform a patent number search to view the patent.

(iii) Contact the competitor directly. If you have reason to believe that one of your competitors has a trademark or patent on a related product but you cannot find the patent via an online patent search of the competitor's product, you may want to consider contacting the competitor to see if they have a patent. Keep in mind that by contacting a competitor, you are immediately putting your company "on the radar," and they will diligently watch your future product developments (i.e., you should only contact them if you have a solid reason for believing they have a patent you cannot find). If they say the product is patented but refuse to provide you with a patent number, they are most likely not being truthful since patents are public knowledge and there is no reason to withhold such information if it is true.

(iv) Preliminary patent infringement "screening" of patents by your BCA team. After you identify one or more patents related to your product, you will want to do a preliminary patent infringement "screening" before sending the patents to your patent lawyer for review. Sending all of the patents you have found can be very costly as a formal patent infringement review by a patent attorney can cost range from $10,000 to $20,000 plus per patent reviewed.

## Steps in Performing a Preliminary Screening of a Patent/Trademark

To perform a preliminary screening of a patent, you should perform the following steps:

**Step 1. Determine if patent term has expired.** In the United States, a utility patent automatically expires 20 years after the earliest effective filing date, while a design patent in most cases automatically expires 14 years after the issue date. To determine if a patent term has expired, you will need to determine the earliest effective filing date and then calculate the expiration date from there. You can use www.PatentCalculator.com to determine the expiration date for a patent.

**Step 2. Determine if maintenance fees have been paid.** If the patent term has not expired, you will then want to check with the USPTO to see if the required maintenance fees have been paid. There are three maintenance fees due for utility patents, as most design patents do not have maintenance fees: 3 years, 7 years, and 11 years. If the patent owner has failed to pay a required maintenance fee, the patent is no longer valid and you can incorporate the patent or trademark without infringing upon the patent.

**Step 3. Self-review of patent claims.** If the patent has not expired (see previous two steps), then you will want to review the patent claims which define the "meets and bounds" of the patent protection. The patent claims are located at the end of the patent and are consecutively numbered starting with 1 and continuing so forth. It is important to note that while a patent may disclose Invention A, Invention B, and Invention C, if the patent claims only protect Invention B, you will not have to worry about infringement if your product relates only to Invention A or C. Reviewing patent claims can be difficult, but with the assistance of a patent attorney you should be able to grasp the concept of what to look for.

## Attorney–Client Work Privilege

Business case developers need to keep in mind that any internal communications regarding the patent and the patent claims are most likely not covered by the attorney–client work privileged – i.e., if a patent infringement lawsuit is filed, the patent owner will be able to discover all e-mails, notes, letters, and conversations relating to the patent not involving your patent attorney. Therefore, it is important to be extremely careful as to what is said within internal communications and preferably keep communications to a minimum. For example, while it may seem obvious some people will make statements such as "This patent looks very similar to our product" when in fact they do not truly know if the patent is close. When in doubt, it is always best to retain a patent attorney to assist you with the infringement review.

## BCA Team's Self-Review

If your BCA team's self-review of the patent indicates there may be some potential infringement issues, you should immediately contact your patent attorney who can help you determine if you do in fact have patent infringement issues. If the formal review by your patent attorney reveals that there may be patent infringement issues for your product, you will then want to determine if the patent is valid or not. Some patents are invalid because the technology was used or known years prior to the filing of the patent application. You will want to bring any known patents, products, or publications that existed prior to the patent owner filing their patent application which could help invalidate the patent.

When infringement on patents, copyrights, or trademarks are included in the proposed project, the BCA team will recommend to the originator of the proposed project that he/she withdraw the project from the business case analysis cycle until the condition have been resolved. If the originator of the proposed project decides not to withdraw the proposed project, the BCA team will escalate the decision to the sponsor. If the proposed project is still not withdrawn from the business case analysis cycle, the situation will be highlighted in the BCA final report.

## SUMMARY OF PATENT AND TRADEMARK PROCESS

As important as it is for the organization's intellectual assets to be protected, it is equally important not to infringe upon another organization's intellectual assets. In this chapter we discussed how the BCA team should investigate if the idea/concept that was considered new and unique to determine if it infringes upon another organization's patents, trademarks, or copyrights. For those ideas/concepts that infringe upon another organization's intellectual assets, these situations are brought to the attention of the originator along with a suggestion that he/she withdraw the proposed project until these conditions are eliminated. If the originator decides not to withdraw the proposed project, the situation is escalated to the sponsor. If the proposed project is still not withdrawn, then it will be highlighted in the BCA final report. For those ideas/concept that are candidates to be copyrighted, trademarked, or patented, action should been taken by the originator to get the concept/idea started through the registration process.

*Special Note*: The patent/trademark process activity should start as soon as the potential patent or patent infringement is recognized. Often this starts in Process Grouping 3 – Value Proposition.

> Protect your innovative capital for it often is the only thing that separates an organization from its competitors.
>
> H. James Harrington

## SUMMARY

Of all the 16 building blocks that make up the TIME PYRAMID if I had to pick only two, they would be BB3 – Innovative Executive Leadership and BB13 – Knowledge Assets Management (KAM). These two BBs are the cornerstone of an innovative organization and creative individuals.

Let's understand how you gain knowledge (see the following table). Analyzing this data you can see that the university systems that we presently hold up as the ultimate knowledge source has become obsolete. Universities structure needs to be very innovative in redesigning their activities and curriculum. Maybe it's better to eliminate the university structure as it has been for hundreds of years and go back to the old apprenticeship concept only this time has the apprentice pay for the experience.

- 10% of what we read
- 20% of what we hear
- 30% of what we see
- 50% of what we see and hear
- 60% of what we write
- 70% of what we discussed
- 80% of what we experience

V. Gordon-*Handbook on Teaching Undergraduate Science Course*, 1999

It has been said that nothing is new. Advances in technology and living conditions are only rearranging things that happened before. It is for this very reason that KAM will be a critical part of all creativity and innovation for at least the next 25 years.

# BB14

## Comprehensive Measurement Systems

*Dr. Sorin Cohn and Ricardo R. Fernandez*

## CONTENTS

*The more sophisticated your process for measuring innovation, the more you can control the apparently uncontrollable.*[1]

(David Simoes-Brown)

This chapter addresses the measurements that are necessary for managing innovation effectively and efficiently for the success of a company in its market environment. First, the chapter puts innovation in its value-creation context, looking at the fundamental ways that its goals can be achieved and the phases of the innovation process. It also summarizes the various ways of characterizing innovation by either its market effects or the aspects of the organization that it addresses.

Innovation management is discussed later in the chapter which underlines the importance of adopting effective models and following the recent ISO 56000 standards guiding on the appropriate system for innovation management and its associated tools and methods. In addition this chapter is dedicated to innovation measurements, starting with the choice of an appropriate measurement framework and the significant indicators. It presents the various types of innovation metrics and discusses the measurement pitfalls that should be avoided.

This chapter presents the criteria for selecting indicators and metrics appropriate for the state of the company, and then shows how to design and update such metrics, taking into account the culture and the life-cycle stage of the company.

This chapter also addresses the creation of balanced portfolios of company-level innovation metrics and devising Firm's innovation Score Cards (FiSCs) for timely evaluation and adjustment of the company's innovation portfolio.

Later this chapter explains the assessment of the company's innovation management: basic principles, various approaches, the process of undertaking it, and the ways the results should be communicated and used for enhancing the value-creation processes of the company.

Lastly the chapter looks at the variety of indexes used throughout the world for measuring (and comparing!) innovation at the industry sector or country level in order to gain more valuable knowledge on industry and country competitiveness in a globalized world.

---

1 Simoes-Brown, D. "*How to Measure Open Innovation Value.*" 100Open, Feb. 2010. Available at: www.100open.com/how-to-measure-open-innovation-value-part-1/

## INNOVATION: GOALS, PROCESSES & IMPACTS

Innovation is about the creation of value. There are two types of values that need to be considered: business innovation which leads to economic value and social innovation that leads to social value. The largest risk to an organization is to stay behind while the competition continues to innovate. The survival of organizations today is directly related to the level of innovation that it can provide in a timely manner. This applies to both for-profit businesses as well as public institutions. Consequently, increasing competitiveness in the world of private business and relevancy in the case of public organizations is not only imperative but also needs to be measured to assure that they know where they stand. The concept of innovation has broadened to be much beyond innovative technologies and basic research to consider a more comprehensive set of sources for value creation including economic, social, and environmental values.

Since innovation is about creating value out of opportunities and ideas, one must consider how to transform these ideas and opportunities to provide that value. It takes a lot of work to make this transformation happen. The value transformation must be perceived from the point of view of the organization, its customers, and other stakeholders. In terms of business, innovation creates economic value, ensures sustainable growth, and enhances competitiveness by

(1) Attracting paying customers with new/better value in products and services;
(2) Surprising the competition through more effective internal and external processes; and
(3) Building resources and capabilities to continue competing and achieving vision.

Innovation is the means to success not an end in itself; and the three fundamental phases in the process of innovation[2] are as follows:

---

2 Cohn, S. "*A Firm-Level Innovation Management Framework and Assessment Tool for Increasing Competitiveness,*" Technology Innovation Management Review, pp. 6–15, Oct. 2013.

(1) The *Research* phase, where money, time, prior intellectual property, and other resources are transformed into "knowledge." Research may be focused on several areas; e.g.:

    a. Environmental context (market and competition) research, which addresses the known and unknown needs, opportunities, and requirements. Constraints and regulations affecting performance within this environment/market must also be considered.

    b. Organization research addressing management know-how and processes.

    c. Science and technology research.

(2) The *Implementation* phase, in which organization uses the acquired knowledge to create "solutions" that may bring value; for example, new or improved:

    a. Strategies

    b. Frameworks that integrate business or social aspects with the environment and the market.

    c. Products, services, policies, programs, and so on.

    d. Organization resources (people, platforms, facilities, tools, partners, and so on).

    e. Organizational processes and methods.

(3) The *Commercialization (Deployment/Exploitation)* phase, when the actual value is being created – by either taking advantage of better strategies, processes, resources, or policies and programs, or by the development and commercial deployment of new/improved business models, products, or services.

(See Figure BB14.1.)

Throughout history, innovation has been the engine of progress and the goal of innovation has been to create value. The value of a company is determined by the economic growth and market position it achieves from creating and selling new or better products and services, all the way to creating new economic entities, industries, and entire markets.[3] Innovation drives new value in the market, thanks to the interplay of discovery "push" and user need "pull."

---

3 Rosenberg, N. "*Innovation and Economic Growth.*" OECD, 2004; Welfens, P., Addison, J., Audretsch, D., Gries, T. and Grupp, H. "*Globalization, Economic Growth, Innovation Dynamics.*" Berlin, Springer-Verlag, 2008.

**FIGURE BB14.1**
Business Innovation Phases.

Source:© 2012, c-IM&E Inc. used with permission from S. Cohn

Companies innovate to create value[4] and to improve their competitive position in the market, with each organization having its own attitude toward innovation, pursuing certain types of innovation and accepting risks associated with change.

Speed of innovation into markets is essential for defending competitive threats and capturing customers and market share. Firms leading in their markets have the luxury of thinking long-term strategically, thanks to the benefits of positive cash flow and the benefits of pursuing higher-risk but high-reward innovation.

Not everything that is new becomes an innovation, and not all innovations are based on inventions, as it is explained in Figure BB14.2. An invention can be patentable for being unique, but does not need to be useful, whereas an innovation must include elements of (i) usefulness that translates into value for the organization, (ii) creativity, and (iii) novelty – at least for the organization creating it.

---

4 Anthony, S., Johnson, M.W., Sinfield, J.V. and Altman, E. *"The Innovator's Guide to Growth – Putting Disruptive Innovation to Work."* Harvard Business Press, 2006.

|  | Value | Examples | Protection |
|---|---|---|---|
| **Novelty** | Limited | Name, color, etc. | None |
| **Creation** | Some but not much utility | Books, clothes, etc. | Copyright or Trademark |
| **Invention** | Potentially high | Technology, algorithm, process, etc. | Patent (limited time) Trade secret |
| **Innovation** | Significantly high | Business models, Internet, Apple Stores, FedEx. | Only through competition; not by legal means |

**FIGURE BB14.2**
Innovation vs. Invention.

**Source:© 2012, c-IM&E Inc. used with permission from S. Cohn**

Innovation is about creating value through changes that affect a wide range of a company's characteristics: from business models and innovation strategies[5] to corporate capabilities and higher value products, from platforms to services and operational processes. Innovation is necessary because (i) customers demand better solutions, (ii) competitors adopt winning strategies, (iii) the market becomes saturated and customers demand different solutions, and (iv) the market gets new regulations or becomes saturated with customers able to dictate prices and conditions of business.

Innovation could address all areas affecting the competitiveness of a company. Strategically, it begins with understanding of the market and the ways by which the firm differentiates itself in its interactions with the market and its customers; that is, its business models.[6] One characterization of the innovations that a company could pursue[7] focuses on the 10 types of innovations described in Figure BB14.3, which enable companies to compete successfully thanks to insidious values that can be developed through intertwined management across

5 Jaruzelski, B., Loehr, J. and Lohman, R. "*Why Culture Is Key.*" Strategy+ Business, Issue 65. Oct. 2011. Available at: www.strategy-business.com/article/11404?gko=dfbfc

6 Weill, P., Malone, T.W. and Apel, T.G. "*The Business Models Investors Prefer.*" MIT Sloan Management Review, Vol. 52, Issue 4, Summer 2011.

7 Doblin, J. "*Doblin Is Now Part of the Monitor Group Recently Acquired by Deloitte.*" 1998. Also see: www2.deloitte.com/us/en/pages/strategy/articles/ten-types-of-innovation-the-discipline-of-build ing-breakthroughs.html

**FIGURE BB14.3**
Ten Types of Innovation Framework.

**Source:© 2012, c-IM&E Inc. adapted from Doblin, J. (1998).**

the entire set of innovations. However, this way of looking at innovations does not address the aspects related to the capabilities of the organization – its culture, its structure, and the processes of coordination.

A major area of innovation for a company is its resources, which comprise

(1) the people forming the company – from the CEO to the lowest level employee;

(2) the partners – all institutions and firms with which the company collaborates in its business processes from investments, technology supply, and development to marketing and sales, including lobbying, and so on.

(3) the infrastructure of the company – buildings, machinery, tools, software, existing product/service technology platforms, and so on.

Corporate *culture* and the ways the organization is structured and behaves are also potential targets for innovation. *Culture is key* for innovation success, and the cultural alignment with business goals and innovation strategies plays a more important role in the firm's success than additional amounts of R&D.

*Corporate processes have* a major impact on a company's state of competitiveness, with each process, including human resource management, administration and legal, financial management, research and development, supply and distribution, production and quality assurance, and customer service, being a target for innovation at one time or another. The same is true for the *innovation management process itself.*

Ultimately, companies distinguish themselves by the values they create, be they financial outcomes, product/service outcomes, customer (experience) outcomes, brand and marketing outcomes, territorial outcomes, or environmental and social outcomes.

A company's innovations can be classified by the market impact they have, as illustrated in Figure BB14.4:

- Efficiency innovations are incremental changes that attempt to do more with less by a more efficient use of capital, infrastructure, tools and, of course, labor. Most established companies do them and Walmart is a typical example.
- Sustaining innovations are those that lead to the improvement of products and services through enhancements and new versions of the already existing ones. For example, just think of the new models of phones or cars delivered year after year to the market by the likes of Samsung, Apple, GM, Ford, Toyota, and so on.
- Expanding innovations lead to new product lines and the increase in classes of customers or new territories (countries) served.
- Business model innovations concern the introduction of new ways of interacting with markets in their entirety. Establishing new business models may lead to market disruptions, especially if they

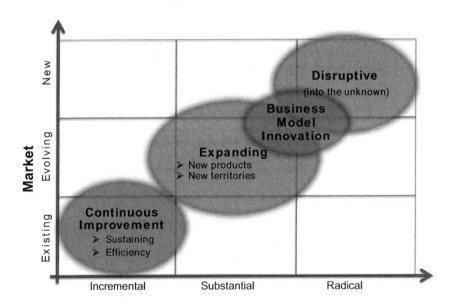

**FIGURE BB14.4**
Innovations and their Market Impacts.

Source:© 2012, c-IM&E Inc. used with permission from S. Cohn are reinforcing the old ones thus leading to market leadership, as happened with FedEx, Dell, Apple, and Google among others.

- Market creation innovations lead to fundamental new business opportunities and economic growth, but they are the riskiest as well and few companies have proven success. Good examples are Amazon, Facebook, PayPal, and so on.

Most companies undertake continuous improvement innovations, some also focus on expanding innovations, while only few dare the risk and expenses of pursuing disruptive innovations. High-growth companies have distinctive innovation approaches[8] outlined in Box A.

---

### BOX A   CHARACTERISTICS OF HIGH-GROWTH COMPANIES

High-growth companies achieve their results thanks to being:

- Change-oriented, with the courage of facing risk to reinvent themselves and create better ways of working
- Outcome-led, with the discipline and wisdom to innovate across key business aspects while ensuring sustainable financial performance
- Disruption minded, looking for aggressive innovations with the potential for creating new markets

In general, high-growth companies exhibit common characteristics, like being:

- Strategic about innovation, with an inclusive concern for all stakeholders and all aspects of innovation
- Rich in future-oriented talent both at the leadership level and in the workforce, with a strong competitive will
- Hyper-competitive, intensely concerned with changing customer needs and the competitors' action in the market

---

8 Abbosh, O., Nunes, P., Savic, V. and Moore, M. *"Discover Where Value Is Hiding."* Accenture, Oct. 2018. Available at: www.accenture.com/t20181023T095450Z__w__/us-en/_acnmedia/Thought-Leadership-Assets/PDF/Accenture-Unlocking-Innovation-Investment-Value.pdf

- Ecosystem conscious, with the focus on harnessing the power of partners and customers to speed-up and create higher value
- Technology exploiting, comprehensively using the latest technologies available to enhance the value of their solutions to the market, making them easier to deliver and be adopted by customers while making their own processes faster and more effective
- Operations-smart, taking care of corporate assets and managing operations effectively to enable continued innovation investments
- Data- and Metrics-driven, taking advantage of external data and astute internal measurements to acquire agility in adjusting strategies and products to market changes while ensuring timely adjustments of innovation activities and influencing behaviors toward higher performance.

It is innovations that drive a company from one life-cycle stage to another: from being a startup to becoming a growing company, and from there to maturity and, for some, true market leadership. It is lack of innovation that leads to a company's decline and only innovation can help a company recover from decline. Of course, the nature of innovations differs from one life-cycle stage to another.

As the pace of technology, economic, demographic, and environmental changes increase, so does the importance of innovations and market dynamics as illustrated by the decline in the average life span of companies.

Why some companies innovate less and are unable to survive competitively? The answer reflects their attitude vis-à-vis innovation and its proper management:

- Failure in market reading and understanding evolving customer needs, which translates into wrong focus: stagnant industry and nonpaying customers.
- Fear of change, coupled with the risks and costs of innovation.
- Short-term narrow-minded CEO's focus on "operations" and stability.
- Lack of coherent strategy and planning.

- Failure to define value proposition and ability to market it.
- A stifling culture that does not reward challenges to orthodoxy and employee participation.
- Inadequate internal resources and inability to partner for success.
- Not understanding the role of innovations and how to pursue them comprehensively and competitively.
- Lack of effective systems of innovation management.

All of the above, and more, attest to the importance of managing innovation methodically and with the right measures for ensuring tangible value creation and sustainable competitiveness.

## INNOVATION MANAGEMENT

### Frameworks for Innovation Management

The fundamental innovation management question that a company's leadership must ask is: "how do we keep our company however old it is to be ambitious and wise enough to keep on performing superbly in our markets?" To manage something well, one needs to understand its context, why it is being done, what needs to be done best at minimal cost, for whose benefits, how it can be done, who can/ should be doing it and with what tools, at what date should it be ready to be of value. To succeed, one needs a model (framework) for managing the resources and activities required coupled with a plan for preparation, for budgeting, for initiation, for execution, for monitoring, for correcting, and for finishing it successfully at the right time – or for terminating it without too much waste if there are no chances for success.

Innovation is complex and multidimensional.[9] How to manage innovation has been for a long time an art, which is now becoming more and more of a science based on objective data, workable models, and proven methodologies. Various management models have been proposed and used for managing innovation activities in firms:

---

9 Clayton, C. "*The Innovator's Dilemma.*" Harvard Business School Press, 1997.

- The basic Linear Model[10] distinguishes "inputs," which can be tangible (resources, capital, infrastructure) or intangibles (culture, knowledge, strategies, and so on), "process," which refers to creation, execution, and evaluation, "outputs," which are the specific results of the innovation activity (products, services, processes, and so on), and finally the "outcomes," which represent the changes in the status of the firm within its market.
- The Innovation Value Chain Model[11] is also linear but takes a sequential approach to the innovation process starting with the "idea generation" stage, the "conversion" stage of selection and implementation, and the "diffusion" stage when the innovation is disseminated across the organization and, eventually, commercialized into the market.

Such models have merits from an "innovator's perspective" managing one specific innovation. Each innovation activity can and should be treated as a project along its linear progress from ideation to implementation to exploitation with all the characteristics of good project management, including leadership, plan, monitoring, and evaluation with suitable metrics, and correcting through feedback loops and pivoting in case performance is not as expected.

There is a fundamental cognitive jump to progress from individual innovation management to managing the innovation of the entire company. This is a multidimensional affair, for which there is need of more sophisticated framework to satisfy the more complex business management perspective.

The Structural Perspective model[12] looks at innovation from a capability, resource, and leadership view in an attempt to balance all critical aspects in the selection and management of innovation from inception to market valuation. The Critical Domains model[13] attempts to address innovation holistically toward business growth by coupling the main domains of innovation balancing results over time against capabilities for

---

10 Davila, T., Epstein J. and Sheldon, R. *"Making Innovations Work: How to Manage It, Measure It, and Profit from It."* Wharton School for Publishing, Jan. 2006.

11 Hansen, M.T. and Birkinshaw, J. *"The Innovation Value Chain."* Harvard Business Review, p. 121, June 2007.

12 Muller, A., Valikanagas, L. and Merlyn, P. *"Metrics for Innovation: Guidelines for Developing a Customize Suit of Innovation Metrics,"* Strategy & Leadership, Vol. 33, Issue 1, pp. 37–45.

13 Anthony, S.D. *"31 Innovation Questions."* Business Week, December 28, 2009.

potential future innovation outcomes, thus enabling answers to the fundamental issues of innovation management:

- Doing the right things.
- Doing those things right.
- Is the organizational environment ready?
- Are there the necessary means and capabilities (resources) available?
- Is the company getting the best from its resources?

The Innovation360 framework[14] is based on the following six basic sets of questions:

- Why? This addresses strategy in terms of target markets and profits, priority innovation strategies, and innovation market impacts to be pursued.
- What? This looks at the types of innovations to be pursued: products, services, business models, organizational structures, management system, or production.
- How? This concerns the leadership styles and the suggested 66 innovation capabilities important for innovations.
- Where?
- When?
- Who?

To innovate successfully, companies need:

- people with minds open to recognizing competitive threats and future opportunities;
- people with the expertise to transform innovative ideas into commercially viable products and services;
- data-driven strategies with realistic action plans to accomplish them, thanks to appropriate facilities, tools, and organization structures supporting innovation;
- people "systems" to nourish a corporate culture of entrepreneurship that dares to risk for achieving worthy goals and has affinity with the variety of cultures in their ecosystems;

---

14 Penker, M., Junermark, P. and Jacobson, S. *"How to Assess and Measure Business Innovation."* Create Space Independent Publishing Platform, South Carolina, 2013. ISBN-13: 9781535160988.

- innovation management practices using proper measurements to ensure progress and timely adjustments when necessary.

All of the above are predicated on having company leadership with compelling will to succeed, business vision, profound market understanding to detect customer issues and translate them into profitable solutions, able to acquire adequate financing and capable to manage the organization, and energize its people by inspiring and motivating by addressing all value-add dimensions of competitiveness in the market:

- The "market knowledge" dimension that concerns the organization's understanding of its market context based on the 7 "W" questions concerning *Why, Who, What, Where, When,* to *Whom,* and *HoW* things happen and are done in the market;
- The "resource" dimension addressing the people, the facilities, tools and partners without which innovation cannot be achieved, again within the context of the 7 W questions;
- The "culture" and the organizational dimension that enables and channels action toward achieving stated goals;
- The "solutions" dimensions – the things that the organization implements: its technology platforms, its processes, its products, services, and policies. These, in unison and in an integrated fashion create the *potential* for creating value. One of the most important of all the processes that further the value creation is the process of managing innovation;
- The "value" dimension that is concerned with the actual realization of value in the organization's environment/market: financial and social outcomes, customers' outcomes, territorial outcomes, environmental outcomes, and so on.

These innovation management dimensions represent the fundamental layers of the Value-add Corporate Innovation Management (v-CIM), as shown in Figure BB14.5.

Effective innovation management requires

- Leaders who understand the importance of innovation and put in place adequate systems of innovation management, including responsibilities, processes and measurements while continuously nourishing the culture of innovation in the organization.

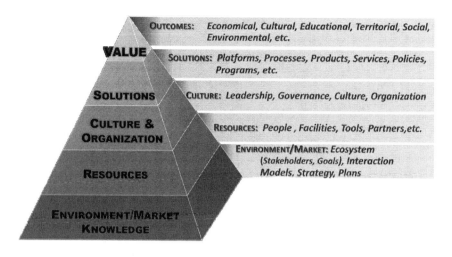

**FIGURE BB14.5**
Value-Add Corporate Innovation Management Framework.

Source:© 2012, c-IM&E Inc. used with permission from S. Cohn

- Knowing well who and what the company is: its vision, its goals, what works well, and what does not.
- Determining where the company is positioned in its market, who are its customers and competitors, what are its business models and its most pressing competitive needs and opportunities.
- Determining what the company really needs to do by selecting carefully the priority innovation targets and ensuring timely availability of funding and the necessary and sufficient resources.
- Organizing a corporate innovation portfolio consisting of various innovation projects and devising a portfolio management plan together with a set of measurements for monitoring and controlling satisfactory progress.
- Executing the innovation portfolio projects, according to project management plans.
- Timely evaluating the innovation portfolio and adjusting it, with some projects being given higher priority and resources, other are terminated or new ones are adopted, while learning and improving.

## BOX B    LEARNINGS FROM AN EXTENSIVE INDUSTRY-WIDE STUDY OF FIRM-LEVEL INNOVATION MANAGEMENT

The extensive 2012 Conference Board of Canada study of firm-level innovation management in Canadian industry[15] – all sectors, all sizes of companies – showed that companies without a system of innovation management had a financial performance that was 35% worse on average than that of companies that had systems of innovation management.

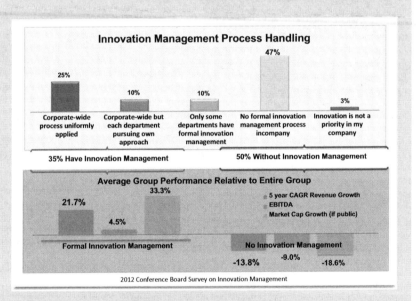

2012 Conference Board Survey on Innovation Management

**FIGURE B**
Performance of Companies with and without Innovation Management Systems.
**Source:** © 2012 c-IM&E Inc, adapted from Cohn, S. and Good, B. *"Status of Firm-level Innovation in Canada: Findings from the 2012 CBI Survey of Canadian Industry,"* The **Conference Board of Canada, June 2013**

At the same time, companies who pursued innovation activities as full-fledged projects did 45% better than those who undertook innovation without the usual project management methodologies.

---

15 Cohn, S. and Good, B. *"Status of Firm-level Innovation in Canada: Findings from the 2012 CBI Survey of Canadian Industry,"* The Conference Board of Canada, June 2013.

> The fundamental issues affecting an organization's performance are not the amount of funding spent on R&D, but its corporate innovation management know-how and capabilities. Success starts with leadership that nurtures a culture of entrepreneurship and pursues innovation *competitively, comprehensively methodically* with the right *measurements* to ensure value where it counts.

Idea generation is not the issue, but organizations consistently waste a lot of resources either pursuing the wrong idea that is not in line with the corporate strategy or not recognizing that the idea could assist in the development of a new market for the organization. This is due to poor management of innovation at the corporate level, and is especially true in the phases of selection, implementation, and deployment. Achieving the innovation goals of high value creation (i.e., both in terms of returns on investments and competitive differentiations) in the face of uncertainty and associated risks requires using an adequate innovation management system with appropriate measurement practices to guide the company along its innovation journey. These issues are so important that the International Standards Organization decided to develop a complete set of innovation management standards.

## ISO 56000 Standards for Innovation Management

Innovation and standards conceptually do not mix. Both concepts are inherently opposite. Innovation is usually related to something new that adds significant value to your product or service. Many times innovation is risky. The conundrum is most evident when one discusses the possibility of standardizing the innovation process. Even though most significant innovations are unique and, each company has its own ways of innovating, one would conclude therefore that the process of innovation cannot be standardized. What can be standardized is the management of innovation. Like any other management activity, it is a process that can be guided by proven methodologies of handling it.

The International Standards Organization (ISO) has undertaken in its Technical Committee TC279 the development of the ISO 56000 standards on Innovation Management.[16] These standards, which are being developed by delegates from over 50 countries in liaison with OECD, WIPO, WTO, ISPIM, and IAOIP among others will align with the pre-existing ISO standards like Quality (ISO 9000), the Environment (ISO 40001), and Information Security (ISO 7001), and so on.

The ISO 56000 standards are addressing both private for-profit companies and public and not-for-profit organizations. Irrespective of their specific goals – be they economic, social, or environmental – innovation management in all types of organizations are based on fundamental principles that concern:

- Realization of value
- Future-focused leaders
- Strategic direction
- Culture
- Exploiting insights
- Managing uncertainty
- Adaptability

The initial set of ISO 56000 innovation management standards consists of the following:

- ISO 56000 – Fundamentals and Vocabulary
- ISO 56002 – Innovation Management System – Guidance
- ISO 56003 – Tools and Methods on Innovation Partnerships – Guidance
- ISO 56004 – Innovation Management Assessment – Technical Report
- ISO 56005 – Tools and Methods on Intellectual Property Management – Guidance
- ISO 56006 – Tools and Methods on Strategic Intelligence Management – Guidance
- ISO 56007 – Tools and Methods on Idea Management – Guidance
- ISO 56008 – Tools and Methods on Innovation Operation Measurements – Guidance

---

16 ISO/TC279. *"Innovation Management,"* Working Document, ISO, N 136, October 30, 2017.

The flagship standard is the ISO 56002,[17] which describes the Innovation Management System. Like all ISO standards, it commences with an introduction capturing the principles at its foundation, the risks and uncertainties of innovation, the concept of an innovation managing system, and its relation to other management systems. Clause 1 addresses the scope of the standard, Clause 2 covers the normative references, and Clause 3 contains the terms and definitions. Clauses 5 to 10 that address the components of an innovation management system are illustrated in Figure BB14.6.

- Clause 4 addresses the context of the organization, which, for a business company, is represented by the market in which the company operates.

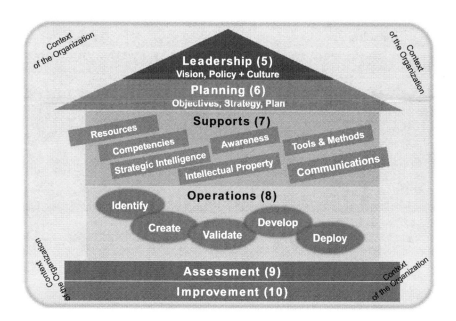

**FIGURE BB14.6**
Major Components of the ISO 56002 Innovation Management System.

**Source: 2019 c-IM&E Inc. adapted by S. Cohn from https://www.iso.org/standard/68221.html**

---

17 ISO 56002:2019. *"Innovation Management System – Guidance."* Available at: www.iso.org/standard/68221.html

- Clause 5 highlights the importance of establishing thoughtful leadership capable of defining the vision and governance of the organization as well as nourishing its culture and operating structure.
- Clause 6 covers the planning necessary to establish objectives, manageable strategy, and operational plans for achieving stated goals.
- Clause 7 addresses the diverse support systems and processes necessary for managing innovation in the organization: from resources and their competencies to strategic intelligence and awareness of itself and of the context, from ways to handle intellectual property (IP) to communications as well as other necessary tools and methods, like those for partnerships, for idea management, for innovation measurements, and so on.
- Clause 8 looks at the major operations involved in managing innovation: identifying opportunities and competitive or relevance needs, creating innovatory concepts, validating them, implementing innovation solutions, and last but not least deploying and exploiting innovation solutions internally or externally through commercialization.
- Clause 9 addresses ways and means for assessing innovation performance.
- Clause 10 looks at the ways by which innovation management can be improved throughout the organization.

The ISO 56000 standards are being published starting in 2019 onward, with suitable addition and upgrades as the market requires.

## INNOVATION MEASUREMENTS

### Innovation Measurements: Role, Process, and Measurement Principles

*You cannot manage something unless you measure it* is a summary of what Lord Kelvin said in 1883.[18] For innovation, as for most activities, success

---

18 Baron William Thomson Kelvin *"I Often Say that When You Can Measure What You Are Speaking about, and Express It in Numbers, You Know Something about It; but When You Cannot Measure It, When You Cannot Express It in Numbers, Your Knowledge Is of a Meagre and Unsatisfactory Kind …"* Available at: https://todayinsci.com/K/Kelvin_Lord/KelvinLord-MeasureQuote500px.htm

is predicated on proper management and progress measurements to enable decisions on progress achieved, what to change and how to do better. Innovation is performed by people whose behavior are impacted by how their performance is assed. Basically, measurements drive behavior. Measurements enable learning for improvement and provide the framework for learning. Of course, good measurements, those that address the important issues with appropriate ways of measuring, drive to success, whereas measurements addressing unimportant issues with poor ways of assessing them drive to failure. This is why it is critical to devise an appropriate framework for innovation measurements – one that points to what are the critical aspects to measure (we call them the "indicators") while enabling appropriate ways for assessing them (we call these the "metrics").

Timely and relevant measurements are critical for management to ensure valuable results despite changes in the environment, the organization, and the technology. Measurements are necessary to understand the status of the "system," be it an organization, a specific project or a portfolio of innovation activities. On the basis of such measurements, one can make the necessary corrections for satisfactory performance. Measurements are also part of the arsenal to develop appropriately the culture of the organization.

Just doing something about (innovation) measurements is better than doing nothing.[19] Notably, no two organizations are the same. Measuring innovation is a combination of *art* and *science* that should be flexible and agile to match the organization's situation internally and externally in the context of its market (environment).[20]

One key measurement issue that needs to be addressed is: "what are the **indicators** (aspects) that one should measure in order to get a good understanding of the situation and to make the necessary adjustments?" Indicators should be chosen to inspire toward specific goals and behaviors in support of the organization's strategy. Determining the right innovation indicators is a critical process in itself, as one needs to cover all relevant aspects of the innovations pursued: capabilities and inputs, the outputs as well as the processes leading from inputs to outputs, including the innovation management process itself. Some indicators

19 Kaplan, S. "*How Do You Measure Innovation.*" Innovation Excellence, Feb. 2014. Available at: www.innovationexcellence.com/blog/2014/02/12/how-do-you-measure-innovation/
20 Malinoski, M. and Perry, G.S. "*How Do I Measure 'Innovation'?!?.*" Balanced Scorecard Institute.

could address strategies and activities, others may address effects and outcomes, while others are specific to capabilities and/or outputs.

Several frameworks for innovation measurements have been proposed in the literature recently, most of them following frameworks for innovation management. One interesting framework[21] is centered on the key questions:

(1) Why do you innovate, with focus on goals, market issues, and innovation strategies?
(2) Where and what do you innovate, which address the domains and types of innovations pursued as well as the specific goals of each innovation activity?
(3) How do you innovate, which addresses the process of innovation management itself starting with leadership, continuing with each of the operational phases of innovation?

The model shown in Figure BB14.7 is preferential because it combines the fundamental domains of innovation management with the perspectives and processes adopted by the ISO 56002 standard on Innovation Management System and with full consideration of the market context within which the organization operates. We refer to it as the "3D Innovation Measurement Model[TM]"

The *Innovation Value Domains* depicted in Figure BB14.7 are as follows:

- Market knowledge domain.
- Resources domain consisting of people, platforms, tools, and partners – all implying funding as *sine qua non* resource.
- Culture and organization domain addressing the leadership aspects, the corporate values and culture, and its structure.
- Solutions domain – what the company creates: its processes, including the innovation management process itself, its platforms, and the products and services it makes available to the market.
- Value domain that reflects what the company achieves as outcomes in terms of economic values, customer values, social values, territorial values, environmental values, and so on.

---

21 Lindblom, S. *"Metrics that Matter – Are You Innovating in the Right Direction,"* Innov8rs Blog, March 2019. Available at: https://innov8rs.co/news/metrics-that-matter-are-you-innovating-in-the-right-direction/

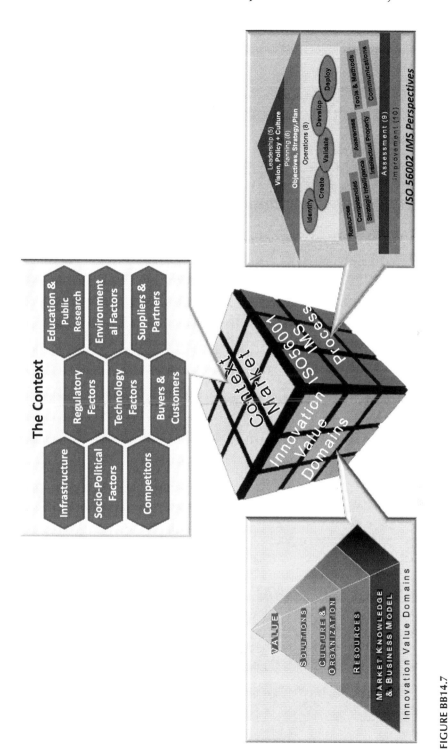

**FIGURE BB14.7**

3D Innovation Measurement Model[TM].

Source: © 2019 c-IM&E Inc. with permission from S. Cohn

The *ISO 56002 IMS Process* perspectives, as stated above (see also Figure BB14.6), are as follows:

- Leadership (clause 5), which covers vision, governance, and culture.
- Planning (clause 6), addressing objectives, strategies, and plan.
- Support (clause 7), which includes awareness, strategic intelligence, resources, IP management, tools and methods, communications, and so on.
- Operations (clause 8) consisting of the innovation phases from identification to creation and from there to validation, development, and deployment/commercialization.
- Assessment (clause 9) for appropriate measurement and learning.
- Improvement (clause 10) for timely adjusting the innovation of the company and its underlying capabilities, processes, and structures.

The Context and Market are dynamic in nature. This includes technology developments, economic, social-political, and environmental factors. Innovation management and its associated measurements must be updated as often as necessary to ensure the company's sustainability, relevance, and competitive success.[22] The high-level process for establishing and updating the innovation measurements and practices in the organization is shown in Figure BB14.8.

- First, the company must reconsider its context and its competitive position in the market to update its strategy, its innovation focus, and its priority activities.
- On that basis, the company must decide what to measure and select the appropriate measurements.
- The measurement process (who, how, when, etc.) needs to be established or updated as well.
- The resulting set of measurements and practices must be communicated and deployed effectively.
- As often as necessary, the company should evaluate the effectiveness of its innovation measurements and adjust them accordingly.

---

22 Richtner, A., Brattstrom, A., Frishmammar, J., Bjork, J. and Magnusson, M. "*Creating Better Innovation Measurement Practices.*" MIT Sloan Management Review, Sept. 2017.

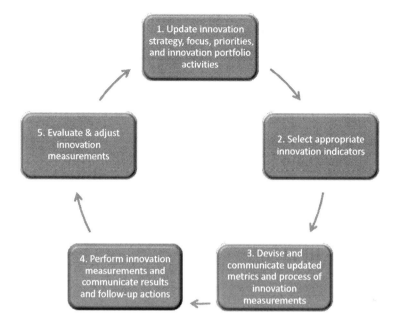

**FIGURE BB14.8**
High-Level Innovation Measurement Process.

**Source: © 2016 c-IM&E Inc. with permission from S. Cohn**

This process is cyclical, with timely re-initiation to reflect changes in the company's context and its competitive position in its markets.

## BOX C   THE SIGNPOSTS OF INNOVATION MEASURE-MENT FRAMEWORK

The Signposts of Innovation Framework[23] positions financial performance at the center because that is considered to be the *raison d'etre* of companies and most companies prefer to measure financial output results. Of course, such a narrow financial perspective limits the scope of measurements, as companies and, definitely,

---

23  Hao, J.X. et al. *"Signposts of Innovation: A Review of Innovation Metrics,"* The Conference Board EPWP#17-01, May 2017. Available at: www.conference-board.org/publications/publicationdetail. cfm?publicationid=7475&centerId=8

public and not-for-profit organizations are looking at other aspects of value beyond the financial ones.

- The Technology signpost is considered a key aspect of innovation capabilities in the company, despite the fact that not all companies are defined by their technologies.
- Digitization is another signpost, addressing the latest adoption and usage of information and communication services.
- Customer Experience and Branding is an important signpost due to the essential role that customers, with their needs and perceptions, play in shaping the innovation goals and processes in a company.
- The Environmental and Social Sustainability signpost addresses long-term shareholder values related to the company's social and environmental impacts.
- The Internal Innovation Networks signpost concerns the core of the business innovation process, from strategy funding, from types of innovation to innovation management issues and organizational structures among so many other aspects.
- The final signpost concerns the External Innovation Network that looks at collaboration and competition within the innovation ecosystem of the company.

One motivation for the development of this framework was the desire to make it operational not only for individual companies but also for entire industry sectors or countries.

## Innovation Indicators

The first question in innovation measurements is *what's to be measured*; that is, what aspects of organization's innovation are significant enough and telling enough to be measured. Innovation *indicators* are those aspects of innovation that can be used as the representatives of progress and how things are done, thus providing meaning to the measurements process. The literature on innovation measurements exhibits a variety of proposals for classifying and determining important innovation indicators. Some are looking at indicators in five areas of importance[24]: mission and strategy, organization, idea generation and development, portfolio management, and scaling. Others are narrowly focused on indicators along the innovation process[25]: product definition, product concept, validation phase, production, market launch, and general innovation management. Interestingly, the recent OECD manual[26] looks at six components: research and development, product and process innovation, marketing and organizational innovations, design, use of s/w in innovations, and the fuzzy area between R&D and non-R&D innovation activities.

More consistently, appropriate indicators can be found by asking insightful questions concerning the domains of the innovation management framework:

- Market knowledge and strategy questions like:
  - Do we understand our customers and their daily journeys with or without our products or services?
  - How are we positioned *vis-à-vis* our competitors?
  - Should the company prioritize market share at the expense of revenues?
  - Are there any techno-socio-political dynamics that will affect our position in the market?
  - Is our innovation strategy aligned with our business goals?
  - How much risk can we afford, and are we having a balanced incremental-substantial-disruptive portfolio of innovations?
- Resource (capabilities) oriented questions like:
  - Are we using our resources optimally?
  - What kind of resources will we need in the future?
  - Are our facilities and tools sufficiently advanced to carry us forward?
  - Do we have the right partners? Do we know how to choose and manage partnerships effectively?
  - Do we have the right channels to market?

24 Almquist, E., Leiman, M., Rigby, D. and Roth, A. *"Taking the Measure of Your Innovation Performance."* Banin & Company, 2013. Available at: www.bain.com/insights/taking-the-measure-of-your-innovation-performance/
25 Dziallas, M. and Blind, K. *"Innovation Indicators Throughout the Innovation Process: bn Extensive Literature Analysis."* ScienceDirect, May 2018.
26 OECD. *"Oslo Manual 2018 – Guidelines for Collecting, Reporting and Using Data on Innovation."* 2018.

- Culture and organization questions like:
  - How focused on innovation is our leadership?
  - Do we have a working environment that enables innovation?
  - Do we know how to collaborate?
  - Is our organization structured for the demands of effective innovation tomorrow?
- Solution-oriented questions like:
  - How can we make our corporate processes more effective?
  - What kind of platforms do we need to build the market solutions for the future?
  - Are our innovation projects meeting the business goals?
  - Do we have a satisfactory innovation management process with an adequate set of measurements to guide progress?
  - What are the risks associated with our innovation projects and how can we mitigate them?
  - Are we failing fast enough to minimize losses and with sufficient learning to advance better?
  - Are we balancing well the demands for more featured products vs. those for getting faster into the market?
  - Do we communicate well internally and with external stakeholders?
- Value-oriented questions like:
  - Do we know how to measure value?
  - How can our margins be increased?
  - How committed to us are our customers and how can we get more value from serving them?
  - Are there other classes of customers that we could serve in the future?
  - Have we covered all the territories that might adopt our market solutions?
  - How can we be perceived to provide more social benefits?
  - How do we affect our environment, and how could we do better?

Many companies continue the industrial age tradition of focusing on:

- "performance indicators" like growth impact of innovation, return on investments, new product survival, and so on.
- R&D aspects, especially concerning intensity of investments, percentage of R&D people, number of R&D projects, and patent outputs.

Limiting indicators to such R&D or performance aspects may inhibit valuable innovation in other value domains that would be more important for enhancing competitiveness; for example, cultural-organizational innovations, collaborations internal and external, business model innovations, environmental innovations, and so on. Overemphasis on performance leads companies to the "ROI syndrome," in which case ROI stands for "restraint on innovation"[27] because ROI measures used in isolation lead to short-term thinking and prioritization of incremental innovations.

---

**BOX D   MEASURING VALUE AND NET PRESENT VALUE**

Creating value is the "golden nugget" of innovation. Without value, there is no innovation. However, the assessment of value depends on the perspective from which it is assessed. To assess value requires assuming a specific stakeholder perspective, be that of the customer/user, the purchaser, the executive management, the shareholder, or society. Value of a product or service can be determined by the willingness of a purchaser to pay for it. It is likewise, with processes. Organizational transformations are more difficult to value due to the uncertainty of its potential benefits and costs to set up.

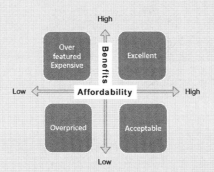

**FIGURE D.1**
Basic Value Analysis Matrix.
**Source: © 2018 c-IM&E Inc. with permission from S. Cohn**

---

27 Langdon, M. *"Innovation Metrics: The Innovation Process and How to Measure It."* An Innovation Labs White Paper, 2008. Available at: www.innovationlabs.com/publications/innovation-metrics/

Value can be measured as a function of benefits vs. costs (or its inverse, the affordability). A Value Factor can be defined as the product of Benefits and Affordability (or the Ratio of Benefits to Costs), where the benefits and costs are assessed according to the established practices of each organization.[28]

The critical aspects of value measurements concern all the facets of costs and deciding on what are the essential benefits and how to prioritize them. This reflects one of the big issues with innovation measurements: deciding where and how value is created. It is here, in deciding on what is important to measure that mistakes are made due to (i) "vanity," that is, the desire to highlight what's personally attractive and (ii) "laziness," that is, the desire to focus on things that are easy to measure. Innovation benefits may be derived from:

- Strategic alignment
- Idea generation and selection
- Diversity of innovation
- Increase in market understanding and business knowledge
- Percentage of sales and profits from new services and/or products
- Sustainability of revenue
- Intellectual property
- Customer satisfaction and loyalty
- New types of customers
- Brand and reputation
- Ease of hiring talent
- Distribution of products and services
- Price elasticity and so on.

Some of the innovation costs are determined by:

- Investments
- R&D
- Ideation
- Incentives for innovation

---

28 Keathly, J. "*Knowing When You've Added Value*," ASQ Quality Progress, pp.16 to 23, March 2019.

- Production
- Marketing and sales
- Opportunity analysis (and opportunities lost) and so on.

A lot has been said about the rationale for selecting Net Present Value of innovations indicators, how to measure and use them,[29] as shown in Figure D.2.

**Purpose**
✓ To measure the expected value of an innovation project or a set of projects
✓ To act as leading indicator for the probability of meeting performance targets in time to allow corrective action

**Definition**
✓ Net Present Value of project(s) in innovation pipeline that involves new products or cost reduction benefits
✓ Initially based on the predicted value of the project(s)
✓ Measured over the profitable life the project(s) as calculated when submitted for approval or updated.

**Advantages**
✓ As a leading indicator, it allows timely action
✓ Already measured during the innovation selection process

**Corrective Actions**
✓ Increase idea generation activities
✓ Revise project selection criteria
✓ Review innovation strategy

**Disadvantages**
✓ NPV is calculated on the basis of forecast that have to be credible and accountabieW
✓ Feedback loop and accuracy correction may be too long

**Balancing Effects**
✓ Tendency to overforecast can be balanced by thorough and timely resource contribution metrics

**FIGURE D.2**
Net Present Value as Innovation Metric.
Source: Adapted from Collins, J. and Smith, D. "Innovation Metrics: A Framework to Accelerate Growth," Prism, Issue 2, 1999. Available at: http://www.adlittle.com/down loads/tx_adlprism/1999_q2_11-17.pdf

However, as Figure D.3 illustrates, care has to be taken in how cash flows are considered and measured in the context of having innovations because the reference situation has to take into account what happens to corporate competitive performance in the absence of innovation rather than assuming a steady-state level of performance.

29 Collins, J. and Smith, D. *"Innovation Metrics: A Framework to Accelerate Growth,"* Prism, Issue 2, 1999.

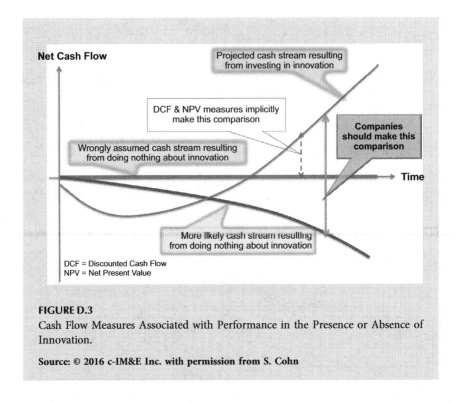

**FIGURE D.3**

Cash Flow Measures Associated with Performance in the Presence or Absence of Innovation.

Source: © 2016 c-IM&E Inc. with permission from S. Cohn

Some companies focus their measurements on specific phases of the innovation process:

- Research (opportunity) phase:
  o Target customer classes
  o Customer pains and needs
  o Competitive situation
  o Market conditions
  o Performance requirements
  o Resource acuity
  o Strategic fit
- Ideation phase
  o Resource creativity
  o Classes of ideas
  o Number of ideas
  o Synthesis
  o Min. value solution
  o Market fit

- Selection and validation phase
  - Return on investment (ROI) potential (gains vs. costs)
  - Portfolio balance (short- vs. long-term)
  - Risks – technical, organizational, customer, and market
  - Protection
- Implementation phase
  - Development platforms and tools
  - Production facilities
  - Development speed and affordability
  - Performance/cost targets
  - Ease of acceptance/use
  - Volume production
  - Time to market
- Deployment and commercialization phase
  - Marketing processes
  - Speed of adoption
  - Sales capabilities
  - Cost of adoption
  - Customer feedback
  - Time to profit
  - Competition impacts
  - Time in market

Proper choice of meaningful innovation indicators that reflect the company's business goals, competitive needs, capability, and project developments is essential for the well-being of a company. [30]

## Metrics for Innovation Management

*Metrics* are the formulae by which we measure the indicators. Some indicators can be measured quantitatively. For example, one can calculate:

- a company's "Growth Impact" as a measure of innovation effectiveness defined by the ratio of (revenue of new products over $X$ time) vs. (Total Revenues over $X$ time)

---

30 Spitzer, D. *"Rethinking the Measurement of Innovation."* IBM Innovation Forum, Zurich, Nov. 2007. Available at: www.slideshare.net/elsua/ibm-iforum-rethinking-innovation-measurement-by-dean-spitzer

- a company's "Return on Innovation Investment" defined by the ratio of (Cumulative Net Profit over $X$ time) vs. (Costs over $X$ time, including R&D, incremental production, plus initial commercialization costs)
- or a company's "Market Understanding" measured via new product survival as the ratio of (Number of new products remaining in the market after $Y$ years) vs. (Total number of products launched in the past $Y$ years).

Also, measuring the results of innovation is not sufficient. It is also necessary to measure its effectiveness, the rate and the efficiency of innovation processes because it is not sufficient to know how well the company has done in the past. One needs to measure how well it is doing in the present and how well it prepares its capabilities for the future. For instance, traditional *process* performance metrics are:

- "Speed to Market" measured via Time-Efficiency of R&D as the ratio of the (Sum of Ideas to Market Launch over past $Y$ years) vs. Total number of new products launched over past $Y$ years.
- "Value to Market" measured via Cost-Efficiency of R&D as the ratio of the (Sum of new product revenues introduced over past $Y$ years) vs. (the Sum of R&D and Product introduction costs over past $Y$ years).
- "Innovation Decision Efficiency" measured as the ratio of the (Sum over all approved innovation projects of the ratio of (Time to Approval vs. Project Cost)) vs. Total number of approved innovation projects.

Other interesting process indicators may look at the percentage of innovation activities that are blessed with specific risk management plans, or the percentage of the organization's executives being involved in innovation activities, and so on.

As innovation is a complex human endeavor, some important aspects of the process of innovation can't be described numerically. Strategy, culture, and management are characterized by uncertainty and ambiguity that can be better handled by *qualitative indicators*, in which case more often than not the associated metrics are based on questions rather than mathematical formulae; for example

- Are we doing the right things?
- Are we doing them right?
- Are we getting the best from the present organizational structures?
- How well are we prepared for the future?
- Does the management system enable collaboration for higher effectiveness and efficiency?
- How meaningfully does the organization measure innovation?

Innovation measures must reflect each company's business goals, competitive situation, strategies, and capabilities within its own industry sector and territorial markets. No two companies are identical, and there is no such thing as a standard set of indicators and metrics good for all companies because of their diverse market positions, business goals, resources, and capabilities.

## Measurement Pitfalls

Metrics drive behavior and enable companies to evolve their culture toward better alignments with business goals and strategies – if the adopted indicators and metrics have been chosen to ensure that the company measures what matters in meaningful ways. If not, use of metrics in isolation or adoption of inappropriate metrics may drive companies in wrong directions or obscure competitive realities that need to be addressed for survival. The development of appropriate measurements for innovation is a function of the company's understanding of innovation and adequate processes for its management. The volatility of innovation focus within the company and lack of proper communication of the company's business goals and strategies also impact negatively on the choice of good innovation measurements.

Typical innovation measurement pitfalls concern:

- Unsuitable framework for managing and measuring innovation – one that addresses only the past or does not include the company's critical domains of innovation in accordance to the company's latest innovation strategies.
- Metrics non-aligned with competitive realities and business goals. This is typical of companies focused on R&D when better results may be obtained by addressing more critical competitive imperatives. Indeed, measuring percentage of resources with high degrees

or number of patents may not indicate real innovation in the same way that big R&D budgets do not equate with differentiating innovation and higher value creation.

- Too few metrics, which denote a narrow focus of innovation, with the consequence of overlooking important aspects of competitiveness. Companies that use too few metrics stand the danger of falling prey to unintended consequences if the chosen metrics provide narrow window understanding of the company's situation and lead to misalignment with corporate goals. For example, metrics that exacerbate the Not-Invented-Here syndrome end up in creating innovation silos and diminish overall innovation capabilities.

- The opposite, that is, companies using too many metrics. The usage of lots and lots of metrics brings higher administrative burdens and waste of valuable resources. Besides, too many metrics may lead to confusion. The optimum appears to be having 6 to 10 firm-level innovation metrics.[31]

- Same old metrics: The consequence to the saying that "what gets measured gets done" requires that indicators and metrics should be changed in synch with the changing competitive imperatives and innovation priorities of the company. Besides, while recognizing that "metrics drive behavior," innovation managers should be aware that humans are good at adapting themselves to play according to "the rules of the game" in order to show well rather than achieving the true innovation needs of the company. Hence, indicators and metrics should be changed from time to time.

- Metrics that are not aligned with the HR evaluation process and vice-versa. HR performance metrics have higher behavioral impacts, and if they do not reflect the innovation goals there should not be any surprise that innovation performance is poor.

- Failure in making the metrics "fun to measure, discuss, and decide on remedial action" along with lack of patience in allowing some metrics sufficient time to impact on behaviors.[32]

---

31 McKinsey Global Survey Results. "*Assessing Innovation Metrics.*" a McKinsey Report, 2009. Available at: www.mckinseyquarterly.com/PDFDownload.aspx?ar=2243

32 Kirsner, S. "*What Big Companies Get Wrong about Innovation Metrics.*" Harvard Business Review. May 2015. Available at: https://hbr.org/2015/05/what-big-companies-get-wrong-about-innovation-metrics

- Lack of alignment across the corporation. This is a problem for larger companies with diverse business units and departments adopting their own metrics that do not align well with the corporate set of metrics.

No two companies are the same and hence companies should use the innovation metrics most suitable for their competitive progress: there is no standard set of metrics applicable to all companies. Companies should choose and design their own metrics.

## SELECTING AND USING INNOVATION METRICS

### Criteria for Innovation Metrics Selection

Innovation indicators must be *SMART*, that is, *specific, measurable, actionable, realistic,* and *time-related.* In general, people behave according to the metrics by which they are being judged. The principles for selecting organization-level innovation indicators and metrics are as follows[33]:

- Alignment with organization goals, operational (business) models and strategies. Indicators must address strategically relevant aspects of innovation in support of business goals and innovation strategies.
- Coverage of all key aspects of innovation in the organization. Selected indicators and metrics must address comprehensively the priority domains of innovation in the company and avoid missing aspects that are critical for competitive success.
- Focus on high leverage areas: strongest impacts and weakest links. It is exhausting to measure everything. For the sake of their innovation success, companies must focus on measuring how they correct their competitive vulnerabilities while taking advantage of their competitive strengths.

---

33 Cohn, S. and Good, B. *"Metrics for Firm-Level Business Innovation in Canada,"* The Conference Board of Canada, Dec. 2013.

- Easy to understand. To drive behavior and lead to progress, metrics must be understood by all participants in the process of innovation all the way from strategic thinking to ideation, implementation, and commercialization.
- Conducive to corrective action. Metrics must enable management to make necessary timely adjustments in the goals and execution of innovation activities, including termination of innovation projects that not show promise. It is better to fail fast, save expenses and learn early to move forward to truly rewarding innovations.
- Addressing of historic, present, and forward-looking innovation capabilities. It is not sufficient to know how well the company did in the past to know how well it will do in the future given the fact that competitive challenges and innovation goals change rapidly in dynamic markets. The company needs to track how well the innovation process is handled today, in real time, and also to ensure it is building capabilities necessary for future success.
- Coherent and consistent across the entire company. While it is natural for each component (business unit or department) in a large organization to prefer its own metrics for driving innovation, misalignments among measurement systems adopted throughout a complex organization impedes optimizing overall innovation efforts. A solution is to rely on hierarchical portfolios of metrics to abstract consistent corporate knowledge from the lower organizational levels.
- Nurturing culture of innovation that drives to higher individual and team performance. Indicators and metrics should be chosen to lead to positive evolution in attitudes and behaviors, including empathy to customer journeys, constructive debates and internal and external collaboration. HR performance evaluation and reward systems must be aligned to innovation metrics to drive positively the evolution of the company's culture.
- Measurable over a period of time transcending short-term fluctuations. Technology changes rapidly, and so do customers and competitive markets. Companies need innovation indicators and metrics that can transcend short market fluctuations.
- Enabling benchmarking. While each company needs to select its own innovation indicators and metrics, most companies appreciate being able to compare themselves and learn about best

practices in their industry sectors. This can be addressed by accepting a few common industry sector metrics while ensuring private use of most other company metrics.

- Avoiding "value degradation." Companies need to change indicators and metrics from time to time to reflect changing innovation priorities and avoid "metric mastering" by people more interested in playing the established metric game.

## BOX E  IS PRODUCTIVITY GAINS A GOOD METRIC FOR CORPORATE INNOVATION?

An interesting aspect of the usefulness of certain metrics concerns Productivity Gains (or losses) as a metric of innovation. Innovation is a complex multi-stage process and overall productivity by itself is an obfuscating metric unless balanced by other metrics in the portfolio. This is so because overall productivity is a "black box" measure as illustrated in Figure E.1.

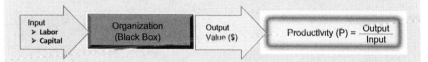

**FIGURE E.1**
Productivity of an Organization.
**Source: © 2016 c-IM&E Inc. with permission from S. Cohn**

As such, productivity is of value only in a historic sense to determine if the organization is creating more value or not. But it does not help in determining where within the organization are the weak links in matters of value creation.

In most complex organizations, there is a value chain that starts with the leadership and includes all the components of the organization contributing to its value creation. The overall productivity is the product of productivities and quality factors of all stages in the organization's value chain, as illustrated for a manufacturing organization in Figure E.2.

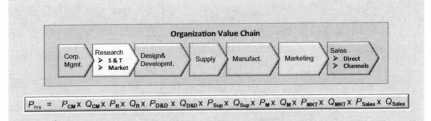

**FIGURE E.2**
Example of Productivity Value Chain.

Source: © 2016 c-IM&E Inc. with permission from S. Cohn

Looking at the overall productivity, one cannot determine if blame for loss should rest with the Management for taking lousy decisions, or the Research that focused on the wrong target customers, or the Design that created an unappealing product, or the Supplier who purchased poor-quality materials, or the Manufacturing line that was outdated, or Marketing that was ineffectual, or the Sales channels which were too weak …

On the other hand, Productivity gains, which are much used by economists, have proven to be a useful metric at industry sector and country levels for benchmarking purposes and analyzing industry and country competitive evolution.

## Designing and Updating Innovation Metrics

One cannot underestimate the importance of choosing suitable innovation indicators and the design of appropriate metrics for the positive competitive evolution of a company. The selection of indicators should be achieved via "intelligent constructive debates" to sift through their advantages and disadvantages, followed by an analysis of potential consequences and trial application before being put into formal usage. As explained earlier, the value and impact of a metrics should be evaluated and its applicability reconsidered in a process like the one illustrated in Figure BB14.9.

(1) Use the innovation management framework and the organization's competitive/relevance situation to consider the important indicator domains.

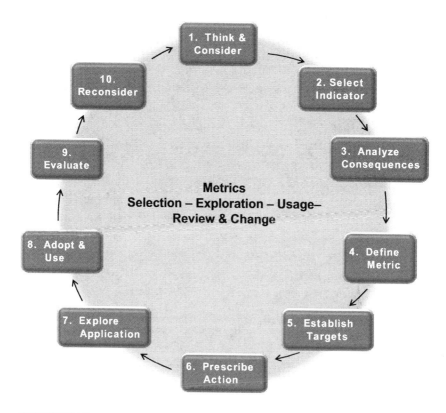

**FIGURE BB14.9**

Process of Identification, Exploration, Usage, Review, and Adjustment of Metrics.

Source: © 2015 c-IM&E Inc. with permission from S. Cohn

(2) Select the appropriate SMART indicators that are of value for the management of the organization's innovation and deserve to be short listed for further analysis toward adoption.

(3) Analyze the potential consequences of using such an indicator, with extra attention paid to the negative ones.

(4) Define the measurable aspects of the indicator and the process of measuring it with an understandable metric.

(5) Establish clear, reasonable, and effective targets of performance *vis-à-vis* each metric.

(6) Define potential corrective actions in cases when the targets are not being met such that the situation is speedily remedied. [(See Box B) on the impact of pre-defined targets and corrective actions.]

(7) Explore the usage of such a metric for the organization and verify that there are no impediments to its acceptance and use.

(8) If the exploration shows positive results, adopt and use the metric. Communicate its adoption to avoid any misunderstanding of the indicator objective, the way it is to be measured (who, how, when, where) and the significance of the level of performance expected. Once metrics are put into usage, they start impacting what the management "sees" and how the people in the company act.

(9) Evaluate timely, in synch with market and company changes, the usefulness of this metric in achieving desired innovation objectives and the fact that it does not lead to any undesirable consequences or that people have become too "comfortable" with it.

(10) Reconsider the wisdom of using such an indicator and its associated metric and, if advisable start looking for different indicators, which takes one back to point #1 above.

It is better to select meaningful indicators with complex associated metrics than employ easy-to-measure indicators that obscure how priority innovation objectives and processes are being addressed by the company.

If selected judiciously, innovation indicators and metrics enable companies to:

- adopt effective innovation strategies and targets in alignment with business goals,
- monitor progress and undertake necessary corrective actions,
- optimize allocation and further development of resources, and
- reward true contributors to innovation value and nourishes a culture propitious to innovation.

## BOX F  PRE-DEFINING TARGETS AND CORRECTIVE ACTIONS

Several industry studies have shown that organizations that pre-determine the targets of performance for their metrics perform, on average, better than those that don't.

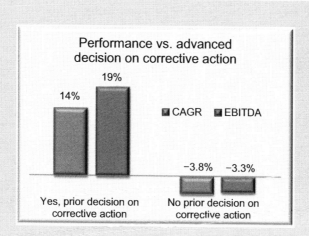

**FIGURE F**
Performance Correlation with Predefinition of Corrective Action.
**Source: © 2015 c-IM&E Inc. adapted by S. Cohn from:[34] Cohn, S. and Good, B.,** *"Metrics for Firm-Level Business Innovation in Canada,"* **The Conference Board of Canada. Dec. 2013.**

Likewise, organizations which pre-define corrective actions in case metric targets are not met perform better on average[35] because they do not lose precious time and resources wondering what is to be done when things are not as required. Figure F captures the results of the extensive study of firm-level innovation management practices undertaken by the Conference Board of Canada in 2012 across all industry sectors and sizes of companies.

## Culture and Life-Cycle Stage Considerations in Innovation Metric Selection

A company's selection of indicators and metrics is a reflection of its culture and the maturity of its innovation management process, and the performance of the company depends on the selection of indicators and metrics appropriate to its competitive market realities, business objectives,

---

34 Cohn, S. and Good, B. *"Innovation Measurement Metrics and Practices: The Manufacturing Sector,"* The Conference Board of Canada Report, Ottawa, Apr. 2015.
35 KPI Library is a Saas – Business Intelligence Solution that automates business metrics reporting – Available at: www.kpilibrary.com

and innovation strategies. Market performance depends on many factors beyond the metrics used; however, it is possible to acquire a better understanding of the relative value of using a specific metric by analyzing the average performance of companies using it *vis-à-vis* performance of all companies in the same study.

A metric's "Relative Associated Performance" (RAP) can be defined as the difference between the weighted average of a performance measure like the Compound Annual Growth in Revenues (CAGR) of companies using that metric and the weighted average performance of all companies surveyed in identical conditions. The RAP value of a metric has little correlation with its popularity. The RAP measure of a metric relates to the culture and the sophistication of the innovation management of companies using that metric more than to the abstract definition of the metric itself.

It is natural for companies to select indicators and metrics in accordance with their life-cycle stage of evolution, their business focus, attitude *vis-à-vis* risk and culture characteristics as described in Figure BB14.10.

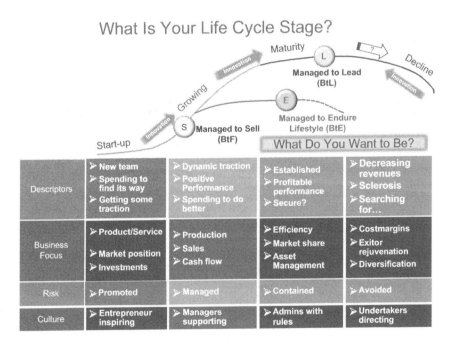

**FIGURE BB14.10**

Major Life-Cycle Stages of Corporate Evolution and their Characteristics.

**Source: © 2015 c-IM&E Inc. with permission from S. Cohn**

At the same time, it is fair to ask how the selection of innovation indicators and metrics impacts the intensity and speed of change in the company's life evolution. That question leads to valuable learning when one undertakes extensive industry studies of metrics used and performances achieved by companies at all stages of evolution, as it is exemplified in Box G.

## BOX G   LEARNINGS FROM EXTENSIVE PAN-INDUSTRY STUDIES

The 2013 pan-Canadian industry study captured usage of diverse innovation metrics for each domain of innovation in conjunction with self-stated levels of financial performance. Participating respondents (70% C-level executives) had the option of choosing which metrics they were using within a set of almost 100 metrics in addition to describing their own metrics.

First of all, this enabled the study to correlate the numbers of corporate innovation metrics used with the self-stated perfor-mance of companies in the study. This is shown in Figure G.1

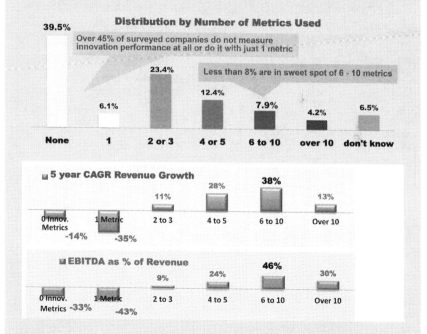

**FIGURE G.1**
Distribution by Numbers of Metrics Used and Average Financial Performance.

Source: © 2015 c-IM&E Inc. adapted by S. Cohn from Cohn, S. and Good, B., *"Metrics for Firm-Level Business Innovation in Canada,"* The Conference Board of Canada. Dec. 2013.

The fact that over 45% of the respondent companies had no metric or just one innovation metric at the corporate level makes one ask the question about how much higher competitive performance would industries have if more companies would undertake innovation management with properly selected sets of 6 to 10 innovation metrics. Some additional analysis of the data showed that the prevalence of 0 or only 1 innovation metric is higher among startups and companies in decline.

The study also analyzed which were the most mentioned metrics and what were their RAP values, as shown in Figures G.2 and G.3.

| Most Used Metrics (416 firms) | | | | Metrics with Highest "Relative Associated Performance" | | | |
|---|---|---|---|---|---|---|---|
| # | Metric | # Firms | RAP % | # | Metric | RAP % | # Firms |
| 1 | Customer satisfaction with new products | 186 | 15.0% | 1 | Executive intensity involvement | 39.4% | 36 |
| 2 | Return on innovation investment | 145 | 13.7% | 2 | Market understanding (% of products still there after x years) | 38.4% | 68 |
| 3 | New product revenue impact | 138 | 32.2% | 3 | Addressable customer innovation | 36.2% | 68 |
| 4 | Product performance improvement | 127 | 1.5% | 4 | Number of R&D Projects | 35.7% | 56 |
| 5 | Value of customer | 123 | 14.2% | 5 | Innovation risk management (% projects with risk mgmt. plans) | 33.6% | 38 |
| 6 | Focus on technology platform innovation | 118 | 12.0% | 6 | Distribution chain improvement | 33.2% | 30 |
| 7 | Quality performance improvement | 108 | 6.8% | 7 | Supply chain improvement | 32.5% | 55 |
| 8 | Customer innovation capture (new classes of customers) | 105 | 17.2% | 8 | New product revenue impact | 32.2% | 138 |
| 9 | Market position improvement | 101 | 14.0% | 9 | Intensity of bottom-up innovation | 30.1% | 36 |
| 10 | Intensity of R&D | 101 | 10.3% | 10 | Resource innovation focus | 29.7% | 48 |

**FIGURE G.2**

Most Used and Highest RAP Metrics in 2013 Conference Board of Canada Study.

Source: © 2015 c-IM&E Inc. adapted by S. Cohn from Cohn, S. and Good, B., "*Metrics for Firm-Level Business Innovation in Canada*," The Conference Board of Canada. Dec. 2013.

| Most Used Pairs of Metrics | | | | Pairs of Metrics with Highest "Relative Associated Performance" | | | |
|---|---|---|---|---|---|---|---|
| # | Pair of Metrics | # Firms | RAP % | # | Pair of Metrics | RAP % | # Firms |
| 1 | Customer Satisfaction + New Product Revenue | 110 | 19.5% | 1 | Executive Intensity + Market Understanding | 65.1% | 16 |
| 2 | Return on Innovation Investments + Technology Platform Innovation | 86 | 22.0% | 2 | # R&D Projects + Platform Innovation Coverage | 51.3% | 27 |

| Metric Triplet with Highest "Relative Associated Performance" | | | |
|---|---|---|---|
| # | Triplet of Metrics | RAP % | # Firms |
| 1 | Executive Accountability + Market Value of Innovation in Pipeline + Market Understanding | 71.6% | 22 |

**FIGURE G.3**

Most Used Pairs of Metrics and the Metric Pairs and Triplets with Highest RAP Values.

Source: © 2015 c-IM&E Inc. adapted by S. Cohn from Cohn, S. and Good, B., *"Metrics for Firm-Level Business Innovation in Canada,"* The Conference Board of Canada. Dec. 2013.

Most interesting, traditional metrics like "customer satisfaction with new products" and "product performance improvements" have much lower RAP values than metrics concerned with leadership ("executive intensity involvement in innovation"), market focus ("market understanding," "addressable customer innovations"), or integration of innovation and risk management. Of course, having two metrics is better than having just one, and three are usually better than two if properly chosen.

In terms of metrics usage at different life-cycle stages of evolution, Figure G.4 shows the preferred metrics of companies participating in the 2013 pan-Canadian study of firm-level innovation.

| Innovation Domain | Startup | Growing | Mature | Decline |
|---|---|---|---|---|
| Strategy Focus | 1. Customer | 1. Customer | 1. Process | 1. Process |
| Financials: #2 after ROI as #1 | 2. Pipeline value | 2. Pipeline value | 2. Productivity gains | 2. Productivity gains |
| Product/Serv. Outcomes | 1. Product performance | 1. New product revenue value | 1. New product revenue value | 1. Product performance |
| People | 1. % Innovation Resources | 1. Innovation Training | 1. HR Management | 1. HR Management |
| Corporate Processes | 1. Sales 2. Quality | 1. Sales 2. Time of R&D | 1. Sales 2. Quality | 1. Cost of R&D 2. Manufacturing |
| Innovation Management | 1. Success rate 2. Decision efficiency | 1. # in pipeline 2. Success rate | 1. Success rate 2. # in pipeline | 1. Decision efficiency 2. Successrate |
| Culture & Organization | 1. Alignment with mission 2. Openness to new | 1. Alignment with mission 2. External collaboration | 1. Alignment with mission 2. Staff turnover | 1. Staff turnover 2. Internal collaboration |

**FIGURE G.4**
Most Popular Metrics by Life-Cycle Stage of Evolution.

Source: © 2015 c-IM&E Inc. adapted by S. Cohn from Cohn, S. and Good, B., *"Metrics for Firm-Level Business Innovation in Canada,"* The Conference Board of Canada. Dec. 2013.

The contrast between startups and growing companies, which usually have strong cultures of innovation, and companies in decline with their entrepreneurial deficiencies is quite telling in matters of preferred metrics. While startups and growing companies focus on customers and pipeline of innovation, companies in decline focus on process and productivity gains. While startups and growing companies focus on innovation resources, innovation training, and alignment with mission, companies in decline emphasize HR administration, staff turnover, and internal collaboration (the latter probably due to silo mentality). Interestingly, both startups and companies in decline focus on product performance metrics, but for different reasons: the startups because they are doing their utmost to build a market position with their new products, while companies in decline are mostly concerned with sustaining the performance of their old products. To avoid decline, companies need to innovate more effectively, which requires them to adopt more of the entrepreneurial attitudes of startup companies, including the metrics that they choose to ensure innovation success.

## CORPORATE PORTFOLIO OF INNOVATION METRICS

### Balancing the Corporate Portfolio of Innovation Metrics

While each innovation project should be associated with its own set of metrics designed specifically for driving people to meet and even surpass the project's specific objectives, at the organizational level, management should design and select a balanced portfolio of *corporate innovation metrics* that can be used for defining the FiSC.

A balanced portfolio of company-level innovation metrics should address the most pertinent areas of the value-add corporate innovation management framework illustrated in Figure BB14.6 – be they areas of weakness that should be remedied or areas of strength that are profitable to develop further for competitive differentiation:

- Metrics addressing market understanding and innovation strategies.
- Metrics addressing the organization's resources – its people, its platforms, and its partnerships.
- Metrics addressing its organization culture and structure.
- Metrics addressing the *solutions* that the organization is creating: its processes, its policies and programs, and its products and services – including aspects of the innovation management process itself.
- Metrics addressing its outcomes: economic, social, territorial, environmental, and so on.

How many metrics should such an organization innovation portfolio contain? Companies that have no metric for corporate innovation either do not care about innovation, are undertaking it blindly or just do not understand the importance of metrics in mastering control of their evolution. Using just one metric runs the risk of having chosen a misguiding one or one that obscures other more impacting aspects of innovation management. In general, few metrics enable only a partial understanding of the situation and may not help in providing the appropriate corrective action. On the other hand, too many metrics may overburden the organization with additional administration efforts and lead to wastage of time and resources.

Studies in various countries over diverse industries and organizational sizes and ages have shown that on average, organizations with 6 to 10 metrics in their corporate innovation portfolio perform better than organizations with fewer metrics or than organizations with more than 10 or 12 metrics. Also, it is not surprising to find countries and industries where a sizeable proportion of organizations do not use any corporate innovation metric or focus on just one.

Noticeably, there is a larger percentage of no innovation metric organizations among either start-up companies (which may be too small to have structured innovation management systems) and companies in decline (which may be in decline because they do not have proper systems of innovation management). Some companies that find themselves in dire competitive situation have chosen to exploit the use of large portfolios of metrics in order to change the corporate culture and redress the competitive situation faster, as shown in Box H.

## BOX H  RECOVERING A SPIRIT AND PRACTICES OF EFFECTIVE INNOVATION USING LARGE PORTFOLIOS OF CORPORATE METRICS

Spooked by Asian competition and realizing that it has lost its market leadership role, a large global manufacturer decided to revive its culture of innovation and insure that innovation is undertaken systematically and methodically throughout its many business units and subsidiaries across the world. This was achieved by creating a strong headquarters unit (with more personnel than a decent mid-size company) dedicated to innovation management and tools. One of the solutions adopted was to develop a whole suite of innovation metrics and corresponding targets. It contained three streams of metrics: Culture, Process, and Action, as shown in Figure H.

| | Financial | Time | Collaboration |
|---|---|---|---|
| **ACTION** | ♦ $ funding for innovation<br>♦ % of Innovation Investments<br>♦ Expected ROI = Financial Innov Budget vs. Expected Financial Outcome | ♦ Innovation time budget (average % of time spent on Innovation)<br>♦ Time Budget vs. Expected Value of Innovation Activities | ♦ # Projects with Partners<br>♦ # Projects with Customers<br>♦ Ratio of Projects based on internal vs. external ideas |

| | Ideation | Value | Flexibility | Innov. Tools Usage |
|---|---|---|---|---|
| **PROCESS** | ♦ # ideas created in team<br>♦ # ideas found or borrowed<br>♦ # ideation tools used<br>♦ % increase in # ideas<br>♦ % ideas/project that are not realized | ♦ Total estimated Value of Innovation<br>♦ Total $ Investment in Innov<br>♦ % Resources to Projects > Threshold Value<br>♦ Avg. Ratio of Value vs. effort for all Innov. Portfolio | ♦ Variety of ideas – product, service – process – bus. Model<br>♦ Yes/No procedure to fast track project<br>♦ % of Fast-Tracked Projects | ♦ % Innov. Projects following Process<br>♦ # projects using Toolbox<br>♦ % Increase in Delivery Precision: Time & Budget<br>♦ Usage of Metrics |

| | Innovation IncentiveSystem | Openness | Risk Taking | Project Performance |
|---|---|---|---|---|
| **CULTURE** | ♦ % staff contributing ideas<br>♦ # people rewarded<br>♦ # people with Innov. Goals<br>♦ # new ideas per year<br>♦ # trained Innov. Coaches<br>♦ # stories communicated | ♦ # ideas shared /person and /business unit<br>♦ # ideas from outside<br>♦ Level of knowledge sharing<br>♦ # conversations on future business | ♦ Ratio of high risk & high return projects<br>♦ Risk Index at beginning of every project (0% to 100%) | ♦ Plan precision<br>♦ Delivery date vs. planned date<br>♦ Real budget vs. planned<br>♦ Time to market vs. plan |

**FIGURE H**
Portfolio of Metrics to Revitalize Culture and Re-Establish Systematic Innovation Management.
Source: © 2015 c-IM&E Inc. adapted with permission from S. Cohn from Cohn, S. and Good, B. *"Innovation Measurement Metrics and Practices: The Manufacturing Sector,"* The Conference Board of Canada Report, Ottawa, Apr. 2015

The initial deployment of such an extensive portfolio of metrics met with resistance due to the onerous burden of undertaking so many measurements at the short time intervals the company deemed necessary to redress its competitive situation before it declined beyond redemption. However, the company survived and revitalized its competitive spirit and even used its upgraded innovation management system for its marketing and lobbying value. Once the shock treatment achieved sufficient success, the number of metrics in the portfolio could be taken down in a carefully managed process.

The process of selecting a balanced portfolio of corporate innovation metrics deserves particular attention due to the major role it has in directing the evolution of the company. The critical steps that need to be followed are:

(1) Identify the critical innovation imperatives. This requires an audit of the company's competitive situation and a deep understanding of leverageable strengths and most dangerous weaknesses.

(2) Determine all the key metrics for each domain and perspective of the Innovation Measurement Framework described in Section 2 that address the critical innovation imperatives identified in step 1. If too many metrics appear to be of value within each domain of innovation, combine them in "layered metrics" that use two or more primary metrics to provide a more telling-at-a-glance measurement for that aspect of innovation, as exemplified in Box I.

## BOX I   LAYERED TOP-LEVEL METRICS

To arrive at a manageable number of metrics in a balanced corporate portfolio, it is advisable to use "layered metrics"; that is, metrics that are built as weighted combinations of primary metrics as exemplified in Figure I.

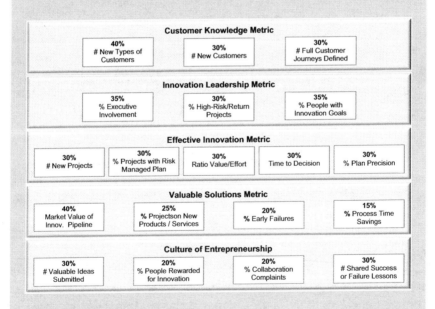

**FIGURE I**
Examples of Layered Top Metrics.
**Source: © 2018 c-IM&E Inc. with permission from S. Cohn**

> Creating and using such top-level metrics require careful consideration of how one distributes the weights of lower-level metrics and, very importantly, its target performance, in addition to ensuring that the meaning and rationale of such metrics are clearly explained throughout the company.

(3) Analyze and prioritize the selected metrics by their potential impacts and other criteria and select a short list of most important metrics based on their balancing capabilities and their potential positive impacts and/or unintended consequences. Ensure that together, the selected metrics are reinforcing each other and reduce unwanted consequences.

(4) Define a highly representative corporate portfolio of innovation metrics consisting of 6 to 10 metrics that are understandable, actionable, and forward looking in terms of capabilities and business evolution.

(5) Determine targets of performance that optimize creative stress for the chosen corporate metrics making sure to identify both short-term (1 to 6 months) and long-term (1 to 3 years) targets. For each metric identify potential corrective actions in case performance is below target.

(6) Establish a schedule for evaluation of the corporate innovation portfolio, together with the responsibilities and processes for performing the measurements.

(7) Communicate the Corporate Innovation Portfolio, together with the established targets of performance, corrective actions, and schedule for reviews and adjustments.

Without a carefully chosen portfolio of corporate innovation metrics, innovation in a company has a great chance of being haphazard, reactive, and downright wasteful. It takes time to build an effective portfolio of metrics and even more time to establish its level of effectiveness and its credibility.

## Devising and Using a FiSC

Many companies use score cards containing balanced portfolios of key performance indicators with associated weights to enable a quick quantitative assessment of the company's performance. The same approach can be used to address innovation evaluation[36,37] using commercial[38] or company-designed metrics, thus creating a FiSC. One vaunted value of scorecards is that they can be used to benchmark innovation within the industry sector, which is true if and only if all companies use the same scorecards. However, no two companies are the same, and care must be exercised to avoid losing sight of the specific innovation situation of a company just for the sake of being able to benchmark with others. Unless properly designed and used, scorecards present the danger of oversimplification in an attempt to provide an overall numerical estimate of innovation performance for making "decisions at a glance." This may lead to hasty decisions and problems resulting from entrenching practices beyond their limited life span of usefulness.

For executives who do not want to be burdened by too much data, it is advisable to limit the organization's FiSC to three key innovation performance indicators:

(1) The Innovation Acuity (IA) index, which measures how well the organization understands its context and how strategic are its selected innovation activities;

(2) The Innovation Enablement (IE) index, which measures how prepared is the organization in terms of its resources, its culture, and its processes; and

(3) The Innovation Value (IV) index, which measures how well is the organization meeting its value growth outcomes.

At the working level, the company's innovation portfolio council (or innovation board) may need to use a more detailed working innovation score card with more than just three indexes in order to better ascertain the situation of the organization and undertake appropriate corrective actions and adjustments in the innovation portfolio, as illustrated in

---

36 Jonash, R. and Donlon, B.S. "*Connecting the Dots: Using Balance Scorecard to Execute an Innovation Strategy.*" Balance Scorecard Report, Harvard Business Chool Publishing, pp. 11–17, March–April 2007.

37 Koehler, H. and MacGillivray, S. "*Measuring and Managing the Innovation Strategy with an Innovation BSC.*" Balance Scorecard Report, Harvard Business Chool Publishing, pp. 20–26, March–April 2007.

38 Innovations scorecard metrics are available at: www.strategy2act.com/solutions/innovations_excel.htm

Figure BB14.11, which highlights the usage of layered metrics even at the working level of managing innovation in a company.

- How often and how impacting are innovation score cards evaluated is as important as how completely representative and well balanced are the chosen corporate innovation portfolios or their associated score cards. Good practice requires that the innovation score card be calculated as often as possible – quarterly or even monthly in competitive situations – for arriving at timely decisions concerning the status of the organization's innovation portfolio and the necessary adjustments and corrective actions. Indicators that are measured to be below target require further discussions and attention by management:
- *Why* such a situation?
- *What* are the potential impacts?
- *How* should the situation be remedied by immediate action items?
- *Who* is responsible for the remedial action?
- *When* should the remedies take effect?

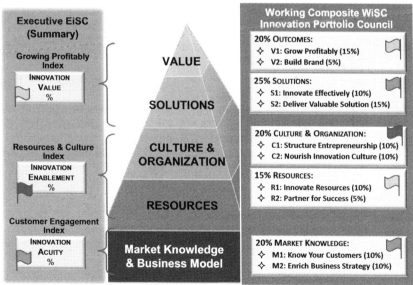

**FIGURE BB14.11**

Executive and Working-Level Innovation Score Cards.

Source: © 2018 c-IM&E Inc. with permission from S. Cohn

Green flags indicate a good situation, while yellow flags denote the areas that require further, albeit not immediate, attention. A good example of using thoroughly designed and effectively used innovation scorecards is shown in Box J.

---

**BOX J   EXAMPLE OF PROPRIETARY INNOVATION SCORE CARD AND ITS EFFECTIVE USAGE**

One of the best examples of representative FiSCs is provided in the literature.[39]

It looks at corporate innovation from four perspectives:

(1) Enablers, which consider aspects of culture, resources, technology, working environment, and communications.
(2) Business evolution drivers, which consider customer understanding, improvements in agility, and execution of innovation activities.
(3) Customer focus and solutions, which address delivery of effective solutions, building brand, preparation for future, and becoming a partner of choice.
(4) Financial values that concern both profitability and business growth.

Some of the metrics used are layered to cover critical aspects of the innovation process. For example,

- "Improving Agility" is a metric that combines responsiveness to customers as well as timely reactions to market changes
- "Delivering Effective Solutions" combines with appropriate weights:
  o velocity in terms of milestones and actions for customers
  o rate of adoption of treatments by customers
  o effectiveness for patients' medical journeys, and
  o return on investment as a percentage of sales.
- "Innovation Execution" combines with judiciously assigned weights

---

39 Cohn, S. and Good, B. "*Innovation Measurement Metrics and Practices: The Life Sciences and Clean Tech Sectors*," The Conference Board of Canada Report, Ottawa, Mar. 2015.

- Ideation capabilities, in itself a combination of percentage of people with ideas and number of valuable ideas.
- Risk management as a combination of number of people trained and percentage of projects with risk management plans.
- Culture of collaborative success as a combination of percentage satisfaction with collaboration and percentage of on-time projects.
- Rate of innovation implementation as a carefully weighted combination of conversion of ideas to tangible solutions and the quality and value of such solutions.

The FiSC scores are calculated every month with an analysis focus on those requiring further attention to determine why they were below targets, what could be the short- and long-term impacts and what must be done to remedy the situation as soon as possible.

Innovation scorecards should be considered in the context of the organization structure – a conglomerate or ministry, a multi-business unit, a government agency, a simple business unit, or just a functional department. Likewise, innovation scorecards should reflect the specifics of the life-cycle stage of the organization – a startup, a rapidly growing organization, a mature one or one in decline. Companies using well-designed innovation score cards in conjunction with effective innovation management systems have a better chance of outperforming their competitors.

## ASSESSING INNOVATION MANAGEMENT

### Objectives and Principles

Innovation management has become a common topic of discussion in organizations independent of their size or activities. Managing innovation is a key prerequisite for value creation and future development. As all other key aspects of the organization's innovation activities, the innovation management itself needs to be assessed on a regular basis in order to:

- Understand better the existing practices and responsibilities.
- Improve its performance toward increasing its impact on the value of the organization.
- Meet specific internal or external requirements; for example, due diligence of the company or qualifications of the organization for further funding, and so on.

The comprehensive ISO 56004 technical report provides guidance on why innovation management assessment should be done, how it could be conducted and the kinds of outcomes the organization should be looking for. The seven principles that stand as foundation for an innovation management assessment are:

(1) adding value to the organization;
(2) challenge the organization's strategy and objectives;
(3) motivate and mobilize for organizational development;
(4) be timely and focused on the future;
(5) allow for context and promote the adoption of best practice;
(6) be flexible and holistic;
(7) be an effective and reliable process.

Innovation management assessments can be done in a variety of ways. Companies should select the approach and the tools most suitable for their situation on the basis of specific objectives pursued, the type of innovation management preferred and the kind of results desired. Assessments may be done internally with or without external assistance or they can be performed by external parties via interviews and/or more extensive surveys.

Some innovation management assessment methodologies and tools are based on the universal understanding that like fish who always rot from the head down, so do companies decline because of their leadership that takes bad decisions, do not nourish a culture of innovation, and do not pursue innovation competitively, comprehensively, and methodically with the right metrics to achieve value where it counts. Because it focuses just on the senior management team, such an approach[40] is less resource-expensive (people and time) and more immediately effective on condition that the

---

40 Cohn, S. and Good, B. "*Competitive Value Guide*": *ISO50501 Compatible Corporate Innovation Management Diagnostic Tool*," The Conference Board of Canada, May 2017. Available at: www.conferenceboard.ca/e-library/abstract.aspx?did=8785

company's CEO and executive team (or their investors) have the wisdom and courage to accept responsibility and assess the company's innovation management by starting with its leadership: how it thinks, how much it knows, how it acts, and how misaligned it is. Other approaches are more elaborate, corporate data oriented, and focused on the process of creating and implementing innovation. Some are concerned with determining the "maturity of innovation management,"[41] others look at paths for growth[42] or analyze innovation ideation, usage of design thinking,[43] the status of innovation projects and innovation failure/success rates in order to provide some measures of comparative performance.[44]

## The Innovation Management Assessment Process

The basic process of an innovation management assessment as guided by ISO/TR 56004 is illustrated in Figure BB14.12, which clearly identifies its three constituent phases:

a. Preparation
b. Execution
c. Analysis and Conclusion.

Proper preparation should start with the alignment of the innovation management assessment scope with the company's strategic objectives before choosing the specific approach and tools to be used. Preparation includes determining the necessary resources (budget, people, tools, etc.) and ensuring their availability at the right time. The definition of the core metrics and their expected performance targets is also part of the preparation phase, as is the planning of the assessment itself and to whom and how the conclusions should be presented.

The metrics of an innovation management assessment may be both quantitative and qualitative addressing, among others:

---

41 Center for Innovation Management Studies, "*IM Maturity: Tools and Assessments.*" Available at: https://cims.ncsu.edu/tools-assessments/im-maturity/

42 GrowthWheel International Inc. "*Get the Tools.*" Available at: www.growthwheel.com/

43 Lewrick, M., Link P. and Leifer L. "*The Design Thinking Playbook: Mindful Digital Transformation of Teams, Products, Services, Businesses and Ecosystems.*" Wiley, 2018.

44 IMP³rove – European Innovation Management Academy. "*Innovation Management.*" Available at: www.improve-innovation.eu/

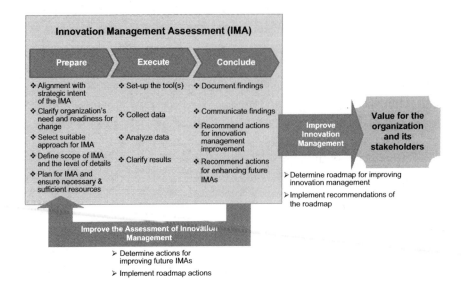

**FIGURE BB14.12**
Innovation Management Assessment Process.

**Source: © 2019 c-IM&E Inc. adapted by S. Cohn from ISO/TR 56004: 2019 Innovation Management Assessment – Guidance. Available at: www.iso.org/standard/69921.html**

- The strategic alignment of the company's innovation management and potential misalignments within the management team.
- How innovation strategies are established and communicated.
- The executive team involvement in, and accountability for, innovation in the company, and how the innovation management process is supported and enabled by the company's leadership
- The effectiveness of innovation management practices in terms of:
  - culture development,
  - idea management,
  - prioritization and resourcing of innovation activities,
  - selection and usage of appropriate innovation metrics,
  - timely evaluations and adjustments,
  - risk management integration,
  - alignment with HR management,
  - training for and rewarding of better innovation,
  - how innovation outcomes are exploited, and
  - how lessons are learned and communicated,
- The efficiency of the innovation management team.

The actual execution of the innovation management assessment starts with the set-up of the assessment team and its tools, with particular attention to the ways quantitative and qualitative data are to be collected. The collected data may require cleaning and the identification of gaps before proceeding to its analysis.

The conclusions of an innovation management assessment should be documented and reported clearly, starting with a management summary and an overview of how the key results should be interpreted and acted upon. The performance of each investigated aspect of the innovation management must be identified based on the metrics used and the ensuing recommendations for improvement should be outlined clearly, with due focus on enhancing value creation, achieving higher alignment with strategy and within the management team, enabling better learning, and enhancing agility and efficiency.

The assessment measurements and results can be presented in a variety of forms depending on objectives and intended audience as qualitative dashboards, quantitative scorecards, graphic bar/column charts, or comparative radar diagrams, as used by Jaruzelski et al.[45] to highlight the impact of alignment with primary innovation strategies.

## MEASURING INNOVATION AT INDUSTRY AND COUNTRY LEVELS

Several innovation measurement models have been discussed in this chapter in previous sections. The intent of this section is to provide the reader with some actual examples of the use of some of these models as applied to both an industry sector and to a country. By understanding how to apply measurement models to industry sectors, the organization can work to better understand how they compare to others, potentially be able to benchmark with the best from the sector to leapfrog their individual competition. At country level, governments can better understand where they are in comparison to other nations and to be able to determine strategies to improve all the industries within that country.

---

45 Jaruzelski, B., Staack, V. and Goehle, B. *"The Global Innovation 1000: Proven Paths to Innovation Success."* Strategy+Business, Oct. 2014. Available at: www.strategy-business.com/article/00295?gko=b91bb

| Historical Progression of Indicators | 1st Generation Input Indicators (1950s–60s) | 2nd Generation Output Indicators (1970s–80s) | 3rd Generation Innovation Indicators (1990s) | 4th Generation Process Indicators (2000+emerging focus) |
|---|---|---|---|---|
| Author notes | These were the easiest to measure but soon it was understood that they were not sufficient to manage the innovation process | In the next two decades, output measures became more popular since there was more emphasis on results and ROI | The 90s expanded the base to include some less objective though important indicators as well as comparisons | In the past decade, knowledge management, open innovation, and market segmentation have emerged |
| Sample measures from that generation of Indicators | • R&D expenditures<br>• S&T personnel<br>• Capital<br>• Tech intensity | • Patents<br>• Publications<br>• Products<br>• Quality<br>• Change | • Innovation surveys<br>• Indexing<br>• Benchmarking innovation capacity | • Knowledge<br>• Intangibles<br>• Networks<br>• Demand clusters<br>• Management techniques<br>• Risk/return<br>• System dynamics |

(Source: Adapted from Milbergs and Vonortas. 2004)[47]

**FIGURE BB14.13**
Historical Progression of Innovation Indicators

Macro innovation measurement models have evolved from the early 1950s to the present.[46] Milbergs et. al. generated the following chart showing the progression of indicators over time (See Figure BB14.13).

One of the most cited and utilized processes for measuring Innovation across industry sectors and at country levels is the OSLO (OECD) Manual. It was initially started in 1990s to provide guidelines for innovation surveys for the measurement globally in 80 countries. The most recent version of the OSLO (OECD) Manual,[48] as initially described in *Innovation Indicators* section of this chapter, examines six components:

46 Adapted from Innovation Metrics: Measurement to Insight, Milbergs and Vonortas, White Paper, 2004

47 Adapted from Innovation Metrics: Measurement to Insight, Milbergs and Vonortas, White Paper, 2004

48 OECD. "*Oslo Manual 2018 – Guidelines for Collecting, Reporting and Using Data on Innovation.*" 2018.

- research and development
- product and process innovation
- marketing and organizational innovations
- design
- use of s/w in innovations, and
- the area between R&D and non-R&D innovation activities.

The significance of this and other recognized Innovation Measurement Frameworks is not necessarily because of its completeness, but more importantly because of its standard methodology whereby comparisons and conclusions can be drawn from these. It focuses on the added value of data collection from all firms, without consideration of their size or innovation activities or results. The data that are collected in a standard format are then grouped by Country, Industry Sector, Revenue, Employees, and Geographic Region.

## Industry Sector Innovation Indexes

Innovation metrics at industry level are in practice either as breakdown of country-level indexes or as summary of company-level measures. The goals of industry indexes are to identify heterogeneity across industries at the macro level, or among companies to rank them and build industry benchmarks, or to present industry trends. We will dive into existing industry indexes in the following section.

One of the most useful aspects used by OECD for the survey data is the standardized functional categories that are used to better hone in on the types of business process innovations that are being reported. (See Table BB14.1.) Similarly once these data are collected, the comparisons that were discussed earlier can be made, but more importantly, now the type innovation that is being compared can be added to the demographics. By narrowing it down this way, processes that are similar in different industries can be more easily compared. As a simple example, the admission process at a hospital can be compared to the registration process at a hotel and to the registration process at a seminar. Of course the complexity levels of these three business processes are different but innovation that takes place in one could potentially be easily adapted to the other.

The types of business innovation can lead to a different variation of comparative processes which can be even more generalized by functional category. This is exemplified by Table BB14.2. By utilizing

**TABLE BB14.1**

Innovation Category vs. Input–Throughput–Output Innovation Measurement Examples

| Innovation Category | Throughput | Input | Output | Notes |
|---|---|---|---|---|
| Technology | Patents | R&D | Receipts of license fees | Very common practice showing level of success |
| Digitization | ICT access index | ICT spending | ICT and business model creation | Shows level of technology use |
| Environmental & Social Sustainability | Number of ISO 14001 environmental certificates | Investment in operational sustainability | Environmental Performance Index | Sustainable environmental goals |
| Customer Experience & Branding | Relationship duration | Spending on advertising | Customer satisfaction | Design Thinking approaches should be considered |
| Internal Innovation Networks (leadership & organization, processes & tools, people & skills, and culture & values) | Number of new ideas created internally | Spending on innovation projects | Number of new products developed from new ideas | Shows activity and commitment but not success |
| External Innovation Ecosystems | University/industry collaboration | Venture capital access (links with government, research & education and access to finance) | Innovators (% of SMEs) | Shows level of open innovation |
| Profit and Revenues | Potential of entire new product/service portfolio to meet growth targets | Innovation budget | % of sales revenues from new products/services | Financial results are a key expected output |

*Source*: Adapted from Hao et al., The Conference Board, May, 2017, "Signposts of Innovation: A Review of Innovation Metrics."

functional categories to make the comparison, one can derive a generic measurement for evaluation that can be more easily utilized to compare not just at a process level but also at a functional level of any similar industry. This provides for a more accurate comparison and the

**TABLE BB14.2**

Functional Categories for Identifying the Type of Business Process Innovation

| Functional Category | Detailed Description of Subcategories | Notes |
|---|---|---|
| 1. Production of goods or services | Activities that transform inputs into goods or services, including engineering and related technical testing, analysis and certification activities to support production | These apply to internal operations that will benefit from process innovation |
| 2. Distribution and logistics | This function includes<br>a. transportation and service delivery<br>b. warehousing<br>c. order processing | The inclusion of Suppliers into the innovation formula usually leads to disruptive industry-level innovation |
| 3. Marketing and sales | This function includes<br>a. marketing methods including advertising (product promotion and placement, packaging of products), direct marketing (telemarketing), exhibitions and fairs, and market research and other activities to develop new markets<br>b. pricing strategies and methods<br>c. sales and after-sales activities, including help desks other customer support and customer relationship activities. | The consideration of the market and especially of competitor direction is of utmost importance. These measures can lead the organization to new products/services and business models |
| 4. Information and communication systems | The maintenance and provision of information and communication systems, including<br>a. hardware and software<br>b. data processing and database<br>c. maintenance and repair<br>d. web-hosting and other computer-related information activities | The application of technology is one of the quickest ways to innovation. The provision of these resources becomes imperative to innovation success. |
| 5. Administration and management | These functions can be provided in a separate division or in divisions responsible for other functions. This function includes | The development of new business models is important and the support of these is crucial to their success. |

*(Continued )*

**TABLE BB14.2** (Cont.)

| Functional Category | Detailed Description of Subcategories | Notes |
|---|---|---|
| | a. strategic and general business management (cross-functional decision-making), including organizing work responsibilities<br>b. corporate governance (legal, planning, and public relations)<br>c. accounting, bookkeeping, auditing, payments, and other financial or insurance activities<br>d. human resources management (training and education, staff recruitment, workplace organization, provision of temporary personnel, payroll management, health and medical support)<br>e. procurement<br>f. managing external relationships with suppliers, alliances, and so on. | Organizational culture is important to measure as well to assure the foundation is laid for innovation. |
| 6. Product and business process development | Activities to scope, identify, develop, or adapt products or a firm's business processes. This function can be undertaken in a systematic fashion or on an ad hoc basis, and be conducted within the firm or obtained from external sources. Responsibility for these activities can lie within a separate division or in divisions responsible for other functions, for example, production of goods or services | Innovation portfolio management that considers replication across business units should be considered |

*Source*: Adapted from Brown (2008), "Business Processes and Business Functions: A New Way of Looking at Employment," www.bls.gov/mlr/2008/12/art3full.pdf and Eurostat (2018), *Glossary of Statistical Terms*, http://ec.europa.eu/eurostat/statistics-explained/index.php/Glossary: Business_functions.

derivation of more adaptable best practices once determined to be in the same functional grouping.

## Country Innovation Indexes

At a country or national level, there are different methodologies that can be used. The most logical one would be to continue with the OECD methodology because of the extent of the coverage of the survey data being collected. The additional data that are required at a national level include information about the policies that the country has implemented and to what extent they are effective

- Has it been fully deployed?
- Does everyone understand how to take advantage of the policies?
- What achievements and outcomes are coming about as a result of those policies?

There are various innovation-related indexes at the country level or at the regional level. We review five major indexes for their structures and variables. The five indexes are:

- *The Global Innovation Index (GII)*, provided by the World Intellectual Property Organization of the United Nations
- *The European Innovation Scoreboard (EIS)*, provided by the European Commission
- *The Global Creativity Index (GCI)*, provided by Martin Prosperity Institute
- *The Global Entrepreneurship Index (GEI)*, provided by the Global Entrepreneurship and Development Institute, and
- *The Portfolio Innovation Index (PII)* on US states and counties provided by Indiana University's Kelley School of Business supported by the U.S. Development Administration.

The limitations of country-level indexes include the following:

- They cannot sufficiently capture the rapidly changing innovation models at the company level.
- A simple ranking of countries based on their innovation capabilities does not sufficiently capture the complexity of innovation activities.

- Macro indexes focus on input metrics rather than output metrics due to the availability and maturity of data.
- Macro indexes of innovation are often not timely.
- Country-specific measures fail to capture the interaction between and among countries.

Despite their shortcomings, macro-level indicators of innovation could still provide useful guidance to business from the perspective of competitive advantages especially with regard to the comparative strengths of innovation systems (external innovation ecosystems), one of the selected signposts of innovation for this project. Moreover, macro indexes could shed light on possible problems at the company level if companies rely too heavily on one segment of the innovation process (i.e., outputs) or suffer from data unavailability. Finally, country of origin could be an indicator that a company is advantaged if it is based in a country that is strong with innovations. (See Table BB14.3)

---

## CONCLUSIONS

Innovation is too important to be managed without good measurements. Only through proper and timely measurements of innovation progress it is possible to ensure accountability for innovation investments and quick remedial of issues to enhance the competitive position of the company.

Proper innovation management pays attention both to traditional quantitative performance indicators and to qualitative indicators of the complex human interactions involved in innovation activities internally and externally to the company. Effective innovation metrics require a strategic and disciplined methodology to decide on the important indicators and devise procedures for measuring them in ways that are clear to all people involved.

Metrics drive behavior and "what gets measured gets done." Innovation indicators should be chosen, and their metrics should be designed and used to manage the evolution of the company to achieve better alignment with business strategies and nourish a culture of entrepreneurship that leads to tangible performance where it matters: in the market.

**TABLE BB14.3**

Approaches for Classifying Government Policy in Support of Innovation

| Policy Approach | Measurement Examples | Notes |
|---|---|---|
| By intention to support innovation capability or activity | Develop a list of capabilities that are related to innovation, such as personnel development and network integration | Government policy can direct and focus national innovation activities either by industry sector or by size of organization depending on their needs |
| By policy objective | These would focus on the result expected from the policy and could also include subsidies for the production of goods or services | Government expectations, representing their constituency, may focus on specific products/services where the country is behind |
| By type of instrument | Using the classification of socio-economic objectives. Note that this approach does not have many studies to back it up and may be difficult for individual firms to respond accurately | The social field is receiving a lot more emphasis these days. It has become a higher priority for large companies which realize that their success must include the success of the communities affected |
| By level of government agency responsible | Local, regional, national, supra-national, and international rules vary considerably; therefore by segmenting the measures accordingly, one may be able to draw more specific applicable solutions | Alignment across government levels is hard to attain unless there are common innovation measures that they share |
| By conditions on the support | Depending on the conditions required for transfers, or support that can be provided on a discretionary (e.g., competitive) or nondiscretionary, on-demand basis | Financial support can be directed to focus on continued policy or on the more flexible discretionary policy that can react faster over time |
| Financial value of support | Different instruments require different valuation methods and consequently respondents may be unable to provide reliable estimates of the financial value of support, other than for basic transfers such as direct grants | The level of support and the effort required to receive it may determine the ability for SMEs to acquire the commensurate support required. The level of "red tape" should be reduced |

*Source*: Adapted from OECD (2015), *Frascati Manual 2015: Guidelines for Collecting and Reporting Data on Research and Experimental Development*, http://oe.cd/frascati and the taxonomy adopted by the OECD's STIP COMPASS database of innovation policy initiatives and instruments (https://stip.oecd.org/)

Metrics indicate strategic priorities and they help drive the company in the right direction if chosen wisely and used for timely evaluation and corrective action. They also help in allocating resources better and rewarding people objectively. However, there are no magic metrics for innovation, but there is science and art in the proper selection of metrics to achieve the desired innovation goals.

Sufficient number of indicators and metrics should be used to provide a comprehensive view of innovation activities in the company. Such indicators and metrics should be adjusted from time to time according to market changes and competitive needs to avoid stagnation and people playing the game for show rather than for value.

# BB15

## Innovative Organizational Structure

Jane Keathley, MS PMP

## CONTENTS

## INTRODUCTION

> In an effective organization there is congruence between purpose, strategy, processes, structure, culture and people, It is the challenge to the leaders to orchestrate this alignment and to still promote innovation and change.
>
> David J. MacCoy

Dr. H. James Harrington points out, "A major restructuring change in any organization should only be undertaken when it will produce a very significant performance improvement and then it must be accompanied with an effective Organizational Change Management plan."

A 2016 Deloitte study found that

> only 26% of large companies (> 5,000 employees) were functionally organized (i.e., sales, marketing, finance, engineering, service, etc.) and 82% were either in the process of reorganizing, planning to reorganize or had recently reorganized to be more responsive to customer needs.[1]
>
> Bersin Josh, 2016

Overall, "92% of the companies … surveyed cited 'redesigning the way we work' as one of their key challenges, making this the #1 trend of the year."

What is driving this need to reorganize? Traditional models of organizational structure, based on functional areas, are not meeting the needs of customers or the workforce in today's environment of innovation. Information technology and instant communications have led to a shift from traditional functional and hierarchical models to network-based models that offer more rapid collaborations across more diverse populations. Effective structures must encourage such interactions, sharing of knowledge, and effective communication between customers, workforce, partners, and management.

## TYPE OF ORGANIZATIONAL STRUCTURES

The following list presents the most commonly used organizational structures. There are advantages and disadvantages to each of them, making it too risky to specify a one-size-fits-all organizational structure.

   (1)  Functional
   (2)  Vertical
   (3)  Bureaucratic
   (4)  Decentralized
   (5)  Geography
   (6)  Product
   (7)  Customer
   (8)  Case Management System
   (9)  Process-Based Network
(10)  Matrix
(11)  Hybrid

In this chapter we will provide general information about the advantages of the most frequently used organizational approaches, as well as some less frequently used models.

## Definitions related to Innovative Organizational Structures

**Customer Experience Index** – Forrester Research's annual survey to evaluate organizations' customer experience (CX) maturity; categories measured include effectiveness, ease of use, emotion, retention, enrichment, and advocacy.

    **Holacracy** – way of structuring an organization that replaces the conventional management hierarchy. Power is distributed throughout the organization, giving individuals and teams greater autonomy to self-organize and take rapid action, while staying aligned to the organization's purpose.

    **Structure** – system that outlines how organizational activities, such as task allocation, coordination, information flow, and supervision, are directed in order to achieve the goals of an organization. Structure can be considered as the viewing glass or perspective through which individuals see the organization and its environment.

## ORGANIZE TO INNOVATE

An organization's structure is directly related to its performance, and the design of the structure needs to be such that peak performance can be achieved. The influence of its structural design extends to the organization's ability to innovate and to the outcomes of each of its key performance systems. This chapter explores ways in which the structures of these key systems – management, product, process, sales and marketing, and customer service – factor into successful innovation.

One of the major benefits of management restructuring is to increase the employee sense of ownership, dedication, and pride within the organization

## MANAGEMENT STRUCTURE FOR INNOVATION

Management sets the tone of an organization and defines its culture and behaviors. The organizational structure, for which management is responsible, defines the division of activities and responsibilities, sets up communication lines (and barriers), and forms the rules for decision-making, all of which contribute to the culture and ultimately to how well the organization innovates.

Organizational structures that foster an innovation culture tend to be less hierarchical than traditional structures, in some cases doing away with hierarchy entirely. They tend to use advanced communication mechanisms that encourage interactions and exchange of information. Innovation in these environments is seen as integral across the organization – everyone's responsibility, to borrow a quality management phrase – and the structure is set up to support innovative thinking and behaviors throughout.

Not surprisingly, there is no one-size-fits-all structural model. A model that stimulates innovation in one organization may fall flat in another. Information about successful models is readily available in business publications; an organization may have to try more than one approach to find (or adapt) the model that is most effective. In general, these models can be grouped into those in which the innovation structure is fully integrated; those that are based on start-up incubators, either in-house or external partnerships; and those that operate alongside a more traditional structure.

## FULLY INTEGRATED MODELS

Organizations with a fully integrated structure ensure each individual not only has the opportunity but also feels responsible for contributing to innovations and problem-solving. Leveraging the varied observations and knowledge of these individuals is a key feature of successful innovation. Methodologies that allow the capture and curating of ideas and feedback, such as on-line collaborative tools, are prominent in such organizations. Each individual is accountable for creating value for customers.

A challenge with a fully integrated model, especially in large organizations, is to keep the model focused and connected to strategic directions. Stronger communication mechanisms may need to be established to keep the organization's goals and objectives prominent, foster capture of inputs and feedback, and effectively link them.

## Start-up Incubator Models

Innovation labs, creativity centers, and corporate start-ups are booming across various industries and academic institutions. Establishing a dedicated "start-up incubator" has become highly popular as senior leaders look for ways to keep their organizations at the cutting edge. The start-up environment lends itself to generating ideas and rapidly moving them forward, bypassing bureaucratic obstacles of the day-to-day business. MasterCard, Coca-Cola, and GE, among others, have established start-up enterprises within their business organizations with goals such as building profitable new entities, becoming more agile and entrepreneurial, and identifying innovative talent.[2] The start-up incubator can take the form of the traditional research and development lab or it may involve partnering with independent start-ups or academia. Once the start-up has a viable innovation, care must be taken to ensure the handoff to operations (e.g., development, manufacturing, sales, and marketing) is done with sufficient interaction and communication for a smooth deployment.

## Complementary or Parallel Models

In a parallel operating system, the organization is divided into two parts: one utilizing a traditional structure and another utilizing a structure designed for innovation. Day-to-day business follows the more traditional model, and a separate innovation system functions as a network-based structure within the established traditional operating system. Certain individuals serve as liaisons between the systems to exchange information, gather inputs and feedback, and provide expertise in customer/user requirements.[3] The Innovation system is able to move quickly to pursue strategic solutions, which can then be integrated into the traditional system more efficiently due to the early and on-going interactions between the groups. The parallel traditional system continues to operate more efficiently on day-to-day activities than the innovation system, as it was designed to do.

## Eliminate Management Structure

A more dramatic approach to structuring for innovation may be to eliminate hierarchical models of management altogether. Hierarchies typically lead to bureaucracy, strict division of duties, and "siloing," all antagonistic to innovation. Allowing individuals to take responsibility and accountability for their own work in a network-based structure can bring the transparency, accountability, and organizational agility needed for innovation.[4] Employees are allowed to focus on outcomes and to self-organize and collaborate as needed. Companies like Zappo's, The Ready, and Toyota have successfully utilized this approach. Org charts appear as role-based teams in nested and overlapping circles. These teams form and reform as needed and are focused on outcomes aligned with the organization's value streams.[5]

## Management Structure and Strategic Objectives

Management must also ensure a structure that is aligned with strategic objectives. Depending on your strategic goals, you may need to build a new division, hire staff with skill sets currently lacking in your organization, or merge units to leverage combined resources and talent. Each of these scenarios is an opportunity to achieve desired strategic outcomes with innovative approaches. Your strategic direction ultimately will determine your structural needs.

## Structure for Product Innovations

"What is it my customers really want (or need)?" is the essential piece of successful innovation, and the organization should be structured to ensure a thorough and deep understanding of user problems, needs, and desires. It is said the reason most innovative products fail is because it turns out as the customer didn't really want or need it. Finding the sweet spot in the middle – where the organization can innovatively solve the customers' frustrations and make their lives easier, simpler, and cheaper – is where the best innovations will arise.

The organization's structure must address responsibilities for gathering and understanding information on the customer perspective, prioritizing the information, and effectively acting on the information. Dedicated research teams, product managers, or sales and marketing staff may be assigned responsibility for direct interactions with users, both current and potential, as well as monitoring other sources such as literature, industry conferences, and social media. Some or all of the responsibility may be outsourced to a partner with expertise in the methods and tools for gathering user insights. Customer-facing methods and tools must be utilized and the appropriate skill sets must be available in these groups. The data and information must be analyzed to understand the message for the organization. The important thing is that the structure holds some group or set of individuals responsible for the on-going task of keeping up with customers' problems and needs, as well as new and evolving ways to address them. This information is where the organization's next opportunities will be found.

This part of innovation is inherently less predictable and resistant to traditional product management approaches. Timelines need to be more flexible and performance metrics may differ from those in other parts of the organization. In the end, understanding the customer's world, maybe even better than they do, leads to more attractive and competitive products.

Transitioning product innovations to development is often a major barrier to the product's deployment. The second most common reason innovations fail is that the product never gets built. Organizational structures set up with direct interfaces between new product information (i.e., research, product management, marketing, etc.) and development or engineering are most successful at avoiding such barriers. These structures allow regular back-and-forth communication as an idea moves from the theoretical, pilot, or prototype phase to an actual deliverable; it is not a one-time handoff.

## Structure for Process Innovations

New and value-adding products, services, and business models must make the most of the investments of time and money needed to achieve them if they are to contribute to the success of the organization. Organizational structure can help.

First of all, a common innovation methodology must be established. An innovation methodology or process lets people know the expectations for innovation and how innovation will get done across the organization. It improves the organization's functional abilities in the environment of uncertainty inherent with innovation. A systematic approach to innovation is critical in building a culture for innovation and ensuring the organization's sustainability.

At a high level, there are a few standard steps, or phases, in the innovation process. The process begins by developing insights into the problem and identifying the opportunity. This is followed by researching the problem and discovering creative solutions. The process needs to have frequent decision points to keep things moving and to focus resources as the solution matures. A step to compare and narrow the list of possible solutions is sometimes included as a formal step in the process. From there, the chosen solution (or short list of solutions) is refined with the goal of achieving the best value proposition for users and the organization. Finally, the innovation process must develop the business model around which the innovation can be executed, including manufacturing, marketing, and commercial sales.

This is also where the cycle begins anew. In a fully functioning system, innovation never really stops. There is constant movement in each part of the process, with a pipeline of opportunities working their way along the process at any given time.

Whatever methodology is adopted, it needs to accommodate the iterative and non-linear nature of innovation. It is typical to loop back to earlier points in the process as information becomes available and more is known about the evolving innovation. That new information may also expose a lack of value in the innovation and result in ending its development, allowing the next idea in the pipeline to emerge as a high priority.

## ORGANIZING THE WORKFORCE AROUND YOUR INNOVATION PROCESS

The organizational structure around which you execute the innovation process must incorporate cross-functional personnel who can bring their varying perspectives and sources of insights. Insular thinking, that is, siloes, is unlikely to give you the fresh ideas you need to be innovative. Matrix organizations and external partnerships that bring together creative thinkers with process engineers, designers with users, opportunity developers and problem solvers with marketers can jump-start the innovation program and must be driven by the organization's structure and innovation process.

Flat organization structures tend to be more effective, in part because they don't get bogged down by layers of decision makers and irrelevant decision factors. Speed and agility require rapid and timely decisions based on objective criteria and data, not bureaucratic decision trees. Allow decision making at the lowest level possible, based on empirical evidence that supports a go/no-go decision to move to the next step. Flat structures and clear decision making policies will provide the speed and agility needed to excel at innovation.

A 2016 study by Deloitte Human Capital Trends[6] supports this movement towards structures based on "networks of teams." Redesigning the way people work was found to be integral to employee engagement, innovation and speed to market. Communication and analytical tools, open information flow, and learning centers are necessary for networks of teams to thrive. Learning, the essential element of innovation, must be embedded in the structure. In this environment, teams come together for a purpose, then disband and reform as needed to adapt to the organization's needs.[1] General Stanley McChrystal used this model effectively during the Iraq war, as related in his book, Team of Teams.[7] McChrystal "created a new structure that allowed for dynamism and flexibility within the overall (military) organizational structure."

> "We have to think of companies like 'Hollywood Movies' – people come together and bring their skills and abilities to projects and programs, they build and deliver the solution, and then many of them move on to the next 'movie' later." – Josh Bersin.

A recent ASQ/Forbes study of 2,291 executives and managers showed that self-described world-class companies are more likely overall to cite strong quality programs as a vital tool to drive innovation. Managing business risks and continuously learning and improving are core to quality systems and essential for innovation. The QMS (Quality Management System) enables an organization to more readily tune in to external and internal customers, identify and appropriately control risks, apply creative problem-solving techniques, and recover quickly from failure – all essential to an innovation structure.[8]

Co-locating key functions may be useful to improve communication and interactions. Under Armour found that bringing designers and manufacturers together under the same roof not only facilitates efficiency and speed to market for their athletic clothing – it also allows rapid adaptations based on early customer evaluations, reducing the risk of manufacturing large runs of new styles that don't do well in the marketplace.[9]

Automating certain processes may bring efficiencies and also free up personnel to focus on other aspects of innovation. Automation is necessary for complex processes and systems (and to remain competitive, in many industries). Organizations that fall behind with technology and automation soon will become endangered. The cost-justification for using automation should be focused on enhancing the skills of the workforce and redirecting their contributions to those innovative activities that require human thinking and brain-power. Automated systems are increasingly able to learn and self-adjust, and "some enterprises have started using intelligent automation to drive a new, more productive relationship between people and machines."[10].

Focusing the organization's process structure on understanding customer and employee needs, managing risk, and maintaining flexibility and agility are keys to the long-term success of your program.

## Innovation through Sales and Marketing Structure

> It's not about having the right opportunities. It's about handling the opportunities right.
> Mark Hunter, CSP; Author, High Profit Prospecting

The sales and marketing functions of the organization play their most significant roles in innovation through their interfaces with customers. Well-developed customer relationships engage the customer and make them feel comfortable conveying the things they like and the things that cause issues for them. Sales and marketing personnel are at the front line in finding and learning about innovation opportunities. The sales and marketing structure contributes significantly to the collection of customer and market data to feed into the innovation cycle.

Organizing the sales and marketing groups to function in a network structure allows them to bring their customer-facing perspectives to the innovation effort and contribute their expertise in ways that staying in a siloed functional unit cannot. The model is increasingly being adopted in government and business, in such sectors as healthcare (Cleveland Clinic) and in manufacturing (3M), resulting in improvements in organizational outcomes such as customer satisfaction and time to output/delivery.[11]

Structural sales and marketing models that go beyond the organization may be used to trigger innovation, such as retaining a marketing research company or creativity consultant to help gather and analyze customer feedback and insights. Co-marketing collaborations with partners are a time-tested model for expanding the customer base and reaching out to new market areas that are ripe for innovation. These collaborations often stimulate innovation by bringing different perspectives of the challenges facing the marketplace and customer. To be successful, marketing collaborations require clear definition of content control and engagement expectations.

As sales models shift to be more technology-driven and purchasing transactions are done on-line, the ratio of external sales agents to internal is changing in favor of internal. Internal sales models offers advantages in scalability, organizational growth due to reduced costs and increased access to customers, as well as the ability to access specific markets such as small businesses.[12] Organizational structures focused on internal sales groups may be challenged to have a complete view of the customer's situation, and companies with this model may need to ensure other means are in place to provide face-to-face access to customers.

Structuring your Sales and Marketing organization for effective innovation means engaging them in all aspects of your innovation program. Sales and Marketing personnel are uniquely positioned to identify and understand your customers' pain points and problems, which are the key drivers of innovation. Setting expectations and supportive structures to capture those insights, and continuing to involve Sales and Marketing through innovation development to delivery to the marketplace are essential to a dynamic and innovative organization.

## Structure for Service Innovation

Ever gotten frustrated at the level of customer service you received? Did you give that organization a low on-line rating? Tell your friends and neighbors about your bad experience? Seems that bad news travels faster than good, and in this day of on-line and instant reviews many organizations have had to refocus their commitment to service in order to maintain customers and recruit new ones.

> It takes 20 at-a-boys to offset 1 unpleasant contact.
>
> H. James Harrington

There is no doubt that having happy and enthused customers are worth the attention and focus you give it. Data show correlations between satisfaction measures and company growth/profitability. For example, Forrester conducts an annual Customer Experience Index (CX). For the years 2010–2015, their data show compound average revenue growth of 17% for companies whose customers scored them highly (CX Leaders), while "CX Laggards" realized only 3% compound average revenue growth.[13] Best-in-class brands included USAA, several banks, Etsy and Zappos, among others.

## FOCUS ON THE CUSTOMER

Keeping the customer front and center, and tying everyone's' perspective back to the customer, is the primary purpose of service structure. It's easy in the day-to-day efforts of running a business to become inwardly focused, making sure production is on track, financial matters are being managed, and personnel are getting the work done and being paid. Strategies may be developed, perhaps focusing on new products or market areas, but customers sometimes become subordinated to all of the other activities going on and this is where things may go awry for the organization.

To shift the focus to a more customer-centric approach, rethink your structures. Start with the customer and list all the possible points of contact they have with the organization. Map each of these points of contact to the internal party or system responsible for receiving and handling the contact. Continue to map your processes from the individual or system receiving the customer inquiry to the steps for responding to them. As you drill down into the organization's processes you should eventually get to product development and delivery work areas and ultimately to the infrastructure processes such as accounting and financing and facilities management.

Viewing the work of the organization in this way allows you to make innovative changes to the structure of your organization and focus it on the customer service experience. It also emphasizes to every employee how their work supports customers and the business. This approach can be transformative – when you see things from the customers' eyes, you can more readily add value and develop enthusiastic customers.[14,15]

Structuring your service organization to minimize complexity and inefficiencies in the customer experience will help build loyal and happy customers. Using technology may be an innovative way to achieve this. Electronic customer relationship management applications (eCRM) provide the technology that allows customers to virtually engage with the organization to submit orders and queries and to obtain information about their account and the company's products. Benefits to the organization are the ability to log and track customer interactions, quickly access information needed to address the customer request, and build customer history data to help provide continuity and consistency in interactions over time.

## Understand the Employee-Customer Relationship

Given the critical-to-success nature of the customer-employee relationship, it may be best to manage them together, not separately. Consider organizational structures that put employee management (i.e., human resources) together with customer relationship management (e.g., operations, quality, or marketing) – this emphasizes the critical relationship between the two and their importance for organization success. You must identify internally who "owns" this relationship and ensure that it is managed as an integrated system. Acknowledge that each customer/employee interaction is unique and develop processes to allow "customized" services for each service interaction.

Furthermore, interactions and collaborations with customers are important sources of innovative ideas and customer delight. Ensuring customers have opportunities to convey and discuss their thoughts – for example, through instant pop-up surveys, focus groups, and prototype reviews – helps to build open relationships and gather the diverse perspectives of your customers. These interactions with customers may enhance the structure for innovation by extending them beyond the service provider to other internal groups, such as product developers, marketing, process improvement experts, and executive management.

## THE BOTTOM LINE

The key to structuring your organization's customer service system for innovative services is to focus on the customer experience. Develop structures that are driven from the customer's point of view and aligned through to back-end work that is not directly facing the customer. Employees are integral to the customer relationship and providing them with good training, tools, and expectations for innovation is a must. Tracking the customer experience with good metrics and acting on the results to add new services that delight them is the bottom line.

## SUMMARY

> We trained very hard, but it seems like every time we were beginning to form up into teams, we would be reorganized. I was to learn later on in life that we tend to meet any new situation by reorganizing. A wonderful method it can be for creating the illusion of progress while producing confusion, ineffectiveness, and demoralization.
> *Charlton Ogburn, Jr, "Merrill's Marauders" (Harper's Magazine, 1957)*

Many structure models have been developed and many of them contribute to successful innovation programs. Each structural type, alone or in combination with others, is the best answer for a certain situation. Your challenge is to find the "right" structure and fit for your organization and then deploy it. Start by looking at the organization from three perspectives: strategic, operational, and tactical.

- The strategic perspective looks at the organization from the top-down and determines the overall shape of the organization. It's a process of moving the big boxes, or key systems, around to determine the right fit.
- The operational perspective deals with the work needed to support the strategic perspective. Review the appropriate mix of operational, managerial, and support processes through a "customer-looking-in" review.
- The tactical perspective is completed with a bottom-up approach and determines the work teams and job designs.

| OPTION | ADVANTAGES | DISADVANTAGES |
|---|---|---|
| 1. **Function**<br><br>*Organized around major activity groups such as R&D operations, finance or HR* | • Increased knowledge sharing within functions.<br>• Ability to build depth and specialization–attracts and develops experts who "speak the same language"<br>• Leverage with vendors<br>• Economies of scale<br>• Standardization of processes and procedures.<br>• Eliminates costly duplication and allows maximum specialization in trained occupational skills because of the individual grouping specialties<br>• Fosters professional identity and career paths<br>• Makes management easier because of the need for competence in a narrower range of skills.<br>• Provides access to specialized skills in other departments | • Difficult to manage diverse product and service lines.<br>• Cross-functional processes cause contention.<br>• Different departments have different priorities; the customer's interest can get overlooked.<br>• Creates major differences between departments.<br>• Fails to develop well-rounded top managers, especially when higher-level management makes the decisions.<br>• Is difficult to trace responsibility for performance.<br>• Is not readily adaptable to change.<br>• Takes longer to resolve conflicts. |
| 2. **Vertical** | • Clearly defined scope of tasks<br>• Limited range of knowledge or skills required to perform effectively<br>• Knowledge transfer along the chain-of-command is enhanced<br>• Competency development within a vertical unit is enhanced<br>• Efficient in stable, predictable environments | • Limited flexibility or exposure to other responsibility areas.<br>• Limited career development opportunities.<br>• Knowledge transfer across the organization is difficult.<br>• Narrow skills base within a vertical unit.<br>• Ineffective in dynamic or unpredictable environments. |
| 3. **Bureaucratic** | • Clear policies and procedures.<br>• Stable organization systems and processes | • Policies and procedures create inflexibility |

*(Continued)*

(Cont.)

| OPTION | ADVANTAGES | DISADVANTAGES |
|---|---|---|
| | • Consistent service and quality levels.<br>• Clear performance expectations.<br>• Clear roles and responsibilities.<br>• Enterprise-wide focus.<br>• Effective strategy deployment.<br>• Optimization at a micro level. | • Potential for long cycle times when process crosses many responsibility areas.<br>• Glacial responsiveness to change<br>• No individual judgment or empowerment.<br>• Performance expectations tend to be internally focused<br>• Cooperation across role and responsibility areas is difficult<br>• Internal focus<br>• Difficult to dramatically change strategy<br>• Potential for suboptimal performance at an enterprise level. |
| 4. **Decentralized** | • Strong customer focus.<br>• Business units responsive to changes in customer needs and market demands<br>• Business units are focused on the needs of their segments.<br>• Self-sufficiency at the business unit level.<br>• Accumulation of customer-related knowledge is enhanced.<br>• Business units empowered to focus competency development efforts in areas which support their own success.<br>• Business units empowered to develop own standards within corporate guidelines.<br>• Accountability and control at business unit level. | • Reduced enterprise focus.<br>• Enterprise-wide ability to act in concert is difficult.<br>• Business units are hard to coordinate when a customer is in multiple segments.<br>• Duplication of resources and inefficiency at an enterprise level.<br>• Knowledge transfer across business units is difficult.<br>• Difficult to maintain consistent functional competency levels across the enterprise<br>• High potential for inconsistent processes, technologies applications and competence levels<br>• Internal tension and competition for resources based on measurement system |

| | Advantages | Disadvantages |
| --- | --- | --- |
| 5. **Geography**<br><br>*Organized around physical locations such as states, countries or regions.* | • Provides a local focus.<br>• Moves decision-making authority closer to the problem.<br>• Permits accountability for performance<br>• Provides mechanisms for the organization to react quickly, such as to competitive changes or new customer needs.<br>• Simplifies coordination among functions | • Difficult to mobilize and share resources across regional boundaries.<br>• Duplicates costly resources (i.e. equipment and personnel) between departments<br>• Encourages competition among divisions<br>• Reduces specialization in occupational skills. |
| 6. **Product**<br><br>*Organized into product divisions, each with its own functional structure to support product lines* | • More rapid product development cycles.<br>• Focus allows for "state-of-the-art" research<br>• P&L responsibility for each product is located at the division level with a general manager.<br>• Positive team spirit develops around products | • Divergence among product lines in focus and standards.<br>• Loyalty to product division may make it hard to recognize when a product should be changed or dropped.<br>• Lost economies of scale when functions are spread out.<br>• Multiple points of contract for the customer. |
| 7. **Customer**<br><br>*Organized around major market segments such as client groups, industries, or population groups.* | • Ability to customize for customers.<br>• Ability to build depth in relationships. | • Divergence among customer/market segments in focus and standards.<br>• Duplication of resources and functions.<br>• Lost economies of scale when functions are spread out among customer/market divisions. |
| 8. **Case Management Network** | • Strong customer focus.<br>• Flexible<br>• Total accountability for customer satisfaction<br>• Job diversity<br>• Eases coordination between functions | • Reduced enterprise focus.<br>• Potential for variability and inefficiencies in the delivery of products and/or services<br>• Stressful work environment due to high levels of interdependence |

*(Continued)*

(Cont.)

| OPTION | ADVANTAGES | DISADVANTAGES |
| --- | --- | --- |
| | | • Requires highly skilled employees<br>• Unclear roles and responsibilities<br>• Dissipates resources<br>• Difficult to maintain strategic focus |
| 9. **Process-Based Network** | • Strategically aligned.<br>• Customer focused<br>• Total accountability for process performance.<br>• Work force aligned along process lines.<br>• All resources to do the job are available within the network.<br>• Lower process cycle time.<br>• Efficient process execution. | • Duplication of resources.<br>• Competing goals across process teams and across levels of hierarchy<br>• Stressful work environment due to high levels of interdependence<br>• Career pathing is complex and there is a potential for glass ceiling to be created.<br>• Reduced critical mass or economies of scale<br>• Dissipation of knowledge. |
| 10. **Font-Back Hybrid**<br><br>*Combines elements of both the product and customer structures in order to provide the benefits of both* | • Customers can buy multiple products with a single point of contact and one account<br>• The organization can better cross-sell its products<br>• Ability to provide value-added systems and solutions when products have become commodities.<br>• Preservation of product focus and product excellence.<br>• Allows for a variety of distribution channels. | • Contention over where resources are allocated.<br>• Disagreements over prices and customer needs<br>• Difficulty coordinating marketing functions that are split between the front and the back.<br>• Conflicting metrics<br>• Information sharing and accounting complexity |

**FIGURE BB15.1**

Summary of Organization Structure Types, Advantages and Disadvantages

The combination of strategic, operational, and tactical decisions will be the basis for determining the "right" organization structure, and if done well, can drive a structure that is highly successful at innovation.

## REFERENCES

1. Berson, J. 2016. http://joshbersin.com/2016/03/the-new-organization-different-by-design/ (May 2016).
2. Alsever, J. Start-Ups … within Giant Companies. 2015. http://fortune.com/2015/04/26/startups-inside-giant-companies/
3. REF: Accelerate HBS Kotter, J. Nov 2012 HBR, pp. 44–58.
4. REF: holacracy.org
5. Robertson, B. *Holacracy* (Henry Holt and Co., New York, 2015).
6. Deloitte. 2016. www2.deloitte.com/content/dam/Deloitte/global/Documents/Human Capital/gx-dup-global-human-capital-trends-2016.pdf
7. McChrystal, S. *Team of Teams* (Penguin Publishing Group; Penguin Random House LLC, New York, 2015).
8. Forbes Insights. *Culture of Quality, Accelerating Growth and Performance in the Enterprise; Forbes Media* (New York, NY, 2014).
9. Halzack, S. Under Armour Debuts Gear Made in the US. Washington Post, January 31, 2017.
10. Wells, M., and Kralj, M. Accenture. 2016. www.accenture.com/us-en/blogs/blogs-case-for-automation (April 29 2016).
11. McDowell, T., Agarwal, D., Miller, D., Okamoto, T., and Page, T.. *Organizational Design the Rise of Teams* (Deloitte Insights, 2016).
12. Martin, S. https://hbr.org/2013/11/the-trend-that-is-changing-sales
13. Miller M. 2016. www.brandchannel.com/2016/07/26/forrester-customer-experience-index-072616/
14. Bitner, M.J., Ostrom, A.L., and Morgan, F.N. *Service Blueprinting: A Practical Technique for Service Innovation* (Center for Services Leadership, Arizona State University, Tempe AZ, 2007).
15. Bollard, A., Larrea, E., Singla, A., and Sood, R. The Next-Generation Operating Model for the Digital World. 2017. www.mckinsey.com/business-functions/digital-mckinsey/our-insights/the-next-generation-operating-model-for-the-digital-world (Mar 2017).

# BB16

## Rewards and Recognition: Traditional and Emerging Methods for Recognizing Innovation Excellence

*Christopher F. Voehl, PMP*

## CONTENTS

## PROLOGUE

TIME's (Total Innovation Management Excellence) overarching message is that people are at the top of the list of any company's major assets and are an integral element to a diverse and thriving organizational culture of innovation.

In their seminal work on Managing Human Resources for Innovation and Creativity[1], Gupta and Singhal advised organizations seeking to innovate adopt the following *four-pronged human resource management strategy*:

1. Evaluate current personnel needs vs. emerging market trends and hire creative people to achieve organizational goals.
2. Find a way to align employees' long-term career objectives with the company's vision.
3. Institute meaningful and measurable performance appraisal systems.
4. Implement recognition and reward systems to bolster employee creativity.

The materials in this chapter are based upon both historical and recent literature concerning the management of human resources (HR) and how this may influence innovation management within an organization. We start with the hypothesis that certain management practices in this area consist of goal recognition and reward for achievement. Also important is an understanding of the five generational workforce categories, along with the creation of a shared understanding of how we can all work together toward creating an innovation culture, by building synergy between experienced workers and those new to the workforce who may have vital information and ideas to disrupt entire industries.

## TIME AND THE FIVE GENERATIONAL CATEGORIES

By popular consensus, this is the first time in modern history where we have the opportunity for five generations to be working side-by-side within a given workplace.[2]

---

1 Ashok K. Gupta & Arvind Singhal (1993) Managing Human Resources for Innovation and Creativity, Research-Technology Management, 36:3, 41–48, DOI: 10.1080/08956308.1993.11670902

2 *Inc* magazine – www.inc.com/john-rampton/different-motivations-for-different-generations-of-workers-boomers-gen-x-millennials-gen-z.html

## Traditionalists

- Traditionalists[3], also known as "The Silent Generation", are valued as the oldest workers in our modern workforce. Having been born in 1945 and earlier, they represent approximately 3% of the current U.S. workforce.
- Their value system embraces civic (and corporate) pride, and have traditionally high levels of dedication, and respect for authority. Most are highly disciplined and demonstrate sacrifice and loyalty above personal gain.
- Traditionalists are motivated by flexible, autonomous work environments, and find reward from working on prestige projects and assignments.
- Traditionalists often require compensation packages including profit sharing, stock options, and retirement plans, in addition to traditional salary plus vacation and benefits.
- However, standard health and insurance benefits may not be a motivating factor if they already have Medicare.
- They appreciate being recognized for their wisdom and contributions (past and present) and are self-motivated by accomplishment of personal goals and objectives.
- During times of change such as mergers, acquisitions, and even downsizing, traditionalists can often be relied upon to bridge the knowledge gap with incoming workers.
- Traditionalists prefer coaching focused on improving their professional strengths and can often be counted on to mentor others as coaches themselves.

## Baby Boomers

- As of the 2016 U.S. Census, Baby Boomers[4] represented 23% of the population.
- For many Baby Boomers (born between 1946 and 1964), that period of post-World War II, prosperity and relative stability defined their eternal optimism and values of equal rights.

---

3 According to the *Pew Research Center*, this generation was born during the period from 1928 to 1945 and constitute about 3% of the current workforce.

4 Pew reports approximately 70 million Boomers will be retired by 2020 year-end.

- This carries over to the workplace where a level playing field is often sought.
- They are often driven to provide their children the best of everything possible.
- Accordingly, many are motivated by salary, promotions, and titles conveying respect and recognition of their career accomplishments (past and present).
- Baby Boomers expect regular performance appraisals to gain feedback on how to do even better, and positive reinforcement of their value to the organization.
- Organizations should be aware that many Baby Boomers expect to work beyond the standard 40-hour work week, seeking recognition for going above and beyond.
- Boomers appreciate individual rewards and earmarks of status, such as trophies, plaques, preferred seating/office space, and items which they can give to others to convey their status such as business cards.
- Unlike traditionalists, coaching boomers is most successful when it's focused on shoring up weaknesses, such as by providing training opportunities designed to help them keep skills up to date to remain competitive in the workforce.

## Generation X

- Analysis of the U.S. Census estimates from 2016 projected Generation X[5] to be approximately 20% of the U.S. population, with that number projected to grow as the Silent Generation and Baby Boomers retire and phase out of the workforce.
- Born during a period of upheaval and national uncertainty (between 1964 and 1979), Gen X workers crave stability yet retain a healthy skepticism, and therefore are motivated by recognition and rewards based on individual performance and results, over which they have a greater sense of control.
- As the generation raised during the greatest technological advances of the 20th century, Gen X workers (many now in their 40s and 50s) seek access not only of top notch technology to

5 Generation X, defined by the Pew Research Center, are those individuals born during the period from 1965 to 1980, are about 45–50 million Americans, the offspring of Traditionalists and/or Baby Boomers.

automate their work, but also the platform by which to share their innovations and advances with their peers.

- Having survived both the dot com crash of 2000 and rounds of layoffs during the Great Recession of 2008, many Gen X workers have re-evaluated their career goals in pursuit of greater work–life balance, flexible schedules, and remote employment opportunities.

- Like their predecessors, traditional performance-based merit increases and promotions can still be motivating factors, but to a lesser degree. They often will not be afraid to shake things up, suggest innovative methods of (how they perceive to be) the best way and can be counted on for routinely coloring outside the lines beyond traditional methods.

- Coaching works best when equally focused on shoring up strengths and improving weaknesses.

## Millennials

- Millennials[6], often referred to as "Generation Y" as a way to contrast with the preceding Generation X, make up the greatest percent of our workforce, at 22% (2016 census). They are estimated to grow to as great as 75% of the workforce by the year 2025.

- Traditional recognition, reward, and incentive programs often do not resonate as powerfully with Millennials as with past generations. They value work–life balance but have come to expect and experience more of a work–life blend.

- According to the 2016 Millennial Survey conducted by Deloitte[7], 16.8% of millennials choose employment based on opportunities for work–life balance, and 11% expect flexibility in the form of telecommuting and flextime vs. the *traditional* 40-hour week.

- However, according to a recent work–life balance survey[8] conducted in 2019, millennials can still be counted on to work approximately 42 hours per week.

---

6 Among the different generations in the workforce, Millennials already comprise the largest group, according to Pew.

7 the 2016 Millennial Survey – https://www2.deloitte.com/content/dam/Deloitte/global/Documents/About-Deloitte/gx-millenial-survey-2016-exec-summary.pdf

8 COMMERCIAL Café survey – https://www.commercialcafe.com/blog/work-life-balance-survey-2019/

- In lieu of this work ethic, and surrounded by technology that makes this possible, upwards of 75% are seeking telecommuting options in pursuit of work–life balance.
- Beginning with the millennial generation, we are seeing a shift in how attitudes and approach to meaningful work, recognition, and rewards are very different from prior generations. This observation is backed by volumes of research, including the 2016 Gallup study "How Millennials Want to Work and Live"[9] highlighting the following:
  - ○ 60% responded on-the-job learning was of paramount importance.
  - ○ Only 50% plan to stay with their current employer for more than a year.
  - ○ 60% report quality of management is "extremely important".
  - ○ 44% are more likely to be engaged by regular meetings with their manager.
  - ○ Those who are meeting regularly (61% of respondents), report they regularly receive recognition. However only 19% receive routine feedback, with merely 17% reporting they receive meaningful feedback.
- These findings suggest more personal and regular forms of mentoring and performance appraisal between manager and employee to ensure individual training development is proceeding as planned, and they have opportunities to apply what they are learning.
- Coaching for Millennials needs to evolve into ongoing conversations regarding what they need to be successful, what barriers they're currently experiencing, which provides management the opportunity to provide more regular, personal feedback and recognition.

## Generation Z

- Generation Z[10], also known as the "I Generation" due to their advanced technological aptitudes, represents the youngest of the five generations in the modern workforce.
- While known for their embrace of technology, it is estimated up to 53% prefer face-to-face communication. If that sounds odd, consider that 62% of millennials prefer F2F communication with their manager.

---

9 Gallup – https://www.gallup.com/workplace/238073/millennials-work-live.aspx
10 Gen Z workers constitute about one-quarter of America's population.

- Widely regarded as the most diverse generation, members of this youngest generation have seen the impacts of economic downturn on their parents' careers and are looking for alternate employment arrangements. Many have already started their own businesses by the time they leave High School! Perhaps this is why many choose to eschew college.
- In contrast to millennials, Gen Z workers spend only 38 hours per week in a traditional office setting. They're also less likely to work overtime; only 7% vs. baby boomers 16%.
- This may correlate with their feelings on work–life balance and overall happiness, where 25% report being unhappy with work–life balance.
- Like every generation that preceded them, Generation Z workers desire personal development and career advancement. What sets them apart is they are not solely reliant on their employer to provide these opportunities, and many express an open distrust of conventional institutions, including corporate recognition and reward programs.
- Regarding coaching, Generation Z workers expect coaching to be a natural extension of the educational arenas from which many have just emerged.

Whether from the Traditionalist, Boomer, Gen X, Y, or Z generation, modern workers have begun to assimilate the traits common to all generations. Most have embraced technological advancements, and many still seek work environments that foster innovation by rewarding excellence and recognizing opportunities for personal development and improvement.

When you stop and listen to them, it becomes clear that a one-size-fits all approach to recognition and reward programs is quickly becoming a thing of the past. The challenge organizations will face is putting policies in place that can be adapted for changing generational demographics and individual needs.

## RECOGNITION AND REWARDS WITHIN THE TIME FRAMEWORK

The challenge facing organizations today is not what to recognize and reward but how. As stated in the opening chapter of this book, every person cannot be recognized in the same way. Rewards and recognition systems must be adaptable *based on the contribution that the individual (or team) made to the innovation being recognized.* If the contribution also benefitted the organization's overall performance, as in the case with breakthrough innovations, the reward should be incrementally commensurate – in other words, a billion-dollar breakthrough should have a bigger reward.

The Rewards and Recognition process should be designed to reinforce the Total Innovation Management Pyramid. As Recognition and Rewards are part of the innovation endgame, at this stage in the process the TIME Pyramid is turned on its axis, with Stakeholder Needs and Values (and organizational direction) driving the adaptive, overlapping phases of the innovation delivery process. When looked at from this perspective, Shared Values are like precious gems being mined at the heart of a mountain.

Tier I – Value to the Stakeholders (the Foundation)
Tier II – Setting the Direction
Tier III – Basic Concepts
Tier IV – Delivery Processes
Tier V – Organizational Impact
Tier VI – Shared Value

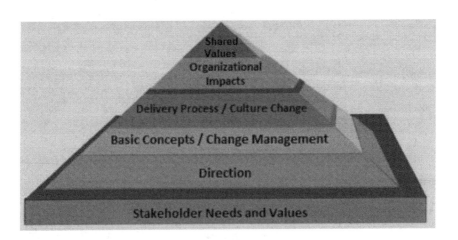

**FIGURE BB16.1**
The Six Tiers of the Total Innovation Management Pyramid (Inverse Model)

Each recognition and reward must reinforce the organization's vision beginning with stakeholder needs and values (Tier 1). Through leadership, vision deployment, direction (Tier 2) and communication of basic concepts (Tier 3), the organization's Change Management practice drives both the deliver process (Tier 4) and culture change. This ultimately results in the realization of:

a. desirable and sometimes unforeseen Organizational Impacts (Tier 5) and
b. Shared Values (Tier 6), including creativity and innovation.

It is true that everyone hears "Thank You" in a different way. We find ourselves in a unique time where Traditionalists, Baby Boomers, Gen-X, Y (Millennials), and Z (iGen) are all potentially working together within the same organization. If you want individuals of wide-ranging backgrounds and levels of experience to take an active role in your innovation culture, you must be able to deliver expressions of gratitude to each individual in a way that is meaningful to them personally. Because of the collapse of traditional corporate employee loyalty and retention programs over the past 25 years, the time where a "pat on the back" had any lasting value has passed, and monetary reward has become such an expectation that it lacks the lasting value of more meaningful, custom-tailored rewards. Not only has the time for a "pat on the wallet" passed, it also invokes certain unavoidable and unwanted connotations in the era of Me Too.

During one of our conversations, Dr. Jim Harrington relayed an example from IBM's halcyon days how one person from each function would be selected each month to have lunch with the president of the division based upon how much money their ideas saved the company. In the glass-ceiling era of uneven compensation and reward structures, this type of recognition tended to level the playing field. Whereas in today's climate, these types of rewards might carry less weight, there are organizations where division heads, VPs and the C-level echelon are still lionized, and their star-power (and their time and attention) might continue to carry more weight as a meaningful reward. There are also a significant enough number of workers in the workplace that are old enough to remember, and younger workers who may still hold these ideals in high regard – for this segment of the workforce, traditional recognition and reward systems still may be significant motivating factors. Programs such as employee of the month, merit-based promotions, and President's Cup awards pioneered by organizations such as AT&T Card Services in the 1980s and 1990s may still be of value when looking for benchmarks to custom tailor your recognition and reward program to suit a diverse workforce spanning multiple generations. The point here is that a one-size-fits-all approach to recognition and rewards will no longer be sufficient for the emerging workforce of the future where the worker is often migratory, moving from organization to organization as a way of finding fulfilment and career advancement.

Dr. Sunnie Giles, in her book *The New Science of Radical Innovation*, examines how mid-level leaders are willing to forgo up to 39% of their annual compensation in order to work for a Quantum Leader (defined by exhibiting leadership competencies which stimulate radical innovation breakthroughs within their organizations). By seeking to forgo a significant bit of their safety net, those inspired by innovation leaders are seeking a higher calling, one where they might be able to effect a tremendous degree of change within their organizations and their industry by being on the cutting edge of the next great advancement – in business, science, technology, medicine, or within niche organizations that exist in the convergence between (feeding from, and in service to) these disciplines by serving as a conduit between business sectors. These smaller niche organizations typically involve nontraditional employer–employee relationships, including the ability to work remotely all or part of the time, which must be considered when seeking ways to motivate people to innovate via recognition and rewards.

**Key takeaways**: If people are willing to work for less, and risk more, for the intrinsic rewards of working for an innovation leader on the next big thing, organizations must facilitate the development of leaders with innovation as a key leadership competency.

Ultimately, it is up to the organization, its culture, and the individuals working within it to determine what constitutes a meaningful recognition and rewards program.

## Relevant Recent Research into Time-Based Recognition and Rewards

In order to fully support the TIME methodology, the rewards and recognition process should continue to include both monetary and nonmonetary rewards, while going above and beyond to include what the latest generations truly value most – time. How to balance expectations for the five different generations in the workforce can be challenging to understand and balance their diverse expectations when it comes to total rewards. These rewards include everything an employee values in the work relationship, including compensation, benefits, work–life balance, performance management, coaching, job satisfaction, and motivation. To address the needs of different generations in the workforce, you first need to define them as individual groups and understand their typical expectations as previously described.

In the 2018 Harvard Business School paper on what today and tomorrow's employees will value most intrinsically, a study of 1,232 graduating university students, "respondents who valued time over money chose more intrinsically rewarding activities and were happier one year after graduation." Their findings extend prior research by demonstrating a "tendency to value time over money is not only predictive of daily consumer choices, but also of major life decisions." In other words, this tendency to value time over money extended not only to their day to day lifestyle choices, but also into major life decisions such as career choice and place of employment.

In order to confirm the theorized correlation and "long-term effect of time and money orientations" on major life decisions and well-being, the authors sought to study individuals undergoing a potentially life-altering critical decision-making process – they studied over 1,000 college grads to see if their time/money inclinations were a predictive factor on their overall happiness one year after graduation. The study focused on career selection as a life-altering decision (Hodkinson & Sparkes, 1997) as well as a predictor of overall well-being (Marum, 2014).

These are not traditional workers motivated by traditional factors. This is an incoming generation of workers raised by parents who devoted the prime working years of their lives to their careers (in many cases at the expense of work–life balance), only to see their careers and retirement savings evaporate in the financial downturn of 2008. Reaching, recognizing, and rewarding this new generation is becoming increasingly difficult, as we're collectively becoming more disengaged in the age of the smart phone. Recent employee engagement research from Gallup[11] is staggering: 87% of employees worldwide are

11 Gallup engagement research – https://www.gallup.com/services/190118/engaged-workplace.aspx

not fully engaged in their work. Whereas "companies with highly engaged workforces outperform their peers by 147% in earnings per share." According to Gallup, these higher performing organizations have rates of employee engagement upwards of 20 times higher than that of underperforming organizations globally.

Whereas organizations in Europe and internationally provide more vacation and leave time per worker, many American organizations have lost touch with an age-old objective of a job well done – time off and away from the job. People are simply happier spending their time with family, friends, and loved ones. In this same study, Ashley Whillans concludes that "the happiest young workers were those who said around the time of their college graduation that they preferred careers that gave them time away from the office to focus on their relationships and their hobbies."

It's become common knowledge[12] that organizations in the European Union award more paid vacation time. Finland has the highest-ranking average of paid vacation time, where employees have approximately 30 paid vacation days annually. That's in addition to nine national holidays.

The Czech Republic, Germany, France, Ireland, and the United Kingdom also have generous vacation plans. Outside of the European Union, Australia, Brazil, India, New Zealand, and Saudi Arabia reward employees with generous paid-vacation plans. Granted the Saudis have a nontraditional approach to profit and loss management. While working in "The Kingdom" on a contract for Saudi Telecom, it had to be explained to the American team that there was no such thing as expenses – as a seemingly endless supply of money continues to flow freely from oil revenues and their population is richly rewarded.

Elsewhere, countries leading this trend provide four weeks minimum paid vacation on average as a mandate – again, this is in addition to national paid holidays. These countries conduct their own independent research into what best motivates and attracts employees to work at organizations within their country based on the most attractive paid-leave, benefit, and compensation packages. Certain countries offer minimum vacation time, as is the case with many American organizations that offer additional paid leave based on tenure.

---

12  https://www.wisegeek.com/what-is-paid-vacation.htm

Some countries do not have any mandatory rules for paid employee vacation time. In the United States, up to 25% of full-time workers have zero paid vacation days. To be fair, American workers do have approximately 10–15 paid vacation days per year on average. While there are a significant number of American organizations who do provide paid-vacation time for their employees, it is entirely up to the organization to decide what the individual paid-leave compensation will entail, who is entitled, and how much paid time off will be rewarded.

**Key takeaway**: Organizations must rethink traditional recognition and reward systems, focus on what their employees truly want, and determine how to practically apply the concept of time as a reward.

### Traditional Methods

In today's exponentially changing business climate, organizations continue to face challenges in breaking the mold from day-to-day execution into innovation. These same challenges are present when attempting to implement or re-vitalize an existing recognition and reward program. It may not be practical or financially feasible to financially reward every employee who contributes to the innovation program in some way. Thankfully there are a myriad number of tried and true methods and ways to reward your employees[13] that don't have to be incredibly expensive. Simple, thoughtful gestures will go a long way to express your gratitude. Employees who feel appreciated tend to be more focused, produce better output, and have greater job satisfaction – they produce more and are happy to do so. This creates a win–win situation for everyone[14].

1. **Praise**

    Using meaningful praise is the simplest way to show that you care, and everyone will appreciate that. Perhaps best of all, praise doesn't cost a thing.

    Handwritten thank you notes are a surprisingly effective and simple gesture. Creating a dialog which invites a response creates a positive feedback loop which can lead to greater innovation efforts, improved

---

13 https://www.businessstudent.com/topics/10-tried-and-true-ways-to-motivate-your-employees/

14 "https://www.zippia.com/employer/10-ways-to-increase-profit-productivity-by-making-employees-happy/"

overall performance, tighter focus, and improving engagement[15].

Stay away from generic e-mails and hallmark cards. This lessens the authenticity of the recognition. In support of an innovation culture, a culture of praise is cultivated by rewarding leaders for creating a recognition culture within their organizations and regularly recognizing employees both for successes, and critically for failures from which valuable lessons learned must be extracted.

**Key Takeaway**: Figure out a way to give empowered employees the "freedom to fail"[16] as Edison once called it, and a method for self-promotion of successes.

2. **Promoting**

In order to cultivate a culture of innovation and recognition, employees are given the opportunities to lead by example and self-promote their work. Innovation leaders must harvest this effort and conduct promotion and marketing activities of the work performed, particularly work in the innovation sphere.

Traditional job-title promotion may also be a logical outcome for employees who demonstrate leadership capacities, leading teams, and pushing the innovation goals of the organization. The leaders of tomorrow are your change agents of today, and cultivating these people from within the organization is vital to the success of any innovation management effort. Provided this type of recognition is done as a part of a clear career path, avoids favoritism and recognizes true excellence, this will ultimately inspire other employees to fulfill their destiny within the organization.

Another method of promoting and recognizing innovation activities is with the use of publicly and/or virtually posted leaderboards. Although this is somewhat a controversial practice, if done openly and honestly leaderboards can effectively promote innovation recognitions by displaying data which encourages healthy completion, by allowing comparison to homogenous samples, that is, their own peer workgroup(s):

---

15 https://positivepsychology.com/flow-at-work/
16 Good companies embrace a culture of mini-failures. Fail often to succeed sooner, and find the silver lining in every cloud. Thomas Edison stated many times: "I have not failed. I've just found 10,000 ways that won't work" and his rule of thumb was that success is 99% failure, as long as we learn from it. "Don't be afraid to make a mistake, but make sure you don't make the same mistake twice" Akio Morita, the Sony Chairman often stated.

- **Demographic or Location** – display the innovations by location, division, workgroup, or team – this is similar to placing Continuous Improvement boards at workstations where the improvement was attained.
- **Data Driven** – use of real time performance improvement data from past projects that clearly demonstrates the organization's transition from improvement to innovation. The data should demonstrate how the organization has used gains from past initiatives such as Six Sigma, TQM, BPI, Lean and Kaizen ... and how the time saved frees up time to work on innovations.
- **Social Sensibility** – through the use of internal social media tools, such as Microsoft Teams, Delve boards, SharePoint, Yammer, or even Skype, employees can view accomplishments, encourage one another, and engage in friendly competition. Participants are able to access real-time updates as the latest innovation accomplishments are posted.

3. **Awarding Greater Responsibility**
   Similar to traditional promotion, increasing the amount of responsibility within an employee's stated performance goals is an effective method for demonstrating confidence in their ability to continue to perform at a high level while also (or in some cases exclusively) focusing on innovation activities.

   Organizations also demonstrate confidence in employees by giving them the room to fail. This is vital to the success of any innovation management effort. By accepting "failure that results in a lesson learned," organizations and their employees become freed from the specter of perceived failure. Appointing one of your Change Agents to lead a team's innovation activities or giving the team the option to self-manage without management interference (except to promote successes and failures) demonstrates to everyone involved the organization has truly embraced a culture of innovation.

4. **Competition**
   Using competition through methods such as gaming provides organizations a way to reward everyone involved by providing a fun way to leverage competition and camaraderie in the goal of attaining innovations. Games help keep people interested and

motivated while working on routine tasks in support of the greater innovation, project, or goal.

This provides further incentives and can significantly lessen the sting of any perceived failure, if bonus points are awarded for harnessing lessons learned from a failed experiment which lead to a breakthrough in subsequent efforts. The individual competition and game mechanics are also open for innovation and creativity. People appreciate, and seek to work for organizations that seek to create a fun and rewarding workplace. For organizations looking for an automated yet engaging gaming experience, software programs such as Hoopla are specifically designed to facilitate this experience. In one example, Hoopla helped an organization increase call volumes by 20%.

Programs such as Hoopla have become a vital aspect of organizations' recognition and reward programs, demonstrating how competition and gaming efforts if strategically approached, can foster increased competition, resulting in greater innovation and improved performance, while contributing to strengthen organizational and innovation culture.

### Innovation Events

Organize regular or even ad-hoc innovation events several times a month. In addition to celebrating recent breakthroughs, meaningful failures and employee promotions (and self-promotions) can be focal points of any innovation event.

Providing food and extending this to appetizers and libations after hours are one way that many organizations reach out to and say thank you to their employees. Ad-hoc events are a way to encourage everyone to take a break from their busy day, to gather briefly and get inspired, or offer inspiration to one another. Innovation events reinforce a culture of innovation and recognition, by demonstrating gratitude to our most important assets.

### Gifts

While as we previously stated, the reward should be commensurate with the level and value of the innovation attained, providing employees with gifts for service in the line of duty is also a great way to recognize and promote a culture of innovation. Gift cards and gift certificates to local retailers, restaurants, and coffee shops are greatly appreciated and a relatively inexpensive way to say Thank You!

If seeking a more personal or personalized way to recognize and reward innovation excellence, keep a log of your employee's interests and hobbies, and reward them with something they are sure to value and appreciate.

Speaking of gaming, who wouldn't love to have a foosball table or a billiards table in the breakroom? These games encourage teamwork, getting up and moving around, and clearing some brain-space for the next innovation inspiration. Some of your employees may enjoy reading – consider if you have the space to provide a little reading nook/library. Important: this must also be promoted by allocating people the time to take a break and enjoy it and encourage people that they have the flexibility to enjoy it during the workday.

Since providing meaningful nonmonetary recognition and rewards has been demonstrated as a tangible and lasting demonstration of recognition, this must be extended to every facet of the organization's innovation management infrastructure. Consider which gifts would be most appreciated by asking your potential recipients – they'll work that much harder knowing their efforts are appreciated and rewarded.

### Trophies and Medals

Members of the military risk their lives for the sake of our country and are awarded with medals of accomplishment and rank. A gold medal at the Olympics is a highly sought-after recognition. People who have completed successfully the Six Sigma black belt exam or those awarded PMP certification receive a lapel pin to display their accomplishment.

Although plaques and trophies are less common in today's workplace, they still represent a viable form of recognition, and if tied in with other forms of reward, can still serve a viable role in any organization's corporate recognition program.

## Flexibility of Time

As previously demonstrated, time is the single greatest reward you can provide to the modern worker – particularly to those that have already gone above and beyond by creating something truly innovative for the organization.

After exceeding expectations, overcoming numerous failures, which ultimately led to the organization's next innovation, the employee(s) who collaborated on this achievement are entitled to a little old-fashioned R&R (we're talking rest and relaxation here not more recognition and reward).

This flexibility of time can manifest in any number of ways, but this is not a one-size-fits-all approach. This must be uniquely tailored to the needs of the individual and the needs of the organization. For example, the working mom being recognized for her innovation efforts would not find value in time off to attend the company's sponsored golf tournament. This person's contributions are valued in terms of time, which she can never get back, to spend with her friends, family, and loved ones.

Here's another example: Your star performer and newly anointed team leader that led the team's innovation efforts is an avid golfer with traditional baby-boomer values. Do you think they would value a paid-day off with their green-fees pre-paid? If you are still unsure you need to ask them (trust me the answer will be a resounding yes!).

For team-based time rewards, you can provide the team the option to create a rotating schedule where each week one person has a 3-day weekend. At Google, they simply hire the best people and get out of their way. Google allows people to self-organize within a 20%-time policy, where employees spend 20% of their time working on what they think will most benefit Google. This freedom empowers them to be more innovative. Incredibly successful and financially rewarding projects have come from this policy such as their multi-billion-dollar AdSense business.

**Key Takeaways**: Organizations need to go beyond dated recognition and reward programs like employee of the month.

Flexible hours, flex-schedules, or providing the ability to work from home remotely during a specified part of the time – all of these are viable, valued options which demonstrate recognition with flexibility of time as the reward. Also, see the footnote on the different types of awards for workers.[17]

---

17 (a) Financial compensation (includes salary, commissions, piecework, organizational bonuses, team bonuses, gainsharing, stock options, stock purchasing plans, benefit programs, and retirement funds); (b) monetary awards (includes suggestion awards, patent awards, contribution awards, best in category awards example best salesperson, best employee of the year, etc.); (c) special awards, for example President's award, group/team rewards; (d) public personal recognition; (e) private personal recognition; (f) peer rewards; (g) customer awards; (h) patent and trademarks; (i) organizational awards.

These tried and true methods can all be immediately implemented and can be custom tailored to co-exist with nontraditional methods. Organizations that go the extra mile to recognize and reward their employees realize greater productivity, and sustained innovation by keeping rates of job satisfaction high, while guaranteeing a harmonized workplace centered on work–life balance, leading to incremental innovation breakthroughs and improved employee retention.

## SUMMARY

We do what we are recognized or are rewarded for doing. Although individuals may have largely routine day-to-day task assignments, if you can provide the space to innovate, then effectively reward and provide the recognition as a hero before their peers, friends, and family, they will take greatly increased pride in their job and creativity and the way it's being performed. We put rewards and recognition at the top of the pyramid because it is the mortar that holds the total pyramid together. We need to continuously sharpen the saw with our recognition and reward programs to consider how rewards and recognition systems need be custom tailored to make the individual change their emotions, thought patterns, and actions related to innovation.

The chapter presented unique challenges, in that it required a great deal of innovation in rethinking the way we approach recognition and rewards. The challenge we present to organizations, and their leadership, from the Board of Directors and the executive committee down to the line level supervisors is to figure out how to do something other than what you're doing today to recognize innovation at all levels within the organization. Now that ISO has included continuous improvement as being part of innovation it opened the door for everyone from the executive committee to the maintenance engineer to be innovative. We feel it is of utmost importance for organizations to change their approach to innovation management and the way recognition and rewards factors into their Innovation Management Program. It is extremely difficult to innovate while simultaneously seeking a status quo of continuing to do things the way we've always done.

In preparing your Innovation Management Plan, you may question where will your breakthrough innovation come from? Which employees should be nurtured in order to facilitate the breakthrough idea that leads the organization to its next level of success? You may question which individual is the most creative, or has the most potential: the individual that is paid to design and develop new products that comes up with a patent, or the maintenance engineer that helps the organization realize that everyone is responsible for finding ways to innovate. Can a factory with broken windows be counted on to consistently yield quality products, let alone the next generation of breakthrough innovations? The factory with very few broken windows is one where the employees take pride in its maintenance and appearance. This leads to greater pride of workmanship and overall quality of the products produced. We hope the factory with broken windows has become a relic of the past.

Regardless of the generational mix in the workplace, create experiences that engage and empower individuals to achieve shared business objectives. It really comes down to establishing, implementing, and maintaining a strategic vision to motivate, coach, and develop diverse employees. As more and more organizations move beyond continuous improvement and its diminishing returns, as the workforce is freed from the shackles of fire-fighting and problem solving, the organization may enter a state where breakthrough innovation becomes possible. To those organizations seeking to implement or re-energize your Innovation Management Programs, we wish you Godspeed and good fortune with your endeavors. This is good work, and an important task, one that requires a great deal of innovative thought and planning in order to attain breakthrough innovation.

---

## APPENDIX A: CHECKLIST OF WAYS TO REWARD PEOPLE

Here is a checklist of ways to recognize and/or reward people:

- ✓ Innovation day – where each function has a booth to show off their best innovation that year.
- ✓ Lapel pins that show the individual has had one of his innovative ideas implemented and the color of the lapel pin can be based upon how many individual innovative ideas the employee has had that were implemented.

✓ Changes in the individual's environment like moving the desk by the window, a new and better computer, painting their work area with a color they prefer, giving the individual a customized chair, or providing accommodations that help them feel at home (without interfering with other workers).

✓ Internal conferences showing off innovations that the organization had implemented. The individual that created the innovation should be allowed to make the presentation if desired.

✓ Recognition plaques that are affixed to the work area of the individual.

✓ Medals for outstanding innovation activities.

✓ Flowers and/or a personalized thank you letter.

✓ Innovation club – employees become members based upon the innovation they have implemented.

✓ Recognition for individuals whose papers have been published and/or presented at conferences.

✓ Pre-paid membership within a relevant association.

✓ A night on the town – the organization picks up the total bill for the individual and the spouse to go out to a dinner and another event (sporting event, movie, or musical concert); this would also include babysitting fees and the cost of a limousine to take them around.

✓ Special reserved preferred parking for a designated duration of days.

✓ Time off with pay for special community service.

✓ Paid time off to attend a school directly related to the individual's work assignment. For example, IBM sent 20 employees to Cornell for 3 months in the summer full time for 2 consecutive years. IBM paid in their normal salary plus travel and living expenses, books, and tuition in order for them to get their BS in electrical engineering.

✓ Find a way to have employees highlighted for their innovative ideas every month, such as on bulletin boards, company newsletter, and/or the company intranet, highlighting the individuals and departments that are meeting their innovation goals.

# TIME Book Summary

Sean O'Brien once said, "You can't fit all people with one size shoe." The same is true for most methodologies and the Total Innovation Measurement Excellence (TIME) methodology is not an exception. Like any methodology, TIME provides one framework that will serve as a skeleton for your cultural transformation. It is like a pair of shoes. We need different sizes, different colors, different heels, and different materials but the basic structure remains the same for all shoes. You need a sole, a heel, an arch, and you need a means to bind together all the individual components. In TIME, we have pictured the elements of a cultural change strategy as a pyramid. This pyramid is made up of 16 building blocks. At first glance, the unyielding strength of the pyramid may mislead you into believing that the building blocks have to be assembled sequentially. In actual practice, none of the building blocks needs to be completely implemented before any of the other building blocks. For example, BB12 - Rewards and Recognition is the top building block in the pyramid, which could indicate that it is the last building block to be developed. But in most cases, rewards and recognition systems will start to be formed very early in the cultural change process in order to reinforce desired behavioral patterns.

Another building block that you probably will want to start earlier is developing a comprehensive measurement system. Frequently, the initial start in preparing a comprehensive measurement system begins during the strategic planning activities in BB3 – Innovation Executive Leadership and in BB5 – Commitment to Stakeholders' Expectations and BB4- Performance and Cultural Change Management Plans. It is our experience that the TIME pyramid provides the basic structure needed to help an organization develop an innovative culture, but there are many different tools and techniques that make up each of the building blocks. The way and the order that these tools are nestled together make a large difference in their impact on the organization.

Another point I want to make is that you don't have to start your knowledge culture change activities across the entire organization at the same time. Frequently, based upon the innovation survey and/or organizational structure and financing, individual cherry picking areas are identified. The innovation survey points out innovative weaknesses between processes, products, management, sales and marketing, and after sales service. One way is to select one or two areas of improvement in the organization's operations. Another way is by selecting a function or two to focus your innovative culture initiative so as to bring about significant visible bottom-line improvement. Typical functions that are considered often for the initial pilot are as follows:

- Research and development – It is often difficult to measure the impact that the innovation improvement initiative is having on the area due to the long cycle times for the design projects and evaluating their impact.
- Product engineering – Frequently addressing continuous improvement problems and minor upgrades to the present product. Normally, it is a good candidate for a pilot.
- Marketing – Major activity is identifying and scoping future customers and trends. Often a high error rate in their future projections as a result is a good candidate for innovation.
- Sales and advertising – produces a continuous flow of innovation activities from these areas. Often innovation in sales and marketing pays off bigger dividends than the engineering-type activities. Currently, sales and advertising has a bigger impact upon competing on present and future products.
- Management – present management methodologies still focus on the caliber and educational level that we had in the 1960s. Little or no innovation has been made in the management process. A difficult area to accomplish anything in but it is a prime candidate for innovation based upon its impact on the total culture of the organization and employees' needs.
- After-sales service – highly impacted area on customer's future dealing with the organization. There is a major need for major upgrading in the way this area is interfacing with the organization's customers. It is a difficult area, as resistance to change is high.

I hope these comments have not left you with a negative impression of the TIME methodology. But like anything and everything, for every positive thing created there is a negative thing generated to offset. Our view of TIME is that the positive benefits far offset any negative consequences. Each of the building blocks is designed to fulfill a need that an innovative culture needs to have.

BB1 – Value-Added to Stakeholders – Like it or not, for for-profit organizations or for not-for-profit organizations whose performance eliminated the potential profit, we work for the Board of Directors who represent small to big investors. It is absolutely imperative that we understand what the Board of Directors expect from the organization. A very few investors are planning on allowing the organization to operate on their money for more than 10 years. If that is the case, then innovative efforts should be directed at short-term continuous improvement and minor improvements to the product, thereby maximizing return on the investment. I realize this is not a popular belief but it is a realistic one.

BB2 – Innovative Organizational Assessment – You need to have a way of identifying improvement opportunities and setting a stake in the ground to measure improvement opportunities. The innovative organizational assessment is an excellent tool to meet these objectives.

BB3 – Innovative Executive Leadership – Too many executives preach one thing then live in completely different work life. In an innovative culture, the primary function the manager has is to encourage free-thinkers and free doers. The level of innovation needs to set the benchmark for the rest of the organization.

BB4 – Performance and Cultural Change Management Plans – The plans we had when Six Sigma and quality were the driving forces within an organization need to change, which means a long-term commitment to innovative thinking and action will not be beneficial anymore. You cannot have a 6-month focus on innovation and then 7th month drift off to a different commitment. You need to plan your activities so that the future trends, such as Artificial Intelligence, are being considered in today's activities.

BB5 – Commitment to Stakeholders' Expectations – You need to define who the organization's stakeholders are. Typically, they would be the investors, management, the employees, the customers, the suppliers, the community, and special interest groups. It's logical to not treat all of these stakeholders the same, as often a positive impact on one stakeholder will have a negative impact on the other. For example, the organization can decide to move all of its product engineering work to India in order to reduce the cost by 70%. This has a major positive impact on the investor but it will have a very negative impact on the 285 people in the basic research and applied research departments. It is easy to calculate the product cost savings from moving the activity, for example, from United States to India. But what is the cost of putting 285 people out of work. Is it $100,000 per worker, $1 million per worker, or $10 million per worker? I have seen legal cases where making a person ill so he could not work has resulted in a $10 million fine. You need to consider all stakeholders when you make a decision, not just the investor.

BB6 – Innovative Project Management Systems – We have seen estimates between 30 and 80% of projects fail to deliver a product on time, within costs, and that meets customer's expectations.. Value propositions are grossly wrong in many cases, and business case analysis is frequently overlooked at the same time. Lucky when marketing quantity and cost estimates for a new product are not worse than plus or minus 20%. We keep pouring more and more money into increasing the bureaucracy and crosschecking of the product. If the project is going to fail, then the right time to stop it is before it begins. This is a real improvement opportunity for the project management community.

BB7 – Innovative Management Participation – The tried and true management approaches that worked so well in the 20th century need to be readdressed to keep pace with an innovative culture. Employees are looking to management to set the role model by applying the same degree of innovation to the management system as applied to the rest of the organization.

BB8 – Innovative Team Building – Any team meeting lasting for 1, 2, or 3 hours is not a meeting that's worthwhile going to. It obviously is the one in which the agenda has not been properly evaluated to see how much time will be really needed. (In a typical 1-hour meeting, all of the decisions are made in the last 5 minutes. Hence it should only be scheduled for the time that is required to complete the agenda.) Many people turn a meeting into a debate and try to win the point even if they do not have the correct information. Such people should not be invited to any future meetings if their behavior remains the same. Instead, their immediate manager should attend the meeting. Action needs to be taken to penalize any individual who comes to a meeting late or does not attend the meeting at all.

Keeping all these negative points in mind, meetings are very worthwhile and a valuable part of the innovative culture and allow individuals to express their ideas through free exchange of information built upon each other's thoughts.

BB9 – Individual Creativity, Innovation, and Excellence – I am a great believer that we should grow our people to the point that they can handle the problems that are presented to them without going to a team meeting. Your employees should come to your office saying "This is what I did to solve the problem" instead of "what should I do about the problem?" Our ultimate goal should be to develop our people to the point that they become self-thinkers who consider all aspects of the situation rather than team members. You can have a good company when individuals exercise their creativity and are empowered to use it.

BB10 – Innovative Supply Chain Management – The United States is now turning more amd more into a service-oriented country driven by financial arrangements. Manual, boring labor, and activites are now being outsourced to Asian companies that have excess labor. This puts a heavy demand and high degree of risk on excellence of suppliers located thousands of miles from the name–brand organizations.

BB11 – Innovative Design – This mainly focuses on continuous improvement of products, services, and processes of an organization. Innovative designing uses tools such as process redesign, process reengineering, benchmarking, and Six Sigma. Many people feel that continuous improvement should not be a part of innovation but the definitions used by ISO include continuous improvement as part of innovation. Studies of present and past patents indicate that 95% of the patents issued fall into the continuous improvement classification. Hence for long-term survival of any organization, a strong focus on expansion and continuous improvement activities is essential.

As you focus on your continuous improvement activities, it's important to remember that service-type organizations, which involve processes and products, often use very different approaches to maximize their continuous improvement efforts.

BB12 – Innovative Robotics/Artificial Intelligence – The development and use of robotics and artificial intelligence is progressing very fast, as developed countries strive to compete with the low-cost labor markets in Asia, Central America, South America, and Africa. The United States is a leader in Artificial Intelligence but the Chinese government has put a great deal of money to help organizations in China take the lead away from the United States. Probably the most extensive use of Artificial Intelligence is related to military applications at the present time.

BB13 – Knowledge Assets Management – Too many people think of Knowledge Assets Management as being only related to patents and trademarks. Certainly patents and trademarks are important considerations but that is only the tip of the iceberg. Knowledge is the problem of all innovations. The vast amount of information and data available today is overwhelming to the average individual. As a result, it is essential that a knowledge management warehouse is maintained to reflect the latest changes in the technology and to remove the obsolete analyses. The knowledge management warehouse should be receiving input from the organization itself in the form of formal reports and from external sources such as conferences, books, newspapers, technical reports, and benchmarking studies.

BB14 – Comprehensive Measurement Systems – Meaningful results in innovation are difficult to measure. Too many of the projects fail because the value proposition is based upon statistically unsound data. We need two types of measurements; one that reflects what's going on today within the organization and one that reflects the consequences of what we're doing today. Area Activity Analysis is an effective approach at defining today's innovation. Activities like restructuring the organization designed to bring about improved performance frequently produce nothing but chaos. Too often we think of innovation as it relates to problem-solving or taking advantages of opportunities, but actually much of our opportunity approaches solutions are driven by the knowledge that we collected.

BB15 – Innovative Organizational Structure – The only way you can justify reorganizing is when it will have a positive impact upon the organization's bottom line. This means that we have to quantify the impact that a reorganization will have on the organization's key performance indicators. The cost of reorganizing an organization is usually underestimated or changed and is not measured. All too often organizations come into existence because of the individuals' pushing for more power. Rotating the executive team between functions often has a very positive impact on an organization's work flow and cooperation. I like to move the executive who is complaining about the way another function is performing into heading up that function's activities at the executive team level.

BB16 – Rewards and Recognition – Don't underestimate the importance of an effective rewards and recognition system.

# Appendix A

## Glossary

- Administrate – To direct and manage resources.
- Area Activity Analysis is a methodology to establish agreed-to, understandable efficiency and effectiveness measurement systems and communication links throughout the organization. It is designed to define and set up all of the internal and external supplier/customer relationships and measurements.
- Artificial Intelligence (AI) –
    - Per Haugeland (1985), an American professor of philosophy and cognitive science, AI refers to "the exciting new effort to make computers think … machines with minds, in the full and literal sense."
    - Per Kurzweil (1990), an American inventor and futurist, AI is concerned with building machines that can act and react appropriately, adapting their response to the demands of the situation.
- Artificial Narrow Intelligence (ANI) or narrow AI – This type of AI, also called weak AI, is designed to perform a very precise and well-defined task.
- Artificial General Intelligence (AGI) or general AI – This type of AI, also known as full AI or strong AI, has the potential of mimicking human cognition, and the decision-making process that a human brain goes through.
- Artificial Super Intelligence (ASI) or super AI – In this type of AI, we reach the Singularity moment where the machine intelligence surpasses human intelligence.
- Benchmark (BMK) – Standard by which an item can be measured or judged.
- Benchmarking (BMKG) – A systematic way to identify, understand, and creatively evolve superior products, services, designs, equipment, processes, and practices to improve your organization's real performance.

- Communicate – To transfer understanding.
- Creative Problem Solving – A body of methodologies for solving often ill-defined problems or to help you search for possibilities and opportunities not readily apparent.
- Customer Experience Index – Forrester Research's annual survey to evaluate organizations' customer experience (CX) maturity; categories measured include effectiveness, ease of use, emotion, retention, enrichment, and advocacy.
- Educate – To transfer knowledge and skill.
- Executive – Person or group appointed and given the responsibility to manage the affairs of an organization and the authority to make decisions.
- Executive management of innovation    The day-to-day tasks performed by executives to drive an organization to achieve their stated innovation goals.
- Explicit knowledge is defined as knowledge that is stored in a semi-structured content, such as documents, e-mail, voicemail, or video media. Also known as hard or tangible knowledge.
- Holacracy – Way of structuring an organization that replaces the conventional management hierarchy.
- Incremental improvement – A change to a product or service that creates a new value proposition to the customer above and beyond just a lower price for essentially the same product or service.
- Innovation – The output of a conscious and purposeful effort to create, be creative, identify, develop, and bring to the customer a new value proposition.
- Innovative executive leadership – Efforts by senior leaders of an organization to change themselves, the way they operate both individually and as the executive team in order to become more creative in their approaches to all areas of their organization.
- Innovation content – A reflection of the relative rations of the mixture of linear problem solving, uncertainty, and creativity required to achieve a given task(s).
- Innovation Vision Statement – The vision statement set by executive leadership to guide the whole or specific parts of the organization as they endeavor to develop new products or services or change the way the business operates.
- Involvement – The act or process of taking part in something: the state of being included in an activity.

- Knowledge is defined as a mixture of experiences, practices, traditions, values, contextual information, expert insight, and a sound intuition that provides an environment and framework for evaluation and incorporating new experiences and information.
- Knowledge artifact – A specific instance of a knowledge asset.
- Knowledge Capital (same as Intellectual Capital) is the intellectual material, knowledge, information, intellectual property, and experience that can be put to use in order to create wealth. It is collective brainpower.
- Knowledge assets – Refers to the accumulated intellectual resources of an organization. It is the knowledge possessed by the organization and its workforce in the form of ideas, learning, understanding, memory, insights, cognitive and technical skills, and capabilities.
- Knowledge management – A proactive, systematic process by which value is generated from intellectual or knowledge-based assets and disseminated to the stakeholders.
- Leadership – The art of motivating a group of people to act toward achieving a common goal. … directing an organization's resources in order to achieve the objectives of that policy.
- Leadership – Is both a research area and a practical skill, regarding the ability of an individual or organization to "lead" or guide other individuals, teams, or entire organizations.
- Linear Problem Solving – Any of the standard methods used to solve problems that have a correct or right answer.
- Management – Defined as being responsible for organization and coordination of the activities of an organization in order to achieve defined objectives.
- Manager – A person who accomplishes tasks through others.
- Mission Statement – Used to document the reasons for the organization's or area's existence.
- Motivate – To draw out the potential of another person.
- Natural Work Team (NWT) or Natural Work Group (NWG) is a group of people who are assigned to work together and who report to the same manager or supervisor.
- Participation – Is the act of taking part in an event or activity.
- Performance – The act or process of carrying out or accomplishing an activity, task, or function against preset known standards of accuracy, completeness, cost, and speed. Performance is deemed to be the fulfilment of an obligation.

- Robotics – An interdisciplinary branch of engineering and science that includes mechanical engineering, electronic engineering, information engineering, computer science, and others.
- Stakeholders.
  - collinsdictionary.com: "Stakeholders are people who have an interest in a company's or organization's affairs."
  - businesdictionary.com: "A person, group or organization that has interest or concern in an organization. Stakeholders can affect or be affected by the organization's actions, objectives and policies."
  - stakeholdermap.com: "A stakeholder is anybody who can affect or is affected by an organization, strategy or project. They can be internal or external and they can be at senior or junior levels."
  - dictionary.cambridge.org: "A person or group of people who own a share in a business."
  - dictionary.cambridge.org: "A person such as an employee, customer, or citizen who is involved with an organization, society, etc. and therefore has responsibilities towards it and an interest in its success."
  - Project-management.com: "Project stakeholders are individuals and organizations that are actively involved in the project, or whose interests may be affected as a result of project execution or project completion."
  - psychologydictionary.org: "A person or company who has an interest in a research project that could be a sponsor, director, service recipient."
- Alan Li: "Stakeholders can be defined as all entities that are impacted through a business running its operations and conducting other activities related to its existence. The impact can be direct in the case of the business's customers and suppliers or indirect in the case of the communities in which the business chooses to place its locations."
- Structure – A system that outlines how organizational activities, such as task allocation, coordination, information flow, and supervision, are directed in order to achieve the goals of an organization.
- Tacit knowledge – Knowledge that is formed around intangible factors embedded in an individual's experience. Often referred to as soft knowledge.
- Team – Two or more entities (people, houses, oxen, dogs, etc.) bound together or dependent upon each other to achieve a specific goal.

# Appendix B

## List of the Most Used and/or Most Effective Innovative Tools and Methodologies in Alphabetical Order

Book I – Organizational and/or Operational IT&M
Book II – Evolutional and/or Improvement IT&M
Book III – Creative IT&M
Note: IT&M = Innovative Tools and/or Methodologies
P = Primary Usage S = Secondary Usage Blank = Not used or little used

|     | IT&M | Book I | Book II | Book III |
|-----|------|--------|---------|----------|
| 1   | 5 Why questions | S | P | S |
| 2   | 76 standard solutions | P | S | |
| 3   | Absence thinking | P | | |
| 4   | Affinity diagram | S | P | S |
| 5   | Agile Innovation | S | | P |
| 6   | Attribute listing | S | P | |
| 7   | Benchmarking | | S | P |
| 8   | Biomimicry | P | S | |
| 9   | Brain-writing 6-3-5- | S | P | S |
| 10  | Business case development | | S | P |
| 11  | Business Plan | S | S | P |
| 12  | Cause and Effect Diagrams | | P | S |
| 13  | Combination methods | P | S | |
| 14  | Comparative analysis | S | S | P |
| 15  | Competitive analysis | S | S | P |
| 16  | Competitive shopping | | S | P |
| 17  | Concept tree (concept map) | P | S | |
| 18  | Consumer co-creation | P | | |
| 19  | Concurrent Engineering | P | | |
| 20  | Contingency planning | | S | P |

(*Continued*)

523

(Cont.)

| | IT&M | Book I | Book II | Book III |
|---|---|---|---|---|
| 21 | Co-Star | S | S | P |
| 22 | Costs analysis | S | S | P |
| 23 | Creative problem solving model | S | P | |
| 24 | Creative thinking | P | S | |
| 25 | Design for Tools | | P | |
| | Subtotal number of points | 8 | 7 | 10 |
| 26 | Directed/Focused/Structure Innovation | P | S | |
| 27 | Elevator Speech | P | S | S |
| 28 | Ethnography | P | | |
| 29 | Financial reporting | S | S | P |
| 30 | Flowcharting | | P | S |
| 31 | Focus groups | S | S | P |
| 32 | Force field analysis | S | P | |
| 33 | Generic creativity tools | P | S | |
| 34 | HU Diagrams | P | | |
| 35 | I-TRIZ | P | | |
| 36 | Identifying and Engaging Stakeholders | S | S | P |
| 37 | Imaginary brainstorming | P | S | S |
| 38 | Innovation Blueprint | P | | S |
| 39 | Innovation Master Plan | S | S | P |
| 40 | Kano analysis | S | P | S |
| 41 | Knowledge management systems | S | S | P |
| 42 | Lead user analysis | P | S | |
| 43 | Lotus Blossom | P | S | |
| 44 | Market research and surveys | S | | P |
| 45 | Matrix diagram | P | S | |
| 46 | Mind mapping | P | S | S |
| 47 | Nominal group technique | S | P | |
| 48 | Online innovation platforms | P | S | S |
| 49 | Open innovation | P | S | S |
| 50 | Organizational change mgt | S | S | P |
| 51 | Outcome driven innovation | P | | |
| | Subtotal number of points | 15 | 4 | 7 |
| 52 | Plan-Do-Check-Act | S | P | |
| 53 | Potential investor present | S | | P |
| 54 | Project Management | S | S | P |
| 55 | Proof of concepts | P | S | |
| 56 | Quickscore creativity test | P | | |
| 57 | Reengineering/Redesign | | P | |
| 58 | Reverse Engineering | S | P | |

(*Continued*)

(Cont.)

| | IT&M | Book I | Book II | Book III |
|---|---|---|---|---|
| 59 | Robust design | S | P | |
| 60 | S-Curve Model | | S | P |
| 61 | Safeguarding Intellectual Properties | | | P |
| 62 | Scamper | S | P | |
| 63 | Scenario Analysis | P | S | |
| 64 | Simulations | S | P | S |
| 65 | Six thinking hats | S | P | S |
| 66 | Social Networks | S | P | |
| 67 | Solution Analysis Diagrams | S | P | |
| 68 | Statistical Analysis | S | P | S |
| 69 | Storyboarding | P | S | |
| 70 | Systems thinking | S | S | P |
| 71 | Supply Chain Management | S | P | |
| 72 | Synetics | P | | |
| 73 | Tree diagram | S | P | S |
| 74 | TRIZ | P | S | |
| 75 | Value analysis | S | P | S |
| 76 | Value propositions | | S | P |
| 77 | Visioning | S | S | P |
| | Subtotal – number of points | 6 | 13 | 7 |

| (P) priority rating | CREATIVE | EVOLUTIONARY | ORGANIZATIONAL |
|---|---|---|---|
| TOTAL | 29 | 24 | 24 |

| | |
|---|---|
| IT&M in Creativity Book | 29 |
| IT&M in Evolutionary Book | 24 |
| IT&M in Organizational Book | 24 |

# Index

Page numbers in *italics* refer to Figures, and in **bold** refer to Tables.